**Dervla Murphy was attacked
by wolves in Yugoslavia**

. . . when she bicycled almost around the world in 1963. She was also nearly swept away by floods and was threatened by bandits. Her exciting story is in
THE BEST OF *BICYCLING!*

What do you know about the record-smashing Keirin racers of Japan? You can read about them in
THE BEST OF *BICYCLING!*

One daredevil reached speeds of 127 miles per hour on his bicycle. It's in
THE BEST OF *BICYCLING!*

THE BEST OF *BICYCLING!*
was originally published by Trident Press.

THE BEST OF
Bicycling!

edited by

Harley M. Leete

PUBLISHED BY POCKET BOOKS NEW YORK

THE BEST OF **BICYCLING!**

Trident Press edition published November, 1970

POCKET BOOK edition published March, 1972

*Please direct all correspondence relating to
the materials in this book to:*

    Bicycling! Magazine
    256 Sutter St.
    San Francisco, California 94108

I

Standard Book Number: 671-78534-6.
Library of Congress Catalog Card Number: 70-102883.
Printed in the U.S.A.

Acknowledgments

Naturally, there are many who love the sport of bicycling. It gives a kingly ease . . . or devilish challenge . . . depending on which portion of the Earth's physiognomy, the uphill or downhill side, you are tickling with your bicycle wheels. Of the many whom cycling fascinates, some return the good they receive in full and overflowing measure. These bright spirits have helped to create and nurture Bicycling! magazine.

Ranking high in this good company is a great roadman and leader in cycling realms, E. Peter Hoffman. Pete edited and published the magazine for seven years with the fervor of true devotion.

The technical contributions of Fred De Long and the travel stories of Dr. Clifford Graves have been of great value and charm.

Bicycle-making titans Ray Burch and H. M. Huffman, Jr., have exerted, through the years, a dynamic and almost fatherly influence on the magazine's economic progress.

In editing this anthology, I have been simply a caretaker, selecting and organizing the inspired work of others. They are too many to list here, but I can and do acknowledge our debt and deep gratitude to them all.

HML

Contents

Touring in the United States

Competition Cycling

Cycling for Radiant Health

Equipment and Techniques

Bikeways and Trails—A New Cycling Frontier

The Romance of Cycling's Golden Age

Introduction

Even if you have never seen a bicycle race or taken a long ride and felt what a graceful and incredibly swift machine a fine bicycle can be, most of you have probably been a part of the cycling world at least once in your life. You know what it is like to coast down a hill on a quiet afternoon or to let your thoughts wander as you pedal through woods, along a seacoast, or on some little-traveled path. For most of you, bicycling was an accepted part of childhood, your favorite way to get around, an added joy to your early years.

For thousands of Americans, this fun has never ended. Through participation in tours and camping trips, racing events, or simple Sunday rides around the block for exercise, bicycling still plays an important part in their lives.

Bicycling! magazine exists for these enthusiasts. It all began in 1961 with a tiny mimeographed bimonthly journal called *American Cycling,* devoted exclusively to reporting bicycle competitions. Gradually, this now all-but-legendary publication became more and more ambitious, and grew by fits and starts in quality and scope. Today it can be bought at newsstands and in bicycle shops all across the nation.

Over the years, hundreds of features on bicycle touring, racing, mechanics, techniques, and all-around fun have appeared in its pages. There have been articles by engineers, conservationists, and doctors, stories from foreign correspondents and sportswriters, remembrances of professional adventurers, and advice for feminine enthusiasts.

We at the magazine thought the best of all this ought to be preserved. So here it is, a book full of vicarious thrills for waiting out the rain and a wealth of invaluable information for when the sun shines. There are times when a bicycle can be a pair of wings, a joy and a wonder. We have sought to capture here some of that pleasure and excitement.

You will find the harrowing tale of Dervla Murphy, a young woman swept away by floods and threatened by bandits in Turkey, and attacked by wolves in Yugoslavia, who, despite these and many more catastrophes, bicycled almost all around the world in 1963. There are bicyclists' portraits of Holland (and how to "go Dutch by bike"), of precipitous canyon roads in Norway, and of the record-smashing Keirin racers of Japan. An authentic bicycle romance, "A Penny-Farthing for Your Heart, Darling," is reproduced from the December 1882 issue of *The Wheelman*. And there are fascinating pieces on a daredevil who reached speeds of 127 miles an hour on his bicycle, a twelve-year-old's own Mississippi bike hike, a professional roadman's training advice, and a race that takes you up stairs, across rain-swollen creeks, and over bales of hay!

For the serious cyclist there is expert technical advice on how to choose a good touring bicycle, with recommendations as to best wheel size, brakes, gearing, frames, and handlebars, and what to pack on a tour; riding in the rain without getting wet; how to carry several bikes on even the smallest car; how to ride a tandem; and much more. The touring sections cover such areas in the United States as northern California, the Potomac River Valley, Indiana, Ohio, Texas, the Ozarks, the Catskills, and the Rockies, and other countries, such as England, France, Norway, Japan, and Canada. There are also racing articles on the Tour de France, the Olympics in Mexico City, and the National Championships, and unforgettable contests in Nevada City, Portland, and Aspen. An important section of the book is devoted to the health aspects of cycling, and how best to use this sport to stay fit.

We are thrilled to be able to share the best of our work with what we hope will be an even wider audience than we now have. We trust that this book will enhance the great and ever-growing sport of bicycling in America.

HARLEY M. LEETE
Publisher

Worldwide Touring:

Adventures on

Two Wheels

INTIMATE JAPAN—DELIGHTS OF RURAL CYCLING

Clifford L. Graves, M.D.
March 1969

When I arrived at the magnificent New Otani Hotel in Tokyo my friends from France, the Nogrettes, were not yet there, but they had left word to wait for them in the restaurant on the revolving top floor, so I went up and sat down at the bar. All of Tokyo was at my feet.

"How are you enjoying your trip?" I asked of the man next to me. He was an American in his fifties, a little overweight and a little underslung.

"It's all right, but I am still trying to get over that cold I caught in Moscow."

"Moscow?"

"Yes, the weather was terrible there. We ran into a snowstorm." He ordered a double Scotch.

"Moscow is a long way from here."

"We are on a round-the-world flight. My wife thought it would be fun because she knows a lot of people in the group."

"How long have you been at it?"

"We started a month ago. This is our last night. Tomorrow we will be back in New York."

"What an adventure. How many stops did you make?"

"Seven. First Moscow. Then Samarkand, Karachi, New Delhi, Bangkok, Hong Kong, and now here."

3

"The trip of a lifetime."

"Yes, and so cheap. The whole fare was only eighteen hundred dollars, everything included. Except drinks." He winked.

"How do you know when it is time for a drink? It must be terribly confusing with all those jumps in the time zone."

"That's a problem. I never know whether to have breakfast or dinner."

"What did you see here in Tokyo?" I was trying to pick up some good tips.

"To tell you the truth, I haven't seen much of it. The traffic is terrible."

"Isn't it everywhere?"

"You can say that again. I've been scared ever since that accident in New Delhi."

"What happened?"

"Our bus ran into a streetcar. Shook us up a bit. My neck still hurts."

"Too bad. But at least you didn't have any snow there."

"Just the opposite. It was too hot."

"How about Samarkand? That is halfway between."

"The weather was all right, but the food nearly killed me. All they give you there is soup, you know."

"No dysentery?"

"That came in Bangkok. I had to stay in bed for two days."

"What city did you like best?"

"Hong Kong. They have a marvelous tailor there. I ordered three suits for the price of one."

"What about Tokyo? Did you ever see so much glitter?"

"I'll tell you tomorrow. We are going on a round of nightclubs because it's our last night."

He got up, downing his Scotch. "My wife is probably waiting for me now. We'll have dinner first. But no more Japanese food for me. The only way to survive in this country is in an American house with a Japanese wife and a Chinese cook."

He disappeared in the crowd.

"Happy you!" shouted the Japanese man across the street when we got our bicycles ready to roll the next morning. We had taken the train to Takasaki, sixty-six miles northwest of Tokyo, to escape the worst of the traffic. We waved at our friend. He waved at us. You might fault him on his grammar, but you couldn't fault him on his sentiment.

This tour was the outgrowth of a chance meeting in Copenhagen last summer. There, at the rally of the Alliance Internationale de Tourisme, Jean Nogrette of Paris ran into Shinichi Toriyama of Tokyo. Both were riding tandem with their wives. Between the Nogrettes and the Toriyamas, a plan was hatched: a tour of Japan. As soon as Jean got back to Paris, he sent me an invitation to join. He also invited a longtime family friend, Anne Marie Potin, a Frenchwoman who lives with her family in New York. The opportunity was too good to turn down. Moreover, didn't I have the obligation to scout the country for a possible huff 'n' puff tour later?

I knew Shinichi Toriyama by reputation. He is a cyclist, a world traveler, a writer, an engineer, a physiologist, and even a film producer, all on the subject of cycling. A connoisseur, he can tell you what kind of steel is best, where to go for a tour, and even how much oxygen you use when you shift from the drops to the tops. His interests run from the purely technical to the highly practical. The Japan Cycle Club has honored him. Bicycle manufacturers use him as a consultant. The government underwrites his scheme of leadership courses in cycling for schoolteachers. Even the Imperial family called him in when the Crown Prince wanted a bicycle. With all these accomplishments, he is a very human person with a delightful sense of humor. His wife, Yoshie, was educated in London and speaks perfect English.

Come late in October, said the Toriyamas. At first that struck me as pretty late in the season. But the Toriyamas were right. The weather was perfect. Sunny days alternated with brisk evenings and starry nights. The only rain we had was a brief shower in Kyoto. On the plains, it was the season of the harvest; in the mountains, the season of the colors. Brilliant reds and yellows stood out against the snow of the mountains. We marveled.

The route Shinichi had planned for us ran across the central mountains to the west coast. We then followed the coast in zigzag fashion until we got to Kyoto on the narrow waist of the country. Here, the Nogrettes and Anne Marie ran out of time while I flew on to Kyushu at the southern tip for another week of cycling on the outlying islands. Altogether I was in Japan three weeks, during which I cycled about a thousand miles.

Almost everybody who comes back from Japan has an unkind word to say about traffic. Admittedly, it can be pretty awful. A few of the major cities are now connected by expressways, but that is the exception. For the most part, traffic crawls along bumper to bumper on single-lane roads that were never meant to carry anything heavier than a wheelbarrow. These are the roads to avoid. What you look for on a bicycle is a little country road. They exist in almost the same profusion as in Europe, although many are not paved. To find paved country roads, you have to have a good map. The maps we used were on a scale of 1 to 250,000, contoured.

Once you leave the main road behind, you have it made. Life passes in review. Children play by the side of the road. A schoolteacher takes his flock on a picnic. An itinerant knife grinder trundles along, his equipment strewn on a sidecar that he has cleverly attached to his bicycle. A farmer leaves his wagon on the road while he works in the field. You detour around it. The rice paddies show evidence of loving care. Schoolboys are making a sketch of a house in the distance. A mother takes her baby for a stroll. Farms are clean and well-kept. Wherever you stop, people are helpful and courteous. This is the way to see Japan.

After two days of fine cycling in the Joshin-Etsu-Kogen mountains, we came to the Shiba Pass. Right away, conditions began to deteriorate. The road, which up to this point had been paved, turned to dirt. Melting snow made a quagmire. The temperature plummeted. Noisy trucks labored past us with heavy loads of gravel. At several points, the road was completely broken up. Mud caked under our fenders in such quantities that we had to remove the wheels to clean it out. Our clothes were scant protection against a wind that came straight from the ice fields. Now and then a bus rumbled by, the occupants staring at us in disbelief. We looked like a bunch of escapees from a Siberian labor camp. Yoshie was near collapse.

We arrived at the summit in heavy fog. Chilled to the bone, we sought refuge in a shelter where several hundred bus travelers had already holed up. In a corner, two girls were ladling out soup from a tremendous pot over an open fire. We fell in and got our share. Revived, we contemplated the descent. It turned out to be even worse than the climb.

The western slope is snow country in Japan. Here, in the middle of the winter, villages are buried under eight and ten feet. In our case, it wasn't exactly eight feet, but enough to turn the road into a swamp. Alternately pushing our bicycles and riding them, we finally reached lower altitudes where the weather was clear.

At this point we came on a bunch of women in baggy trousers who were hauling loads of gravel in wheelbarrows. One of them had built a little fire to keep warm. From my position in the rear, I could see that she was trying to hand Helen something as the tandem sloshed past. What could it be that this woman, stooped beyond her years, wanted to give away? In a moment, I saw. A flower! Here was an eloquent expression of human resilience under grim conditions. Bent by ceaseless toil, hounded by constant drudgery, chained to the most frugal existence, this woman nevertheless recognized the spirit of adventure and responded to it. Helen was so surprised, she forgot to hold out her hand.

When you arrive at a Japanese inn, or *ryokan,* you leave your shoes in the vestibule, pick out a pair of slippers, and aim for the dimly lit lobby. Here, you immediately become the center of attention. Two or three pretty girls in kimonos emerge out of the darkness, relieve you of your baggage, and flutter off to your room while you flippity-flop after them. Registering can wait. You go down a long corridor, up some steps, around a corner, and down another long corridor. Finally you get to your room. It is completely bare except for a very low table and maybe some cushions. Even your slippers are not allowed here. You kick them off and enter on stocking feet.

You look around. The floor is covered with straw mats, or *tatami*. Each *tatami* measures six by three feet. That is sleeping space for one person. The capacity of the room is therefore the same as the number of *tatami*. A nine-*tatami* room is about average for a *ryokan*. Sometimes, all six of us slept in a nine-*tatami* room. Opposite the door through which you have entered is an alcove with a window that looks out on a pretty Japanese garden, the size of your room.

You look around some more. There is a refrigerator! Just as you open the door to see what is in it, your kimono girl is back with steaming napkin, a pot of green tea, and some cookies. The tea is tasteless, but the cookies are delicious. Now the girl helps you into your kimono and asks when you want dinner. She has to know because she serves you in your room. There is no dining room in a Japanese *ryokan*.

When the hotel could spare two rooms, we put the men in one and the women in the other. This arrangement never failed to dumbfound the kimono girls who simply could not understand what was going on. They had heard of crazy things Americans do, but never anything as crazy as this. We tried to explain, and they just giggled.

After your tea, you suddenly realize how cold it is. The only heating system is a tiny electric bulb under the table. So you look for the hot bath, or *ofuro*. It is a Japanese institution. In the larger inns, they have a separate *ofuro* for men and women, but in the smaller ones, they don't.

When I got to the *ofuro* in the Hamadaya Inn in Omura, I found a young woman already in it, but she did not seem the least bit disturbed, so I pretended that I wasn't either and I slid in at the far end like a native. That is, after I had thoroughly soaped and doused *outside* the pool, where the temperature hovered around 50°. I must explain here that the water in the *ofuro* is always very hot. It is supposed to stay around 116°. With that much difference between water and air, great clouds of steam are constantly billowing up with the result that the whole room takes on the atmosphere of a boiling caldron. Nevertheless, I could make out that my companion was a shapely creature in her early thirties. She had her hair done up in a bun and her arms folded across her chest.

Presently, a kimono girl toddled in with a deep tray that held two heavy-bottomed glasses full of *sake*. This tray she deposited on the choppy waves with the utmost gentleness. I gave the tray a little shove toward my companion, and she picked up a glass. I was next. "Kan pai!" The kimono girl refilled our glasses. "Kan pai" again. This could go on a long time except that the water felt awfully hot. Moreover, the wine was beginning to go to my head. Never have I felt so completely relaxed. It was as if I were floating in a nirvana, a different world with softer outlines, heightened pleasures, greater contentment.

Dinner is a production by itself. You start by sinking down on a cushion and folding your legs under you. Now there is a knock at the door, and the girls sidle in with a deep bow. The price of the meal is determined not so much by what you eat as by the number of girls who wait on you. A three-girl meal was about par for us.

First comes a black lacquer bowl with clear liquid in which float bits of fish and rice. Then follows the *sashimi,* slices of raw fish that you dip in soy sauce. Next comes *tempura,* prawns fried in butter. Now comes the *pièce de résistance:* the *sushi.* It is a vinegared rice ball, spread over with a thin piece of raw fish and wrapped up in a leaf of dried seaweed. Your dessert is soup, which you drink. If there is anything left in the bowl, you pick it up with the chopsticks and pour the rest down your throat. The *ocha,* or tea, is something that you can skip. All through this repast, the girls keep an eye out to make sure that you don't fumble with the chopsticks. Or with your legs.

It is time to go to sleep. The girls clear the table, sweep the *tatami,* and make your bed. You sleep on a *futon,* a thin mattress that is put on the floor. Over you goes a quilt, and at the top goes the *makura,* or pillow, very hard and small. Amid much giggling, the girl tells you never to put your head pointing north because that is the region of the dead. You crawl in while the girl turns off the light. "O-yasumi nasai."

At seven o'clock the next morning, she is back. "Ohayo

gozaimasu," she gurgles as she opens the shutters and closes the window. Pretty soon, the room begins to stir. People sit up, rub their eyes, stagger to their feet. It's cold, but the *ofuro* soon takes care of that. The bedding is cleared and breakfast brought up. Two boiled eggs, toast, and coffee. Now comes the bill. It varies from six to twenty dollars each, depending on the *ryokan*. Time to pack your bags.

Downstairs, you retrieve your shoes while the kimono girls flit all around you. You put your bags on the bicycle. A dozen children quickly gather. The boys have blue uniforms, and the girls have sailor dresses, neat as a pin. One of the boys comes forward and says that he speaks a little English. He would like to practice it on you. You tell him that Japan is a beautiful country. Your bags are in place. You wave good-bye. The boys wave good-bye. The girls wave good-bye. The kimono girls wave good-bye. The bystanders wave good-bye. Everybody waves good-bye. You are off and running.

You look at the map. Ouch! Everything is written in Japanese characters. It's like studying hieroglyphics. In the absence of clear information, you pay close attention to the terrain. You watch for the rivers, the mountains, the valleys. When you get lost, you ask. If they don't understand you, you point at the map. Often, they will drop everything to go with you. Failing that, they will draw a little map with incredible speed and nimbleness. The Japanese are a staccato people. They do everything quickly.

Still, you miscalculate. After our travail on the Shiba Pass, we were sailing along a pretty valley on our way to the coast when we ran out of steam and daylight at about the same time. Our goal was the Akakura Hotel on lofty Mount Myoko. How to find it in the dark? We knocked at the door of a lonely farmhouse. A smiling girl in her teens opened the door. Yes, we were on the right track, but we still had nine hundred meters to go. About three thousand feet. That's nothing, I thought. But then it developed in the further conversation that the nine hundred meters were not as the cyclist cycles or as the falcon flies, but as the rocket rises! The hotel was nine hundred meters *above* us. We sent a flare up, and the hotel sent a Jeep down. The bicycles we left behind. We arrived one jump ahead of the ski crowd.

The Akakura Hotel treated us well. It is, in fact, one of the most luxurious hotels in Japan. The next day, we hiked all over the mountain so that we could have an extra night to relax in a real bed. Soon after leaving this choice spot, we reached the coast at approximately the same time as the crab fleet. Every village had huge pots of crabs on display, usually with a barker to invite you in. Jean Nogrette drooled. At one of these emporiums, we consumed a dozen crabs each.

Jean was exceedingly useful at eating time because of his sharp nose for restaurants. As soon as he spotted one, he would have us gather around for a look at the outside showcase which displays plastic models of the various dishes with price tags attached. You make your selection and point at it while the waitress looks over your shoulder. This system never failed, and we dispensed with it only once. That time we wanted rice only. We looked it up in the dictionary and found that rice is *ine*. Bring us some *ine*, we said with considerable aplomb. The waitress burst out laughing. *Ine* is rice in the field. Rice on your plate is *gohan*. It was like asking for a pig when you want pork chops.

Cycling through an industrial city in Japan is murder, but cycling through a village is a ball. Because the shops are open to the street and because the streets are very narrow, you are right on top of the action. On your bicycle, you could snatch an apple without coming to a stop. All the shops are indescribably cluttered. Merchandise is stacked three-deep on the shelves that are so close together you can barely squeeze through. There are fish shops, sweet shops, fruit shops, vegetable shops, flower shops, book shops, tailor shops, dress shops, shoe shops, bike shops, but no butcher shops. Meat is too expensive. Book shops always have at least a dozen freeloaders who read their favorite magazine and then return it to the shelves. Sometimes you find the salesman, sometimes you don't. Once, too hungry to leave empty-handed, I roamed through a grocery till I walked in on a woman nursing her baby.

Like all huff 'n' puffers, we quickly discovered what

we liked best in the grocery shop: *an-pan,* a bun with a sweet paste in the center. Each country offers its own delights. In England it was yogurt; and in France "hak-kelak," which was Bill Vetter's translation of *chocolat au lait,* or a chocolate milk. No matter how bad a food sounds, you eat it after a couple of hours on a bicycle.

The Japanese name for bicycle is *jitensha,* the wheel that rolls by itself. Our wheels did roll by themselves for the next ten days. Pushed by a steady tail wind, warmed by a radiant sun, entertained by the sights, sounds, and scents of this hospitable land, we gradually made our way down the coast and along Lake Biwa to Kyoto.

Kyoto is a city of over a million, and they were all on the streets when we entered the suburbs at nightfall. Trucks, buses, and streetcars thundered past in a clangor of noise and confusion. Sidewalks were jammed. All forward progress stopped at a star-shaped plaza with streets taking off in six directions. We knew the name of the hotel where Jean had made reservations, but we had no idea where it was. Without a map, we were lost.

Help came in the form of a charming girl, no older than fourteen, who volunteered assistance. She knew the hotel and directed us in the meticulous but labored English that is typical of the Japanese. You could tell that she was thrilled to be understood. We thanked her and took off. Slowly we threaded our way through the choked streets, over narrow bridges, and under the garish arcades that Kyoto is famous for. Now riding, now walking, we must have covered at least two miles when we saw the girl again. How she ever picked us out in that throng, I will never know. But she did. Flushed and winded from running after us for half an hour, she blurted: "Oh, I am so glad I found you." Then, pointing, she continued: "The hotel is *that* way, not *that* way!"

Then she melted into the crowd.

I spent the next day helping Jean with the shipment of his tandem and laying my plans for the following week. From all I could gather, I should see Kyushu, the south-ernmost island. It's about four hundred miles from Kyoto, a journey that would take at least a day by train and boat. That would be a day wasted. Moreover, I knew that trains in Japan rarely carry vans. My bicycle would have to go by slow freight. Under these circumstances, I decided to fly.

That Japanese trains are unable to take your bicycle as accompanied baggage is a severe handicap for the cycle tourist. A similar difficulty arose at the boats. Although I was always able to talk my way past the gate, I suffered some anxiety and annoyance as a result. Looking back on this experience, I can see that a folding bicycle would be a clear advantage. Many folding bicycles that are now on the market are not suitable for touring, but a few are. I have seen one that had ten speeds, twenty-seven-inch wheels, and Campagnolo joints at the hinges. I would advise anyone who is going to tour the Orient on a bicycle to look into this.

It was after dark when I arrived at the remote airport of Omura, which serves the island of Kyushu. My fellow passengers quickly cleared the building, and I found myself alone, saddling up. Only one employee was still on duty. I asked him whether he could direct me to a *ryokan*. Yes, he could, but it was four miles away. He drew a little map. Clean-cut and well spoken, he took a great interest in my trip. Just as I got ready to leave, he hurried away and quickly returned with four little cupcakes, daintily wrapped. I offered to pay him. "No, no," he said. "This is our way of saying welcome."'

Outside, I faced a pitch-black night. Black and silent. The country was deserted. A narrow, twisting road took off across the fields. I switched on my light and followed its nimble beam. Without it, I would have been utterly lost. Eventually, I arrived at the *ryokan*. Since I was the only guest, the kimono girl smothered me with attention. I have already told you about the *ofuro*. I had an excellent dinner, a lively conversation (with the help of a dictionary), and a restful night, all for the price of six dollars. I thought of all the big impersonal luxury hotels where I had paid twenty dollars just for a bed.

Japan has 100 million people in a country the size of California, and about 80 percent of these live on the main island of Honshu. The three smaller islands are much less congested. On my ride across Kyushu, I hit traffic only once.

The first day out of Omura saw me over land and

sea to the pretty little town of Matsushima. On the second day I cycled over the seven bridges to Kumamoto and then to Mount Aso in the center of the island. Here, on the slopes of a gigantic extinct volcano, I found a fabulous youth hostel. The director took me on a tour of the building. It has four hundred beds, a cafeteria, a gymnasium, a library, many classrooms, marvelous grounds, and a fifty-mile view over the crater. The hostel has a number of bicycles for rent, the gift of the Japan Cycling Association. I might say that the situation in Japan is much like the situation in America: millions of utility bicycles, few touring bicycles.

On the third day I reached Beppu, ready for the jump to Shikoku the next morning. A swift and luxurious steamer made the eighty miles in just over four hours. At Matsuyama I had my first glimpse of the Inland Sea. Tucked between Honshu and Shikoku, this magnificent waterway is 150 miles long and from 15 to 30 miles across. It is dotted with hundreds of islands that are maintained in their pristine condition because the entire area is a national park.

Now began one of the most delightful travel experiences I have ever had. Starting from Matsuyama, I cycled several hours to Imabari, then took a hydrofoil boat across the sea to Onomichi, then cycled for several hours to Fukuyama, then recrossed the sea by hydrofoil to Mataguma, then cycled through the country to Kotochira and Takamatsu. From Takamatsu, it was another four-hour crossing on a luxury boat to Kobe. For anybody who contemplates a bicycle tour of Japan, this is the area to explore.

It was at Imabari that I almost came to grief. I had asked of a travel agent in Matsuyama what the road was like. This man, who could recite all the air schedules by heart, had to admit that he had never been to Imabari! After I started, I found that the road was partly under construction. Much delayed, I finally reached the outskirts after dark. Not wanting to overshoot, I stopped at the first cluster of houses. Everything was dark except for one house that looked as if it might be a *ryokan*. I walked in and found myself in a dimly lit room with a bar and a couple of girls in Western dress at the far end. They quickly surrounded me.

I tried to explain that I was looking for a hotel. The girls giggled. One of them spoke a little English. I gathered that this was not exactly a hotel but there might be one in town, three miles down the road. How will I find it in the dark? The girls called in some other girls who materialized out of nowhere. Everybody talked at once. After much chattering, laughing, and scurrying around, one of the girls got on the phone. Mushi, mushi. A long conversation. Now another phone call, even longer. Then an urgent request for me to pick up the phone. Hooray. The voice spoke English. I was talking to Mr. Hidefumi Shiga, secretary of the Municipal Assembly. Yes, if I would continue on the road I was on, I would come to the town square where he would meet me. Meanwhile, he would send out a messenger to look for a hotel room. I thanked the girls in the most gracious manner possible and backed out. My watch told me that my séance with the giggling girls had taken nearly an hour.

At Kobe, my trip was almost over. All that remained was to cycle to the airport and fly back to Tokyo. The Kobe airport also serves Osaka and Kyoto, the three cities having a combined population of four million. I therefore expected to see something like Chicago's O'Hare field. Imagine my dismay, after a hectic ride from Kobe, to find two small and rickety buildings at the end of a long and bumpy detour through an industrial section that looked worse than Watts. Only the skeleton of a large, new building had as yet been completed. Hundreds of people were milling around. Taxis came and went in droves. Long lines formed everywhere. The roar of planes mixed with the blare of a loudspeaker. It was a scene of utter chaos.

I fought my way to the ticket window. Could I get on the next plane for Tokyo with my bicycle? Impossible, said the girl. The bicycle would have to go as freight, maybe the next day. Just sell me a ticket, then, I said. She did. I wormed my way to a cramped and dismal freight office where a dozen trucks were noisily jockeying for position. Over the din, I collared a nice-looking young fellow. How about my bicycle?

"Just leave it here. We will get it on the next flight. You have an hour. Would you like to join me for a cup of coffee?"

I might say that coffee is rapidly replacing tea as the national drink in Japan.

We made for the restaurant. There was a long line, but my friend talked his way past it. Inside, eight small tables were sagging under the onslaught of a hundred people. We sat down next to a young woman who was teaching her six-month-old baby how to eat spaghetti—a masterful performance.

"It is always this busy here?" The knowledge that I would soon be on my way made me relax.

"Worse. You should be here tomorrow."

"How can you stand it?"

"I am happy here because I am doing something useful. Japan is building for the future."

He broke into an engaging smile.

WILD PONIES—AN ENGLISH JOURNEY WITH NINA

M. BAGLEY
September 1968

Nina was two years old when we first struck out for the hills, and my enthusiasm for that early venture was clouded with doubts as to whether she would take to the bike game so young. But in her large round eyes I thought I saw a gleam that had once appeared in my own, when I had looked to the rim of the mountains and felt an itch in my feet. So I heaved the bike onto the car roof rack, and over familiar local roads, motoring, headed for adventure.

An overcast was breaking when we topped the first rise, and the Black Mountains National Park rising beyond Herefordshire's Golden Valley was an irresistible invitation. I drove into the Olchon Glen, a box canyon enclosed by Cat's Back Ridge and 2,200-foot Black

WILLIAM W. VETTER

Camped at 2,000 feet in Black Mountains National Park.

Mountain, and while I unloaded the bike, Nina spent a happy time throwing stones into a creek and sailing sticks through a culvert.

I had Nina strapped into a lightweight seat over the rear wheel, and as a counterbalance I had the saddlebag fixed to the handlebars. We set off on a rough track, heading for the Cat's Back, with Nina wondering why I couldn't rise the scree that formed the first two hundred feet of the ascent.

Huge slabs of rock littered the narrowing gully, and a red grouse chuckled "Go back! Go back!"—a warning that went unheeded. Herds of wild ponies roamed the ridge above us, and when we were clear of the gully, whinberry plants formed a carpet of ocher, red, rust, and pale green.

There had been rockfalls near the summit, and I had to unseat Nina and carry the bike. The rougher the climb, the more she seemed to enjoy it as she scrabbled up the steepening mountain, now a thousand feet above the gully.

During rest periods she invented a game; small stones and rocks became automobiles and buses, and she filled them with gas through reed stalks that grew around the many tiny streams.

The summit was a dramatic finale to the climb, and it was not hard to see why it had been given the name Cat's Back. The backbone ridge varied from two to twenty feet in width, and the mountain fell away for around twelve hundred feet on either side. We found a small plateau where I set the tent up with a view out the flap over the heat haze that prevented us from seeing clear across the Midlands of England.

But we were in the company of wind and small clouds, and while we sat there, two elderly ladies came hiking from somewhere, stopped to listen to Nina's account of her adventure, and after eyeing the bike with amazement they went on with their hike in the sky, leaving us alone again on the roof of Herefordshire, though we soon had a sparrow hawk and several ravens circling around and below us. Nina was fascinated by being able to look down on birds in flight, and became dizzy watching miniature trees and farms rushing beneath their outspread wings.

After a vicious descent, with the rear wheel trying to overtake the front and reclimbs to carry Nina down the worst parts, we cycled the narrow road that circles the Olchon Glen. Then we motored home, windburned and tired, but looking forward to the next time.

We didn't have long to wait. A few days later we were on an old but silent bike I had borrowed from Nina's grandfather, and inside half a dozen miles we were climbing Wonder Hill on the eastern side of Hereford county. Early fall colors were rampant along those narrow winding roads, bits of rust and russet among buff and burnished gold, spots of vivid red and shining green berries everywhere on that misty, spider-webbed September morning.

Unable to resist a track that bounds up some impossible hill, I dismounted and pushed Nina toward what appeared to be a lost land, a land that might have existed in an old book, for rough meadows and ancient gnarled apple trees abounded there, and twisted timbers in farmhouses, barns with wavy roofs covered in moss and tired sheep dogs lazing in chicken-scratched dust. Where the track rambled on along the hill, a dark stand of trees sent a finger of oak and elm across it, a green tunnel full of the smells of retreating summer, and when we found the road again, we went flying along the Ridgeway, a high road on the backbone of Marcle Hill.

The old bike carried us, it seemed, like one of the first airplanes, for the wind whistled through the spokes as we leaned around corners, the valley swaying far below. Down, down, we dived, rushing with magnificent ease, rising, dipping over humpbacks, before plunging finally to the valley, tall trees spinning away and pale blue scabious flowers like bits of summer sky rushing along the banks. Houses, gates, farms, and red-and-white Hereford cows rushed up to meet us, all resuming normal size as we touched down again at my in-laws' home.

"That," said a windblown and excited Nina, "was a nice ride."

It was the last day in September when I took her into what is called the Welsh Desert, and for once that five hundred square miles of bog and moorland had been dried by a long hot summer. The triple Elan dams supplying Birmingham City with water were reduced to less than half capacity, and dried mud and shingle covered acres of what had been a green valley. I pushed the bike across a moonscape of bleached rock and cracked mud flats, and Nina's face was alight with joy at so many stones to throw into what she called a big puddle.

After tears over being strapped back into her seat, I blazed a new trail up the mountain so that I could follow an ancient track once used by cattle drovers. All grass had been burned a buff color, the stones were dry and shiny amid thick dust, and the sides of this magical pathway were gold, yellow, and crimson with the leaves of the willow herb, a plant that stormed the shimmering air with a fleecy white seed. We sat there and ate our food, and afterward, Nina, tired and sleeping, lay in the shade of a fence post and my rain cape, while a fence wire pinged in the heat and a lark chirped once, as if too weary for further song.

A breeze whispered past in the dust, and we trundled on through a forest of stunted, wind-tortured oaks and silver birches that were tinted myriad colors. I walked the bike where the track clung to the edge of a rock outcrop, and the sun burned Nina's face, so that her flushed cheeks contrasted vividly with the blue of her eyes. Below us the waters of the dams had receded to reveal Shelley's garden, though what would be left of the house where the poet had once lived still lay below water. Odd stone walls and rot-blackened rhododendron stumps were a gaunt reminder of what had been a place of beauty, where a stream had chuckled between green lawns and where it has been said that Shelley sailed paper boats made with high-value currency notes.

But Nina was wilting as an angry red sun began to dip below Drygarn mountain, so we raced down a steep road to the small town of Rhayader, where we collected the car and drove back home, dry-eyed, red-faced, tired, but gloriously happy.

Nina put a lot of bike miles behind her during that long hot fall, and even as late as November we were heading up the Gospel Pass, named after ancient monks, a tiny mountain road climbing to a lonely sixteen hundred feet. Nina was building up to a heavy cold, but she insisted on a bike ride, though it was unusually silent without her chatter and continuous "What's that?" as I toiled up the divide.

To our west the Black Mountains fell away for over four hundred feet to a scarred plateau that was another thousand feet above the Wye river valley. Thick mist was climbing toward us as we set off on what was for me a muscle-straining walk-cum-ride along a sheep track that circled the Gospel summit. Nina was silent and sad in her seat, listless and seeming unaffected by Rhos Dirion, Rhiw-y-fan, and Rhiw Wen mountains falling in great sweeps through the misty sunlight.

But suddenly she came alive again when we rejoined the road and went swishing down to the mountain village of Chapel-y-ffin. Mist came pouring over the ridges, huge towers of it tumbling toward us, so that Nina's face became constraint with awe. As the dramatic light faded, colors turned somber and eventually black as the still, sheep-bleating night swallowed us and the valley.

In the headlamp glow, bracken hanging from the rocks and banks on either side of the road looked like giant hands or claws, and lights from lone farms told us we were not really alone in the world. Our cycle lamp was a warm, friendly glow in the dark, and the swish of tires on the road was a reassuring sound. After motoring home Nina sleepily said: "Tomorrow we'll go up a different mountain." I wondered where along those high roads and tracks, we had lost her cold.

My journeys with Nina have been numerous and varied, like the mid-winter day when we came back from the wild, eerie hills of southwest Herefordshire, back from a fire I had lighted by the roadside in a glowing, cold dusk, with old sticks crackling and a billycan boiling. We left that lambent firelight on the lonely hill where I met a friend I had not seen in ten years, left it to him and went rushing along on the bike, down the valleys of dead summer and up the hills to the frosted sky, meeting and passing folk, yet seeming to be isolated from them as if the bike were a time machine traveling in a different plane.

With so many miles behind us I often wonder what those wide eyes of Nina's really saw. She certainly has her own original descriptions for what passes before them. As I was pushing her up one of many unridable hills, I watched her puzzling over insulators on telegraph posts. They were maroon and white, and suddenly she exclaimed: "Milk bottles and jam up there!" Another time she was staring into a clear blue sky, her hands behind her back and a look of infinite wisdom on her face as she pointed to the daylight moon and said: "Look, a tiny hole!" I picked up the bike, feeling that there were a good many miles between me and the world of a child.

Nina is four years old now, and she has to share her biking miles with her baby sister, but I still take her on occasional trips, just the two of us.

TRUFFLE TOUR OF FRANCE

CLIFFORD L. GRAVES, M.D.
December 1966

"What a charming place," said Bill Barnes, bringing his bike to a halt on the shaded plaza of a French village where nothing had changed for three centuries. "But not a sign of life. I wonder where we could get a cold beer."

"I think I see a café," said his wife, Frances, pointing to an ancient house, half askew, with a small table and two chairs under a little canopy. "It looks like the coolest spot in town."

They sat down. A door opened, and a pleasant young woman with two small children clutching at her skirt came out to meet her unexpected guests. Meanwhile, Bill had been studying his phrase book.

"Avez-vous deux verres de bière?" he asked discreetly.

"Be sure it's *cold*," said his wife.

"Bière froide," said Bill, hoping for the best.

"Mais oui, monsieur" was the instant reply. She smiled on her way back into the house.

Bill was flushed with success. "You see! She understood me perfectly. All you have to do is start talking."

The beer tasted good, even though it was not exactly cold. They ordered another. The second glass went down as quickly as the first.

"I think that we should eat something. We haven't had a bite since lunch," said Frances. Lunch? She tried to remember when that was.

After a careful consultation of the phrase book and a long discussion with the woman, they settled for a cheese sandwich. It was delicious. "Say, this place deserves at least three stars in the Michelin guide," said Bill. "I wonder what she will charge us."

But when Bill went over to settle the account, the pleasant young woman held up her hand, shook her head, and explained that this was a private house. She was

22

delighted to have an American couple as her guests. Especially a couple *au vélo*. Bill and Frances were dumbfounded. No phrase book, not even an unabridged dictionary, contained the words they were groping for.

That was the huff 'n' puff tour of France this year. Always the same warm greeting, always the same spontaneous hospitality, always the same sincere goodwill. It was this unique rapport that gave the tour its flavor.

Who were these huff 'n' puffers, where did they come from, how did they get their idea, what was their object, why did they go to France? The story goes back two years, when forty people gathered at Bantam Lake youth hostel in Connecticut for an experimental tour of New England. Because these forty people came from all parts of the United States and even from Europe, they chose to call themselves the International Bicycle Touring Society. This first tour was so successful that it had to be repeated the following year. In fact, to accommodate all the applicants, the society organized two tours in 1965: one on the coast of Maine and the other in Wisconsin. In 1966 there were enough huff 'n' puffers for three tours: New England, the Blue Ridge southwest of Washington, and France. Far from being a deterrent, the bicycle proved to be a big attraction.

The French tour had been carefully planned by Jean and Hélène Nogrette. Monsieur Nogrette has his own public relations firm in Paris, and he is widely known as a financial columnist. From their intimate knowledge of France, Jean and Hélène decided that the best area for our tour would be the Midi in the south-central part of the country. It is a region of winding rivers and secluded valleys, of deep ravines and colorful gorges, of vast caves and immense forests, of smiling vineyards and giant rocks, of heathered tracts and round-topped mountains, of Roman ruins and medieval towns, of storied castles and moss-grown churches, but above all it is a region of little roads and leafy lanes which meander merrily from hillock to hillock and from village to village. It was on these little roads and in these little villages that we saw France as it should be seen: fair, fresh, and friendly, proud of its past, poised for the future.

The Midi is famous not only for its natural beauty

and historic interest but also for its food. One of the
delicacies peculiar to the Midi is truffles, a growth of
fungi on the root of the oak. To harvest truffles, a farmer
sends his pigs into the field because pigs can smell truffles,
no matter how deep. When the pig starts digging, the
farmer comes running. As they finally appear on your
plate, truffles are minute specks of black material in liver
paste. You have to have a magnifying glass to see them.

We met in Paris at the gare d'Austerlitz on a splendid
afternoon in mid-September. While Jean busied himself
with the ticket agent (he always acted as our purser), we
busied ourselves greeting old friends and new. Except for
Jim Grambart who had met with a slight accident in
Holland, the group was complete: Leonard Gohs, an
advertising man from New York; Captain Lodeensen, a
writer from Bermuda; Ted Paulson, an architect from
California; Charles Horn, a lawyer from Dayton; Fred
De Long of Exide Batteries in Philadelphia; Captain Dan
Henry, late of American Airlines; Bill Vetter, a photog-
rapher from Washington; Dr. Medwin Clutterbuck, a
dentist from the south of England; Malcolm Jackson, a
freelancer from Indianapolis; and "Happy Thought" Joe
Dietrich of Los Angeles. We also had six couples. Besides
the Nogrettes, the Jack Ludlams of Atlantic City; the
George Twitchells of Hartford, Connecticut; the Bill
Barneses of Greenville, Delaware; the Bill Parises of
Oceanside, California; and the Steve Halls of the U. S.
Air Force in Wiesbaden, Germany. In age we ranged
from twenty-four to sixty-two; in experience from veteran to tyro; in enthusiasm from high to sky-high.

Our French contingent ran from Jacques Faizant, a
well-known novelist, to Sylviane Couve de Murville, who
is a niece of the French foreign minister. At one time or
another, we also greeted Lyli Herse of the famous bicycle
firm; Léon Creusefond, president of the French Federation
of Cycle Tourists, and his wife; André Rabault, editor of
Le Cycliste, and his wife; André Charasson; Henri Gerard; and many local cyclists who would often travel great
distances just to be with us for a few hours. These impromptu meetings on the road were among the highlights
of the tour.

Like every railroad station in the major cities of Europe, the gare d'Austerlitz is more than just a station. It is a social center where people go to get a haircut, buy flowers, meet a friend, enjoy a drink, or just sit and watch the world go by. A man who was watching the world go by over an *apéritif* in the station restaurant nudged his neighbor. "Sacré bleu. A bunch of Americans. With bicycles! What do you think of that?"

"Oh, I read about them in *Le Figaro* this morning," said the other, who looked more like an intellectual type. "They are on their way to Brive."

"Yes, but on bicycles! Why should they want to be on bicycles? I bet they all have big cars at home."

"Of course. In America everybody has a big car. I have been there. Everything is big in America. After dinner, instead of giving you a finger bowl, they make you take a swim."

On the Toulouse express, which covered the three hundred miles to Brive in just over four hours, we divided our attention between a six-course dinner, the fleeting landscape, and the stories of our transatlantic flight. These stories all centered on the bicycles because bicycles are unclassified objects to the airlines. When you call them and ask whether they will take a bicycle, the answer varies all the way from "Sure, bring it as it is" to "Yes, but you will have to crate it." Air France, which is ordinarily most cooperative, gave Bill Vetter a bad time, but Icelandic welcomed him. Pan American, which has a reputation for fussiness, took the Twitchell tandem sight unseen. TWA was giving Malcolm Jackson the runaround until he mentioned that Air India had already okayed his bike. In general, the people who made no preliminary inquiries fared best. The worst they had to put up with was a startled look at the ticket counter. In defense of the airlines, it must be said that not one bike suffered damage worth mentioning.

Our reception committee in Brive was headed by Monsieur Roland Rassow, local notary public and cyclist extraordinary. Since our next day was free, Monsieur Rassow had arranged a full program. At noon, we would be received by the mayor in the city hall. The morning was reserved for a visit to the museum, and the afternoon for a ride to the famed monastery at nearby Aubazine.

These events came off without a hitch, but we will remember Monsieur Rassow more for his shorts than for his activities as an impresario.

On the ride to the monastery, Monsieur Rassow overheard Sylviane say that her brand-new saddle was a pain. Sylviane is an extremely well-bred girl, diffident, demure, and decorous. That evening, while we were all sitting in the bar which also had about a hundred locals, Monsieur Rassow walked in, waving his shorts. "Here is what you need," he said to Sylviane in a voice that could be heard to the farthest reaches of the room. With that, he turned his shorts inside out, rubbed the chamois lining, held it about four inches from Sylviane's nose, and continued: "Just feel how soft this is. Like sitting on foam rubber. Why, I remember in Paris-Brest-Paris five years ago . . ." And then followed a long story about Monsieur Rassow's posterior while Sylviane alternately blushed and blanched.

In spite of such contretemps, Sylviane always found the right words at the right time, a quality that served her in good stead when she acted as interpreter on the guided tours and at the receptions. Only once was she thrown for a loss. In the little town of Egliseneuve-d'Entraigues, we stayed in a hotel with four stories, all alike. That is, you could not tell what floor you were on except by counting them as you went up the stairs. In France, room numbers and floor numbers have no constant predictable relationship. Well, on this night, we had had an exceptionally drawn-out dinner after a hard day on the road, as a result of which one of our men, who shall remain nameless, decided to go to bed early. Tired, sleepy, and somewhat unsteady, he went up the stairs and stopped at what he thought was his room. Finding the door unlocked and the blankets turned down, he sank into bed without so much as turning on the light or looking for his pajamas. An hour later he felt somebody tug at his arm and whisper: "Mon Dieu, what are you doing in my bed?" It was Sylviane.

We cycled 750 miles in two weeks, mostly under a dazzling sun. The first week we found ourselves in gently rolling country, the valleys of the Dordogne and the Lot. The second week we entered the mountains of the Massif

Central where you can expect snow in late September, but the worst we got was a light drizzle on the last day. Our most severe climb was from Aurillac to Salers over the pass of Peyrol, 5,200 feet. We had a sag wagon but only one person needed it.

On the road we were mostly in twos and threes. Everybody set his own pace. After the last man was off, the two service vehicles would leave. One of these was a Volkswagen for Hélène Nogrette who would go ahead to the next hotel and make all the room assignments so that there was no delay when we arrived. The second vehicle was a one-ton panel truck, supplied by the Touring Club de France and driven by a bright-eyed shaggy-haired Sorbonne student named Jacques Clanche, who was quick to get into the spirit of things. "You all look so happy," he observed with a twinkle in his eye. "This cycling must be better than raspberries." Jacques was in charge of our baggage. In the morning, he would pick it up, and in the evening, he would deliver it to our rooms. You can't have it any better than that.

If the physical pace was not demanding, the social pace was—at times. At every overnight stop, the town notables were there to greet us with a *vin d'honneur,* which is the French equivalent of a cocktail party but with more speeches and less babel. Moreover, at a *vin d'honneur* you always learn something of the wine you are drinking, its name, its origin, its creation (in France, you do not *make* wine, you *create* it). In Bergerac we were welcomed in the twelfth-century vaults of the Convent de Bricolet by the consul of the wineries, Monsieur del Perier, who in everyday life is a judge of the superior court. Monsieur del Perier, in splendid medieval costume, told us in the presence of several hundred guests, half a dozen reporters, and at least one television crew that wine is to be enjoyed in four distinct and separate steps. First, you look at it. Second, you smell it. Third, you taste it. And fourth, you brag to your friends about it. A wine-tasting ceremony of the Chevaliers de Tastevin rates somewhat above a christening and below a diplomatic reception in France.

Later that same day we were guests of honor in a fantastic setting at the Château de Borde. Imagine a

stately château, not too old but full of dignity, surrounded by sweeping lawns, massive trees, and luxuriant
shrubbery. Visualize a huge swimming pool by the side
of the château with a spacious terrace and several large
serving tables. Picture a hundred animated people from
the worlds of finance, commerce, diplomacy, and bicycles,
mingling, talking, eating, drinking, swimming, or standing
by a crackling fire in a recess of gigantic proportions. And
all this because the owners of the château were friends
of friends of the Nogrettes. You could hardly say that
the French lack warmth.

Even more touching were the receptions by the local
bicycle clubs. At Aurillac, the Vélo Club Montagnard invited us to a simple but impressive *vin d'honneur* at which
the principal speaker was their dean, seventy-six-year-old
Pierre Canal. Monsieur Canal, who has cycled more than
half a million miles in his lifetime, built his speech on the
theme that the French have not forgotten what the Americans did in the last two wars. "Dear friends of liberty,"
he said after complimenting us on our decision to tour
France by bike, "twice you have come to rescue us from
a ruthless and savage invader. Twice you have come to
retrieve our liberty and our honor. Twice you have come
to shed your blood on our soil. This we can never forget . . ." Tears welled up in his eyes as he sank back
in his chair.

Another poignant experience awaited us in the village
of Boussac. Boussac is too small to have a bicycle club
but it did have at this moment an interesting visitor
sixty-nine-year-old Léon Boscus, who is a dedicated cyclist
and a brother of the mayor. We first saw him about five
miles before the village, waiting for us under a sign
Welcome to the Americans. After we had exchanged
amenities, we cycled en masse to the village where there
was another sign, stretching across the road: WELCOME TO
THE AMERICANS. He introduced us to a waiting delegation
of the mayor, the priest, the doctor, the butcher, the
baker, and all the other officials, following which we
gathered in the churchyard where three long tables sagged
under tremendous quantities of bread, cheese, wine, apples, pears, figs, and all sorts of goodies. Soon we were
joined by the rest of the population of the village, men

WILLIAM W. VETTER

Lyli Herse and her early-morning exercise group.

women, and children, to the accompaniment of speeches, songs, and the sound of movie cameras. It was difficult to tear ourselves away from so much kindness and graciousness. What Léon Boscus demonstrated to us, charmingly and touchingly, was that there *is* such a thing as fellowship of the open road.

Neither did we lack for official recognition. Shell Francaise offered us a gourmet dinner at the Hotel de la Muse in the gorge of the Tarn. The Société des Caves in the famous town of Roquefort arranged a tour and a sumptuous luncheon. The Touring Club de France delegated its deputy director general to present us with their gold medal at the meeting of the Alliance Internationale de Tourisme in Martigny. And one memorable evening in the great hall of the Château Mercues, the president of the Federation Française de Cyclotourisme presented us with two medals that had been struck especially for the occasion by the Ministry of Sports: one for the group and the other for an individual in our group. Our unanimous choice for the individual honor was Gertrude Ludlam, a gallant little lady with the heart of a lion and the grace of a kitten. With only a year's experience, Gertrude has already become an unreconstructed cycle tourist.

Another radiant personality among the women was Lyli Herse, daughter of the famous bicycle maker. Lyli had just come from Paris-Brest-Paris, the famous 750-mile trial in which her father had sponsored the winning team. I asked her for the secret of the success.

"Our two men were out front after the first ten hours," she said, "and we never let them out of sight. I fed them rice balls, laced with apricots and marinated in kirsch water."

"Rice balls? I never heard of that."

"They are my own invention. A cyclist needs quick energy in a low-volume low-residue food. The rice balls are perfect. They ate at least 150 of them."

"How would you like to make some for us?"

"I'd love it."

We planned a picnic, but the job turned out to be more complicated than I had thought. All during our rest day, Lyli toiled and moiled. First she had to buy the ingredients, the pots, the pans, the butane stove, the flour, the kirsch, and a very special kind of milk. Then, the mixture had to simmer for three hours while Lyli and Sylviane thought up all kinds of excuses for the strange noises and smells that came from their room. Finally, the next morning, the finished product had to be taken to a rendezvous in the mountains, along with the bread, the cheese, the tomatoes, the fruit, the wine, and the menu that Jacques Faizant had drawn for the occasion. The rice balls were delicious, but even more delicious was the sight of Lyli, hustling and bustling in the bright sunshine while we praised her handiwork with unfeigned enthusiasm. She sparkled.

Evenings, over a Pernod before dinner or a Verveine afterward, we settled the problems of the world, but one thing we never settled was whether a tourist should use tubulars or clincher tires. About half of us used tubulars. In fact, I did so myself but I learned several lessons. I the first place, you should mount only the highest quality of *silk* tubulars, and that is not cheap. Secondly, you should glue the tire with the greatest care. A tubular tire that is held by tape only has a tendency to slide on the rim when you descend long hills with a full load. Thirdly, you should carry at least two spares. Bike shops in most of the European countries want nothing to do with repairing tubulars. With this long list of possible troubles, why should anyone ride tubulars on a tour? The answer is in their responsiveness. Before I left, I rode my bike first on clinchers and then on tubulars for an honest comparison. Without trying to analyze the many factors involved (if I could!) I will only say with the Frenchman who was arguing whether women should have the vote: "Yes, there *is* a difference."

After our final banquet in the Panorama Hotel at Le Mont Dore, most of our people went straight to the station for the night train to Paris while I cycled to Clermont-Ferrand to catch a train for Switzerland. I started in a light drizzle on a pitch-black night with the wind and the grade against me, but when I got to the top of the pass after half an hour, the clouds broke, the wind died, the rain ceased, and the moon came through. That moon remained my sole companion for the rest of the evening, and it acted as a catalyst for my thoughts.

What was outstanding about our trip? The enchanting country? The romantic châteaus? The ancient churches? The quaint villages? The quiet roads? The invigorating exercise? The faultless arrangements? The cozy hotels? The lively companionship? Yes, all that. But there was something else. Because of the way we traveled, we met people that we never would have met otherwise. People from all walks of life. The high and the low, the rich and the poor, the proud and the humble, the boastful and the sober, the genuine and the spurious. People like the shepherd on the Sauveterre, the winetaster in Bergerac, the aged cyclist in Aurillac. These were people who had something to tell us. We will always remain in their debt.

Lanny Salsberg breathes in the fresh Canadian air.

GOD IS ALIVE AND WELL
ON THE CANADIAN PRAIRIE

LANNY SALSBERG
February 1969

I set out from Vancouver on a lightweight racing bicycle called the Dawes Galaxy, which has a ten-speed Simplex gear and, if the winds are right, will take you 125 miles a day. I was searching for Canada. I pedaled most of the way to Kenora and hitched a ride in a Stanley Tool Company van to Parry Sound and then bicycled the last leg home to Toronto, and somewhere along the way I found what I was looking for.

I discovered a personal relationship to the vast country whose existence had previously been drowned out by the obsessive rhythms of urban life. For five weeks I was an emissary from the bright lights and beautiful cacophony of the city, among people for whom a University of Toronto student with long hair and a strange vocabulary was a kind of foreigner; in the end, the land and its people absorbed me.

To millions of rural Canadians the weather is more than a matter of whether to wear galoshes or carry an umbrella. It's a central factor to survival. The rain that pursued me for my first two weeks out of Vancouver depressed me and slowed my progress; for western farmers it seriously delayed the harvest, caused the grain to start sprouting, and came close to ruining the crop.

And rain is only one factor. Michael Ramsey, a long-faced, steel-haired Scotsman who farms grain and beef near Strathmore, Alberta, told me how he was hailed out in the middle of August: five hundred acres planted, and only thirty harvested. "What would city people do if they had to live on a fraction of their salary for a year?" he asked me.

I descended on the Ramseys' farm about 7:00 P.M., four hours out of Calgary. Mr. Ramsey and two of his teen-aged children were working on a corrugated-metal granary. I just stood there, thinking that at best I would have a shed to sleep in and at worst I would be ordered to leave. A small noisy dog yipped and played about my feet until Michael, Jr., came over to me. I explained how I had gotten there and said I needed a covered place to put my sleeping bag. Michael relayed my request to his father and returned to say I could sleep in the bunkhouse.

The bunkhouse had two beds and an oil stove that gave off a heavy odor of kerosene. After dumping my stuff inside, I went back out to the yard. Mr. Ramsey was stapling together curved sheets of metal to form a hollow cylinder for storing grain. He said he sure as hell didn't need another granary, there were two standing empty already, but he had no harvesting to do, and sure he had the metal; he might as well use it.

When it became too dark to work, we all went into the house for coffee. Mrs. Ramsey kept piling plates of toast and Kraft cheese and jam on the table and Michael and his sister Sheila brought out their homework, and it was all in the tradition of western hospitality.

After the senior Ramseys went to bed I sat around talking with Michael and Sheila and their older sister Susan, who's going to be an X-ray technician. Susan told me she had to spend four months in Edmonton taking her course and she didn't want to be away from home so long. Last summer she and Sheila went to Expo with a group from Strathmore High School; Susan found Expo interesting but had strong reservations about the city. "There's so much mixing up of different people," she said. "I stayed with a girl in her apartment and she was going out with a boy from Trinidad!"

When I went back to the bunkhouse, the moon was shining crisp and sharp in the clear sky. In the morning Michael summoned me for breakfast. Mrs. Ramsey served me eggs and toast and coffee while Sheila and Michael, dressed like well-groomed students at any Toronto collegiate, watched out the window for the school bus. After breakfast, Mr. Ramsey drove off somewhere to pick up a part for the tractor. Susan helped her mother clean up the kitchen, and Mrs. Ramsey made me honey sandwiches before I cycled off.

So who cares about Prairie farmers?

The point is that we in southern Ontario inhabit a kind of urban wilderness isolated from the *real* Canada. In the country they don't indulge in our passion for soul-searching about a national identity. Attachment to the land is an identity, and the land that constitutes Canada is quite distinct from any place else in the world. Metro Toronto is media-land; we build our lives in terms of images.

We want symbols of a national culture—*Let us have Canadian films!*—just as we wear symbols of affluence, work with symbols of production, and play with symbols of recreation. This is where it's at, this is groovy twentieth-century mass urban culture, but this is not Canada.

Statistically the drift to the city is an unarguable trend of the twentieth century. Here in the metropolis our faith in statistics and our access to the means of self-publicity lead us to believe that we are the focus of Canadian life. But a striking division still exists: on one hand, city dwellers who accept change as absolute and concede control to a proliferating network of organizations; on the other hand, a stable rural society living in scattered units, wary of change and resentful of mass control. Urbanization may be dictating the direction of the twentieth century, but a trip across the country reveals that not everyone wants to be urbanized.

All the western towns I visited still had a spiritual link with the farm. Every radio station broadcast detailed reports on the harvest, and in Calgary grown men with responsible jobs wore cowboy boots and ten-gallon hats.

I spoke to many young people on farms along the way: a young girl near Montey Creek, British Columbia, who taught me to ride a horse; the three children of the Ramsey family outside Strathmore, Alberta; a boy at the University of Saskatchewan who came from a farm outside Swift Current. They look and dress very much like us, they go to school, they often attend the closest university, but they wish to stay on their farms. Many had visited Toronto or Montreal and expressed distaste for the crowds, the dirt, the senseless bustle. ("If you stand still on the sidewalk, people actually push you along!")

It's the kids in middle-sized towns like Kamloops or Moose Jaw who feel restless and trapped, because ~~y~~

have neither the stability of the land nor the frenetic excitement of the city. During the course of an afternoon in Kamloops, which is the largest community between Vancouver and Calgary, I talked to a girl working in a sporting-goods store who eulogized the cosmopolitan attractions of Winnipeg; I had my sunglasses repaired by a young optician who confided, in an undertone, how much he hated the place, hated the country-and-western-music station, hated the provincialism, hated everything about it.

The middling towns may be dull, but the big city has failed to realize everybody's dreams. There's this malaise: Groups believe that we are hurtling toward self-destruction, by suffocation or dehumanization or loss of contact with anything meaningful. In the interior of British Columbia, for example, groups of urban middle-class families have tried to set up self-sufficient communities in the wilderness. The hippies, alienated children of the bourgeoisie, also long to escape from the corruption of the cities and establish (or reestablish) a mystical communion with nature. Very few have, but they express a dissatisfaction that many of us feel.

Dependence on the land produced western conservatism, which can be pretty ornery, and western fundamentalism, which can be pretty funny. Farming is partly a science, partly a business, and certainly a mystique. Farming is a religion. A Calgary radio station features four hours of Bible broadcasts on Sunday morning, starting with former Premier Manning and ending with Billy Graham; and lots of people out there must be listening. Planting a crop requires faith in the climatic conditions that will produce a harvest, because without that faith the risk would be unthinkable.

In politics, the western conservatives maintain that change will come when conditions are right, in the manner that grain grows out of the earth. An ardent Social Creditor tried for about two hours to convince me that everything is basically all right, that the Vietnam war is somehow a solution to itself, that *most* people aren't poor. When the discussion had run its course, he said in the most earnest tone, "Just let me ask you one question: Don't you believe that people are good?"

The federal government is often regarded as a sort of

national busybody representing the interests of eastern financiers. Not only is God alive and well on the prairies, but the Antichrist (personified by the Bay Street Boys) gives constant battle.

Westerners are constantly talking about their hospitality, their openness, their friendliness (compared with eastern coldness, pushiness). E.g.: "Just take whatever you want. We don't stand on ceremony here." And they do come across. Many people put me up and invited me into their homes with no other reference than the account I gave of myself and the fact that I was there. Westerners are conscious of their inexperience, even proud of their innocence.

In Swift Current, a farmer with one of those gnarled, leathery faces sat opposite me in a beverage room and immediately ordered me a beer. He was silent for several minutes, staring at the tabletop and apparently formulating his question. Finally he looked up and said, "Why is it that so many people have long hair?"

However, this innocence implies a tendency to stereotype people who by their appearance or language or religion identify themselves as "different." The hippies with their (to a Westerner) outlandish clothes and hairstyles inspire a kind of terror akin to the Yellow Peril. All the kids who hitchhiked this summer, in fact every boy who traveled out west with longish hair, encountered at some time a reaction of fear and hostility. Highway restaurants posted signs forbidding entrance to hitchhikers, small-town police tried to bust them for vagrancy, and among themselves hitchhikers would pass on stories of the "bad vibrations" in this or that town. My bicycle seemed to act as a guarantee of wholesomeness—that is, I was doing something healthy, all I needed was a haircut. But I was upset a number of times by the little brainwashed children who stood around and chanted "hippie" at me.

Frequently, I heard anti-Semitic remarks made by people who seemed perfectly decent and hospitable. A man from Revelstoke who bought me lunch at the top of the Rogers Pass mentioned that he had lived in Winnipeg. "Wouldn't go back," he said. "Too many Jews to suit me." On another occasion, a college student in Calgary launched into a tirade about "how the Jewish mind works."

But beyond pettiness and prejudice stretches the land, immense, varied, expansive: cathedral-like mountains and monotonous prairie and secretive forests of the Canadian Shield. What I've been saying is something pretty simple, that we miss the land. Not the actual cultivation of it, not "Let's dig holes in the soil and weave our clothes out of treebark": these are pipe dreams you might have after too much pot or too many busts or too much hassling. I'm not advocating immediate evacuation of the cities and the end of technology. But we might feel better if we recognized that the land belongs to us, that it is eternal, that it waits silently for us to discover it. When we do, the land will suggest its own possibilities.

> There was a time in this fair land,
> When the railroad did not run.
> When the wild majestic mountains
> Stood alone against the sun.
> Long before the white man and
>   long before the wheel,
> When the green dark forest was
>   too silent to be real.
>   (Gordon Lightfoot,
>   "Canadian Railroad Trilogy")

I crossed the country, or three thousand miles of it, on the Trans-Canada Highway. At times I resented the road simply for being there, for carving a gash through all that wilderness, for bringing with it the shoddy artifacts of twentieth-century civilization. The railway running alongside had a powerful romanticism that the highway lacked.

Riding along, I would sing Gordon Lightfoot's "Railroad Trilogy" with its locomotive rhythm, and I began to identify with the men who built the railway, and gradually the pride and hope and regret of the song was interwoven with my own journey.

God is alive and well on the Canadian Prairie.

The songs of the future have been sung,
All the battles have been won.
On a mountain top we stand,
All the world at our command.
We have opened up the soil,
With our teardrops and our toil.

I was singing out those lines from Lightfoot's song one afternoon as I bicycled down the hill into Sicamous, British Columbia, and something happened that seems to summarize many of my reactions to the trip. I started to cry. Nobody would have been able to tell because I was coming down the hill very fast and the wind was blowing in my eyes. But it wasn't just the wind or the dust.

I cried, in part, because I was lonely. I had left friends behind me and knew no one until Winnipeg. I felt at the same time a sense of exhilaration at the 2,500 miles that lay ahead of me before I reached home, the friends I had not met, and beyond all those miles and people the challenge of a vast emptiness as yet untouched by roads or gas-station-motel-café units with jukeboxes and trailer hookups and synthetic food. And there was my country, which has not managed to grasp a vision of itself, which is casually selling control of its land and its destiny to the business interests of a blind, rapacious, and relentless giant.

It was a very sentimental moment.

Reprinted from the Toronto Daily Star.

NORWEGIAN ADVENTURE

M. BAGLEY
May 1967

We had landed in Norway during the early hours of the morning, yet we felt that all the eyes of Oslo were on our short pants and lightweight bikes, and our small saddle-bags containing all we needed to cross the country at its

A snow tunnel on the 400-foot Reindeer Road over the Hardanger Moor. Built where heavy drifting is likely to occur and right out in the wilderness, they are weird, other-planet-like things to cycle through. Damp and cold, they creak in the thin wind and send strange echoes after the rider.

widest point. We rode silently away from the harbor, like ghosts in the gray dawn, heading out on the Honefoss road.

"We're going up already," John said, and I looked up at the hill and the pine trees closing down to the highway.

"Is that so!" I muttered, beads of perspiration clinging to my eyelashes and running down my face.

We fetched up on top of the rise, stood our machines against a tree, and took in the valley spread out before and below. The rising sun hit a rock face, and it glinted redly through the pines. This was our first real bike tour, and we took a good look at the scene.

"Think we can make it?" I said slowly.

John lifted a plastic bottle from its handlebar cage and took a long pull at the air-cooled water. He grinned. "We just done a thousand miles nonstop. What're you worrying about?"

"Anybody can do a thousand miles by rail and steamer, but there's three hundred pedaling miles between us and Bergen."

We'd had an overnight rail journey up from central Germany into Denmark, and a second night on the steamer up to Oslo. We'd scheduled three days to cross Norway, a day return by rail to Oslo, and three days pedaling down the Swedish coast to Copenhagen. We didn't have too much time to lose.

"How far've we come?" I said, digging out our road map. "Twenty miles. There's another eighty to Nesbyen. We've got to go."

We sailed down a long hill into the valley, cold air hitting us and bringing moisture streaming from our eyes. John hit a small stone, and it whirred from his wheel. We leaned around the bends, the valley swung below and raced up to meet us, and the road twisted down to a lake.

We had to stop. It was warm there, and the fall was turning the grass to gold. Rowanberries hung from the trees around the lake, vivid red splashes against the deep blue of the water.

"Could stop here all day," John said.

"Yea, if we had cash and a pass that said we didn't have to be back on base in seven days' time."

The sun grew warmer, and by midmorning we had passed Honefoss, a lumber town and the only place of any size between Oslo and Bergen. We rolled on over the concrete road, going easy along the valley floor. Our machines were very light, our one and a half cubic feet of space in the saddlebags being sufficient for a complete change of clothing packed in tight, pants, shirt, sweater, shoes stuffed with socks. Then we had sheet sleeping bags for the youth hostel beds, small face towel, razor, soap, pajamas, and a pack of plasters in case of accidents. Also a small loaf of bread, cheese, jar of jam, biscuits, and as many bars of chocolate as we could cram in. Side pockets on the saddlebags held tools, spares, patches, glue, and strapped over top were our rain capes, windcheaters, and road map.

Bottle cages held two plastic bottles to the handlebars, and we had a canvas bag strung over them containing fruit which we could eat while on the move.

We rolled on over the concrete road, heading into the hinterland. The pine forest crowded in, the pale trunks standing clear and straight against the dark shadows in the thick of the trees. We had ten gears to choose from, and two nights without any real sleep did little to rob our legs of the strength to push a high one. The first hundred miles looked like being easy, but then we ran out of road.

We stared in disbelief at the shovelfuls of grit and rocks a road repair gang was dumping into ruts and holes in what had now become a dirt road.

"We can't ride on this!" John yelled, steering between a heap of stones and an amused Norwegian's shovel. "Ask 'em what it's like up ahead."

"Taler de Engelik?" I queried, but the road gang just gathered around us and smiled. I tried again. "Bergen?" I said, pointing at the grit and then up the road.

"Bergen," a big fellow grinned, his face the color and texture of fir bark at sundown. I had a feeling there was a joke here somewhere that I didn't understand.

"It's all right," John whispered, "they think we're asking them if this is the right road to Bergen. They are not saying it's like this all the way there."

Twenty miles on, we looked at each other and then at the continuing dirt road, but slate-blue lakes, the forest, and the wildness of this Hallingdal valley took our minds off the slower pace. There was plenty of room to ride around the bad patches, for we saw no more than ten automobiles right through that day.

We came to Nesbyen youth hostel in the late evening. It was a pleasant wooden building, black with tar, the window frames, doors, and eaves painted white. Our sleeping quarters were in a small cabin standing in a paddock at the back of the main building, and this cabin contained about a dozen bunks grouped around a huge stove. We reckoned they must have quite a winter if it needed around sixty square feet of iron to heat such a small area.

There were two wardens at Nesbyen, elderly ladies whose bright eyes glinted from behind thick-rimmed spectacles. They set us up with a meal of cheese and cold meat and bilberry jam, and we drank quarts of coffee, after which we settled back to enjoy a conversation of very few words, though much was conveyed. It was all done with our eyes and hands, and the language barrier collapsed during that enjoyable hour spent in their quiet, pine-scented room.

They pointed to the next day's date and we indicated our destination on the map. Their eyebrows shot up, and the look in their eyes spoke of wonders along our route. "Fossli!" they whispered, and we gathered that this was a place to test our cycling skills. How right we were. That "Fossli!" was to live in my memory forever, along with two aged faces expressing apprehension and concern.

When we awoke the next morning, we lay listening to the strange, beautiful silence of Hallingdal in the fall. The sky was a cold, bright blue, the first sunlight shone redly on the tips of the mountains, and we watched it creep down to the tree line. And then the first sound cracked the hush, the chop of an ax somewhere in the forest, and it released us from the spell of stillness.

We dashed out to douse our sleepy faces in a tub in the paddock, and the water tingled like an electric current. Icy dew flew off the grass and seemed almost to burn our legs. We could smell coffee coming from the house. The road to Fossli beckoned through the pines. It seemed unreal. yet more than real, like in a dream.

Fifteen miles northwest of Nesbyen we reached the village of Gol with its Wild West atmosphere, especially around the general store and the boardwalk at the dusty roadside. Then, like pioneers setting out for the unknown, we headed west up the valley through Al and Hol and on to what is called the Reindeer Road. This took us over the Hardangervidda, a barren moorland plateau, and we climbed above the four-thousand-foot contour. We came to within a few miles of where the road reached the Hardanger Fjord and sea level, yet we lost altitude only very slowly, slithering unsuspectingly toward Fossli.

A roar came whipping up out of the core of the earth and stopped us. There were no danger signs, no fences, nothing but the lip off Hardangervidda and heaven knows how many hundreds of feet between us and the foot of the waterfall. John could stand on the edge and look over, but gripped by a hellish vertigo I could only creep up on my stomach and peep down.

I saw the road plunge, curling and twisting around sheer rock like a partly uncoiled spring, and I could almost hear those old ladies whispering "Fossli." We checked our brakes, mounted, pointed our bikes at the edge, and went over.

Sometimes I dream of that moment. The canyon seemed to suck us down, and we went skidding around hairpin bends, tensed up with wonder and fear. John disappeared ahead of me, and suddenly a large battered truck filled the space where John had been, coming insanely toward me and filling the road completely. It rocked and lurched and roared like a maniacal lion, and I looked for John on its vicious, tooth-like fender. Somehow he must have got by, and somehow that was what I had to do.

I flung the bike toward a dark drop at the roadside and went bouncing over great wheel-busting rocks. Everything vanished in a cloud of dust as the furious truck went leaping and bucking up the pass, and I swerved back onto the road, not daring to look at the drop beneath my pedals.

I pulled up around the corner, trembling and prickly with sweat. John stood, mopping his brow. "Missed him!" he said quietly, and we went slowly down to Eidfjord and the fjordland. It was more picturesque perhaps, but not so adventurous as that wild, silent hinterland with its grand climax at Fossli.

THE PERILS OF DERVLA MURPHY

CLIFFORD L. GRAVES, M.D.
January 1969

When I wrote in this magazine two years ago that it was no longer possible to go around the world by bicycle because of international tension, I had not counted on a young woman—repeat, woman—who brought off the most difficult part of such a journey, alone and unaided, in 1963. This woman is Dervla Murphy, an Irish nurse, who has written an eloquent and fascinating account of her travels.

Dervla did not come by her idea overnight. On her tenth birthday she got a bike and promptly fell in love with it. She also got an atlas. Between bicycle and atlas, she hatched a plan. Someday she would cycle from Ireland to India. People laughed, and Dervla lay low. Twenty years later, she crossed the Channel and turned her wheels into the teeth of a howling snowstorm at Dunkirk. It was the beginning of a fantastic journey on which she nearly lost her life twice and her honor once. But she made it.

No visionary, she selected her equipment with care and common sense. Her bicycle was an Armstrong with quarter-inch tires and a nearly flat handlebar. Without her baggage, it weighed thirty-six pounds; with it, sixty-four. To prevent trouble with the derailleur, she took it off. As an additional precaution, she sent spare tires to the various cities along her route. She bought a gun and learned how to shoot it. She studied her atlas and decided to go through Paris, Milan, Venice, Zagreb, Belgrade, Sofia, Istanbul, Tehran, Meshed, Kabul, Peshawar, Rawalpindi, and Delhi. With several arduous side trips, this 4,500-mile trek took 175 days and cost $175.

Whenever day was done, she looked for a place to sleep. She slept in European youth hostels and factory dorms, in dark bungalows and Indian pagodas, in Kurdish coffeehouses and Iranian teahouses, in Afghan mud huts and Turkish caravansaries, in police barracks and army caserns, in governor's residences and royal palaces, in Himalayan shelters and nomad tents, and finally on charpoys out in the open. What she learned was that after a day on a bike, you can sleep anywhere, any way, in any company.

Dervla knew that if she wanted to get to India before the heat of summer, she would have to leave in the dead of winter. Unfortunately, the winter of 1963 was one of the worst. Within days, her gay adventure turned into a grim struggle for survival. In Grenoble, she had to give up. The road disappeared under a mountain of snow. She took the train to Turin, beat her way across the Po Valley, and entered Yugoslavia on a day so cold that her hand froze to the handlebar.

Night was falling as she entered Nova Gorizia, the first town on the Yugoslav side. Walking her bike along the dark and deserted streets, she asked a girl for directions. Where to stay? The girl explained that tourists could only stay in official hotels, which are very expensive. Sensing Dervla's alarm, the girl continued without a moment's hesitation: "Come with me. My friends would love to meet you." The farther Dervla penetrated into the undeveloped countries, the more kindness she met.

Of her trip across the interior of Yugoslavia, Dervla remembers only barren mountains, frozen plains, and ice-bound roads. After four days of this, she stumbled into Belgrade, more dead than alive. Here, the weather seemed to take a turn for the better, but she had hardly started again when she was forced to accept a lift because black ice made two-wheeled travel hazardous. The truck ride was a nightmare. When progress on the main road became impossible, the driver switched to a side road where his truck finally gave up the ghost in a collision with a tree. Thankful that she was still alive, Dervla left the disabled driver and her bicycle in the truck and started walking toward the village in the dead of night.

She had barely gone a mile when she was almost bowled over by a heavy object that came tumbling out of the shadows and fastened itself to her shoulder. Fearful growling told her that her attacker was either a wolf or a dog crazed by hunger. A second animal was trying to sink its teeth into her ankles while a third stood by, ready for the kill. Not for nothing had Dervla practiced the quick draw. Her first shot killed the animal hanging from her shoulder. A second shot wounded the one at her feet. Suddenly she was alone. Her ammunition gone, she ran the rest of the way and collapsed on the steps of the local gendarmerie.

As she approached Istanbul, sudden thaws converted massive snowbanks into raging torrents. Mountains of water came rushing down the Morava, lapping at its banks. Dervla's road was on the levee, only inches above the floodwaters. Suddenly a tremendous wave crashed over the levee and washed Dervla down the embankment, bicycle and all. Soaked to the skin, she could think of

nothing but her bicycle. When she picked herself up, she
found it hanging in a tree.

Much to her surprise, she crossed the Iron Curtain with
nary a flurry or a fanfare. The customs house on the
Yugoslav side was deserted. She dragged her bicycle
through one of the numerous holes in the fence and presented herself at the Bulgarian customs house. This, too,
was deserted, but a persistent search led to a room where
a policeman was fast asleep with a kitten on his lap.

"Excuse me, sir. Would you mind stamping my pass-
port?"

She showed it to him. Her visa, obtained in London
with much difficulty, limited her to a stay of four days.
The policeman burst out laughing and gave her a visa
with no time limit at all. Then he poured her a brandy
and wished her a happy trip.

Her route now lay to Istanbul, across the Bosporus, and
into Asiatic Turkey. As the temperatures became milder,
the country became wilder. Shortly after crossing into
Iran, Dervla had to use her gun again.

She was resting by the side of the road at a hairpin
bend when three gnarled and elderly men approached,
each one carrying a spade. Just as she made ready to greet
them, two of the men seized her bicycle while the third
one threatened her with his spade. Dervla backed off,
grabbed her gun, fired in the air, and then took aim at her
attacker, but before she could shoot again, all three men
started running, dropping spades, bicycle, and everything.

Some travelers believe it is better not to carry a gun,
saying that it causes more trouble than it cures. If Dervla
had used her gun in Adabile, she would still be languish-
ing in an Armenian jail. She had just finished lunch on
the plaza when a constable came to tell her that she was
in a restricted zone and needed clearance at the police
station. He told her to follow him. After a long walk
through a disreputable part of town they came to a house
that did not look at all like a police station. Inside, it
looked even less so. It was a private house, completely deserted. The policeman locked the door, put the key in
his pocket, and made his intentions unmistakably clear.
Dervla was in a precarious position. If she used her gun,
she would be arrested for assaulting a policeman. They

hang people for that in Armenia. So she used her knees, her nails, and her teeth. With her attacker temporarily disabled, she grabbed his trousers, retrieved the key, and darted out the door. It was her closest call. Ironically, it came not from a stealthy foe in a dark alley but from a guardian of the law on the main street in broad daylight.

In Tehran she was told that the road to Afghanistan was closed to women since a Swedish girl who tried it in a car had been killed by bandits. Undismayed, Dervla wheedled a letter out of the American Consul, asking the Afghan government to waive the rule for Dervla. "After all," she pointed out, "if visas had been needed in 1492, America would never have been discovered." Her argument worked, and for the next two weeks, she cycled a thousand miles through the Dasht-i-Kavir over roads that would have wrecked a Jeep. Gradually, her bicycle began to develop ailments. In the only bike shop between Tehran and Kabul, two mechanics administered first aid so enthusiastically that the patient almost died. In Iran, no mechanic uses a screwdriver. He hammers the screw into place.

Although Dervla had been warned repeatedly that Afghanistan was a hazardous and primitive country, she never saw a bandit. On the contrary, the people were kind and considerate. In the Tangi Sharo gorge, when she fell asleep by the side of the road in the full glare of the midday sun, a wizened old man built a tent over her so quietly that she never woke up. Yet, an American tourist who traveled this route by car and ran over an Afghan infant by accident was almost killed by irate tribesmen.

Traffic was limited to camel caravans and an occasional overloaded and undernourished bus. In this strangely beautiful country, Dervla saw only one private vehicle. It was a Jeep, driven by an American AID official.

"What the hell are you doing on this damn road?"

"Riding my bike."

"I can see that. But what the hell for?"

"For fun."

"Are you a nut? Gimme that bike and I'll stick it on the back. You get in here and we'll get out of this goddamn frying pan as fast as we can. This track isn't fit for a camel."

"When you are on a bike, it doesn't feel like a frying pan. Just look around and you will have to admit that the landscape makes up for the shocking state of the road. I *enjoy* cycling through this country. Thanks for your kind offer."

"You *are* a damn nut."

Kabul, the capital of Afghanistan, would have been full of interest but for the presence of thousands of Americans on AID missions. Dervla was not long in evaluating them.

"Today I met a twenty-five-year-old American boy in the museum who was typical of his kind. To them, travel is more a *going away from* than a *going toward,* and they seem empty and unhappy and bewildered and pathetically anxious for companionship, yet are afraid to commit themselves to any ideal or cause or person. I find something both terrifying and touching in young people without an aim, however foolish or wrong they may be. This young man was pleasant and intelligent but wasting his time and resentfully conscious of the fact. He did not want to return home, yet, after two years, he is weary of travel, probably because he always holds himself aloof from the people—not through hostility or superiority but through a strange unawareness of his own identity."

Kabul was a disappointment after Herat, but on the other side of the Hindu Kush beckoned an enchanted valley with the legendary village of Bamian. Dervla tackled the 10,380-foot Shibar Pass on her bike, but her tires were ripped to pieces and her brake blocks torn to shreds. She had no choice but to continue by bus.

On this bus she suffered her only serious injury. At the start, the driver agreed on a fare of ten afghanis a head, but on the road he raised it to twelve. Pandemonium broke loose. All the occupants grabbed their weapons, and one man tried to climb over the seats to get his hands on the driver. In the ensuing fight, the irate tribesman fell on Dervla, delivering a hard blow to her chest with the butt of his rifle. The result was several fractured ribs, which plagued her for weeks. But Bamian made up for it. Isolated from the outside world for centuries, it will forever be a fairyland.

At the Pakistan border, Dervla was suddenly back in civilization. The customs house had a fan, the officials were in uniform, and the roads were marked. But the people were no longer proud tribesmen. They were Orientals, living in unbelievable squalor in the oppressive heat of a sadly overcrowded country.

Dervla was now within striking distance of a place she wanted to see above all else: Gilgit. From Rawalpindi to Gilgit is only two hundred miles as the crow flies. But crows don't fly to fifteen thousand feet. And that was the height of the Babusar Pass leading to Gilgit. Even though it was now early June with temperatures regularly over 100°, the Babusar Pass was still closed. There was only one way to Gilgit: fly.

The flight was a nightmare. The pilot could not afford to waste one ounce of gasoline, and he stuck close to the ground. Soon they were flying in the shadow of 26,000-foot Nanga Parbat. Dervla was more puzzled than impressed. Here she was looking out over a fantastic panorama of snowcapped peaks, and yet she was not half as excited as when she saw those same peaks from her bicycle. Modern man cheated himself, she reflected, when he removed all physical effort from the act of travel. Today, a person can tour the five continents with less effort than his grandfather used in visiting the next town. Today, we *see* more. But does it *mean* more?

In Gilgit, high in the Himalayan mountains, Dervla fell in love with the beauty of the country. It was another world.

For a month, Dervla was a prisoner of Gilgit. She could not tear herself away. Finally, the calendar told her that the pass should be open. Alternately hiking and cycling, she followed the gorge of the Indus River to the foot of the pass. Temperatures in the gorge reached 120°. The only way she could survive was to start at dawn, travel till noon, find a shady spot, and sleep till four. One day, she ran out of water and nearly died. She observed her symptoms with more interest than alarm. First, she stopped sweating, then she felt cold, finally she fainted. She lay unconscious for hours, then dragged herself the few remaining miles to the village of Chilas. It took several days to recover.

Now came the Babusar Pass in all its glory and vastness. As yet, the pass had not been crossed, but an old man told Dervla as she left that a pony caravan had come through a few hours earlier. The first six miles took four hours over a recognizable track. Then, as a blistering sun gave way to snow flurries, Dervla could not see the far side of the glacier, and the surface seemed highly treacherous. The only thing to do was to try to find a way around. Crawling and jumping from one rock to another, she finally reached the top with the bicycle wrapped around her neck. The sun was setting rapidly, and there wasn't a moment to waste. She had to get on or freeze to death.

She started the descent, only to come to a ravine where a bridge had been washed out. Her path was blocked! Searching desperately for a clue, she picked up the tracks of the ponies just as she came to the end of her strength. She climbed back toward the glacier, followed its edge, and spotted the caravan a mile below. There was no time to follow the trail. Instead, Dervla slid down the glacier, sending her bike down first. The men greeted her with shouts of glee and astonishment. The Babusar Pass had been crossed by the bike.

The rest of her journey back to Rawalpindi was a 120-mile coast. As she approached the city, the heat once more struck at her savagely. Yet, she persisted. Three weeks after leaving Gilgit, she reached Delhi, but the price was high: dysentery. It ended her travels more effectively than floods, heat, snow, or ice.

What to make of this feat? Dervla Murphy was a young woman with a vision. Her vision was clear. She wanted to see the world. She could have gone by train and by bus, but she chose the bicycle because of its unique advantages. The bicycle opened uncharted ground. It brought her close to the people. It made her see more clearly, feel more keenly, think more critically. In short, it helped her to understand herself.

THE DAY MY BICYCLE
SAVED MY LIFE

CLIFFORD L. GRAVES, M.D.
March 1968

Early in the morning of Saturday, December 16, 1944, I was awakened by the sound of distant gunfire. From my sleeping bag on the floor of a schoolroom on the Belgian-German frontier, I could see that it was raining. That was nothing unusual. But the gunfire? We were supposed to be in a quiet sector.

The schoolhouse in Bütgenbach had been our home for two weeks. I had a mobile surgical team, and surgical teams rarely stayed two weeks in a field hospital. Our job was to clean up the first-priority casualties and move on to the next spot. But at that moment there was no spot on the First Army front. The fighting at Bütgenbach, after the fierce battle for the Hürtgen Forest, had slowed. If there was any doubt about the plans for our sector, it was promptly dispelled by the arrival of the 106th Division. The 106th was fresh from home. A fresh division always went to a quiet sector. We were going to stay put for a while.

It could be worse. Bütgenbach wasn't Paris, but it had a schoolhouse with a roof and that was more than you could say for most buildings in that area. The only thing that was really lacking was water. The pipes had burst when the freeze set in. The freeze was followed by a thaw and then another freeze. In the resulting flood, hundreds of icicles began forming in the john. We used to go there at night, just to shine a flashlight.

In my pleasant state of half consciousness that morning, I thought of those boys of the 106th Division. They were old and wet. I was warm and dry. I even had my bike with me, although in a crate. What a ridiculous article to take along. But who could have predicted all this jumping around? The bike had looked good to me when I bought

it on the London black market. In the months before
D-Day, I became attached to it. So I got this crazy idea
to put it on the surgical truck. But it had to be disguised.
I had the sergeant build a box for it, a solid box so you
couldn't see what was inside. I took a lot of ribbing on
that box. People were always asking me what was in it,
and I'd say surgical equipment, although I don't know
what kind of surgical equipment would fit into a box of
that shape. And here I was six months later with the bike
still in the box. I pictured myself on a beautiful day in
spring, opening the box and taking off for a ride through
the Black Forest. That is as far as I had got in my dreams
when I heard a commotion in the school yard. I got up
and made my way to the next room where the night crew
was gathered over coffee and a cold breakfast.

"What's up?" I asked.

"They just brought that fellow in," said the other team
chief. He pointed to a stretcher where a lieutenant was
trying to get a transfusion started on a poor guy with his
legs blown off. I took a quick look and went outside.
had an uneasy feeling that something was afoot. But what.
It was unthinkable that the Germans would attack now.

The gunfire had become louder but the village looked
no different. Then, just as I started to go back inside,
saw a radar truck barreling toward me. Our building was
on a sharp corner. The truck missed the corner, skidded
on wet pavement, and landed on its side. I hurried over
to help, but it wasn't necessary. The driver crawled out
unhurt.

"Get back, Major," he said. "I am going to set this
thing on fire."

"On fire? What's the idea?"

"I just don't want the Krauts to get their hands on it.

"The Krauts?"

"Yes, the Krauts. The last one I saw was a mile up the
road."

He was now too busy setting the thermite to answer
any more questions. I got back to the school yard at the
same time as a Jeep with a colonel of the 106th Division

"Get out of here," I heard him shout. "German tanks
are coming down the road."

And that was the beginning of the Battle of the Bulge for me.

How the Germans mounted this battle is one of the great military feats of all time. With infinite cunning and incredible luck, the German generals massed twenty-five divisions on the Belgian frontier, and they managed to do this without dropping a single hint to the Americans. On that fateful morning when I was dreaming about my bike, these twenty-five divisions hurled themselves at three American divisions over a sixty-mile front. To add to the shock of the attack, the Germans dropped parachutists in American uniform behind the lines. On December 16, the 106th Division had been in the line one week. It just buckled.

Within three hours, the Germans had torn a huge hole in the American defenses. Through this hole, they poured their armor, a total of ten divisions. Altogether, a quarter of a million men. When it was all over six weeks later, 150,000 of these were dead or wounded. But the Americans suffered almost as much. In number of troops engaged, in number of casualties, and in terms of potential disaster, the Battle of the Bulge was the greatest battle the American army ever fought.

"Get out of here," the colonel had said. But how? We had only three vehicles for 150 men. One of these vehicles was my surgical truck. The second was an ambulance, and the third the water truck. I located my sergeant.

"Sergeant, throw everything out of the surgical truck and load it with the casualties and the men. On the double."

Never have I seen a job done so thoroughly. In five minutes, the equipment was out and the men in. At the same time, the ambulance and the water truck were loading. I'll never forget the sight of the water truck careening through the gate with two dozen GI's clinging to the sides. At any other time I would have laughed myself silly. But this was no time to laugh because when I looked around as the last vehicle pulled out, I could see that half our complement were still milling around in the yard. There was no panic. Just a sort of quiet desperation.

"Sergeant," I said, "help me break open that box."'

The bike was there just as I had packed it. All it needed was air. I started pumping with might and main.

"Sergeant," I said between gasps, "I am getting out. Tell the men they are on their own."

They did not need to be told. The yard was rapidly emptying. Most of the men were captured a few minutes later.

I advanced cautiously toward the gate. In the direction of the front I could see six tanks, about half a mile away. It was now or never. I jumped on the bike and sprinted down the street. If the tank drivers saw me, they mistook me for one of their own. At least, they did not fire a shot. My road led to Malmédy. At first I did not see a living soul but later I began to overtake what can only be described as an army in retreat. Ambulances, Jeeps, armored cars, and half-trucks mingled in great confusion. Many of these vehicles had become disabled and acted as roadblocks. The rain had stopped but the clouds were hanging low. It was the most dismal scene I ever hope to see.

I arrived in Malmédy just as the 44th Evacuation Hospital began to evacuate. On foot. I knew quite a few of the doctors there, and I saw one of them running down the street while he was trying to put on his pants. Here was comedy and tragedy all in one. A mile out of town I passed Battery B of the 285th Field Artillery Observation Battalion. That was the battery that was overwhelmed by the Germans a few hours later. The Germans herded the men into a field and mowed them down with machine guns. Two hundred Americans died in that infamous assault.

Between Malmédy and Spa it was a struggle. The retreating elements of the 106th Division ran headlong into the advancing elements of the 7th Armored, resulting in the most monumental traffic jam of the war. A tank sergeant looked at me in utter amazement and asked where the Krauts were. I told him to keep right on going and he would see plenty of them. A little later German planes came over. I dived for the ditch, bike and all. A bomb landed nearby and buried two dental officers that I had been talking to moments before. By the time we dug them out, they were dead. I pushed on.

I reached Spa at noon, having gone twenty miles in

three hours. To my great relief I found my team and the surgical truck intact. Spa was First Army headquarters. It was full of generals who knew less than I did. I found my commanding officer in a state of great agitation.

"We had given you up for lost," he said. "How did you ever get out of Bütgenbach?"

"On a bike."

"On a bike? Incredible. I'll recommend you for the Silver Star."

"I am more interested in a cup of coffee now."

"There isn't a cup of coffee in all of Spa. We are retreating to Huy."

"Where do you want me to go?"

"I just heard that there is a lot of pressure on Bastogne. Can you go there today?"

Bastogne? The name didn't mean a thing to me. I went to the motor pool. Our surgical truck had survived some rough treatment in the strafing attack, and the driver was lost. I grabbed the first GI I saw.

"Can you drive us to Bastogne?"

"Bastogne? Where is that, Major?"

"Never mind. You just drive."

It took the rest of the afternoon to round up my team and to scrounge some maps. At the last moment, just as we were pulling out, I remembered that I had left my bike at First Army. We chased back, picked it up, and took off.

The map told me that we would have to head south along a line parallel with the front and about twenty miles to the west of it. The route lay through Stavelot, Vielsalm, and Houffalize. With luck, we would be in Bastogne that night. Little did I realize that we were heading for the eve of the battle that was now rapidly taking shape.

At Stavelot, darkness overtook us. The road was now completely deserted. It also seemed to get narrower with every mile. I had done a lot of navigating in the blackout in England and I thought that I was pretty good at it. But somehow I must have taken a wrong turn. I did not know it, but we were actually heading back toward the frontier.

Even though we were going at a snail's pace, my driver had great difficulty keeping the big truck on the road.

To make him feel a little better, I complimented him on the job he was doing.

"Thanks, Major," he said. "This is the first time I have driven one of these."

He had barely finished speaking when I thought I could hear gunfire over the roar of the engine in low gear. At the next bend, we came on an eerie spectacle. Less than a mile away, an isolated farmhouse was burning fiercely. What was this? Saboteurs? An accident? A wanton act of destruction? Whatever it was, I could see trouble. I told the driver to turn around.

"Sir, I can't turn this baby around. The road is too narrow."

He was right. The road was barely twelve feet wide with trees on both sides. Backing up under those conditions was out of the question. Going forward seemed risky. We needed a crossroad to turn around. Where to find one? Our truck was poorly designed for scouting.

Then I thought of the bike. Remembering my getaway in Bütgenbach, I figured that I could go on a limited reconnaissance by bike with a lot less chance of attracting attention than the noisy truck. I jumped out.

"Hand me my bike."

The light from the fire helped me find my way. The crossroad I was looking for was not far. Hallelujah! I scurried back to the truck, told the driver to follow me, and guided him into the intersection. It was in the midst of this maneuver that I heard a rumble of engines and saw three dark shapes silhouetted against the dying flames. Tanks.

My first reaction was relief. At least we had protection. But my second reaction was concern. The tanks were bearing down pretty fast. What if they did not see us? I could visualize a ghastly collision. Somehow, I had to head off those charging monsters.

I whipped my bike around and started toward the tanks. The confrontation took place about a quarter of a mile from our truck. I stationed myself in the middle of the road and waved my handkerchief. Thank God. The lead tank slowed, and I yelled at the top of my voice for him to stop.

The driver throttled his engine, opened the turret, and stuck his head out.

"Stop!" I yelled again. "There is a truck up ahead. Give us a chance to turn around."

The tank driver said something that I could not understand. I came a little closer and repeated what I had said, only louder.

The tank driver spoke again. This time I did understand what he said. He said to get out of his way. In German.

I wish I could recount the thoughts that raced through my head in that anguished moment. All of a sudden, the whole desperate situation became clear to me. This was a raiding party. These were the tanks that had set the farmhouse on fire. Here I was talking to a German tank at a distance of ten yards. My knees began to shake, my heart to pound, my throat to choke. If I had known that Hitler's orders were to shoot all Americans instead of bothering with prisoners, I would have collapsed altogether.

One thing was crystal clear: the tank sergeant mistook me for one of the parachutists in American uniform. How to keep him from discovering the truth? I had to say something in German. I knew a little German but hardly enough to open a conversation under these trying circumstances. Moreover, what little I knew drained out of my system in a wave of black despair. I don't know how long I just stood there, transfixed. Then, since the next move was obviously up to me, I hit on a word that the Germans themselves are very fond of, a word they use over and over, a word that can be used as filler in almost any any conversation. It is the word *ja,* meaning "yes."

"Ja, ja, ja, ja, ja, ja!"

With that, I jerked my bike around, raced back to the truck, and told my driver to beat it. He excelled himself.

For all I know the tank sergeant thinks to this day that he was talking to a friend.

GOING DUTCH

MARIUS LODEENSEN
November 1967

From the cockpit of our Boeing Clipper we looked down on Holland's crisscrossed polderland, resembling a Mondrian painting of multicolored rectangles, taking in the whole of the country in one sweeping glance.

"Ever been there, Gordon?" I asked.

"Except for a fuel stop at Schiphol airport, no," he replied.

I switched on the auto pilot and pointed over his shoulder. "There's the IJssel Lake that used to be the Zuider Zee. It's now halfway pumped dry. When you walk on the cobblestones through the old fishing villages, you feel as if walking in the past. Let me show it to you sometime . . . on a bicycle."

"It's a deal, Lodi," Gordon agreed. "But let's do it on a tandem so you can do the work and I can enjoy the scenery."

And that is how we set out to see Holland.

Holland is a wet country, a land of water, milk, beer, and gin. In a jet you can cross it in fifteen minutes, in a car in three hours, on the bicycle in two days. It's a picture-postcard land with the accent on the diminutive: a land of dikes, canals, reclaimed land, industrial towns, medieval castles, agricultural villages, a blending of the centuries with relics of the past framed in today's progress.

The sky is mainly overcast, the light is soft—the velvet light of the Dutch Masters, the "Rembrandt light" as my friend calls it. Everything has a scrubbed look. Touring in Holland is like traveling through a park.

Sparkling and foamy is Holland's beer, fragrant and potent the gin, or *jenever*. Discovered in the seventeenth century by a Dutchman named Sylvius, gin is the traditional Dutch treat. New *jenever* (Jonge Klare) is taken with sugar, old *jenever* (Oude Klare) straight, and four

Navigating a canal over a suspension bridge for those afoot and awheel—on two wheels, that is.

borrels make all women ravishing and all men friends or enemies, depending on one's temperament.

Cycling is the Dutch way of life. Courting couples ride hand in hand, mothers with babies in wicker baskets, delivery boys on three-wheelers, cabinet ministers with bowler hats and briefcases. And Granddad, puffing a cigar, straddles his bike as a horseman sits his mount, stately and dignified. The country is as flat as a desktop, distances are small, and it is handy to get around. Five million Dutchmen cannot be wrong.

Gordon and I disembarked from the Pan American Clipper at Schiphol airport, Amsterdam, thirteen feet below sea level. Our tandem was waiting for us. W. E. Powell of Birmingham had built it with a combination four-speed Sturmey-Archer hub gear and a Benelux derailleur, giving it eight speeds of wide range. It looked splendid in light blue finish, and after unwrapping it in the customs office (no duty, as we were on a tour), we mounted at once and rode off.

Immediately, we found ourselves on a country road flanking a canal complete with apple-bowed Dutch barges, ducks, coots, and an occasional angler.

While I made an adjustment on the seat and handlebar posts, Gordon said, "You know, Lodi, boring through the troposphere in a blowtorch you really see nothing. This is the life. Look at those beautiful barges!"

"Of course, Gordon. What did I tell you? Look at that row of ducks sitting on a log across the canal. Watch what will happen when a barge comes by."

Just then, a long black low-in-the-water barge came chugging along. Flowering geraniums in pots shaded the cabin ports of the white deckhouse. The skipper stood in the stern, his arm wrapped around the tiller; the wife hung the washing on a line amidships. Two small kids played in a pen on top of the cabin, and a tiny, cocky dog with his tail curled over his back ran yapping along the gunnel. As the boat passed, the stern wave, rolling along the shore behind it, heaved the ducks from their perch with much indignant squawking and swishing of tails.

We followed the coast of the great inland lake, formerly the Zuider Zee. Since it has been cut off from the North

Sea, the water became sweet, the herring disappeared, and the people, clinging to their old way of life, turned to catching eels. But soon this will cease. When the entire lake has been reclaimed, only some narrow streams will be left for draining the adjacent land. A way of life will vanish to yield to the press of industrial "progress."

Circumnavigating the IJassel Lake, we rode through tiny villages with step-gabled cottages hugging the dikes or leaning drowsily over the placid waters, behind every white-curtained window a row of flower-pots. Around the squares stood booths with jars of pickled herring, and bunches of smoked eels hung from the overhead.

Coming to one of the villages, we stopped before a small café, Het Zwaantje (The Little Swan). I suggested a drink.

"Why not?" said Gordon. "But be sure they have *croquettes.*" (*Croquettes* are patties with succulent filling of meat and sauce covered by crunchy crusts, and Gordon had fallen in love with them upon first acquaintance.) I watched the light on the trees and the houses and two great gray horses pulling a farm wagon. A fat man in a white apron walked up to our table.

"Vier croquetjes en twee glazen bier." I ordered.

"Als het U blieft!"

Like full-rigged ships, three and four abreast, women strolled around while the men took their ease on wooden benches lining the waterfront.

Here you see the most beautiful costumes of the many varieties found in Holland. The traditional dress represents an old heritage. It changes from village to village but always in character with the people, and various symbols identify social position, marital status, and religious denominations.

The following day found us cycling over the pumped-dry polderland to Urk, once an island and home of the great herring fleets but now sitting high and dry on the dike. Grizzled fishermen repose on the stoops of their cottages, sucking clay pipes. With red-and-white-striped shirts, bolero-type jackets, baggy pants with silver buckles, and visorless caps, they are a striking lot.

I asked one of them if his belt buckles had any significance.

"It's the custom," he replied. "These buckles belonged to my father and my grandfather."

"And will your son wear them someday?" I asked.

"Nee meneer," he said; and I thought I heard a touch of regret in his voice. "Soon it will be all over with the fishing." He pointed toward the harbor. "That's my son; he is engineer on that tugboat."

I saw a youngster in blue overalls standing at the wheelhouse. He did not look over seventeen.

Dark-hulled boats with high stems unloaded their catches. Sturdy men hauled tubs full of squirming eels to the weighing sheds. Some men sat cross-legged on the decks measuring the eels in an elongated dish. Twenty-eight centimeters is the legal limit. If too small, over the side they go. The others are smoked and become the perfect tablemates to a glass of cold beer or a *borrel* of gin.

Eels are a tough breed as will be attested by anyone who has ever tried to kill one. Their longevity has been mentioned by writers of antiquity; some in Caesar's pond attained the age of sixty and were so much a part of the national scene that Crassus made a funeral oration at the death of one. Eels are omnivorous, eating everything in sight, dead or alive.

All this does not interest the men of Urk. What they care about: Is the eel long enough?

Leaving Urk, we cycled along the dike and through the ancient town of Lemmer—home of the Lemmer Aak, the peaked, round-gaffed vessels so familiar in old Dutch paintings—to Friesland.

Our finest cycling we found here, over winding cycle paths, along reed-grown ditches, the wind murmuring in our ears. Fat black-and-white cows stood in the lush meadows, and overhead, plovers flew their mad gyrations, singing their fluted songs. The pastures stretched out to the distant horizon, with here and there the crossed arms of a windmill relieving the flatness of the scene.

The windmill is part of the Dutch scene, or was.

The wind has always been Holland's ally. It filled the sails of the scrubby fleet and blew it over the flooded land to the relief of the siege of Leiden, held by the army of the Duke of Alva during the Eighty-Year War with Spain.

It provided motive power for merchantmen bringing goods from all over the world to the towns of Zuider Zee. It drove the windmills pumping water from drainage canals, grinding wheat, sawing wood. The graceful contours of thousands of mills dominated Holland's meadows.

Now most of them are out of service, their wings stilled, their language silenced. These windmills, like signaling posts, had their own "sail code." By the position of the arms and sails, millers signaled events such as feasts, salutes, births, and deaths, and during the war even relayed information to Allied fliers.

Holland's windmills will live on in names like Molenaar, Mulder, van der Molen, Molenenk—all meaning "miller."

We paid a short visit to Alkmaar, home of the famous cheese market.

As a restless, life-hungry boy, I cycled to school dreaming of far horizons, distant lands, thinking only the strange, the unknown, could give meaning to my life. I had no eye then for beauty close at hand. In those days, boatmen poled barges loaded with fat yellow cheeses through the canals to Alkmaar, where white-coated porters carried them to the weighing tower.

The boats are gone now, the cheeses arrive by truck, but otherwise the activities have changed little. On barrows painted in bright colors, the cheeses are carried to the weighing house, an ancient structure dating from the fourteenth century. It was originally a chapel dedicated to the Holy Ghost and used as a hostel for poor and needy travelers. We found hospitality there, too.

In the guild room underneath the weighhouse we met the porters, who from time to time repair there for a bottle of beer or a *borrel*. It is all very *gezellig;* they don't believe in punching time clocks in Alkmaar.

Little cupboards lined the walls. Rough wooden tables and benches, rubbed smooth by generations of elbows, filled the center of the old room. Gordon and I sang old Dutch folk songs with the porters, while strains of operetta arias, from barrel organs cruising around the marketplace, wafted through the slitted windows.

It's a great show, and if you want to see it, oil those wheels of yours and go there. You will not be disappointed.

As for me, I returned to the land of my youth and I saw it through another man's eyes. I looked for things that were not there and I saw much I never knew existed. Remembrance, that elusive residue of past living, is a *fata morgana*.

And Gordon? "I must come back here," he said.

When to go? Not during July and August when thousands of holiday seekers choke the roads and crowd the hotels. If you like to admire the famous bulb flowers around the coastal villages and towns north of The Hague, you should go in late March or early April, but the weather is changeable then. The month of September is my favorite. The weather is at its best and the tourists are gone.

In many towns you will find an office of the VVV (Vereeniging voor Vreemdelingenverkeer). Here you can book a room at a price you can afford and obtain maps and particulars.

Never does a cyclist feel pushed off the roads, as he is given priority over motor traffic at all intersections. All roads, even the highways, have cycle paths adjacent to them. But for real cycling, take the cycle paths (indicated on the road signs in red), away from all motorized traffic.

Do not fail to take at least one day to cycle through the national park De Hooge Veluwe, situated in the center of Holland. Here you ride over narrow paths through forests and open stretches of dunes and heather. If you start on a weekday and early, you might surprise a herd of mountain sheep silhouetted on a rise against the pale northern sky giving you the impression you are on the African veld.

The best maps are those of Michelin in three sections, north, middle, and southern Holland.

MEXICO IS A MUST

ROBERT STREETER
March 1965

> It is a winsome, sunlit land; artistic, intellectual, extraordinarily picturesque, and with a character and individuality peculiarly interesting to the thoughtful traveler. It is a felicitous blend of the cold North and the lower tropics; of Persia, India, Arabia, Spain, and the Holy Land; where the people are amiable, friendly, and helpful, and a country where travel is cheap, comfortable, and safe, where life presents an aspect of tranquility distinctly appealing to the hurried Northerner.

Thus began T. Phillip Terry, compiling an enormous amount of material through painstaking research and cumulative experience into the unparalleled classic *Terry's Guide to Mexico* (Boston and Hingham, 1938).

Those of us who are attracted by the lure and strangeness of lands afar—indeed, those of us who are merely after something exotic—can find it south of the border, a scant distance away. During the summer of 1960, I ventured to Mexico, often said to be the perfect place for retirement. Having cycling in mind instead, I chose to begin the trip by traveling via rail from the border entrance at Nogales, Arizona. By rail, one can travel the entire distance from Nogales to Mexico City for less than thirty-five dollars first-class, seeing the beautiful western coast of the country en route as far as Mazatlán, thence heading southeast past San Blas and on to the high central plateaus and Guadalajara in the state of Jalisco.

It must be borne in mind that the worst possible time to *cycle* in Mexico is during the summer months. Some travelers might prefer other modes of transportation during this time, owing to off-season advantages, but, in general, the torrential rains and oppressive heat experienced at that time of the year render the winter months far more favorable—for cycling anyway.

With that in mind, one can start off on the bike wherever it is desired. The baggage car, handled by agents of the Ferrocarriles del Pacífico, accommodates the bicycle, though somewhat precariously, with rumors of thievery constantly in the air. I began cycling in Guadalajara, having an obsessive aim in mind to eventually cross the Guatemalan border in the subsequent weeks ahead. A traveler has a multitude of roads to choose from in that area, and it might be said that the wisest action is that of gradual acclimatization, not only to the climate and altitudes in the country but also to its foods. This I did not do! Thus, rather than spend any extensive but easy "loafing" and general "knocking around" as a start, I attempted to cycle to Mexico City as fast as the wheels could turn—facing 90° temperatures, multithousand-feet elevations, and the weight of an unnecessary amount of touring equipment, including spare freewheel, chain-set parts, and odd sundries not related, such as a five-pound bowie knife.

This writer "finished" on that particular visit after a very short time of two weeks, having become alienated from foodstuffs as a result of "Montezuma's Revenge," dysentery. The remembrances of *that* series of ill-timed misfortunes shan't be mentioned for lack of space and magnitude, but the main thing to pass on is for travelers to avoid water and salad foods. Bearing this in mind on another trip two years later, no such misfortune as the "Revenge" presented itself. Moreover, such an illness can be particularly unpleasant in the remoter areas of the country, since it is not always possible to locate a physician, and total incapacitation can result.

Incessant disregard for the safety of themselves or anyone who treads in their paths can be said for the bus drivers in Mexico, where vehicles are passed at tremendously high rates of speed on the left *and* the right sides, regardless of the road conditions! At times, the cyclotourist might desire to alleviate such a condition by traveling *on* a bus rather than alongside it. If this is the case, he will be in for a genuine, hellish, hair-raising experience, and possibly a catastrophic one at that, in that speed limits do not exist, and seemingly have never been thought of, for that matter. Most second-class buses have roof carriers upon which a montage of Mexicana might be seen, and a cycle can usually be strapped amidst the medley, while the rates for carrying it vary. By and large, one can cover great portions of Mexico this way, cycling in the most interesting areas. The pre-Aztec pyramids at Teotihuacán, thirty-five miles northeast of Mexico City, is a good example: that civilization dates as far back as 350 B.C., and is said to have been "bigger than Athens or Rome."

As far as knowledge of the Spanish language is concerned, one can, in most cases, get by with a portable Berlitz "pocket interpreter" and usage of the few most necessary phrases. Visits to the tiendas where bicycles may be found will usually find new experiences within, for the people in and about such establishments are quite keen on the latest cycling equipment, and were surprised to see such seldom-used apparatus as the twenty-six-tooth chain wheel, as was my case. Thus, although frank, candid discussions on the merits of the Moulton bicycle or Campagnolo "Sport" derailleur, for example, would not arise (unless the traveler has mastered his Berlitz reader quite well), one will nevertheless encounter bona fide enthusiasts.

The guide to Mexico published by the California State Automobile Association is recommended for those who are considering traveling under any mode in Mexico or the Latin-American countries, since the guide is published yearly, and consequently kept up to date with revisions on road information. In addition, numerous hotels and motels are recommended by the association, though for the most part the less expensive establishments are usually not mentioned. Rather, one should also refer to the truthful guidebook *Mexico on $5 a Day* by John Wilcock and John Foreman, published by Arthur Frommer, Inc.

I personally believe that for the cyclo-tourist Mexico is a unique and interesting country, be it the southern peninsular region of Baja California, the mountainous central plateaus, or the jungles of the Yucatán. One can spend months in the central parts of the country alone; but alas, time is finite, and one should therefore consider the advantages of motorized transport at times, even airplanes, which will generally carry a cycle as the complement of baggage. The travel in that land can be pleasant whether solitary or by group, and for those interested in life about us, visiting Mexico is a must.

THE CYCLING SCENE IN THE LAND OF THE RISING SUN

E. PETER HOFFMAN
February 1969

When we think of cycling nations, France, Belgium, Italy, and other European countries come to mind. But in the Far East, on an island in the Pacific Ocean, a most industrious people are making advances in cycling which may soon surpass any land in the world.

Hiroshima and Nagasaki brought an end to a terrible war, but for the Japanese it was the beginning of an unprecedented period of growth.

When the war ended, Japan lay in ruins, completely devastated by incessant air raids and finally by atomic attack. The people were plunged into extreme despair, industry was completely paralyzed, and the government was a financial and political shambles. Rehabilitation progressed slowly. Confusion reigned. Public unrest threatened to explode. The people had little hope until the bicycle came to their rescue.

In July 1948 the Japanese government passed the Bicycle Race Law, establishing a system of bicycle racing, accompanied by pari-mutuel betting, called the Keirin. Its purpose was to give the masses a healthy moral impetus through sportsmanship and a dream of fortune through the totalizator betting system. But the plan was much broader in scope and provided that the Keirin should also contribute to the improvement of the bicycle and other machine industries, increase and bolster the export business, and develop and aid in the financial condition of local autonomous bodies.

The Keirin was an immediate success. The first four-day session was held in Kohura City on Kyushu island and drew twenty thousand visitors daily. The profit from the sales of betting tickets amounted to 20 million yen (today, $1.00 U.S. equals 360 yen). Within a decade, staggering sums of financial aid have been derived from Keirin for the promotion of domestic industries, social-welfare projects, and sports activities through profits obtained from the sale of betting tickets.

Today, Keirin is playing an important part in many new fields, particularly in social welfare and the development of the nation's sports programs. Japan's antituberculosis and anticancer programs have been directly dependent on Keirin racing. The government's budget for

Training on the rollers at the Keirin College.

Tense riders await the start while thousands of betting spectators hold their breath.

these activities was very limited, yet, in three years, Keirin racing provided 330 million yen for the development of national sports. These include subsidies to the organization of Asian Athletic Games and the Japanese Olympic team, as well as 500 million yen for the promotion of the nation's health programs. Furthermore, many social and welfare corporations and fire and police departments received another 330 million yen during the same period.

While all the money was flowing into the government coffers—and the people were enjoying a healthy outlet for their emotions—the standard of Japanese bicycle racing was increasing by leaps and bounds, bringing them into the headlines in world competition, particularly in sprinting.

Not any bicycle racer can be a Keirin racer. Keirin racers are selected from among a large number of applicants from all parts of the country by strict moral and physical tests conducted by local Keirin associations. Those who are thus selected must then attend the Japan Keirin College, where they learn bicycle racing laws, mechanics, tactics and techniques, and physical conditioning for three months. At the termination of the course, prospective Keirin riders must pass an examination before they are qualified to race. During the course of instruction, the greatest emphasis is placed on gentlemanly attitudes and good sportsmanship. At present, there are more than 4,500 male and 430 female professional Keirin riders.

To implement Keirin racing, fifty-three first-class velodromes have been built throughout the country. Seating capacity runs from ten thousand to fifty thousand persons.

The income of Keirin racers depends upon the prizes offered for each race and upon their regular pay for participating. Generally, every Keirin rider has the opportunity to race ten days each month, and his average monthly income is about 100,000 yen ($280), which is comparable to the salary of any section of a first-class commercial firm in Japan. The more successful riders may earn up to 160,000 yen ($445). The highest amount ever paid was to Mr. Hirama Deiki who earned 19 million yen ($52,777) in 1967.

But Keirin racing is only a part of cycling in Japan. A project of unprecedented size, an entire integrated sportsland focusing mainly on cycling is now being constructed on the Izu Peninsula. The cycling circuit of this project is the grandest ever designed and built anywhere in the world.

One of the main features of this facility is a racecourse consisting of two units of 5 kilometers and 3 kilometers in length, which may also be used in combination as an 8-kilometer circuit. Two tracks, one 333 meters and the other 400 meters, will be incorporated on the grounds. Besides their use for official racing, these tracks will provide a training and testing area for cyclists. In the smaller track, pacing lamps are imbedded in the surface of the pavement below the pole line, and the light will move swiftly forward at a speed controlled by the trainer in a control cabin above the track.

There are also two tracks and a research laboratory to study the physical conditions of cyclists in action. One track has a 200-meter section completely covered by a shed to test riders free of any influence of wind. A camera, installed inside, moves alongside the cyclist, photographing his every movement along the entire 200 meters.

Another circuit in the human engineering research center employs a telemetric device with a number of microwave bands which will transmit the cyclist's physical condition to a monitoring machine while he is in action.

Such facilities are good evidence of the serious intent of the Japanese to improve their standards, and learn more of the human machine in cycling.

The cycle-sports center will also include a "cytel," a 150-room hotel for cyclists, perched on top of a hill commanding a view of the entire facility and the famous Mount Fuji. The center has a variety of buildings of characteristically symbolic design, among which are a grandstand of eight hundred seats, a tower, an administration building, a restaurant, ticket booths, a house for rental bicycles, bus terminals, and a spacious parking area for more than twelve hundred vehicles. Other sports facilities will be added in the future, along with a children's circuit and a medical clinic.

When completed in 1970, the cost of the entire project will have reached 6 billion yen ($16.7 million), all provided from Keirin racing revenues.

A Japanese couple touring on secondary country roads.

If this all seems a bit fantastic, you are just beginning to get an idea of what is happening in Japan. In the bicycle industry the advances are just as impressive.

It was inevitable that the Japanese would sooner or later make inroads into bicycle trade around the world, and their export market had been steadily expanding. In the calendar year 1967, over 750,000 bicycles worth $14 million and component parts totaling $18 million found their way into countries on every continent. These figures represent respective gains of 49 percent and 21 percent over the previous year.

The biggest market is the United States, which accounted for 41 percent of Japan's total exports. At the same time, Japan became the top exporter of bicycles to the United States, replacing Britain which had held this distinction for many years.

Behind this marked export expansion are extensive and all-encompassing technical and market research study programs. Above all, the quality and performance of the Japanese products has been vastly improved. Japanese components are being given such high ratings that European demand is growing strong.

Although touring in Japan is not highly organized, interest is increasing rapidly. Clubs are just now beginning to emerge throughout the country. Most touring is done in and around resort and scenic areas where roads are good and the vistas breathtaking. In recent years, hosteling has become extremely popular. Many modern hostels have been built within the last few years, a few with the capacity to sleep up to three hundred visitors. The Japanese Cycling Federation has been buying bicycles for rental use at many of the hostels, and with a government subsidy, leadership classes in cycling are taught to groups of interested schoolteachers.

Utility cycling in Japan is extensive. Everywhere you see people on their way to work, to school, to the shops, etc. These are usually short jaunts, and the bicycles are klunkers. But the heavy volume of bicycle traffic has brought the development of extensive bikeway systems, even in crowded downtown areas. In some cities, bicycle lanes separate cyclists from auto traffic by a raised concrete curb or steel guardrails, as commonly found on

American freeways. In many instances, the dividing strip is several feet wide and landscaped with trees and shrubs.

Cyclists around the world are beginning to look to Japan for technical advancements in bicycle design and physiological breakthroughs, as an emerging power in cycle racing, and as a new and exciting horizon for bicycle touring.

Touring in the

United States

The huff 'n' puffers discover a world of natural wonders on their California cycle tour.

HUFF 'N' PUFFERS DISCOVER CALIFORNIA

CLIFFORD L. GRAVES, M.D.
December 1967

Where can you find the road of your dreams through the land of your fancy to the mansion of your wishes? In California!

Where can you find a full month of sunshine with the air crystal clear and but one day of rain? In California!

Where can you find a thirty-mile downgrade through an enchanting forest with a foaming river your only companion? In California! Reason enough for the huff 'n' puffers.

We gathered in San Francisco, not once but twice. The second time was an encore or, more accurately, a rerun. That was the only way to accommodate all the applicants. The two tours were identical in routing but separate in time. The choice of season could not have been better: late September and early October. The country fairly beckoned.

At starting time on the parking lot of the Del Webb Townehouse, the scene resembled nothing so much as a cross between a reunion of the classes of '36 and a bicycle rally. Bikes, bags, and bellhops were flying in all directions while a brightly painted bus was getting up steam in a far corner. This bus was the key to the tour.

"See America by Bicycle," it said in foot-high letters on the outside. Inside, bicycle racks replaced seats, tires dangled from the roof, and overhead nets carried pannier bags instead of suitcases. The southernmost end held in addition a large tool kit and a first-aid bag. Supplied for the occasion by the youth hostel group in San Diego, this unique vehicle was used to carry the huff 'n' puffers without delay to the areas where they were to cycle: the redwood country and the Sierras.

As on previous tours, huff 'n' puffers came from all sections of the country and from various occupations: publisher, industrialist, housewife, airport manager, missile builder, nurse, social worker, surveyor, doctor, photographer, contractor, freelance writer, airline pilot, boilermaker, magazine editor, architect, dental surgeon, packaging specialist, fashion expert, press agent, freeway planner, painter, all within an age range of twenty-two to sixty-seven. From England came Medwin Clutterbuck, and from France the Nogrettes and the Gerards. About half of these people had never been to California. How to show them the highlights and yet stay on side roads had been neatly solved, partly by careful routing, partly by the use of the bus.

Our first day was a cinch: a jog by bus across the Golden Gate, up Highway 101, and into the pretty town of Cloverdale. Here, the afternoon had been reserved for a shakedown cruise to the Italian-Swiss winery at Asti, but we were so busy greeting a delegation of well-wishers that we had a late start. Among the well-wishers were Al Kaiser and his family (later to earn the merit award for performance above and beyond the call of duty), Jerry Michaels and a group of San Francisco hostelers, and Clifford Franz and his wife, who joined us at intervals throughout the tour. When all these people mounted their bicycles for the eight-mile run to Asti, the line stretched as far as the eye could see—and even farther on the way back.

The winery treated us well. We had a conducted tour, a walk through the gardens, and a taste of many wines in the sampling room. It was at this point that I found myself standing next to Medwin Clutterbuck, our British mem-

ber, who was muttering something under his breath
between drinks.

"What was that, Med?" I asked.

"Damn George the Third!" he answered with a twinkle
in his eye.

The next day we were to cycle sixty miles across undulating country to the coast. A pattern quickly emerged.
A few people would leave early, the main group would
leave at a reasonable hour, and a few people would
leave late. On this particular morning, I was not with the
late section but with the late-late section. Even the bus
had left. Finally I grabbed my bike. What's that? Both
tires were flat.

I tried to figure out how I could have two flats just
from riding to the restaurant, but when this search led
nowhere, I quickly removed the tires and mounted my
spares. Another shock. The air ran out as quickly as I put
it in. Evidently, my spares were defective. Looking at my
four flat tires, I could see that I had a problem because
in a little town like Cloverdale you might as well ask for
a grand piano as for a sew-up tire. How to get rolling
again? I could expect no help from the bus because it
was long gone.

It was now noon, and I had to think fast. Suddenly I
remembered that Al Kaiser had offered his services in an
emergency. Al lives in Santa Rosa, thirty miles south of
Cloverdale. I called. Hooray. Al had sew-ups. Not only
that, but he would put them on the next bus. Within an
hour, I had my tires. That evening, Captain Dan read me
the lesson. "Never use *old* tires as spares. Always have
new ones."

The Heritage House at Little River that evening restored my spirits. The hotel stands in a superb spot on a
high cliff overlooking the coastline where a pounding surf
sends clouds of spray high into the air. The combination
spray and mist gives the light a wondrous quality, clothing
each receding promontory in a veil of mystery. In the
beautifully appointed dining room, the conversation ran
mostly about more mundane things:

"I ate lunch three times today and I am still hungry."

"I thought you said we were going to have a head
wind."

"We talked to a guy in the vineyards. He said to try Charles Krug."

"A kitten chased me all the way through Boonville. I finally had to carry it back myself."

"That ride through the redwoods was fabulous."

"I could have gone another twenty miles without any trouble."

"We stopped to see the demonstration forest at Navarro."

"The man at the grocery said that they have had a month of fog on the coast."

"I am so hungry, I could bite anything that doesn't bite me first."

"Did you see that dairy where they have the electrical milking machines?"

"I took at least twenty pictures today."

"A woman stopped us and asked where we get all that energy. She said that she takes three different kinds of vitamins and she is still tired."

"What a relief not to see any billboards."

"I got a free ride. Stuck close to the tandem all day."

"We stopped to look at a peacock, and the woman showed us the whole ranch."

Gradually, the conversation became a little more coherent.

"I like cycling," said missile expert Bob Fox, "because it gives you an immediate goal. You see a hill. You start to pant. You go into a sweat. You wipe your brow. You blow your nose. You reach the top. You have fought your battle. And you get your reward immediately."

"I like cycling," said social worker Dick Kline, "because it gives me a chance to do a little thinking. I figure it is the cadence of my feet. It clears the cobwebs. It opens the eyes. It sharpens your perception. This morning I suddenly discovered how to handle a difficult situation in the office. And I wasn't even trying."

"I like cycling," said Leonard Gohs, an advertising man, "because you are not trying to outwit the other fellow like in tennis or golf. Cycling is complete mental relaxation. If you want to be competitive, you can compete against yourself."

"And I like cycling," said Henri Gerard, who owns an

insurance agency in Paris, "because it has brought me in contact with all you nice people."

From Little River we headed south. This was our longest day, seventy-one miles. But the scenery made up for it. Everywhere, the road hugs the heavily indented coast. On our right, the turbulent surf. On our left, a rising grassland. In the distance, the stately redwoods. Highway 1, the wonderful one, is still completely unspoiled. No gas stations, no hot-dog stands, no belching trucks, in fact, no human habitations for mile after mile. The only people we saw all morning were some laborers who were tarring the road. When they saw what the tar was doing to our tires, they stopped their truck, motioned us over, and spent half an hour wiping our tires clean. Instant friends.

At Anchor Bay we stopped for a picnic. Here, the forest touches the foreshore in a happy blend of shade and shingle. Here, the silence was broken only by a colony of sea lions. And, here, we relaxed over sandwiches, tea, fruit, and cheese. Here and elsewhere, the non-Californians were captivated with the discovery that they could bask in the sun one minute and shiver in the shade the next.

It was a tired group that gathered for dinner that evening at the Timber Cove Inn, a modernistic hostelry on the cliffs north of Fort Ross.

Later that evening, we were joined by David Brink. David is a Berkeley student who distinguished himself by winning the 4,000 Meter Pursuit championship in the nationals last summer. He stayed with us for four days, and his presence naturally touched off the question of how fast a bicycle rider can go.

In the road race, speeds can reach 28 miles an hour. On the track, the record for one hour of continuous unpaced riding now stands at 29.493 miles. A sprinter who covers the last 200 meters in eleven seconds travels at 40.500 miles an hour, but only for eleven seconds. The record for one hour of racing behind a motorcycle on the track is 51 miles. The all-time speed record for a bicycle that is riding immediately behind a windscreen on a car is 127.342 miles an hour but not for long. This fantastic performance was brought off by Jose Meiffret in 1962, and it is not likely to be repeated soon.

From Timber Cove to Guerneville, we had a choice of many routes. The Skaggs Springs road is the most beautiful but the hardest. The Cazadero road rises steeply from Fort Ross to give magnificent panoramas of woods and water. A third route goes down the coast to Bodega Bay and then loops back. This was the route taken by Henri Gerard, Med Clutterbuck, Jean Nogrette, and Captain Lodi. These four arrived at Occidental in a more or less limp condition, owing to the heat of day and the effort of the ride. Fortunately, they spied one of the famous Italian restaurants and they immediately decided on a break.

"My feet hurt," said Med Clutterbuck. "I think I'll have a cup of tea. That always helps."

"Tea? How could that cure your aching feet?" said Jean Nogrette. "Take my word for it. The best drink in America is root beer."

"Ah, la bière coupe les jambes," said Henri Gerard. "Beer cuts my legs. I must have a glass of ice-cold orange juice."

"Gentlemen, if you know what is good for you," said Captain Lodi, "you will join me in a short beer."

To each his own.

At Guerneville we found five iced watermelons waiting for us, courtesy Al Kaiser. The next day we again had a choice of routes. Mountain Home ranch in the hills of Calistoga was only thirty-five miles away, but three of us decided to make a detour and see the geysers. On the map, it looked easy enough. Just a thirty-mile loop. What the map did not tell was that the first fifteen miles go up 2,700 feet, and the second fifteen miles down again.

No sooner had we left the main road than the climb began. Trees disappeared. Houses disappeared. The only thing that did not disappear was the sun. It got hotter with every mile. We passed over a cattle guard. Ping! One of Carl Schedwin's spokes broke. He replaced it with incredible speed. Up we went through a dozen switchbacks. Rounding one of the bends, we saw for the first time the mountain that confronted us. Holy smokes. But Steve Young had a word of cheer: "Do you see that house at the top?" he said. "It's a restaurant where we can have a tall cool beer. Let's go."

Climbing a mountain on a bicycle is a good bit like digging a deep hole or shoveling a big pile of snow or swimming the English Channel. You bite off a little at a time and don't worry how long it is going to take. The trick is knowing your pace and your endurance. That is where experience comes in. The best climbers are the ones who adjust their pace automatically while thinking about something totally different. It is a mental discipline as much as a physical exercise.

We toiled on. Another cattle guard. Another spoke. Gradually the top drew nearer. Now we could see great billows of live steam shooting up from cracks in the earth. We had been told that these geysers are the only ones in this country to be commercially exploited, but we were no longer interested. All we were interested in was that long cool drink. I looked at my watch. Two hours since we started. Now a short down, followed by a long up. Finally, an easing of the grade, the top, the house, and a big sign: CLOSED FOR REPAIRS. Three grouchy geezers galloped glumly past the gushing geysers.

Meanwhile, at the Mountain Home ranch, the huff 'n' puffers were already in the swimming pool. Others had gone for a horseback ride, and Joe Dietrich was soaring serenely in a sailplane he had rented in Calistoga. Never on a single track, we indulged in water-skiing on Lake Berryessa, canoeing on Lake Tahoe, fishing at Mammoth, hiking in Yosemite, rock hunting on the Yuba, and dancing the light fantastic in the casinos on Lake Tahoe.

After another day of glorious cycling through the Napa valley, over the top at Angwin, and down the Pope valley, we arrived at the Steele Canyon lodge on Lake Berryessa with our next objective, the Sierras, 150 miles away. This stretch we did by bus. To be in the best position for a run down Highway 49 on the following day, we had to stay overnight in the hot-dog hamlet of Sierraville, a crossroad community without sidewalk but with plenty of cowboys and cattlemen. What Sierraville lacks in sophistication, it makes up in atmosphere. When I presented myself for the first time in the dingy bar where Sid normally holds forth, a testy old bartender greeted my inquiry with the counter-attack: "Sid? He ain't here. But there is a real cheap place next door."

The next day more than repaid us for our sufferance. In the clear air of that mile-high country, the climb up Yuba Pass was unmitigated pleasure; and the thirty-six-mile down-schuss on the other side surpassed anything we had yet seen. With every mile, the walls of the canyon become steeper, greener, and lovelier until the road crosses the river and begins to rise again. This is gold-mining country where settlements like Sierra City and Downieville are silent reminders of a turbulent past. Most of us reached the whimsical town of Nevada City before being picked up by the bus for the final miles to Lake Tahoe.

At Lake Tahoe we had a day of rest. The lake is famous not only for its natural setting but also for its gambling casinos, a circumstance that could not fail to impress the huff 'n' puffers. In spite of this distraction, a quorum made the seventy-one-mile ride around the lake on a day so clear, you could make out individual trees on the opposite shore. Others were content to go sailing, walking, shopping, or sight-seeing.

Our next goal was Mammoth Lakes, almost two hundred miles to the south. To take the sting out of the bus ride, we decided to ride the first thirty-five miles by bike. These were miles along the Nevada shore and over the Kingsbury grade with its spectacular view of the Owens valley. At Minden, we were to be picked up by the bus.

Everything went according to schedule except that at Minden a head count showed Dr. Coutts missing. We knew that he had started that morning, but nobody had seen hide nor hair of him since. What could have happened? Dr. Coutts was probably the most conscientious member of our group. He was also the most tenacious cyclist, in spite of his sixty-seven years. His acquaintance with a bicycle goes back only a few years. In search of a way toward physical fitness, he decided to try a bicycle at an age when other men retire to the shuffleboard. It was a case of love at first sight. His first tentative probings quickly led to a regular five-mile run before breakfast, and this in turn to the Grand Prix des Gentlemen, which is a fifty-miler for adults in San Diego. Delighted to discover that he could ride his bicycle a little better and a little easier every day, he worked out a routine that included a five-minute mile, a four-minute mile, and eventually a three-minute mile. His next step was a tour with a group of Houston, Texas, riders through the Rio Grande valley. Now he was ready for his postgraduate work. On the California tour, he rode as if he had been riding all his life.

But how could he have gotten lost on that run from Lake Tahoe to Minden? If he had had mechanical trouble, he surely would have flagged a passing motorist. If he had had an accident, we surely would have heard by now. We made all sorts of wild guesses, none of which got us any closer. It was a mysterious disappearance, to say the least.

At this point, the Minden sheriff stuck his head in the door of the bus:

"Dr. Coutts just called. He is in Reno. He'll be down as soon as he can get a taxi."

Reno was forty-five miles away. Finally we figured it out. Dr. Coutts had turned north instead of south when he left the hotel. Undaunted by the 8,933-foot Mount Rose summit, he had pedaled on and on until he found himself in a strange town with no sign of the huff 'n' puffers. Finally smelling a rat, he had wheeled into a service station and asked with feigned unconcern: "Say, what town is this?"

"Why, you are in Reno."

"Excuse me. I thought I was in Minden."

A slight case of misorientation.

As soon as he had rejoined us, we took off for Mammoth. Here we found ourselves in the rarefied atmosphere of the Sierras, but we were well looked after by the Stanfords, themselves huff 'n' puffers, who ran the Tamarack Lodge. Among the delights at the Tamarack Lodge is the view of the waterfall, a five-hundred-foot cataract from Horseshoe Lake to Twin Lakes. Another delight came when Bob showed us his slides of the huff 'n' puff tour of the Blue Ridge in Virginia.

The next night, still at Tamarack, we discovered Hot Creek. It is a stream where hot water from the bowels of

Climbing the barren eastern slope of 9,946-foot Tioga Pass.

the earth mixes with cold water from the ice fields. In the resulting currents and countercurrents, you can find water of any temperature. Once you have found it, your job is to stay with it. This is not as easy as it sounds. Moreover, you may discover that your feet are in cold water while your hands are in hot or vice versa. We found ourselves floating in this pool of surprises on a pitch-black night when every little star stood out like a jack-o'-lantern's eye. We were enchanted.

From Mammoth to Yosemite, the road leads first to Lee Vining and then over the 9,946-foot Tioga Pass into the park. We tackled this stretch in different ways. Captain Henry, Dick Kline, and Med Clutterbuck cycled the entire 110 miles without blinking an eye. A slightly less vigorous contingent including Jewell Paris took the bus as far as Lee Vining and then cycled across the pass. Still others decided to mix their cycling with hiking. After a picnic at Tenaya Lake, they put their bikes on the bus and struck out through the woods. I was in this group, an experience I would not have missed for anything. Unaware of the difficulties of the trail, we promptly got lost, beat through the bush, fought boulders and rocks, stumbled back on the trail, and barely managed to reach the valley. How thankful we were that night for a hot shower and a comfortable bed.

And so, after a final day of cycling over the roads in the park, this tour came to an end. On the Saturday between the first and the second tour, the combined groups had the good fortune of being guests of Peter and Sandra Hoffman in their charming home in Oakland. We admired Peter's photographs, we praised the elegant furnishings, we enjoyed the excellent wine, and then Captain Dan Henry read us a poem he had written on the spur of the moment. This poem is so expressive of the huff 'n' puff sentiment that I quote it here in part.

> There are roads that make us happy
> There are roads that make us blue
> But the roads that we've been traveling
> Are the best we ever knew.

From Mountain Home to Berryessa
These were roads as roads should be
For they brought complete fulfillment
To a touring man like me.

For a road is more than paving
More than ribbons o'er the land
More than just an easy pathway
All of this we understand.

If we were all musicians
And this tour a music score
It would be the sweetest music
We had ever heard before.

Not just brass or fifes or fiddles
Not a horn or drum that's low
But the fullest orchestration
A symphony of all we know.

SAFARI TO MAUI

NATALIA PURITON
April 1969

When did the wild idea first strike us to go on the safari
by bicycle and foot?

Perhaps it started the day Jock, my husband, took up
cycling as part of a physical therapy routine after a
severe illness. Then we gave our three daughters bicycles
for Christmas: Regina, aged thirteen; Lisa, eleven; Sanna,
eight. And eventually the bicycle bug bit me, too.

We began the planning of our safari many months before the event. Now, mind you, the expanse of "forest
primeval" we planned to conquer was not Africa or South
America, but Maui, one of the four major islands in the
Hawaiian chain. Still, there were many uncharted, unin-
habited, unpaved, remote areas of the island, and the idea

of our thoroughly modern family, accustomed to life's amenities, taking off with bicycle bags holding all our earthly supplies, and nothing but our ten legs and five bicycles for locomotive power, was startling enough, perhaps even foolhardy.

But it was also adventure. And we had never visited any of the neighbor islands, although Honolulu had been our home for almost thirteen years.

Our supplies began to pile up. After many rehearsals, we were ready. We divided, by weight, the various necessities for the trip for each member of the family to carry. On each bicycle we arranged a tote bag to hang on the handlebars so that each of us might carry his or her toothbrush and other personal items. Then on the back of the bikes, beside the small built-in rack, we attached one or two canvas pannier bags (named after the pair of wicker baskets hung across a mule's back for carrying produce in many parts of the world), and in these we carried all our camping supplies.

Jock was made "Master of the Bikes." He was responsible for our collection of maps that marked the County Beach Parks, state parks, secondary roads, cutoff mileage roads, etc. He had the largest packs—coming to twenty-nine pounds, exactly—which comprised most of the air mattresses and cotton blankets, tools for bike repair, air pump, and our fine light nylon tent which could fold up into a square and weighed only a few ounces. Even the collapsible poles were of lightweight metal and weighed almost nothing.

My department was the mobile kitchen, of course. I carried a whole set of light aluminum cooking and eating kitchenware that could be contained in one medium-sized canvas tote bag. Fitting into each other like components of an old Chinese puzzle box were a set of pots and pans with removable handles that could double as fry pans or cooking or mixing bowls and coffeepot; five aluminum plates, five plastic cups, five sets of spoons-knives-forks that hooked into each other; a tin matchbox, spatulas, can opener, candles, soap powder. My packs came to twenty-one pounds.

Regina also carried twenty-one pounds, which included

some of our mosquito netting, nylon ropes, part of the small tent, blankets.

Lisa and Sanna carried their personal effects and the smallest camping items, one of which was our family-created lantern. Our lantern was made, for reasons of weight, from a large plastic container (in which sherbet comes). We set a tiny candleholder with a peg center, and a candle on the peg, within the plastic container, put the cover with a drilled hole on it and, *voilà!* there was light. (We had many a card game and reading session around this makeshift lantern.) The girls' packs came to only twelve pounds each.

We had written to the Parks Board on Maui so that we would have camping permits waiting for us. Our bikes, first, and then our family were loaded on the plane in Honolulu and twenty-five minutes later we were on Maui.

Maui! I took a great, wide, long deep breath, and looking at my family, I saw their lungs expand, too. And the delight on their faces. And the exhilaration. And the incredible wonder we were really starting out, at last.

We pedaled down the highway toward the largest towns of Wailuku and Kahului, laughing, all dressed alike in one of the sets of blue and yellow shorts and shirts that I had made. (We also had handmade rain ponchos tucked in our kits, and bikini swimsuits.)

The first day we covered thirteen miles. Thirteen miles past Maui's pineapple fields and cornfields and sugar acres, in Maui's air smelling like one wide green pasture of grass and cattle, with tropical ginger and guavas tossed in for a bonus. We stopped the first night at Waiahu Park, sharing the lovely beach with twenty-five joyous boy scouts who built the fire for our steaks, gave us rice and vegetables, and generally treated us like visiting relatives.

We stayed for two days, swimming in the turquoise-and cobalt-blue water, hiking along the shore for magnificent seascape views.

Maui is shaped something like a turtle, and we were aiming for its head, the northwestern portion, which comes eventually to Lahaina, the old whaling port, and Kaanapali. the famous resort area.

We started north toward Fleming Beach, on the third day, hoping to have lunch at Pineapple Hill Restaurant for a special splurge. When I look back upon the audacity of this goal, I don't know whether to howl with laughter or weep.

The early miles of the road we took were paved, and we pedaled along contentedly, passing unbelievable little hamlets (are there really villages left in the modern American world like this?), past old sleepy plantation towns with modest homes and exotic flower gardens.

Then we began ascending, higher and higher. Since every twist of the ascending road gave us a more spectacular panorama than the last one, we didn't mind the effort it cost us in pedaling upward, until, with a jolt, we discovered we had gone only four miles and we were hot and thirsty and tired, and had already run out of water. Our packs grew impossibly heavy, our thirst more acute, the road, now unpaved, more and more steep and difficult. Should we go back? We checked our maps and it seemed to us we were about at the point of no return on these West Maui Mountains; it would be as far to go back as to go on. Besides, we had a goal of completely encircling the island of Maui, and encircle it we would!

Then, abruptly, as if we had just turned a page of the *National Geographic* and walked into its farfetched color perfection, we stepped into a forest area, outside Moleheia, lush and jade, with a stream bubbling its improbable wonder. Our feet cooled, our faces washed and refreshed, our water bottles filled again, we felt somewhat encouraged and so continued, higher and higher, up all the way, "hiking" our bikes, since it was impossible now to ride up the steep, rough, rocky, tortuous heights.

By 4:00 P.M. we were blistered, aching in every joint, parched with thirst again, starved for food, too weary to think, and hurting tears began to flow. Sanna kept dropping her bike, simply unable to handle it and herself any longer.

Suddenly a car was there on the road behind us, and we were explaining our plight. The driver had room for one person and one bike. We loaded Sanna and her bike and equipment in the car, and the driver promised to drop her off at the bottom of the mountain where the paved road began.

Through the next hours of our climb, when dusk settled

over us, there were times when I wondered if we would ever reach paved roads again. But through the unbelievable kindness of five people, as yet unknown to us, two cars returned in the dark of that rutty wild mountain pass to rescue the rest of us that night.

Perhaps only a Stanley meeting a Livingstone in darkest Africa could know our exquisite joy at that moment. We stayed in a hotel in Napili Bay, and the next morning, the girls strung some Job's tears into seed leis and presented them to our rescuers. And what could be more appropriate than Job's tears?

We traveled only four miles to our next stop, Honokowai Beach Park. This beach park, like most of the Parks Board camping spots, has good rest rooms, clean showers, electric lights, wide expanse of lovely beach, barbecue grills, all simply ideal for our purpose. What a glorious virgin beach it was stretching out for miles, with picturesque rocks here and there where we could swim, sun, run, find shells—or just sit and be quiet with the earth.

We set up our small tent, which took us only about fifteen minutes, with one four-foot pole in the center and single stakes at the ends, all tied to a pin stuck in the ground. The only hard work in this kind of camping, we found, was blowing up our mattresses. But once that was done, we enjoyed the rest of the chores and the freedom of camp life. We did our laundry in the nearby water tap, and strung up our clothes on a line attached to the tent which we had brought for this purpose. And of course I unpacked the pots and pans to start preparing dinner.

We took a jaunt into nearby Kaanapali Beach and visited the elegant hotels Maui Hilton and Sheraton Maui and all the splendid man-made resorts, and in the morning, we cycled on level roads into Lahaina, the old whaling town, where we visited the historic sites: the old prison where boisterous whaling crewmen were often incarcerated; missionary houses; the courthouse; cannons abandoned here from a Russian ship of the last century; and the famous old banyan tree that looks as if it would spread itself from there to Molokai.

We also took a side trip to Olowalu to see the ancient petroglyphs etched into the cliffs about three hundred years ago by passing Hawaiians. There were the weird "stick" figures throwing nets, riding horses, holding spears. We felt the Hawaiians walking. We later read the accounts of the old Maui as recorded by Jack London, Robert Louis Stevenson, and Mark Twain, and felt that we had written the accounts ourselves, for so little about Maui has changed.

August 19 . . . we are off to our next campsite. What sheer joy it is. It is a new world we have walked into. Not just the natural beauty, not just the adventure, but the comradeship of the road. We go nowhere but some stranger, who quickly becomes a friend, stops to talk with us, to offer us fresh pineapple from a field, or to give us water or whatever we might need. Bus drivers don't honk, instead they wave and smile. Auto drivers don't hurry us on, they stop and chat.

We got as far as Camp Pecusa that night. Seventeen miles of paved road the next day brought us to Kalama Beach Park. Here Maui has flattened out, but is still pretty, and the beaches incredibly magnificent. We have the park, unusually neat and clean, all to ourselves. How is that for an impossible dream in this day and age?

We have become experts at fire-making, gathering wood for dinner and breakfast, discovering coconut fibers for starting a fire with ease. The sunset slashing the sky to scarlet and purple that night, and the tints of apricot at dawn the next morning were worth the whole trip, even if we had seen no other splendor.

We have, also, by this time, discovered where all the convenient grocery stores are. There is nearly always some sort of grocery near a big camp, in the closest town or settlement. And so we do our shopping for one dinner and one breakfast only, each day. If we have food left from a meal, we often leave it on a picnic table for the next person who passes that way.

The next night at Hookipa Park, after many miles of uphill climbing, we experienced our first rain. It was a test for our small low tent, and although the rain came down in torrents, we were snug and dry inside.

Our memory of Hookipa will always be entangled with a darling of a man who was the caretaker there. He brought us fresh doughnuts, fresh pineapples, and ripe avocados for breakfast the next morning. More than that, when we went on to Kaumahina State Park, turning some corner that brought us into Hudson's *Green Mansions* . . . wild and lush and dense, towering trees, bush, flowers . . . and frozen with a sudden burst of cold weather, who should come rolling up in a station wagon but this same caretaker with his fiancée, and a whole feast prepared just for us.

Alone, after our guests had gone, with only our small glow of candlelight, this cold overgrown spot seemed to us without a doubt one of the most remote and eerie spots on earth.

We were glad to be on our way next morning to Hana on the eastern tip of Maui. We had been warned about the road to Hana—rough, rutty, narrow, corkscrew turns, lots of traffic—but by this time, veterans of the road that we were, we pooh-poohed the whole idea of difficulty.

It is a rough road. At least I think it is. I seem to remember turning and twisting and falling into ruts. But the absolute breathtaking beauty of this section of the island blots everything else from one's mind. You were saturated with the freshwater springs, silvered waterfalls, the astounding natural swimming pools, the wild guavas, the fresh wild raspberries. The scent of flowers, fruit, and wild growth lies over the land like a net to entrap the visitor, so that you are prepared to let the rest of the world go, and just stay in Hana forever and get drunk with Hana's particular intoxication. We even worked out the mishap of a flat tire on one of the bikes so that we were not delayed in our goal very long, and sang all the way into the village of Hana, past green pastures with cocoa-colored cattle, and at last to our first glimpse of beautiful Hana Bay.

It was perfection. A lone little fishing boat at the pier, the other boats bobbing around in a bay that has something of Spain or Italy about it, the red-roofed old-world buildings in the distant village, the brilliance of the air and the blue of sky and sea!

We shopped at once at Hasegawa's General Store, where one can get anything from rubber boots to epicurean delights. The camp at Hana is ideal. We settled in and took part in the whole wonderful atmosphere.

We went to the Saturday night movies along with everyone else and congregated at Hana Park for music and fun afterward. We visited Waianapanapa Caves and Falls, entering into its aura of antiquity, its ancient stone walls, the caves with dripping pools, and the legend of princesses and princes. These waters supposedly turn blood-red in April, which is the anniversary of the time a princess named Popo-alae was supposed to have had her head bashed in against the stone—by either her own jealous husband or an enemy of her people, depending on which story you choose.

We spent Sunday morning at Seven Sacred Pools, bringing along our picnic lunch. At least the legend surrounding these pools is lighter of heart, for the *alii* (royalty) used to bathe here. And here, also, the legends say that the mother of Maui, the demigod for whom the island is named, used to wash their tapa cloths in these pools.

Since one pool cascades into the next, we all tried sliding down the wet rocks, chuting out from one pool to the next and the next and the next, and then we watched, breathless, while a native Hawaiian dived from one pool to the next to the next!

We reached Ulupalakua (by truck over the worst of the hot dusty rough road) and as we started unloading our bikes, the almost unbelievable sight of a roundup, complete with island *paniolos* (cowboys) with lariats and whooping and hollering came into our sight and sound. We had forgotten that much of this part of Maui is ranchland. We stood transfixed, watching them until they were out of sight.

It took eight more miles of dusty road on our bikes before we came to our stop, Kalama Beach Park. We stayed here two days, to swim and relax and rest.

When we pulled into the airport the next day, we felt exhilarated at the knowledge that we had really circled the island of Maui, most of it by bike and foot. We stored our bikes here while we took a side trip up to Haleakala by rented car at sunrise.

It was pouring rain and bitterly cold. We were dressed in our sweat suits, the type athletes wear and which we often wore to sleep in, for warmth and protection. Over these, we wrapped all our blankets, and alone in the dark . . . it seemed alone in the whole island world . . .

we approached the crater. We reached the summit of ten thousand feet, watching the moving clouds, the gushing winds, fog coming from our breath, as if we were in a December storm in New England.

Of course we saw only white-gray fog. But it was Jock and my Silver Wedding Anniversary, and storm, rain, hail, dark of night, or outer-Mongolian blizzards could not deter us from our rightful goal, a look at Haleakala, the largest dormant volcanic crater in the world. So we stayed in the car and waited.

The fog never completely rolled away, but at least we caught a glimpse of the moonlike crater with its pocked face filled with strange and weird inner craters. We also found one of the famous silversword, the plant that grows here and nowhere else on earth.

Then we returned to our car and began the roller-coaster descent. At about the five-thousand-foot level, the clouds lifted a little more and we were able to see panorama after panorama, down into the old fire pit of Haleakala, House of the Sun. We could understand from here that the crater's topmost rim drops down to the floor of the crater three thousand feet.

The last night we stayed at Baldwin Park, a lovely place with all the bright lights of Wailuku glimmering across the sea. Our last night! But we have done what we set out to do. We have cycled and walked almost two hundred miles around the island of Maui.

Water has a new significance in our lives, so have roads, climate, food, friendships, kindliness, beauty, nature, sky and sea and mountains. A piece of our heart will forever be left in Hana. A smaller piece in each lovely park. We feel rich in spirit, rich in body and in enthusiasm and accomplishment because of our trip. How many can say that at the finish of a vacation? And we did it all for $1.45 per person per day!

On my kitchen blackboard I have written: Maui, we love you.

I hope we will remember what we have learned. I do hope we will.

GENTLE JOURNEY—THE POTOMAC RIVER VALLEY

E. Peter Hoffman
March 1969

In 1828 President John Quincy Adams lifted the first shovelful of earth near Little Falls, Maryland, and the Chesapeake and Ohio Canal was born. Today, 141 years later, we can retrace the route into the American past, not by barge and mule, but on modern ten-speed bicycles.

Following the Potomac River Valley from Georgetown in the District of Columbia to Cumberland, Maryland, a total distance of 184.5 miles, the Chesapeake and Ohio Canal is a memento of the days when canals were the chief means of commerce. Built during the years between 1828 and 1850, the "Big Ditch" began as a dream to tap the wealth of the West. Plagued by the forces of nature, continuing financial problems, and conflicts with the railroad, it was abandoned in 1924.

Rich in the history of our growing nation and the quiet beauty of the Potomac Valley, the canal was acquired by the Federal Government in 1938 and is administered by the National Park Service. The canal is divided into two divisions. The Georgetown Division, extending 22 miles from Georgetown, D. C., to Seneca, Maryland, was restored soon after acquisition, and is well maintained and heavily used. The Western Division, stretching 160 miles from Seneca to Cumberland, Maryland, is a National Monument. Facilities are being developed, but conditions are still primitive.

The rewatered sections of the canal and the numerous remains of lift locks, aqueducts, dams, culverts, and lockhouses serve as reminders of the days when the young republic was establishing links with the frontier. The communities that sprang up along the canal are rich in history. River crossings of major armies during the French and Indian, Revolutionary, and Civil wars may be viewed from

The Potomac River Valley offers beauty, calm, and quietude for nature-loving cyclists.

many points along the canal. The canal also runs through Harpers Ferry National Historical Park, Fort Frederick State Park, and Antietam National Battlefield Site. Signs along the canal and a museum at Great Falls, Maryland, open daily, help to tell this story.

The towpath is an elevated trail varying in width to twelve feet, built of earth and stone, treaded in places with shale or crushed stone, eroded in other places to expose rough fill stone. Much of it is slippery or muddy when wet, but it dries rapidly after rain. Most breaks in the towpath have been refilled, but some remain. The path is clear of growth and follows the canal for its entire length. Night travel, especially alone, is not recommended.

Cyclists can travel the entire length of the towpath. However, the going is difficult in several places. A bicycle path provides a detour around Widewater, and a county road bypass is recommended around the slack water above Dam 4 during the spring when the Potomac River level is high. Catoctin Creek Aqueduct is in very poor condition and a detour around it is suggested. Bicycles should be pushed across all aqueducts.

Bike-in camp areas are available along the canal at Carderock, Swain's Lock, Violet's Lock, Mountain Lock, and Antietam Creek. All are available on a first-come, first-served basis, but permits are required at the first three listed. Organized groups must make advance arrangements for camp-outs. All gear must be carried into these camp areas by bike, since there is no direct vehicular access.

They are also a number of campsites along the canal between Harpers Ferry and Cumberland. The spacing of the campsites is such that cyclists can plan overnights according to their riding ability. Camping is prohibited along the canal except at designated camp areas. You may picnic anywhere.

Park Rangers and U. S. Park Police are the protective force of the park. They patrol the canal regularly and are on duty to help you and to enforce park regulations. Consult them if you are in any difficulty or have questions about the canal.

SMALL BIER—TOUR OF OHIO'S BACK COUNTRY

MARIUS LODEENSEN
September 1967

We didn't see aquamarine lagoons, lapis-lazuli coral reefs, and amphitheaters of slopes embracing bays of turquoise-green. Nor mountains thrusting their peaks into a white-streaked sky.

We saw a land of red barns and gentle hills that rose and fell like Atlantic rollers. In white-fenced meadows grazed mares, little foals nuzzling their bellies. The corn stood proud and shiny and the golden heavy-eared wheat swayed in waves, blue cornflowers peeking through the grain.

"Ohio!" exclaimed my friends. "You won't find much of interest." One shook his head. "It's an agricultural state," he said. "Nothing but factories and crowded highways and flat farmland. I've been there."

I haven't, not to the Ohio my friends seem to know. I saw the Ohio that Tony Pranses showed the International Bicycling Society's cyclists who answered Tony's call. For cycle touring Ohio is a small bier, but a mighty refreshing one.

Tony knows Ohio. He steered us away from the hub-bub, the four-lane expressways, and those factories and onto the little byroads that nobody knows but those who live there.

Tony is an organization man. Every evening he gave each of us a detailed route instruction sheet. "You won't find those roads on maps," warned Tony, puffing his pipe and looking imposing with a black Kentucky-Colonel necktie.

How right he was. Every one of us got lost at least once and I numerous times, but it mattered not, for all the roads were happy roads and one was as good as another.

Two farmers sit on a bench before a general store in

the middle of nowhere. We dismount and put our bikes against the giant maples laying their cool shadows over the front of the clapboard building.

"You cycling?"

"Yes, a group of us are cycling through the state."

"Two people just passed here on one bike! How far do you fellows go every day?"

"Oh, about fifty or sixty miles."

"Sixty miles! I'd be dead before I'd get out of town."

"Not if you had the right type of bicycle. Look at this fifteen-speed beauty. With such a machine you can zip up any hill—even the Alps."

A shaking of heads.

We open the front door and a little bell tinkles. There's an open space in the front with a great potbellied stove and chairs around and a couch with the stuffing out. Horse bridles hang on a stanchion. Cans of food, ointments, shirts, pants, sunglasses, bags of fertilizer, and breakfast foods bulge on the shelves along the walls. Everything you can get here, everything you could want and assorted junk you could possibly not.

Munching a small blueberry pie, a woman sits on one of the chairs. Another woman enters the store, carrying a bundle in her arms.

"Say, Mary, you ain't seen my new baby yet, has ye?"

The pie-munching lady glances gingerly at a remarkably unattractive infant: "My, my, ain't he the cutest thing!"

We buy Cokes, admire the baby, and eat blueberry pies. Tony takes a picture, the rest of us slouch in the chairs and get the lay of the land from the miniskirted storekeeper. Then we are off again, riding past pale-green tobacco plants in neat rows in small plots, manicured and prim. We ride through covered bridges, heavy-beamed, dark-shadowed, the wooden roadbed rumbling under the wheels of an occasional automobile. It's hot, almost 90° in the shade, but we don't feel the heat as long as we keep moving. We pass through settlements of frame houses with open porches and hanging swings and strange names such as Steam Corners, North Liberty, Scioto-Darby Creek, Basil's Village.

I do not know if it was the bobtailed hedge warbler that twittered so sweetly by the roadside, or what species of songbirds joined in a choral symphony as we rode by. Ohio birds deserve an honorable mention in this chronicle. The birds passed their *joie de vivre* to all who cared to listen. Larks piped their fluted songs over the meadows and blackbirds squawked indignantly from telephone wires. We even saw an eagle soaring high over a wood.

We overnighted in little towns, not besmirched with the fingerprints of progress. Still, quiet towns with shadowy avenues and clapboard houses, the branches of maples and sycamores brushing the upper stories. Voices of families on the open porches drifted into the street, young couples walked hand in hand, and on the not-too-closely-trimmed lawns lay tricycles and children's toys.

You could look through the open front doors into hall-ways with gold-framed mirrors, hatstands, and little tables with the telephone. French doors led into living rooms with unmatched chairs, Grand Rapids vintage. Watteau landscape prints graced the red-bricked fireplaces choked with family photographs. And flowery carpets on the floors. I lived in such a home once and I thought this world had long since vanished.

The Malabar Farm in Pleasant Valley (well named) was a must stop. Here, Louis Bromfield lost the fortune he won by writing thirty-four novels, seven of them filmed. I do not know if you care for his books (I don't), but as a farmer, Bromfield can certainly be classed among the world's most unsuccessful. A pretty girl guide took us around and into the author's study with an enormous semicircular desk where he worked. A tiny door led into the garden so that his six boxers, which had the run of the house, could come and go as they pleased. Pictures of movie stars, writers, and public figures covered the walls. Many of these had been guests here, much to Bromfield's disgust, as the guide informed us.

I wonder how many of Bromfield's books will endure. Perhaps *A Good Woman,* a portrait in acid of a woman who destroyed those she loved (a theme later taken by Phillip Wylie for his notorious *A Generation of Vipers,* a scathing study of selfish, frustrated womanhood). Maybe Bromfield felt annoyed by those movie stars, or perhaps he got his material from them. Who knows?

Dan Henry (Captain Dan Henry, formerly of American

Airlines), feeling sorry for me getting lost so often, marked the road one day. Dan does this for the New York Cycling Club for trips through Long Island. He draws circles with arrows in yellow paint at road intersections. If you think this is easy, you are mistaken. Dan took me along to buy the paint.

"I want some yellow road-marker paint," said Dan to the salesman.

"Fine. How many gallons do you need?"

"To be exact," said Dan, "about a pint, but seeing it comes only in gallon cans, let me have one."

I wondered what the salesman thought we were up to.

President Harding's home was also on the list. I recall that wooden house with the white-columned front porch the President had added to deliver his campaign speeches from. A monument of bad taste from an era not noted for finesse. The house contained a conglomeration of fringe-shaded lamps, statues of seminudes, oversized chairs, chocolate-sweet landscapes, and miscellaneous bric-a-brac. In the adjacent museum, we admired collections of papers of state, medals, fraternal orders, decorations, dog collars, used pipes, tennis rackets, chinaware, gold clubs, and—I almost forgot—the President's bicycle.

Harding was an avid cyclist (or so they say), and times being what they are, he should go down the ages as the last Chief Executive who propelled himself on two wheels (in tandem that is). Of course, we had a group picture taken with Tony holding Harding's wheel.

I could go on telling you how it was, but I know that what I have seen is of more interest to you than your trip to the Grand Canyon is to me. Join one of the tours mapped out every year by the Huff and Puff section of the I.B.T.S. You will not regret it.

AUTUMN IN VERMONT AND NEW HAMPSHIRE

HARTLEY ALLEY
December 1968

There's only one way to experience the thrill of an International Bicycle Touring Society tour: you have to be there, and on your bicycle.

Most of us arrived at the Red Mill a couple of days early, giving us plenty of time to adjust derailleurs, check tires, make friends, and trace our route on Mobil maps. The Red Mill, a friendly little hotel that was indeed at one time a grist mill, is situated in the village of Wilmington, Vermont, the starting point (and finish) of the autumn tour of New England. Our route was to take us on a great circle of Vermont and New Hampshire—two weeks of pedaling fifty miles a day, stopping overnight at cozy, well-kept motels, and eating heartily at small-town restaurants.

There were twenty of us who were to make all or part of the ride. We ranged from retired banker to baseball umpire, including doctor, lawyer, housewife, engineer. Luckily everybody had sense enough to be riding a ten-speed. When you're honking up a three-mile hill, which seemed to happen almost daily, you envy the guy next to you with his thirty-six-inch low gear.

Harry Barnes had scouted our route and set up the accommodations. A finer job could not have been done. Route 100 took us north for three days through the Green Mountains and Vermont's famous ski areas—Mount Snow, Sugarbush Valley, Pico Peak, and Stowe. Then we swung east through the relatively flatter northern part of Vermont, crossing the Connecticut River into New Hampshire at North Stratford. Then south on U.S. 3 along the river valley to Franconia, our Sunday layover spot. (It rained all day on our day of rest. As luck would have it, this was the only rain of any consequence during the entire two weeks.) What do you do on a rainy day? You send out for beer and snacks, turn the bikes upside down, and have "a clean and repair the bikes" party.

The next morning we headed into the White Mountains and the toughest climb of the trip. We warmed up for the day by sweating our way up to Franconia Notch. All stopped in Lincoln for a second breakfast, there being no restaurants or towns between Lincoln and Conway, our stop for the night. This thirty-mile stretch over the Kancamagus Pass is a cyclist's dream. It goes up for eight long miles and down for twenty-two. All of us managed to get over the mountain, one way or another. Most of the women got off and walked. Most of the men, hardened by a week of strenuous cycling, made a solemn vow to conquer this eight-mile monster by pedal alone. But many of the men, myself included, rested at the overlooks, giving the lame excuse that we just "had to take pictures of the lovely scenery"—and indeed it was lovely. Rob Van Ravenswaay, a strong-legged engineer from Pennsylvania, set his bike in a rather high gear and attacked the long grade Tour de France style. He made the hill nonstop, but just as he reached the summit his derailleur came apart. Having proved his legs stronger than his bicycle, Rob retired for the day. With the help of our full-time sag driver, Warran Cropp, a new derailleur was rounded up and Rob was back on the tour the next day.

Jim Eads, the youngest and ablest male cyclist on the tour, climbed the big hill twice in succession, as he said, "for the exercise." But this got him more jeers than cheers —he made us feel old.

From Conway we headed southwest past Lake Winnipesaukee, stopping overnight at Meredith, New London, and Keene, New Hampshire. The final four days of the trip were rather easy cycling, with the exception of the climb over Hogback Mountain, which is just five miles from Wilmington, Vermont, the end of the two-week tour.

Through we traveled on state or national highways most of the time, there were very few places where there was danger of being "blown off the road" by heavy, fast-moving traffic. It's true that Vermont's Route 100 is a narrow road, but cars and trucks are few and far between. We had the road to ourselves most of the time. In New

Hampshire we encountered much more traffic, but we were saved by the six-foot-wide paved shoulders that we found along most of the route. It was as if the highway had been designed by a member of I.B.T.S.

Most of us found that the hills bothered us less and less as the tour progressed. Much of this was, of course, because we gained strength as we piled up the miles. But some of the riders developed elaborate systems for taking the mind off the pain of hill climbing. John Russell said, "I do most of my sight-seeing going up hills. At slow speed I don't have to watch the road as carefully as at other times. I take a good look at the foliage and the mountains and I listen to the birds and before I know it I'm at the top."

Ray Cormier and the writer used this hill-climbing scheme: With the bike in lowest gear, you do one hundred turns of the pedals sitting on the saddle, then you honk (stand on the pedals) for one hundred. Then you shift to the next highest gear and repeat the routine. Then back to the lowest gear, etc. Most of us found that climbing with a group is easier than bruting it up the hill alone. The competitive instinct comes into play and keeps you on the bike long after you feel like quitting. Involved conversations, on any subject except hill climbing, are a good psychological aid. Isn't there an old cycling adage to the effect that "you're not really hurting until you're so winded that you can't talk"? At that point presumedly you should get off and walk.

In spite of the calorie-burning effort that we expended on the daily fifty miles, nobody seemed to lose weight. Nobody cared. When you ride on an I.B.T.S. tour you soon develop the appetite of a soldier on a forced march. Any restaurant that served us buffet style took a loss. Rediscovering the hunger pangs of youth, longtime weight-watchers went back for seconds on mincemeat pie—with ice cream. And between meals many of us "kept up our strength" by munching on apples or gorp—gorp being a mixture of equal parts of salted peanuts, raisins, and M&Ms, an all-purpose ration which you eat from a pocket as you pedal along the highway.

On one occasion we were forced to prepare our own dinner, having stopped for the night at a lakeside lodge that was a good distance from the nearest restaurant. We chipped in three dollars each and sent the sag wagon to do the shopping. After a couple of beers we sat down to a magnificent steak dinner, prepared under the watchful eye of Dr. John Flick, our chef in cycling shorts.

Problems of logistics, where to stop for lunch, and last-minute changes in route were ably handled by Macy Allen, our road captain. Mr. Allen's expertise in getting us seated without waiting in crowded restaurants was much appreciated.

Perhaps the best part of an I.B.T.S. tour is that you have a real chance to get away from it all. It's just about impossible to carry business problems along on the tour. Life is simplified. You have one task for the day; with your own muscles you must propel yourself from one point on the map to another point fifty miles away. There is a great satisfaction in being able to do this.

COVERED BRIDGES—
BUCOLIC ROMANCE
OF AN INDIANA TOUR

JOHN FLICK
March 1969

"The night before we started," said Ralph Schumacher, "I looked around and saw all those old people and I thought this would be a cinch. The next day they all ran off and left me!"

Ralph, at twenty-five, was the youngest member of the International Bicycle Touring Society's tour of southern Indiana, and a newcomer to bicycle touring to boot. He learned that in bicycling, there ain't no such animal as an "old person."

The tour of southern Indiana was a well planned and executed seven-day 326-mile loop designed for the most discriminating cyclists. There was terrain to suit all tastes and ambitions. There was scenery to satisfy the most ardent traveler. There were quaint towns and interesting

The covered bridge—Indiana's archway to adventure.

shops to delight the explorer. And there were meals to
tantalize the palate of an Epicurean. Hartley Alley, the
tour organizer, was a diligent and thorough planner.

The tour began and ended in Bloomington, and the first
day ushered us through hilly Brown County. Nashville, the
Mecca of the county art colony, was the lunch stop. Nashville was beautiful in a very quaint, old-fashioned way.
The Nashville House, where we took our meal, was full of
bucolic antiquery—cider presses, butter churns, spinning

wheels, etc.—with large portraits of old farm characters adorning the walls. Fresh biscuits, hickory-cured ham, and chestnut pie was the day's menu. We rode on to Columbus for the night.

The country canine was out in force one day in particular, and it was interesting to see the various means our group had to repel attacks. Russ and Helen Miller had squirt guns filled with ammonia fastened to their wrists with rubber bands. Russ Meinke had a fire extinguisher which he carried in his water-bottle cage, claiming it would stop any dog at twelve feet. Rose Graham had a large horn with a rubber bulb which gave forth with a startling blast, which had an added advantage in alerting dog owners to the activities of their aggressive pets. Some riders carried little tubes of Halt, designed especially to discourage man's best friend, while others resorted to grabbing their pumps —using them as clubs.

One day in Madison proved too short to see all the town had to offer. This charming community on the bank of the Ohio River was like something out of the old South. Beautiful and stately mansions stood against the background of the great river where boats and barges plied the endless current. The President Madison Motel was our inn for the night. The dinner featured king crab, a tasty treat which shan't be forgotten soon.

We visited Hanover College with its breathtaking view of the Ohio River. It had threatened rain this day, and we were prepared for the worst. Fortunately, our rain gear wasn't needed, and even the muddy skies could not dim the natural beauty of the area.

Salem was our destination, but before we got there, an exhausting hill presented itself. At the top, the word "Sprint" was painted on the pavement. Hartley's humor was lost on most of us who were struggling just to keep our bikes moving.

Toward the end of the tour we were all inveterate "food-oholics." There's nothing like healthy exercise to create a healthy appetite. The little country stores were finding us regular visitors, loading up with all kinds of good things to eat. At a little store in Tampico we were served fresh coffee and offered Amish homemade peanut brittle. This delicious candy was stored in big barrels and made in disks two feet in diameter. We left with bulging pockets.

The tour ended much too soon, a fate shared by most bike tours. With such a grand group of people, there's very little that can spoil such a trip.

CYCLORAMA—OZARKANA

E. PETER HOFFMAN
February 1969

The lore of the Ozarks is filled with legends that spread a magic carpet for the imagination. In this egg-shaped empire with its sixty thousand square miles of territory, there are thousands of romantic tales that act as interludes in the solemn dramas of folklore. Folklore—and folk life—are part and parcel of pastoral life. With the coming of science, they fold their tents and slink away.

When social workers first entered the Ozarks, they found that instinctive caution is deeply seated in the hillman's nature. It is an accredited folkway to outwit changing conditions cautiously like a cat playing with a mouse. Belief and practice in the back hills may have strange imprints of inconsistency. A man may jokingly refer to some household superstition, but you don't find him burning sassafras wood in the fireplace or ignoring a chain letter. His creed may be as antique as his walnut furniture, but he clings to it like a tenderfoot riding a raft.

This inconsistency in behavior is probably responsible for the apparent break in the traditional morale of the hillman. He saw the handwriting on the wall and realized that his way of life must go. He decided to crush pride with the heel of necessity and accept government aid. He adjusted his logic as best he could and tried to save face by accepting employment on Federal projects. He had come to the end of his primitive trail of freedom, and necessity forced him onto the regimented highroad.

In the 1930's folk life in the Ozarks rapidly began to

disappear. Its departure may be likened to the stranger who stopped at a mountain cabin to inquire of the location of a hillbilly's still. The moonshiner's son offered to direct the man to the still for a quarter, but asked payment in advance. "I'll pay you when I get back," said the stranger. "But," said the boy, "you ain't a-comin' back."

The hillman is not the long-whiskered, tobacco-chewing illiterate the movies and comic strips have pictured him to be. He had differed from the average American because of his century of isolation, but good roads, improved methods of transportation, and better schools have almost completely leveled this inequality. The hillman has lost many of his distinctive traits, and the majority have become standardized middle-class Americans.

But it is still possible in some sections of this romantic land to turn back the clock and listen to the hum of the spinning wheel, the creak of the loom, the groan of the waterwheel at the mill, the rhythmic poetry of the cradle in its golden sea of grain, and to enjoy the generosity that springs from the heart of every true hillman. This is the background of a people nurtured in solitude and unspoiled by the workaday commercial world.

Discovering the Ozarks, its beauty, folklore, and people, is best done by bicycle. The International Bicycle Touring Society, a unique organization of cyclists headquartered in the United States, penetrated the Ozark region in southern Missouri last fall. The terrain had been thoroughly scouted and the route carefully planned. Accommodations ranged from modern motels to rustic mountain lodges where crackling fires in huge stone fireplaces dispelled the pleasant weariness of the day's cycling. Meals were taken in private dining rooms decorated with collections of antique guns and by quiet streams which gurgled like cider from a hillbilly's jug. Mouths still water at the memory of fresh-baked corn bread and sugar-cured ham. Food for lunch was often bought in country stores—cheese and biscuits, wild-berry jellies, sausage flavored with sage, spicy molasses cake—to be eaten in the quiet of some secluded hollow.

The general store in the Ozarks has long been a conglomeration of almost everything hillmen eat, wear, and use. Tart Tuttle's store in Woodville is a typical example of early merchandising. The ramshackle building stands in the shade of a large tree, known in the neighborhood as the Old Drunk Walnut. Many years before, a pioneer had built a distillery by the tree and dumped the mash waste out the door. The effect of the seepage was miraculous. The tree got hilariously drunk and never sobered up. The leaves on the tipsy limbs curled like an outlaw's trigger finger.

Inside, stick candy keeps company with plug tobacco, and bolts of calico sometimes get too familiar with the vinegar barrel. Boots and shoes lie tangled on the counter. Hats and overalls collect dust on sagging shelves. You can find snuff for pleasure and pills for pain in fly-specked showcases patched with cardboard.

Out front the "store-porch jury" would assemble to sprawl in the welcome shade, discuss current topics, pass judgment, and whittle time.

Country stores in the tradition of Tuttle's are becoming increasingly hard to find, but biking on the back roads uncovered many similar outposts of the past.

Cycling also unlocked many doors where tourists in shiny, high-powered cars would have encountered cold indifference. "In many instances we were welcomed as if we had been mountain folk all our lives," reflected one rider. "The bicycle seemed to break down barriers which people from the outside normally experience."

Within the I.B.T.S. there is no such thing as an outsider, and it is the very nature of the group's consistency, with members from all parts of the United States and Europe, that makes these tours so popular. Doctors, lawyers, and candlestick makers—nowhere will you find such a group of individualists sharing a common bond so completely.

The highest point in the Ozarks is 2,823-foot Mount Magazine, and most of the country is at considerably lower altitudes. "Just folds of little green hills with occasional peaks protruding from them," wrote one historian. But the Ozarks are marked with deep, rugged hollows, steep ridges, and winding roads. Low gears in the 30's found favor with the huff 'n' puffers, the name affectionately given I.B.T.S. riders.

"It was a perfect time of year," said one female member of the tour. "As far as the eye could see, this unspoiled wilderness was spotted in reds, yellows, rusts, and greens. This array of brilliant color was slowly creeping over the hills. Day by day we could see nature change before our eyes."

There were exciting dashes down canyons where the classical gang of freebooters—the James boys—once rode, but on a different loyal steed. There were rides under dripping trees that sheltered Confederate troops during long-forgotten skirmishes. There were rides along ridges where odes to Billy Joes have been sung for countless generations.

The heritage of the Ozarks will soon be remembered only in song and folklore. The relentless onrush of modern society has sent its contaminating fingers up the canyons and over the ridges like a thick ground fog. But glimpses of the romantic past may still be seen, and will best be found on a bicycle.

PAKATAKAN IN THE CATSKILLS— THE GREAT EASTERN RALLY

DENSLOW DADE
September 1968

Last June 7, Barrett Caldwell retired as school purchasing director in Volusia County, Florida, stepped onto a pair of bicycle pedals, and rode into a brand-new life at sixty. Twenty-five days and fifteen hundred miles later, he piloted his up-bar machine into Arkville, New York, receiving plaudits and first prize for cycling the most miles to the Great Eastern Rally.

Others, too, had cycled creditable distances to reach Pakatakan Lodge in the beautiful Catskill Mountains, headquarters for the weekend sponsored by the New York Cycle Club. Sandy Figuers and Bob Gearhart had ridden from Arlington, Virginia. Jim Eads rolled in from Philadelphia, 130 miles in one day. Frank Bollag arrived Saturday from Manhattan, 145 miles distant.

One hundred and fifty men and women from fourteen states, from all walks of life, with backgrounds and interests as varied as A to Z, eagerly gathered in their common love of cycling. Adventurous, individualistic, friendly people with stories to tell and new experiences to share.

Now to get down to brass tacks. (Ooops—what a metaphor!) I was one of those lucky enough to start my weekend early, and headed toward Pakatakan Lodge on Thursday, July 4. Approaching rally country, the cheering sight of a long line of bright colors stretched out on the road before me, and soon I was shaking hands with old friends. This particular group had been on its first long ride and were already sunburned and happy.

Cyclists are great folks with cameras, and that evening we saw many excellent slides. The first of three beautiful Peugeot bicycles brought to the lodge by Ron Kreiger of Franklin Imports was auctioned. Then the floor was cleared for dancing.

Early Friday morning the hardy ones took a before-breakfast ride, an event that must be fun because so many do it; a nice brisk ten miles without benefit of coffee or bacon and eggs. All hail!

The ride around Papacton Reservoir was the high point of the day. The road winds sixty miles like a snake on LSD. The wind is in your face one minute, it cools the small of your back the next. The road goes every direction of the compass but somehow takes you from Margaretville to Downsville. (The latter may have been so named for the two-mile downhill run that ushers you into Main Street. Glorious!)

It was on this day that many learned that the female of the species is more deadly. "I'm not in good shape," said Ethel Robertson innocently. "Don't let me hold you back." We disagreed with the first statement, were apprehensive of the second. Ethel quickly disappeared from view—ahead of us—and we haven't fully recovered since. It's a cruel blow to the masculine ego to discover that such cute little feminine creatures as Trudy Kuerner and Nancy Burghart can do you in on the road. I once tried to stay on Nancy's wheel, not knowing she was women's National Champion.

It must have been awesome to little Downsville, this

invasion of a hundred bikophiles. Lizzie, the proprietress of the luncheonette, smiled happily as the first of the colorful crew filed in. "Ach! No more! No more!" she soon cried in anguish, and the overflow had to be content with raiding the nearby grocery store.

There were alternate routes back, including mountain climbing for the hardier. That night hungry riders wiped out an entire generation of roast chickens at the lodge where Mr. and Mrs. Beland and pretty waitresses served an excellent table.

Saturday there was a twenty-five-mile round-trip tour to Roxbury, a delightful little hamlet where a professional auction was afoot. The country auction is a sport where the hunters are the hunted, if you follow me.

On the way back to the lodge, Lenore Yalisone, of Wilmington, Delaware, had trouble crossing some railroad tracks. To illustrate how important it is to cross tracks at a full right angle, one of our strongest and most experienced riders promptly spilled at the same spot. The male ego suffered another lesson in humility.

The entire route was plainly marked with Dan Henry's now famous arrows (see article on page 252), which were just one of Dan's many contributions to a successful rally.

There is a local legend that once you put a foot in the Delaware River you will never leave the place again. Perhaps the legend holds some truth, for all of us have left a part of our hearts at Pakatakan.

RIDE OF THE FALLING LEAVES

E. PETER HOFFMAN
January 1969

Bicycle clubs are the big thing this year, and when two or more get together for a joint ride, fun is sure to follow.

There are clubs of all types and descriptions, catering to the young and the old, to the fast and the slow, to the long-distance riders and the "Sunday in the park-ers."

Crisp, tantalizing days and the pageant of autumn color
make cycling the pinnacle of pleasure.

Getting together with a group of friends for a ride can be one of the most enjoyable aspects of cycling, and the intraclub rides, with new faces and through unexplored terrain, can be the highlight of the year.

Such a ride was recently held in Indiana in conjunction with the annual Leaf Festival in Louisville. The promoting club was, fittingly, the Louisville Wheelmen, who scheduled the event, sent out invitations, and provided following vehicles (sag wagons) to aid the weary or those having mechanical problems.

The ride began in Brownstown and headed out over picturesque roads to Freetown, crossing several hundred bridges. Then on to Stonehead, which has been a crossroads since early times, and to Nashville by way of Brown County Park.

Nashville is a quaint little town, built on the theme of yesteryear. It boasts of old-time stores, courthouse, jail, and other buildings in the motif of the past. Here you can buy herbs and stone-ground wheat, and such items as early cooking utensils and coffee grinders. Nashville is also an artists' colony and oil paintings can be bought along the sidewalks. It's a great place to tour by bicycle.

Riders gathered on the courthouse lawn for lunch, some buying fish and chips at Volunteer Firemen's booth, then relaxing among the swirl of fallen leaves for which the ride was named.

Approximately one hundred riders participated, but it was hard to get an accurate count; many joined in along the way or departed before the ride ended, exercising the freedom that cycling so generously offers.

If you are interested in joining a bike club, write to the League of American Wheelmen, 2921 Simpson Street, Evanston, Illinois, for the names of groups in your area.

A bite to eat, a catnap in a golden bed of leaves, pleasant talk—all part of a club run. And what could better capture the feeling of rural America than the country store at right, with covered porch, ancient gas pumps, and, of course, a Coca-Cola sign.

TOURING THROUGH TEXAS

ROSE GRAHAM
March 1968

West-central Texas, popularly called the Hill Country, is a rock-studded land on a great natural terrace, known as the Balcones Escarpment. It is the homeland of a President and is sometimes called L.B.J Country. It is also called, in the phrase of a brewer, the Country of 1,100 Springs. Texas travel folders rather modestly describe it as a country of rolling hills and sparkling brooks.

Yet it is a land of extremes. The earth hardens and cracks in the heat. When the rain comes it is most likely to come in torrents—"gully washers" they call them.

It was late in the evening as we approached the departure point for a bicycle tour of that area and our windshield wipers worked furiously to lick away the rain. We wondered if the rains were likely to continue. It had already been raining for eight consecutive days. Captain Dan Henry, a New Yorker who came to Texas to join the tour, puzzled over his careful packing for the trip and thought perhaps he had forgotten something—a boat.

Soon we were in New Braunfels, a German community, celebrating the Wurstfest, and we forgot the rain, enjoying the wurst (sausage), and oomph-pah bands and the biergarten. We would stay here for two days of *Gemütlichkeit* —good-time fellowship in the German manner.

The weather was somewhat threatening next morning, though we didn't worry about it for a while because we were being elegantly entertained in the beautiful third-generation home of Mr. and Mrs. John Langston, parents of tour member Dr. John Langston. Pat Langston, John's wife, knows well the appetite of a bicyclist and prepared a bountiful breakfast of ham and eggs, grits, and home-made biscuits.

Breakfast over, the sun came out. We eagerly mounted bicycles for a day on Old River Road, which crosses and recrosses the Guadalupe River between high cliffs to Canyon Dam. The river, running fast after the abundant rainfall of several days' duration, attracted many canoeists and we stopped several times to watch their race down the rapids. Spanish-moss-draped live oaks and frost-tinted red cypresses overhanging the river completed this picturesque route. The day on Old River Road was a foretaste of what we were to enjoy all through the tour.

"Beautiful, just beautiful." We were to hear this refrain often. "Beautiful" perfectly describes the scenery: green valleys overlooked by hillsides ablaze with the reds and yellows of oaks, pecans, cottonwoods, and sumacs contrasting with the evergreen of the cedars, shin oaks, and cypresses . . . rugged granite outcroppings on bare crests of hills . . . blossoming fire against a velvet sky . . . a breathless glimpse of running deer . . . woodland glades . . . frothy cascades, quiet lakes, and charming villages. "Ideal" describes the weather: warm, bright sunshine; gentle, cooling breezes.

The Wurstfest lived up to its expectations of good fellowship. A twenty-eight-mile criterium bicycle race was added last year to the festivities, and this year the number of entrants increased from nineteen to thirty-two. After cheering on the racers and saying goodbye to those who could not join us for the entire tour, we left the Wurstfest and began our journey.

Since our start to San Marcos was made in late afternoon, we traveled the twenty miles' distance at a rapid clip. Here we rode on the old San Antonio Road parallel with the Balcones Escarpment that separates the Hill Country to the west from the rolling farmlands to the east. The rise of the fault line was two hundred feet above us on our left; to our right in the low-lying valley young oats and wheat sparkled like green emeralds in the brilliant sunlight. The air was sparkling fresh. We passed abandoned stores that once enjoyed a brisk trade during the days of the cattle drives along the Chisholm Trail. Old stone houses along the way are still inhabited and rock fences enclose sheep and goats. Arrival in San Marcos was just at sunset.

We could just see the campus of Southwest Texas State College, President Johnson's alma mater, as we approached the Aquarena Springs Motor Hotel. The hotel, located on the fountainhead of the San Marcos River, with its balcony rooms overlooking the Aquarena Springs and the garden rooms exposed to the rugged hillside, provided comfortable and pleasant accommodations. Touring members gathered at poolside to see Paul Port jump into the motel pool, but remained spectators when Paul pronounced the water too frigid for swimming. A fine dinner by candlelight with large red napkins gracing the table readied us for a good night's rest. The non-Texan in our group slept so well that he missed breakfast call the next morning, so Joe Blatch became the unofficial waker-upper. A bright red smile and the mating calls of the many beautiful mallard ducks greeted early risers.

Before beginning the day's travel, we enjoyed the sightseeing attractions at the Aquarena. A glass-bottomed-boat journey over the crystal-clear waters of the springs provided a unique view of the native vegetation and the huge catfish, bass, and perch. Aqua-maids and Glurpo, the clown, entertained in an underwater show at the Submarine Theater.

To flatlanders, as most of the touring members were, the ride to Wimberly was indeed an uphill ascent. The uphill slopes were made easier by services from Walter Graham, our faithful sag-wagon driver, who served cooled drinks along the way. The sturdier troop pushed on five miles past the junction to Wimberly to the magnificent, scenic Devil's Backbone, a state lookout over the Blanco river valley and the rugged Guadalupe River. The scenery at this lookout at the time when we saw it indeed rivaled that of Shenandoah Valley. Captain Dan marveled at Texans keeping this beauty spot a secret from the world and wrote a poem, "There Is a Texas No One Knows." To those who had struggled up Devil's Backbone, the scenery was enough, but there also came the reward of a continuous ten-mile downhill ride to Wimberly.

Wimberly is another spring-fed locale whose key industry is dude ranches. We enjoyed our overnight stay at the Holiday Hills Inn Resort. The hospitality of the ranches has made the Hill Country a new resort-land. A family-style meal, singing around the piano, Ping-Pong, and dancing to the jukebox were all a part of the evening's entertainment. We are already planning a return visit to enjoy horseback riding which is also available on the 360-acre ranch.

Next morning, ringing of a cattle bell by the innkeeper beckoned us up to a hearty breakfast. Upon his friendly advice, we also changed the day's route to Blanco. The route he suggested took us along a quiet, narrow, winding road that crossed over small streams through remote scrub-brush goat country. The route change also made possible a delightful rest stop at one of those wonderful old-fashioned stores with a potbellied stove in the middle of the room and fruit in a barrel. Someone said high-button shoes could have been purchased had we asked. We could read on a blackboard the average rainfall for the past several decades.

Blanco's high-school band was warming up as we left that small town on a rather chilly morning. The sun was soon warm, kingfishers were chattering, and we were happy pedaling up hills, coasting down, alongside Blanco River. This road, as well as the road from Wimberly to San Marcos that took us over Devil's Backbone, is being beautified by local businessmen in the area to honor President Johnson.

We left this trail to take Hye Road, which was really just a tree-shaded lane so untraveled that the only sound was that of a helicopter passing overhead. The Hye Store, where the President mailed his first letter when he was four, has become nationally known, but its character has not greatly changed. It still serves the community as a post office, feed store, and grocery. We purchased the makings for a picnic lunch here: summer sausage, cheese, crackers, apples, and chocolate milk. Hye Store is only two and a half miles from the L.B.J. Ranch and we had to wait until a likely spot to eat presented itself. Ranch Road 1, which goes by the "Summer White House," did not offer a roadside park and Secret Service men seemed to have us under surveillance. We contented ourselves with looking at the beautiful white-faced Hereford cattle, the well-kept cemetery, and the ranch house itself. The selected picnic spot was found near Stonewall in the middle of the Pedernales River on a smooth flat river rock with the water rushing by. The meal became a moment to be programmed into our memory banks.

Now we were well on our way to Fredericksburg, but first we went through the famous Stonewall peach orchards. Unfortunately, peaches were not in season.

Fredericksburg is remembered for the barbecue at the Red Barn, the pastries purchased at the German bakery, the interesting old-world architecture, and the cordiality of the people we met. Two charming ladies, descendants of some of the original settlers, proudly guided us through the Pioneer Home and Museum.

The trip from Fredericksburg to Kerrville was the longest, the most difficult, and the most rewarding. We ventured off the route on the itinerary to find ourselves on bladed dirt roads with many good-sized rocks protruding from the surface. Cattle guards which had created fear in the more timid riders were nothing as compared to crossing streams which flowed over limestone rocks. It was primitive country that produced such unexpected sights as a beautiful stone barn and an old stone Gothic church. A highlight of the day was a visit with Ace Reid, rancher, humorist, and creator of "Cowpoke" cartoons. Our efforts to reach Draggin' S Ranch, which Ace says he cartoons to afford, became monumental. The private road to the ranch is three or four miles off the main thoroughfare and is adequate for horses and four-wheeled heavy duty Jeeps, but hardly the kind usually selected for travel on lightweight bicycles. We overcame many obstacles, including a large bull who might have become inflamed (but didn't) by our red shirts, to reach the Reid's beautiful contemporary house which straddles a flowing stream. Mr. and Mrs. Reid entertain often and many of their guests are well-known personages, but, weary and disheveled, we were royally received. The refreshments which were provided thoroughly revived weary bodies and frayed nerves. Though it gave the townspeople a bit of a shock to see Ace unloading bicycles out of his horse trailer in front of the Purple Sage, the trip out of the ranch into Kerrville by Jeep with the bicycles in the trailer was indeed a welcomed service.

Dancing in the lavish private club at the Inn of the Hills in Kerrville did not tire us for the next day's bicycling. A picnic stop along a stream at Camp Verde, a brief refreshment stop in Bandera, and some *really* steep climbs up several hills were the memorable activities of the day. Happily, the night's lodging had been arranged at historic Kendall Inn, formerly an important stagecoach stop. Kendall Inn's gracious dining room was an appropriate setting for the last evening's meal, which Dan Henry helped make a special occasion by toasting wine and giving tribute to the joys of the tour.

So it went. From the thrill of panoramic vistas of the roller-coaster ascent and descent of riotously colorful hills to quiet, narrow roads through scrub-brush goat country to primitive and virgin country along a running stream to roads enclosed by granite cliffs on either side, the Hill Country offers endless delights.

PHANTOM OF THE ROCKIES

PAUL SCHWEMLER
January 1969

> *Are you considering a tour of some far-off mountains at high elevations? Have you ever been aware of the strange effects of such elevations on the individual? If not, it is strongly recommended that you read this, as it describes not only a fantastic bicycle tour, but a series of inexplicable events that occurred to an otherwise mature and reliable adult bicycle tourist.*

It all started when three of us, Art Flanagan, Bob Guyan, and myself, drove to the little Colorado town of Buena Vista, far from our beloved haze of Whittier, California. Here we were to begin a planned trip of the mountain area; a trip that, unknown to us at the time, would bring us face to face with the Phantom of the Rockies.

We pedaled gaily off through the high valley, warming over the 9,346-foot Trout Creek Pass and stopping for lunch at the well-named town of Fairplay, at 10,000 feet.

Much of this trip was through historic mining country, and the names of towns, creeks, etc., are thus reflected. No doubt Fairplay had a two-gun constable.

The afternoon ride was over the modest Kenosha Pass and down very good roads to the foothill community of Bailey (foothill, that is, to the next hill). After purchasing groceries for the next three meals, we set off for the campgrounds which, through some delighted confusion, necessitated backtracking some eleven miles to an identified area possessing a fast-running stream and a little green shed. Since some of the natives were drinking the stream water, so did we. Art cooked his delicious can of hash; Bob his package of macaroni and cheese; and I my can of stew. Yes, we ate like kings—of the road.

The clear mountain air contributed to relatively peaceful sleep. Of course, Art's mattress failed to hold air, so he slept "down to earth." The next morning, with over eighty miles behind us, we packed up for another go at it. Perhaps it was the night air, or perhaps it was the mountain water, but this was to be the first of our encounters with the Jekyll/Hyde of our crew, Art Flanagan. Our route through the rolling hills took us to the little town of Conifer, where we were to head north. Art is a fantastic downhill man, so he preceded us down to Conifer. When we arrived, no Art. We waited for some time and then became concerned. Did he turn and leave no message? Was he run over by a frustrated ex-bicyclist? In desperation we flagged down a passing automobile and requested they look for Art. After siesta and a casual lunch, we spotted Art puffing back up the road to Conifer. It seems he had "just missed the sign." In fact, he was well on his way to the flatlands of Denver when the information reached him.

The road north was one of those glorious gentle downhill runs through a valley to the low (geographically) point of the trip, the little town of Evergreen, at 7,040 feet. This town, deep in the foothill section, was a bustle of preholiday activities.

Art purchased a new heavy-duty air mattress to replace the faulty one. For the uninitiated, sleeping without an air mattress is like reclining on a gravel driveway. And poor ol' Art had suffered.

The three of us then walked across the busy street to

take the main road heading north. Well, that's what we thought. A three-mile-long hill ensued, and when Bob and I reached the top—no Art! I finally coasted back into town and searched it thoroughly. Had he been hurt? Misled by one of the talented small-town girls? Who knows? The jinx was with us. I finally gave up and sweated back up the hill. Bob and I then went on. At the town of Bergen Park we turned west. "Go West, old men," and we did. This was the beginning of the *big* hill. Weather and scenery were with us, so it was just a dandy climb up the Mount Evans road. The meandering mountain road gently deposited us at the 10,650-foot campsite of Echo Lake. We located a palatial shelter house and campsite, met some very nice folks, and inquired about our lost soul to the rangers. They checked all other local campgrounds without avail. Oh, yes, after several days one becomes incompatible with oneself in a sleeping bag, so through the generosity of a camping family I reveled in a hot-water bath from a dishpan. Don't laugh—it's better than none!

Suddenly before sundown the Phantom Flanagan appeared. He, by some strange force, had turned 180 degrees in Evergreen and had gone out of town in the wrong direction; back toward Denver again, as if some mysterious force were attracting him. How strange things happen! We again cooked fantastic meals—Bob his macaroni and cheese; Art a can of some unidentifiable pottage; and myself likewise.

The mountain winds blew cold, and a chilly night it was. No smog—it would have frozen. The next morning we left our heavy panniers at a University of Denver High Altitude Station and headed up the final fourteen miles of Mount Evans. This was, appropriately, Labor Day. The road is quite good, but gradually shows the effects of extreme weathering as altitude is gained. Above approximately twelve thousand feet, the winds become terrible. The road is very rough and winding and, although not unreasonably steep, became a real challenge because of the wind. Each switchback was a thrill, for the wind would change and try to catapult us over the edge. Low gear became necessary, not due to the incline, but to improve control of the bicycle. Low gear was a thirty-nine. The humor of this climb was registered in the shocked and surprised looks on the faces of motorists. There we are, sweating up a wild hill; a descending car lurches, the driver grabs his camera and snaps us as we struggle by!

The end of the road came none too soon, terminating in a parking area equipped with a small restaurant, lookout, and gift shop. The thermometer stood at 35°, which, combined with the wind, drove us inside after a few pictures. This was truly the high point of the trip, and is a never-to-be-forgotten experience. The elevation is 14,260 feet, the highest road in the United States. At its peak is a laboratory for the study of cosmic rays.

The downhill ride (after warming up in the restaurant to the point where sensitivity of the fingers and feet was regained) was a real blast—in every sense of the word. The usual "free-fall" downhill technique was impossible due to the buffeting winds and the roughness of the road. Every corner was cautiously negotiated, at times riding on the wrong side of the road to stay away from the edge. Coasting at a considerable speed down a rough road means the bike is sometimes airborne, which, when coupled with a gusty crosswind, results in a most interesting lateral movement. Highly recommended for those who like thrills. We were back at our 10,650-foot campsite in one hour and ten minutes. It had taken us three hours to make the climb.

We loaded our camping gear and dropped down the hill through the interesting town of Idaho Springs. Part of the downhill run was accompanied by a little rain squall, so Art and I donned our rain capes for the first time during the trip. This gave Art the opportunity to become acquainted with his English import—a brilliant yellow plastic cape, cut for bicycling, which was to be a friend in need.

A little refreshment in a local restaurant and we were on our way. The day was waning, so we headed to a campsite on the top of a hill, five miles away. Art chose to ride up the hill leisurely, while Bob and I pushed on. At the top of the hill we entered the camp and set up. Art didn't show. The Phantom had struck again! Where he went, we had no idea. However, camp was made amid threatening winds and spasms of rain. We shared the entire park with two brothers who were having a camp-out, so after setting up my plastic tube tent under some big trees, I joined the boys in song and brew while Bob intelligently retired.

During the night I learned about locating tube tents. The idea (in spite of what the books say) is to have one side lower than the other so that *when* the rain leaks in (not *if*), it will run to one side and out the end (you hope). This was a great accidental discovery, as only my nylon jacket was along the "trough" side of the tent. Bob, having a hearty dislike for stubby tubes, chose to sleep out. The result was a sleeping bag which was pounds heavier with moisture by morning.

Early the next day we set off in a drizzle. Passing several parks, I paged Art—loud and clear—but to no avail. Gone! After a half hour of riding in cold rain, we stopped at a quaint general store for a warming cup of coffee. The manager (a little lady from Whittier, California) received a phone call from her neighbor who, seeing our bicycles, called to say that our Phantom had stopped by last night and believed he was lost! He had pushed on. A clue! We covered our wet feet with plastic bags and pushed on. At the interesting community of Nederland a resident said our Phantom had been seen eating in a local restaurant. We were gaining on him!

By the time we reached Allenspark we had really been through it—rain, hail, sleet, and snow! We pulled in and inquired about a restaurant. About then, from the depths of a service station, we heard a howl from our Phantom! He had stayed in a motel in Nederland and was warming himself. While doing so, he managed to blow his tire by the process of too much inflation. That's the way it goes!

We then rode several blocks farther to Fay's Café. This turned out to be a sizable establishment managed by a charming hostess who was really great. We ended up hanging wet socks and shoes in front of her fireplace, storing bikes in her shed, and tripping around lightly in our bare feet attempting to restore circulation. The guests took all of this in good spirit and were very sympathetic (and right then we reveled in sympathy). This was a bright spot in what was the only unpleasant day of the trip. After much food, talk, fire-warming, and finally redressing in multiple layers of clothing, we took to the winter wonderland outside. Snow rested heavily on the trees, slush on the roads, and merrily we plugged onward. After slushing along for an hour, the weather cleared and we were able to remove the first layer of garments. With this we entered the notable town of Estes Park, gateway to Rocky Mountains National Park.

While checking the motels, we rode together until Art said he wanted to check another establishment and would be right along. Bob and I, at the direction of a very helpful store clerk, located a tire tube for Art and checked in at an interesting little rooming house. I think these, if clean, are more interesting than motels. There is a good possibility that you will meet other characters like yourself. Estes Park is simply a "Main Street," so we knew we couldn't miss Art. After a bath, we partook of nourishment at a local restaurant. We strolled the street, knowing that our Phantom would show—but alas, no show! Incidentally, it was cold weather and the other folks in town seemed confused by my attire of jacket, slacks, and bare feet in zorries (my shoes were drying in front of the heater). Well, I can't help it if they're restricted by convention! Sleeping in a motel on this cool night gave us a chance to clean up, dry out, and reorganize for the days ahead.

The Trail Ridge Road, highest continuous road in the United States, was closed by snow, but the rangers at the park office thought it would be cleared by noon the next day. So the next morning we started out of town, sans the Phantom, for the Trail Ridge Road over Rocky Mountains National Park. As it happened, the road crews kept clearing the road just ahead of us, so we weren't delayed. Not that we were blasting up this mountain in any hurry. About halfway up, at Rainbow Curve where the wind was cold and strong, we stopped for pictures and I noticed my rear tubular tire had slipped on the rim and all tread was scrubbed off near the valve. If you want fun, change tires when your hands are numbed with cold, the bike is fully loaded, and the tire glued on in a very effective manner!

As we climbed, we entered a snow-covered wonderland. At the 12,183-foot crest we stopped for pictures and were assisted by some college boys who were working for the road-clearing department. They were also bicycle riders and could appreciate our feeling of accomplishment. Then on to the restaurant and store at Fall River Pass where we ate, warmed ourselves, and contacted the rangers' office regarding our lost Phantom. Sure enough, he had just entered another gate at the base of the park. It would be dark before he reached the top. Woe is he; and that's our boy Art! We asked the ranger to contact Art and tell him to get a ride and check in with the police department in Granby, our destination for the day.

Then out into a wild blizzard—the wind and snow again! On with all the clothes—bandanna around the face in true highwayman style, and away we blew! Those first few miles downhill were *very* challenging, but soon we were below the storm and on a fantastically thrilling downhill run. We rocketed through a descending valley, across an open plain, and into the thriving metropolis of Granby. We stopped by the police department (the constable's home) and explained our Phantom problem. His cooperation was assured. No Art that night. Was he high in the mountains in a snowdrift? Far down over some precipice? Who knows? The next morning, while trying to locate a highway patrol car to issue an all-points bulletin, who should walk out of a restaurant but Art, our Phantom! He had cycled partway up the hill, ridden in a truck "over the hill," and cycled into Granby at night to stay in a motel. What a guy! So off we started again. Well, almost. Art had wired for more cash, which was to be in the Granby bank by 9:00 A.M. It was now 8:00, so he said to go ahead, he would catch us. With this guy, anything can happen.

Bob and I rode through awe-inspiring country, past nationally famous ski resorts, and then attacked the delightful Berthoud Pass. By noon we were at the 11,307-foot summit and soared downhill like flying eagles into lowlands of the 8,000-foot variety. After some nourishment in a small town, we were rolling through the foothills toward our afternoon objective. It soon hove into view and we had the pleasure of ascending the 11,992-foot Loveland Pass. Actually, I think this was one of the most enjoyable climbs of the trip. The road is one of the classic long-loop switchback type where the feeling of accomplishment was strong every time we would swing around a hairpin turn and look down and back along our route. This, to my mind, is an important factor in hill climbing.

Atop Loveland we were given some fresh peaches by a chap with a truckload, and we asked him to pass our destination point on to Art, who hadn't showed. We also repeated the request to the highway patrol officer on duty. Another memorable downhill flight and we were soon at our destination. We had the campgrounds to ourselves. The water had been turned off for the winter, but we obtained some nearby. After cooking a scrumptious dinner on my Primus stove, I rode off to a nearby park to see if Art was there by mistake. Alas, our Phantom had disappeared again.

Since the weather was cold, and getting colder, I inserted my silk liner into my sleeping bag and slid down in my two and a half pounds of down. (Now *this* is really sleeping, especially after two passes on the same day.)

By morning there was a lacework of frost on the sleeping bag and our water was partially solidified—I believe they call it ice. Never fear, we filled up on warm, nourishing food before heading on. We warmed at Dillon, cruised through Frisco, whipped by Kokomo, and were not so soon at anticlimactic Climax, atop the 11,314-foot Freemont Pass. The mining operations (molybdenum) are huge, with processing facilities all over the hills. The general store is all-encompassing.

Then down we went! Soon we were at Leadville, tucked away at 10,152 feet. This is a very interesting town recommended for all bicycle tourists. I went to check in with the police regarding our wayward boy and the desk gal said, "You must mean that gray-haired man on a bicycle who was through here about an hour ago and photographed our policewoman who issues parking tickets!" Well, how about that? The Phantom was ahead of us!

I had become fascinated with the "old roads" visible throughout the mountains and this day was no exception. A sign identified the Leadville Stagecoach Road. This appeared to be about a six-foot-wide strip of dirt and rock, faced on one side by the sheer mountain and threatened by a drop-off on the other. Stone bankments were still visible. I would hesitate to ride that road on a bike, much less in a stagecoach!

By late afternoon we pulled into our camp end point, to be greeted by our Phantom. He had already showered away the road grime and was relaxing. We followed suit and discussed the thrill of a trip as great as this. The experience of this tour is hard to describe, as is the true massive beauty of the snowcapped Rocky Mountains. It helps one realize how great is this land of ours.

So closed the saga of our Phantom and the story of a very challenging and fantastically scenic tour—468 miles, four of the state's passes over eleven thousand feet, the highest automobile road in the world, and something well over seven miles (vertically) of hill climbing in seven days.

Anybody interested?

Competition Cycling

Between Seo de Urgel, Spain, and Perpignan, France, tour riders are encouraged by clapping villagers. This is a typical Spanish look for a French Tour de France.

BLOOD AND THUNDER IN
THE TOUR DE FRANCE

ELIZABETH BOURQUIN
September 1968

For the French, the Italians, the Germans, the Belgians, and the Swiss, the Tour de France is truly the "greatest show on earth." It is a show with hundreds of actors and thousands of spectacular sets. Its stage is the heart of Europe, from the peaks of Chartreuse and the Massif Central to the Plains of the North. It passes through great cities and countless picturesque villages. It is a three-week run with thousands of extras—some eight hundred reporters, scores of doctors, nurses, trainers, and representatives of commercial sponsors who, day after day, follow the cyclists in hundreds of vehicles of all descriptions. It is a fabulous extravaganza, rich in human conflicts and tragedies, watched by fifteen million spectators who, enthralled, crowd along the roads, not to mention many millions more glued to their television sets, who see "live" the daily drama as it unfolds.

This year's 2.915-mile race almost didn't get off the ground. The civil disorders and strikes that besieged France in May and June left the Tour's fate in doubt until a few days before its scheduled departure. But the Tour de France is something more than a bike race—it's an institution. Even in 1958 when de Gaulle surged to power and saved the country from the brink of civil war, it was "Le

141

Tour" that commanded the headlines. The country's political troubles were relegated to the back pages while the
exploits of Charlie Gaul, cyclist, not Charles de Gaulle,
politician, jumped from the front pages.

So it was that after weeks of doubts the Tour de France
got under way. The Tour appropriately started in the
famous spa of Vittel. It was, indeed, already known as the
"mineral-water tour," since, for the first time, strict anti-
doping measures were in effect. These were to cause the
sensational disqualification of, among others, the famous
French veteran Jean Stablinsky.

With many of the superstars, including World Champion Eddy Merckx of Belgium, five-time winner Jacques

ASSOCIATED PRESS

*The giants of the tour: Roger Pingeon (closest to camera),
followed by Lucien Aimar, Rolf Wolshohl, Franco Bitossi,
and Jan Janssen, who later won the race.*

Despite broken nose and leg injuries, French star Raymond Poulidor tries desperately to make up lost time.

Anquetil of France, and Italy's Felice Gimondi and Gianni Motta, deciding not to ride, it looked like an open race. The French hopes were riding with Roger Pingeon ("Pinpin"), last year's winner, and unlucky Raymond Poulidor ("Poupou"), a great cyclist who in the past has often come tantalizingly close to winning, only to be beaten by his compatriot but bitter rival, Anquetil. With Ferdinand Bracke (current holder of the coveted World Hour record) and Herman Van Springel, a solid and reliable rider who came close to beating the phenomenal Eddy Merckx in the greatest of all single-day classics, the Paris-Roubaix race, the Belgians had good reason to believe they would win the Tour for the first time since Sylvere Maes' victory in 1939. The Dutch had Jan Janssen, a remarkably calm and confident rider (winner of the Tour de Hollande, the Tour d'Espagne, and second in the 1965 Tour de France). Although he hadn't a single *maillot jaune* (the jersey worn by the race leader), he told an interviewer forty-eight hours before the final decisive stage, an individual time trial against the clock between Melun and Paris, "I can win this Tour. And I think I will."

The opening days lacked in excitement, and without substantial attacks on the road, the stages finished in massive bunch sprints as the race wound its way down France's western seaboard. Van de Berghe, a relatively unknown Belgian rider, held the *maillot jaune* for ten consecutive stages. Then, shortly after the halfway point, some spectacular maneuvers by a few individual cyclists—and some spectacular tragedies for others—roused the passions of spectators and cyclists alike, and the battle for the highest honor in the world of cycling began in earnest. Not until the final seconds on the final day would the winner be known.

For the French public, cyclists, like movie stars and skiers, are heroes and idols; each of their sporting exploits, every event of their personal lives, is scrutinized and discussed with passion. For France, the big event of this Tour was the presence of Poulidor and Pingeon, their highly popular favorites. They rode for the same team. Pingeon, everyone agrees, accomplished some unprecedented feats during the tour. His greatest moment came in the eighteenth stage, between Saint-Etienne and Grenoble.

The weather was bitterly cold and icy rain made it particularly tough. Pingeon, a man with delicate health and a history of bronchitis, feels much less at ease in these kinds of conditions than most of the other riders. Yet, he repeated his exploit of the Pyrenees with even more gusto. With Grenoble still forty miles away, he launched a brutal attack, and again, there was no one who could match him. Not even Lucien Aimar, a strong climber and winner of the 1966 tour, could hold Pingeon's wheel.

"Pingeon is the best!" screamed the headlines in the French press. But the race was far from over, and it remained to be seen if Pingeon could increase his advantage before the tour passed through the Alps.

The next two stages, still in the mountains, proved inconclusive. Nine men—Van Springel, San Miguel, Janssen, Bitossi, Aimar, Bracke, Wolfshohl, and Pingeon—who had an almost equal chance of winning the tour, since they were separated by only two minutes on general classification, simply kept a close watch on each other, conserving their energy.

Pingeon's previous superefforts had evidently exhausted his sting, and his big lead was slowly whittled away as he watched, defenseless.

On the morning of Sunday, July 21, the last day of the race, nobody could predict who would emerge the winner. Pingeon still had a chance. Janssen and Bracke were among the favorites, although most observers were betting on Van Springel, who at this point held the lead.

The last ten miles of the final forty-mile stage from Melun to Paris was an individual time trial—an unprecedented ending—which would decide the winner after three thousand miles and three weeks of racing.

At the "cipale," the brand-new velodrome of Vincennes, tens of thousands of fans jammed the stadium. Many Dutch had come all the way from Holland on the chance that Janssen might bring their country its first victory in the Tour's history. Janssen's pretty blonde wife, Cora, was sitting in the bleachers with their three-year-old daughter, Karina, surrounded by wildly excited Dutch friends.

Riding this last leg against the clock individually, the riders entered the stadium singly and their times were recorded on a big electronic board. The crowd let loose a

tremendous roar as Janssen, one of the first of the favorites to finish, entered the arena. His time was by far the
fastest yet, but his rivals were still speeding toward Paris—
and their times were still an unknown factor.

Janssen felt sure his time was better than that of
Pingeon, Bracke, and the others, with the exception of
Van Springel, whom he had considered from the start his
chief rival.

Then into the velodrome streaked Van Springel, and
his time immediately flashed onto the board. Janssen had
won! And by a mere thirty-eight seconds.

Janssen, bursting into tears and laughter in the same
moment, was kissed, hugged, pushed, and pulled, and
then carried off on the people's shoulders. His wife at
first couldn't believe it. "He has won!" a friend screamed.
"No, it's impossible! It's too beautiful!" his wife shouted.
Then, with much difficulty and the help of several policemen, she and Karina made their way through the delirious
crowd. Husband and wife fell into each other's arms,
laughing and crying. The crowd, after their first outburst
of enthusiasm, had started to sing a sixteenth-century victory song, "Il a gagné le flot d'argent" (he has won the
flood of money).

And no song could be more appropriate. Being the
winner of the Tour de France means not only a tidy bundle
but enough contracts to fill a short career. And for many
of the winners of the less glamorous prizes, the various
maillots jaunes, the stage victories, the *grand prix de la
montagne* (champion of the mountains), the most aggressive racer, etc., the Tour will bring rich rewards, providing enough money to invest in a café or sports shop—or
to live on until the next big race.

One thing is certain. In spite of its enormous strains
and its heartrending tragedies, the Tour de France is, for
true cyclists, a habit they cannot break. As Louison Bobet,
the great Swiss rider who won the Tour several times in
years past, said: "Lying on a beach during the Tour, your
ear glued to a transistor radio, is just murder. . . ."

MEXICO '68—THE FRENCH ARE MASTERS OF THE VELODROME

E. Peter Hoffman
January 1969

Surprises were many in the Mexico Olympics but none more exciting than those in cycling. The Italians, heavily favored, performed like fish out of water, managing to salvage some self-esteem only at the last minute. The French, on the other hand, seemed to have inherited wings from the Aztec gods, and proved themselves the masters of the velodrome. World champions, who in cycling are more highly esteemed than Olympic gold medalists, found themselves out of the running in several events.

The United States team, a product of a totally different competitive environment than that of the Europeans, fared about as expected: far down in the placings and a long way from winning medals.

The thin air at Mexico City made exceptionally fast times commonplace, and existing Olympic and world records fell in rapid succession. The performances, impressive as they were, gained added luster, through this unusual phenomenon, setting standards that, once back down to earth, will be extremely hard to match.

The first cycling medal of the 1968 Olympics went to the Holland team, which, repeating its Tokyo performance, again took home the gold. The fine Dutch team, formed by Marinus Pijnen, Fedor den Hertog, Jan Krekels, and Gevardus Zoetemel, covered the 100 kilometers (62½ miles, riding against the clock) in 2 hours, 7 minutes, and 49.9 seconds, an average speed of 47.881 kilometers per hour (27.8 mph).

The current world champions in this event, the four remarkable Pettersson brothers of Sweden, won the silver medal, finishing more than a minute down on Holland. Italy took the bronze medal.

The United States team of John Howard (Missouri),

TIM MOUNTFORD

The Italian pursuit team, pregame favorites, were beaten into third in a controversial competition.

Oliver Martin (New York), John Allis (California), and Jim Van Boven (California) finished in twentieth place (behind all the European teams; thirty teams competed) with a time of 2:24:13.5.

Mexico didn't get into the medal picture, but their fifth place finish was far better than expected, topping most of the strong cycling nations.

Pierre Trentin, displaying brilliant form, brought France her first gold medal in cycling at Mexico, beginning domination in the track events. Trentin's 1:03.91 over the 1,000 meters established new Olympic and world records. The previous Olympic mark was held by Italian Giardoni Sante at 1:07.27, and the world mark was held by still another Italian, Gianni Satori, at 1:04.61.

The best Satori could do was a fourth place, while Niels Fredborg of Denmark won the silver medal and Poland Janusz Kierzkowski the bronze.

Jackie Simes of Closter, New Jersey, was the United States' 1,000-meter hope. Simes won the silver medal at the Pan-American Games in Canada with a time of 1:09.94, one of his fastest ever. In Nexico, Simes rode 1:05.67, a phenomenal world beating time by normal standards, but in the rarefied air of Mexico City it was good for no better than twelfth.

Trentin's speed over the 1,000 meters was 56.330 kilometers per hour (34 mph).

The individual pursuit provided many upsets and new world and Olympic records to boot. The first surprises came in the opening round of qualifications, when World Champion Jiri Daler of Czechoslovakia failed to make the top eight and was eliminated. Out, too, were Colombia's strong Martín "Cochise" Rodriguez and West Germany's ace, Rupert Kratzer.

In the quarter-finals, Denmark's Mogens Jensen defeated the heavy favorite, Cipriano Chemello of Italy, stopping the clocks at 4:37:54, the fastest time of the games, bettering both Olympic and world marks.

In the finals Daniel Rabillard gave France its second consecutive gold medal in cycling by defeating Jensen, who had to settle for the silver medal and his new records, which will no doubt stand for many years.

Rabillard's victory was just as brilliant as that of his countryman, Pierre Trentin, who earlier won the 1,000 Meter Time Trial. The new gold medalist is a newcomer to the pursuit specialty. He began racing only last year and barely made the French Olympic team.

"I must admit I am surprised," Rabillard said after receiving his medal from Count Jean Beaumont, French member of the International Olympic Committee. The blond, blue-eyed, boyish-looking cyclist then added with a smile: "It all went so smooth I cannot believe it."

Xaver Kurmann of Switzerland took the bronze medal.

Dave Brink of California was eliminated in the qualifications, placing eighteenth out of twenty-two. His time of 4:55.40 established a new United States record.

The French took their third gold medal in track competition when Daniel Morelon swept aside Italy's Giordano Turrin in two straight heats, with 200-meter times of 11:27 and 10:68. Morelon, twenty-four, won the silver

medal in the Games in Tokyo and is the reigning World
Spring Champion.

The bronze medal went to Frenchman Pierre Trentin,
who two days before had taken the gold in the 1,000-meter
time trial.

The United States had two men in the sprint competition: Tim Mountford of California and Jackie Simes of
New Jersey. Simes did not ride the sprints in the Olympic
trials, but replaced Jack Disney at the discretion of the
coaches.

Both boys made it into the eight-finals where they lost
their first heats, Mountford to Pkahakadze of the Soviet
Union and Simes to Verzine of Italy. Two repechage
heats stood between them and the quarter-finals. Both boys
won their first heats, but were eliminated in the second,
Mountford by Loevsijn of Holland and Simes by Barth of
East Germany. Simes rode the third-fastest 200-meter
time of the Games, 10:72, and Mountford the fourth
fastest, 10:79, yet their speed could not overcome the experience and tactics of the Europeans.

In a dramatic turn of events, Denmark was awarded the
gold medal in the team pursuit after defending-champion
West Germany, who again won the event, was disqualified
for an infraction in the finals. Italy beat the Russians for
the bronze medal, and no silver medal was given, pending
a decision by the Federation of International Amateur
Cycling.

The infraction originated when Jürgen Kissner, one of
the German riders, pushed his teammate Udo Hempel in
the next to the last of the twelve laps, thus giving him
unlawful help.

The coach of the West German team, Gustav Kilian,
complained to the jury against the disqualification. His
protest was not accepted.

Giuliano Pacciarelli, Italian secretary of the international jury, told the German coach, "One of your boys
made a mistake and you must pay for it."

"This is the greatest robbery of all time," snapped
Kilian.

The German coach said that when Kissner dropped out
of the quartet he held his hand up because he was afraid

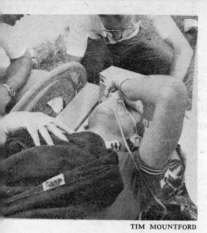

Pursuitist Skip Cutting (United States) was one of the many riders needing oxygen after their events.

TIM MOUNTFORD

Tim Mountford (right), United States' hope, was matched against World Champion and eventual gold medalist Daniel Morelon of France in the early rounds. Morelon won the heat, but Mountford moved on after winning his repechage.

BARRY NORBACK

that Henrichs, one of his teammates, would bump into him.

"There was no pushing whatsoever," Kilian added. "We are filing a new protest to the jury and we are insisting on at least the silver medal which we already won by eliminating Italy yesterday."

While about two thousand spectators crowding the open-air Olympic velodrome were booing and jeering, the jury met to debate a written protest introduced by West Germany officials.

Claude Jacquat, Swiss member of the international jury, proposed that the gold medal be confirmed for Denmark, that no silver medal be awarded, and that Italy retain the bronze medal.

In the qualifying rounds, Italy broke both the Olympic and the world records, recording 4:16.10. The United States team of Dave Chauner (Pennsylvania), Skip Cutting (California), Steve Maaranen (Portland), and John Vande Velde (Illinois) were eliminated in the preliminaries, recording 4:32.87, placing seventeenth.

Taking two gold-medal winners and putting them on one bike could only mean another win for France, making it four out of five in the track events. The powerful duo of Morelon and Trentin defeated Jan Janssen and Leij Loevsijn of Holland in two straight heats, 10:3 and 9.83 seconds, the fastest times ever recorded in tandem competition (9.83 is equivalent to approximately 44 mph).

"If somebody is to be surprised that we came back as a cycling power, it is not me. I knew we would make it," the French trainer said.

Excitement reached another high point in their heats for third and fourth. After losing to the Belgians in the first heat, the Italian duo obstructed them in the turn, almost forcing them off the track during the second round. The Italians crossed the line first, but were disqualified. The Belgians came back in the third heat to gain the bronze medal.

The United States pair of Jack Disney and Chuck Pranke of California met defeat right from the beginning losing the first heat to Belgium 10.4, and the first repechage to Austria, 10.26.

Piefranco Vianelli, 1964 gold medalist, saved the day

for the Italians by winning the last cycling event of the 1968 Olympic Games, the road race.

Vianelli covered the distance in four hours, 42 minutes, and 49 seconds, crossing the finish line all alone 1 minute and 24 seconds ahead of silver medalist Leif Mortenson of Denmark. Sweden's Gösta Pettersson finished third.

One hundred and sixty entries from forty-eight countries took the starting flag for the first of eight 24.525-kilometer laps on the twisting, nearly flat circuit.

From the start the Italians worked brilliantly as a team. There was an Italian in every break, while eventual winner Vianelli remained protected in the field. With two laps to go the bunch was together again, but not for long. Holland, Norway, and the Soviet Union soon had men away and it wasn't until 24 kilometers from the finish that Vianelli made his move, working with Mortenson of Denmark. But the Italian was too much for the others and

Hurtling around the final turn of the Olympic velodrome at nearly forty-four miles per hour, the Italians (top) fight their way ahead of the Hungarians to win their heat.

slowly he pulled away to win, with a comfortable margin to spare.

The twenty-two-year-old Italian, who hopes to turn pro next year, was all smiles after the grueling test.

"I owe it all to my teammates," he said. "They did all the pulling throughout most of the race, allowing me to come on strong in the homestretch."

"The Italians are just too good," said Mortensen, the second-place finisher.

Colombia, one of the prerace favorites, didn't come through as expected. Martín "Cochise" Rodriguez was the best-placed Colombian, finishing ninth. Alvaro Pachón, overall winner of last year's grueling Tour of Mexico, a test of over 2,000 kilometers, in which many Europeans competed, wound up well out of the picture in fifteenth.

As for the United States, it was their poorest showing. Of the six men who started, only one, National Champion John Howard of Missouri, was able to finish. Howard was forty-fourth, ten minutes behind the winner.

KALEIDOSCOPE OF
COLOR, COURAGE, AND CUNNING—
NATIONAL CHAMPIONSHIPS

E. PETER HOFFMAN
November 1968

In the blackness of night the thin thread of white concrete stood out in stark relief, the speeding cyclists a multi-colored blur of bright jerseys and glittering wheels, straining arms and legs and faces contorted with herculean effort. This was the 1968 National Championship, held in Disney's land, California.

Disney's land, however, is not to be confused with Disneyland, for even though they are only a few miles apart, they are completely different worlds. While one was created by the imagination of a man named Walt, the other was established by the speed and cunning of a man named Jack. The Jack Disneys are a remarkable cycling family in Southern California, and the Encino Velodrome has long been Disney territory.

When the National Championships opened on August 30, 1968, Jack Disney had already justified this claim. Jack had won the Tandem Sprints and the Match Sprints in the Olympic Trials the previous week, qualifying for the United States team in both events. The six-time National Champion was now eyeing the coming races with enthusiastic abandon.

There were others, too, who had staked a claim on the national title, and the drama soon unfolded under the lights at Encino, California—the beautiful 250-meter track said by visiting international coaches to be "one of the finest concrete velodromes in the world."

Four men—Dave Chauner, John Vande Velde, John Ward, and the defending National Champion Dave Brink —moved into the 4,000 Meter Individual Pursuit semifinals after the early-morning qualifying heats. Notably absent was Skip Cutting, second in last year's championships, who was disqualified in the preliminaries for dropping below the pole line on too many occasions.

Chauner and Vande Velde appeared in the first ride and provided the most exciting pursuit of the championships. For the entire sixteen laps, neither could gain a discernible lead over the other, and both crossed their respective finishing lines at what appeared to be exactly the same moment. When the stopwatches were read and time recorded, it was found to be a dead heat—5 minutes, 11.9 seconds, for each. Now it was up to the judges, for in the finals, times are not the deciding factor, but rather, the one who actually crossed the line first would be the winner. The verdict went to Chauner by *two inches!*

Ward provided Brink an easy ride (5:23.3 to 3:33.1), and the defending champion was able to conserve his energy for the final against Chauner. Brink won the final without much fanfare, disposing of Chauner 5:10.1 to 5:16.3, and taking the title for the second consecutive year, while Vande Velde defeated Ward for the third spot.

The battle for the most coveted of titles—the 1,000 Meter Sprint, where acceleration and top speed, tactics and experience, aggressiveness and nerve, play equal parts— took on a new light when the current champion, Jackie

Simes III of Closter, New Jersey, failed to take the line to defend his title. Simes' action, or rather the lack of it, was a disappointment to all. It was speculated that he feared losing his title in competition. In the end he lost anyway, and his reputation suffered more of a blow than physical defeat would have brought.

The championship was now wide open, and there were many top-flight men to contend for it.

Into the semifinals advanced Tim Mountford, a twenty-two-year-old lad from Sherman Oaks, California—a Pan-American Games sprinter and winner of the first sprint berth on the current Olympic squad. Qualifying, too, was California's Jack Disney, who, at thirty-eight, is undoubtedly the most remarkable cyclist in the United States. His record is the envy of young and old alike, and Jack is not content unless he is adding to it. Advancing to the semifinals also was Peter Senia, Jr., of New York—the 1967 National Junior Champion—and Bobby Phillips, a popular sprinter from Maryland. It was going to be one of the finest competitions on record with or without the presence of Simes.

Mountford defeated Senia in two out of three, but not without difficulty, and in each ride only inches made the difference. Phillips, in his first ride against Disney, won a dubious call, and the crowd made it known that they were not pleased. Disney came back easily, however, in the next two rides to take the series, burning up the track with 11.7 for the last 200 meters.

Disney and Mountford advanced to the finals for first and second—two good friends fighting for the same crown. Senia and Phillips rode first, to decide third and fourth positions, with Senia winning the series two out of three. Then, with the enthusiastic crowd shouting for their favorite, Mountford and Disney took the line.

The first round went to Mountford, who, going from the front, held Disney to a half length. It was do or die for Disney now, for a second win would give Mountford the championship. Mountford again took the lead, and they slowly circled on the high banking, watching each other intently for an opening—the slightest chance to gain an advantage. Mountford initiated the sprint, diving hard to the pole, causing Disney to back off, and gained several lengths before Disney recovered. But Disney, riding at his best from behind, overtook Mountford coming out of the final turn and just nipped him at the line. It would take a third ride to decide the finals.

Mountford led once again, but Disney caught him off guard and jumped by underneath, opening a gap which Mountford could not close. Disney won the championship by a clear five lengths, again riding 11.7 over the final 200 meters. It was his seventh National Sprint Championship —a record of victories not likely to be equaled.

The grand finale of the National Championships has traditionally been the Ten Mile Open. This event, although not held in international competitions, has become the highlight of the championships here. In recent years it has been hotly contested by the nation's best riders—a fast, action-packed race from start to finish.

This year the field settled down almost immediately into a long, unbroken pace line. Smoothly and like clock-work, the lead riders swung up the banking to let the long line roll through, dropping in again as the last of the riders passed beneath them. Only when the pursuiters, and Brink in particular, took their turn at the front did the pace increase. But this increase was enough to lose a few off the back each time around, and soon the lapped riders were being called out.

As the weaker riders were eliminated, the pace increased. There were no breakaway attempts—only a pulsating of the pace as the stronger men took the lead.

With three laps to go, the pressure slackened somewhat as riders jockeyed for sprint position. Brink found his way to the front, and began to roll it out. But Steve Maaranen, the defending Ten Mile Champion, whose timing and strategy won him the event last year at Portland, repeated his brilliant move, coming around Brink on the bell lap and gaining the pole position. Around the last turn Brink began to gain, and as they came to the line he was moving up fast. But now Simes, who was on Maaranen's wheel, found himself boxed in, with Brink on his right and the pole on his left. He chose to ignore the pole—it was his only chance. Dropping beneath the pole onto the flat, he streaked by Maaranen and was first to cross the line. But his illegal move was obvious, and he was disqualified.

Maaranen was again the Ten Mile Champion and Brink, once again, the bridesmaid.

Outstanding performances by Gary Campbell of Southern California and Hans Nuernberg and James Ochowicz of Wisconsin sparked the junior competition. So close were the points standing that the entire championship rested on the outcome of the final event.

Campbell, whose older brother Buddy has long been a top competitor in Southern California, had won the Five Mile and the Half Mile races, and was second in the One Mile—going into the final race, the Two Mile, with nineteen points. Ochowicz was second in the Half Mile and Five Mile races, and third in the One Mile, having thirteen points prior to the Two Mile final. Nuernberg won the One Mile race, was third in the Half Mile, and fourth in the Five Mile, gaining twelve points. Thus, all three had a chance at the Junior Championship as the final event began.

It was a tough fight, with Nuernberg first, Ochowicz second, and Campbell third. Only three points separated the top three places on final classification, and Campbell emerged the new champion.

As in 1967 Nancy Burghart of New York walked away with the Women's Division in all three categories: the 3,000 Meter Individual Pursuit, Match Sprints, and the 23 Mile Road Race. In the pursuit, Nancy recorded 4:16.3. Judy Hess of Michigan was second, 4:22.7, and Donna Tobias of Northern California third, with 4:25.0.

Jeanne Kloska, also from New York, gave Nancy her closest fight in the sprints. Both gals are tough competitors and ride as hard as, if not harder than, the men. Kloska finished second in the sprints, with Alice Disney (Jack's wife) third.

Out on the tough Agoura Road Course, the same route used by the men in the Olympic Trials, Burghart showed she had endurance as well as speed, and won handily from a strung-out field.

One thing you can be sure about the juniors—they grow up fast! In 1967 Jim Van Boven won the Junior Championship, and soon afterward entered the senior ranks, making the Olympic road team just one year later. Second to Van Boven last year was Southern Cal's Tracy

Wakefield, a little younger in age, but not far behind in talent.

Wakefield dominated the Junior Championship this year, and romped off to a solo victory on the final lap of the six-lap, 49.4-mile race. Wakefield launched his attack on the final climb over the long hill, just prior to the finish line. Said George Barbour of Ohio, who finished second behind Wakefield: "I was out in front going up the hill— and then Wakefield came by me so fast I couldn't believe it!"

Both Wakefield and Barbour finished well ahead of the field, which had regrouped for a tight sprint won by Steve Dayton of Indianapolis, Indiana.

After two long and unexciting 110-mile Olympic trial races over the now familiar Agoura Road Course, the prospects for a hot National Championship race were not promising, unless you were to believe the weatherman. To make matters worse, several Olympic team members had not ridden in their respective state championships, and thus were not qualified to enter the nationals. Dan Butler, Mike Pickens, Dave Mulkey, and Oliver Martin were not among the starters. Yet, gloomy as the prospect seemed, the race was by far the best of the three, with the action beginning immediately.

Before the sun had risen over the rugged hills to beat down mercilessly upon the riders, Olympian John Allis was at the front forcing the pace. For the entire first lap he jammed ahead, while cold, unlimbered legs strained to keep pace behind him. Allis, perhaps the most aggressive roadman in the nation, is never content with an easy ride, and the fifty-strong field found his thinking this day no exception.

Early in the third lap, the first break developed. Emile Waldteufel, a relatively unknown rider from San Francisco, and Dave Sharp, once a top-class rider but out of competition for several years, had gained a minute on the peleton. Two men against fifty, on a hilly course, with seventy-five miles to go, were given little chance. But this break was to set the stage for the entire race, and the courageous effort of these two gave life to an event that otherwise might have developed into a monumental drag.

Fortunately, Waldteufel and Sharp were not as skepti-

Dave Sharp begins the aggression that, with Emile Wald-teufel (center in dark glasses), developed into their coura-geous break.

cal of their chances as the field, and they worked together well, putting all their hopes in the success of their early bid. They were lapping the 7.9-mile course in 19½ minutes, the field in 21, a gain of 1½ minutes per lap. By the sixth lap their lead had increased to just under five minutes.

But Sharp was weakening on the climbs, and their pace slowed. For two laps they held the field even. Then, on the four-hundred-foot climb approaching the finishing line John Allis took off in pursuit. He opened a gap of one hundred yards on the field before Bob Parsons, the defending champion, countered his move. Going with Parsons were Peter Kendall (Southern California State Champion), John Howard (Missouri State Champion), Jim Van Boven, Ed Perales, and John Aschen.

At this point, the field fragmented and fell far behind. The chase was on in earnest. Allis was caught just ove

Running helpers on both sides hand up food and drinks as the leaders tackle the long hill.

the hill, and the seven pursuers settled down to bringing back Waldteufel and Sharp. Now it was the pursuers, and not the leaders, who were gaining 1½ minutes per lap. By the end of the ninth lap, the gap had been cut to 2 minutes.

Sharp had weakened and was dropped by Waldteufel, whose only chance now was on his own. The field overtook Sharp on the tenth lap, then dropped him on the hill. Completely shattered, he retired.

Heading up the hill on the eleventh lap, Allis dropped off the back of the peleton, no longer able to cope with the climb. "If nothing else," he shouted to us as our truck passed him, "this course blows my mind!" And no one could blame him for his sentiments at this stage of the game.

Perales, too, came unhinged toward the top. Chasing hard on the entire last lap, he was able to get back in, only to be dropped once again—this time for good.

Lunging across the line, John Howard dethrones second-place Parsons to become the new National Champion.

As the final lap began, Waldteufel was in sight of his pursuers but holding to a 25-second lead. Only a super-human effort could hold off the field now, and Waldteufel had already given it all he had. With half a lap to go, he was caught, ending a brilliant effort which had almost found a new champion.

The previous week, Parsons had won the Olympic Road Race with an attack on the big hill on the final lap. He was expected to repeat his performance again today. But it was Howard who took the initiative, forcing the pace from the front in his strong style, pushing gears much higher than the others. Waldteufel was the first to come off the back, and Kendall soon followed.

Four men remained together as they crested the hill and began the descent toward the finish line. It was Howard who led out the sprint from five hundred meters—a long, rolling dash in a 108-inch gear. Parsons and Aschen came up on Howard's left, and then Van Boven moved up on his right, but none could outdistance the strong man from Missouri.

Howard had beaten the nation's best, and no one could question his victory. He was the new champion.

"I wasn't worried about Parsons on the hill. There were three of us there who could stay with him," Howard gasped breathlessly after the race. "It was the sprint that had me worried. I didn't know if I had one!"

It was an upset for the California boys, whose climbing ability has dominated national road racing for many years. "It just goes to prove," said Walter Gimber with respect, "that *good* bike riders can come from anywhere!"

ASPEN ALPINE CUP

E. Peter Hoffman
September 1966

In the thin air above twelve thousand feet Chris van Gent, past National Champion of Holland and a top-ranking professional in his time, stood on the mountain with checkered flag in hand, looking down to the graveled switchbacks below.

Standing along the roadside a handful of spectators were bundled against the wind, which blew unhampered across the treeless summit, chilled by the snowpack that had survived the summer heat.

An entourage of team cars loaded with bicycles and spare equipment waited to move down the pass, while all eyes strained to see who would be the first to top the defiant mountain.

The scene might well have been on the Col du Tourmalet in the Pyrenees, or on the famed Mount Ventoux where many epic Tour de France battles have been won or lost, but it was not. The weathered sign read, "Independence Pass, Colorado, Elevation 12,095 feet." The event was the Aspen Alpine Cup race.

My excitement almost overwhelmed me as I struggled to brush the heavy coat of dust from my camera lens. Riding on the top of the press wagon over the graveled road had caused more than a few unpleasant moments. Now some ominous raindrops added to my picture-taking problems. The sun had long since disappeared behind the dark clouds, and a storm was soon to break.

A few miles before, I watched as the race leader was hopelessly dropped and the peleton was split once and for all by two men who were now fighting shoulder to shoulder up the twisting road, neither willing to concede an inch to the other. If they were to finish together, the out-

E. PETER HOFFMAN

Aspen Cup cyclists have a beautiful setting for their race.

come of the entire tour would hang on the final sprint, so close were they in general classification. But I am getting ahead of my story.

The Aspen Alpine Cup has the terrain and the potential to become our "National Tour." Already the race has assumed an unexcelled position, offering riders a 50 percent reduction on all meals and free accommodations in Aspen's best motels for five days preceding the race, in addition to food and lodging during the event. Travel expenses were offered to many of the nation's top riders and the list will be expanded in coming years. Several nationally prominent manufacturers (outside the bicycle industry) have expressed their interest in the race, whose budget this year exceeded $4,000.

My flight arrived in Denver in the wee hours of Friday morning and I caught a few winks at the home of Bernard Witkin, owner of Big Wheel Ltd. Bernie's General Manager, Chris van Gent, was technical director of the race, and three of us left for Aspen at midday, driving over much of the course the tour was to follow. One thing was for certain—it was not going to be an easy race.

In Aspen we met Bert Bidwell, the race promoter and local entrepreneur. Bert had arranged for our accommodations, and I took full advantage of my excellent room by turning in early.

At the crack of dawn on race morning I was up and about, although the race did not start until 10:00 A.M. I wanted a chance to talk with some of the riders, many of whom were already on their way to breakfast.

Three men in particular stood out as race favorites: Stu Baillie, John Marshall, and Bob Parsons.

Baillie had won a decisive victory the week before by being the first to the oxygen-starved 14,264-foot summit of Mount Evans, an ascent of 6,264 feet in twenty-eight miles. He was expected to be the climbing star of the tour. Baillie placed second in the National Championships in California in 1965, but did not ride in the Aspen race last year.

The winner then was John Marshall, and he looked extremely fit. Marshall is a rider of fine ability whose reputation has not extended far outside the mountain state area. He, too, is a man to be feared in the mountains and has the sprint which Baillie lacks.

Parsons was by far the most experienced of the three: a Pan-American Games silver medalist, past national road champion, and after his remarkable victory at Nevada City two weeks previously (see article on page 181), he was in excellent form. However, the drastic altitude change for Bob who lives at sea level and was now to be racing at eight thousand and twelve thousand feet, remained an unknown factor in predicting his performance.

It was generally believed the California boys would dominate the criterium and flat opening stages of the tour, while the local climbers would attack in the mountains in the closing stages. Battle Mountain, Tennessee Pass, and Independence Pass, the latter containing eighteen miles of graveled road open only in the summer months, would tell the story before the riders finished back in Aspen.

From the balcony of the historic Opher Hotel I watched the start of the nine-mile, fourteen-lap criterium which began the day's racing. As expected, the Californians were constantly at the front, with Parsons winning the first stage with ease, and also the Garmish-Parten Kirchen

Cup presented by Aspen's sister city of Garmish, Bavaria, for the leader of the most laps.

Although the race continued nonstop to Glenwood Springs after the criterium, time bonuses were awarded through sixth place. The importance of these bonuses, and those to follow, would have a decided effect on the outcome of the race.

Followers of last year's event will well remember the scorching pace set over the downward miles to Glenwood Springs, but this year the pace remained moderate. The wind was not at their backs and the knowledge of the 130 miles which lay ahead, plus two major climbs before the abandoned mines of Leadville would signal the end of the first day's racing, led to more conservative action.

The inhabitants of the unsuspecting town of Glenwood Springs (much less their police force) were scantly prepared for the 45-mph downhill sprint on the main street at noon hour that hot Saturday. In a hair-raising finish, in which the traffic-clearing patrol car was engulfed by the field in full sprint, Eric Dowty emerged the stage winner, and the race had a new leader.

I joined several of the riders for a quick lunch and an hour later we were off again, threading our way along the Colorado River deep within the walls of Glenwood Canyon, and then out onto the flatlands of Eagle County where, for the first time, the field split in two. It was not the pace so much as the record heat, and those who were seen off the back at this point were never in contention again.

The traffic following the tour was making it difficult to get ahead of the riders after stopping for pictures, so I drove on through the sleepy town of Minturn at the base of Battle Mountain and waited on the lower slopes of the climb which would be the first real test of the tour.

The crawling line of following cars heralded the approach of the peleton far below, long before the riders could be identified. Three men were ahead of the rest, and I assumed them to be Baillie, Marshall, and Parsons.

But, no, Parsons wasn't among them and was instead struggling one hundred yards behind! It was Pat Dennis of New Mexico that I had mistaken for Parsons, and with Baillie and Marshall they were slowly widening the gap.

With race leader Dowty well out of the picture now, and Parsons in grave trouble, the race had taken a new turn.

But far up the mountain Dennis lost contact, and Baillie and Marshall topped the climb with a spirited sprint with Baillie taking the prize.

On the descent Dennis rejoined the leaders, but Parsons had lost too much ground and was fated to ride the re-remaining miles alone.

Hardly had the bottom of Battle Mountain been reached when the climb over Tennessee Pass began, a deceptive, unspectacular ascent which would bring the riders to within a few miles of their day's destination.

Here Dennis cracked completely, eventually overtaken and dropped by Parsons, who, looking desperate, was fighting for every precious second of time. But the leaders had already gained a three-minute lead over their biggest threat.

Marshall was suffering, too, and had cramped miles before on the summit of Battle Mountain. Baillie, aware of his companions' condition, attacked hard several miles from the finish. If he could take a few seconds out of Marshall and win the stage and the time bonus, he would become the new race leader, and so he did, gaining a full minute before the finish.

That evening as the riders relaxed in the lobby of the Vendome Hotel their talk was mostly of the road that lay ahead. The graveled, rutted crossing of Independence Pass had taken its toll of equipment the previous year, and not one rider had escaped without trouble. Several punctured as many as five times.

But the big question in my mind was whether or not the Coloradans were really better climbers than the boys from the West Coast. Although California was not well repre-sented, Parsons was undoubtedly one of their best, and he had taken a humiliating beating at the hands of Baillie and Marshall. Could he be excused for the occasional "bad day" every rider may suffer, or was he simply outclassed? The answer was found the next day.

The road out of Leadville drops gradually for many miles, paralleling the impressive range of snowcapped mountains which would soon challenge man and machine. At the point where the Independence Pass road leaves the

With the 14,340-foot peak of Mount Plata looking on, the pace remained moderate as the climbers of the tour were content to hold their attack for the rough road that lay ahead. Had Baillie been aggressive during these early miles on Independence Pass he might have taken the fight out of Marshall and Parsons, who dropped him so decisively once the gravel was reached.

main highway the conditions change abruptly. For fifteen miles the road climbs from one valley to the next, higher and higher until directly ahead lies a sheer wall of granite rock, a thin line etched up its face. Here the pavement ends and there was no relief from this bone-jarring, nerve-shattering hell for the next eighteen miles.

I had returned my borrowed car of the previous day and hitched a ride with a colleague from the Aspen *Times,* a local paper assigned to cover the race. We were given permission to precede the riders over the pass, keeping a good distance ahead because of the dusty conditions. From a point several hundred vertical feet above, we watched as the peleton reached the graveled road, and here the battle began.

Immediately the field splintered, and after the first quarter-mile two riders were already well away. The dust still hung in the air and it was difficult to make out who they were, and my question of the night before kept running through my mind. I expected to see the climbing aces of the tour, Baillie and Marshall, for it was hard to imagine either of these two being dropped so decisively. I was surprised again, for Parsons was in the lead, grim-faced, showing the determination of a man out to win, with Marshall on his wheel.

At first I feared Baillie had had mechanical trouble, but such was not the case. Instead, he was struggling in despair through the gravel which was to be his Waterloo, unable to match the pace of the leaders, and falling farther and farther behind. But Baillie's troubles had just begun, for on the descent he crashed hard and rode into Aspen bleeding and beaten.

As Baillie had shown his inability to ride on the gravel, Parsons was showing his strength in the mountains, and three hundred meters from the summit, he dropped Marshall and was over the top with ten seconds to spare.

The descent into Aspen was truly a nightmare. We followed Marshall part of the way and he was having a great deal of trouble keeping his rear wheel in line, sliding and skidding through the rough turns.

If Marshall could overtake Parsons and finish with him in Aspen, the tour would be his, but Parsons had the taste of victory in his mouth, and knew his opponent was close

For Parsons, a hard-earned victory.

E. PETER HOFFMAN

behind. It was an epic contest, with the course dropping over four thousand feet in fourteen miles, with a flat five-mile run into town.

Back up the mountain many individual battles were taking place, but it was the red, white, and black jersey of Bob Parsons that the large crowd welcomed into Aspen. He had come from behind to win a splendid victory, displaying the ability that makes him a champion.

PORTLAND'S FINEST HOUR

E. PETER HOFFMAN
October 1967

The red, green, and blue surface of Portland's new velodrome shimmered in the near 100° heat. Around the perimeter of the steeply banked track the flags stirred only slightly in the gentle breeze. In the grass-covered infield scores of officials smartly attired in their fresh white uniforms attended to a myriad of details. Two large circular canopies provided shelter for a collage of riders in multicolored jerseys, shining bikes, spare wheels, and a seemingly inexhaustible supply of fresh fruits, cases of orange juice, yogurt, milk, and ice cream. The bleachers were overflowing with spectators, many of whom had never before seen a bike race, while local television crews prepared to broadcast the races live and in color. Portland and the Pacific Northwest were about to witness their first National Amateur Bicycle League Championship, and the Alpenrose Dairy, hosts to the big event, had gone overboard to make it one of the finest on record.

The Nationals are the high point of the racing season. Here the nation's best meet face to face; where speed, endurance, strength, bike-handling ability, tactics, nerve, and the will to win are tested in a few short moments which can mean triumph or defeat. Years of training, sacrifice, and hardships have been devoted to attaining the skills needed to win a national crown. It's no wonder, then, that the excitement of the National Championships reaches a fever pitch.

The 4,000 Meter Pursuit is one of the toughest and most physically demanding races of the championships. Two riders compete at a time, and starting on opposite sides of the track, each attempts to overtake the other. Qualifying heats are run against the clock, with the four fastest times going into the semifinals. From there on out the man who is up on his opponent at the 4,000-meter mark is the winner. David Brink of Berkeley, California, a friendly, easygoing six-footer and current National Champion, had recently shattered the American records in the Pan-American trials, lowering the mark to 5:05.9 from 5:10.6 set in 1965 by Skip Cutting. In the qualifications he recorded the fastest time with 5:14.8, with Cutting a close second at 5:15.4.

In the finals the two appeared to be evenly matched. Brink took an early lead but Cutting soon pulled him in. At the halfway mark Brink was in command again and this time he didn't relinquish his position. He finished in 5:12.3 to Cutting's 5:18.5. Dave Chauner of Rosemont, Pennsylvania, was third.

Nothing can surpass the sprints for thrills and this is the most sought after crown, for sprinting is the optimum challenge, the test of all one's resources, both mental and physical. From the quarter-finals on, the riders compete in two-man heats and must win two out of three to advance.

The object of the sprint is simple: first man across the line wins. How long it takes to get there is of no importance. Thus develops a cat and mouse game where tactics and alertness can be more important than sheer speed.

Faking, balking, and blocking techniques are an essential part of the game. If both riders decide neither wishes to take the lead, they may come to a complete stop, balancing motionless for minutes at a time until one of them falters and is forced to move ahead. Generally a three-lap event, the actual "sprint" usually begins with about three hundred meters to go.

Three men have dominated the sprint event over the last twelve years. At thirty-seven Jack Disney of Monrovia, California, is one of the oldest men in the sport. Disney was National Champion from 1954 to 1958 and again won the sprint title last year. A racing family, Disney's wife, Alice, also competed in the championships, as did their young daughter Jackie.

Jim Rossi of Chicago, Illinois, is another of the long-time greats. Rossi took over the championship in 1959 and held it until 1963, again, as with Disney, a truly remarkable feat. Rossi, now the father of three girls, is always a tough contender.

The youngest of the big three is Jackie Simes of Closter, New Jersey. Possessing the style and class of a world beater and perhaps the finest sprinter the country has produced in modern times, Simes held the crown in 1964 and 1965 and raced in Europe in 1966.

Simes was the favorite to win, but if Disney and Rossi weren't enough to give him trouble, there were plenty of others. Carl Leusenkamp of Maryland, an up-and-coming sprinter of great promise, had just returned from winning a bronze medal in the sprint event at the Pan-Am Games. Another bronze medal winner, Tim Mountford of Sherman Oaks, California, was determined to outshine Simes. Sam Zeitlin, and Preston Handy, both from New York, were also potential champions.

After some very fine riding Simes and Leusenkamp were matched in the finals for first and second, with clubmates Mountford and Disney battling for third.

Mountford showed no mercy and beat Disney handily

*Chuck Pranke leads Niel King out of the last turn in the
sprint preliminaries.*

in their first two rides. Disney, the defending champion and
the man who has held the sprint crown more than anyone
else in United States history, had failed to place.

As Simes and Leusenkamp rolled off the line and into
the first turn, Leusenkamp blew a tire and tumbled off the
track. Unhurt, but with nerves stretched even tighter, they
started again. Slowly around the top of the track they
circled, high on the forty-one-degree banking almost twenty
vertical feet above the infield, watching each other like cats
about to pounce on their prey. Leusenkamp, now in the

E. PETER HOFFMAN

Balancing motionless on their bikes, Carl Leusenkamp (foreground) and Preston Handy attempt to force each other to take the lead.

lead, twisted around first on one side and then on the other, always watching Simes who was stalking him with deadly intent.

Leusenkamp was first to jump but Simes was on him like a bolt of lightning. Around the final turn their bikes were almost horizontal to the ground as they screamed toward the finish at forty-five miles per hour. Simes' phenomenal speed took him well into the lead on the last long straight and he won the first round in great style.

When Simes crossed the line in the next heat, his arms

were flung high in the air, for he had beaten all comers and was the new champion.

Although the sprint title is the most sought after, the Ten Mile is traditionally the main event. Fourteen men took the starter's gun in what was to prove one of the hottest contests of all times.

Immediately, Pursuit Champion Dave Brink and Oliver Martin of New York City broke away and soon gained over half a lap on the field.

Cutting initiated a chase taking Simes and local lad Steve Maaranen of Portland with him, and the three quickly pulled away from the rapidly depleting field. Now there were three separate groups going flat out, all trying to catch each other.

Cutting, Simes, and Maaranen overtook Brink and Martin, and slowing to recover they were overtaken by the remainder of the field. But Brink was not happy with this and continued to attack savagely, trying to get away once again. With this kind of aggressive riding the first five miles were covered in 10:56.

At last Brink's efforts were successful and he broke clear, this time with Cutting and Maaranen. Again the leaders achieved a lead of a half lap. Rossi, the defending Ten Mile champion, retired and the field was falling apart fast. It looked like the die was cast. But Simes was not yet ready to lay down and die. Out of the field he came like a jet dragster with Martin hanging desperately to his wheel, and before the disbelieving crowd could catch their breath the pair had joined the leaders.

Maaranen took the lead with two laps to go and was still commanding this position when the bell sounded signaling the last lap. The crowd was ecstatic. In modern-day terms they were "blowing their minds." Maaranen was still out in front as they rounded the last turn and they were all bunched together in the homestretch. But Maaranen did it! He beat the fastest men in the country and the roar of the crowd must have rattled St. Peter's Gate. Brink was second, Simes third, Martin fourth, and Cutting fifth.

It was indeed a happy day in Portland.

"What Maaranen did for Oregon cycling," said Simes after he had recovered, "can never be repaid."

The junior races were no less exciting and provided some of the tightest sprints of the meet. Unlike the seniors, the juniors compete at various distances with an accumulated points standing deciding a single overall champion.

When the final score was tallied, John Leedy, Chula Vista, California, and Douglas Downen, Hollis, Long Island, New York, were tied for second with seventeen points each, and Peter Senia, Jr., of Brooklyn, New York, had won by the skin of his teeth with eighteen. It was a cliff-hanger all the way.

After winning the One Mile and Five Mile races and tying for second in the Half Mile, Senia failed to qualify for the Two Mile race, the last junior race on the program. Senia had earned eighteen points, and now had to watch from the sidelines.

Leedy was then in second spot with twelve points. If he could win the Two Mile race, he would have nineteen and the championship would be his.

But Downen won with Leedy a close second—just missing his chance for the overall title.

Leedy was not going to let Downen get away with such a dastardly deed, and he beat him in the runoff to break the tie for second. Hans Nuernberg of Kenosha, Wisconsin, was fourth and Eddie Van Guyse of Chicago, Illinois, finished fifth.

There was little competition for Nancy Burghart of the Bronx, New York, and she had no trouble winning both the sprint and pursuit races.

Jeanne Kloska, Massapequa, New York, was second in the sprints, and Jack Disney's wife, Alice, was third.

Second in the pursuit was Judith Hess of Dearborn, Michigan, with Ann Perales, Paramount, California, third.

Seeking glory under the shade of arrow-straight Douglas Firs on the slopes of Mount Tabor, the roadmen tackled a tough 1.7-mile course containing a long hill and a fast descent.

Burghart again made a shambles of the ladies' championship. She rode away from her competition early in the race and lapped them all before the finish.

The only excitement came when a battle developed between Kathy Fitzpatrick of Granada Hills, California, and Pat McClellan of Bellevue, Washington, for third place.

After catching McClellan, Fitzpatrick beat her to the line by a few inches, much to the obvious delight of her proud father who seemed to get the lion's share of the congratulations. Jeanette Hawley, Portland, Oregon, was second.

The newly established Junior Road Championship found itself a worthy champion, but only by a fluke of fate was the eventual winner allowed to compete.

Jim Van Boven of Belmont, California, had placed sixth in his state road championships a month previously in which the first five riders qualified to ride the Nationals. Only if one of the qualified riders withdrew could Van Boven take part. And so it happened. Van Boven would get his big chance.

The junior race was over the same course ridden by the seniors, but covered only thirty-six miles. It was fast from the beginning and Van Boven was one of the most aggressive pace setters. Lap after lap they jammed up the hill until their number dwindled to thirteen.

Five miles from the finish Van Boven attacked hard, splitting the field in two. With him went Larry Holm and Tracy Wakefield, two top contenders from Southern California, sprinter Eddie Van Guyse from Chicago, Bill Hawley, the Oregon State Champion, and George Barbour from Columbus, Ohio.

When the sprint developed, Van Boven timed his move perfectly and became the first Junior Road Champion in the racing annals of the Amateur Bicycle League of America. Holm was second, followed by Wakefield, Van Guyse, and Hawley.

All hearts were with Eddie Torres, a United States Army private stationed at Fort Sheridan, Illinois, who transformed what had been an uneventful race into an exciting suspense-filled drama. For it was Torres who, with 39 miles remaining of the original 102, escaped from the field in a courageous solo bid for the title and soon built a lead of 1 minute, 52 seconds.

"Who is Edwin Torres?" the crowd asked as, lap after lap, his chances of upsetting the championship looked increasingly brighter.

Riding strongly and with little apparent effort, Torres was cheered by admiring spectators at every rise and turn. To all outward appearances it looked like the heat and

Juniors going into the turn.

the eighty-five miles already covered had taken the fight out of the Torres' pursuers. Bob Tetzlaff, the defending National Road Champion, retired with fifteen laps to go. Of the four Pan-American team members competing, none had generated any action: Nick Zeller was out with cramps; the usually aggressive tactics of Mike Pickens and Dan Butler had not materialized; and Bob Parsons was looking tired. With only ten laps remaining Torres was easily maintaining his lead. It looked as if this unknown rider from Puerto Rico might pull off the coup of the year.

But Torres' dream of victory was not to be. With sudden and unexpected fury, Parsons, Butler, and John Aschen exploded from the field. Sprinting up the long hill, they sliced thirty seconds off Torres' lead by the summit. Within one lap the trio had caught him. Torres could only watch in anguish as they passed; his reserves expended, he could not match their faster pace.

In the chasing group, cramps had overcome strong-man Pickens who climbed from his bike, disgusted and downhearted. The remainder of the field was struggling hopelessly. All but Torres, still holding his own in fourth place, were lapped just twelve miles after the devastating attack.

Aschen's presence with Butler and Parsons was the second big surprise of the race. The eastern rider was hardly expected to perform well on the hilly course. Now, with the end in sight, he was challenging two of the nation's best climbers on their own grounds.

But two laps later the torrid pace was more than Aschen could take and he lost contact with the leaders. But he didn't give in. Maintaining a steady pace he caught them as they slowed in the final laps.

Aschen's reappearance now did not worry either Butler or Parsons.

"We knew we could see him off on the final climb to the finish," Butler said later. "We hardly noticed his presence."

So as it stood, either Butler or Parsons would be the new champion.

Parsons was the favorite to win if it came to a sprint, a fact all too well known by Butler. Butler's only chance was to get away from Parsons on the hill, and they both knew that also.

"I jumped a couple of times," said Butler after the race, "but Parsons was always right there on my wheel."

The finish was tailor-made for Parsons, who with head down and fighting all the way beat Butler by ten lengths with Aschen trailing far behind.

"Butler had me worried," admitted Parsons on the victory stand, the stars and stripes of his new championship jersey in fresh contrast to his mile-weary expression. "He rode a real tough race." And real tough racing well sums up the 1967 National Championships.

INCREDIBLE NEVADA CITY

E. Peter Hoffman
August 1966

Incredible! Superlative! Magnificent! How else could Bob Parsons' win at Nevada City be described. For against the finest of the nation's roadmen-climbers, Parsons simply rode off and left them gasping. But what makes his victory truly a monumental accomplishment is that it was his fourth consecutive win at Nevada City! On a course that you must see to appreciate, requiring the maximum in fitness and ability, only the very best are there at the finish, and Parsons left no doubt who should claim the top honor.

In the early stages of the race Parsons remained inconspicuous, seldom setting the pace up the hill, but always in a position to counter any threatening move. For many the battle was the hill itself, and by midrace only twelve of the riders remained together. Canada's Bill Wild, aggressive in the opening laps, was out with cramps. Bob Tetzlaff, the only other man to win Nevada City (claiming that honor twice in a row) was left by the roadside, ill from his own efforts. Olympian Bill Kund had retired, and the list grew constantly with each successive lap as the pace over the hill continued to wear down the top names in cycling.

Parsons was undoubtedly the favorite of the crowd, but none could really expect him to win this classic of classics

Parsons leads Brink through the crucial corner at the bottom of the hill.

for a fourth time against such overwhelming odds. The field still contained many men who had won first-category events earlier in the year: hard, tough riders like Dan Butler, Dave Brink, Ward Thompson, Charlie Greenlaw, and Ed Renger. Fritz Liedl, Mike Penkert, Mike Cone, Dave Allen, and Dave Lampi, the last two showing great promise this season, were all in there and looking strong.

But when the decisive attack was launched, it was Bob Parsons at the front, and taking Dave Brink with him, they pulled steadily away from a shocked and helpless field.

"I knew from previous experience that the first man through the turn at the bottom of the hill would command the uphill sprint," Parsons told me after the race, and twice before he had risked life and limb to get through that treacherous turn to win. "I didn't want to be in that situation again," said Bob, "and knew I had to get clear of the others before the end of the race. When the time came to go I wanted to take someone with me, in case the field should be able to chase. I didn't want to be out there all alone with too many laps remaining." Parsons had planned to let Dan Butler in on his plan, but Butler was having mechanical trouble with his derailleur, so Parsons chose Dave Brink instead.

"Dave was looking tired," said Bob, "but the time was right, and I told him to get on my wheel because I was going."

And go they did! Gaining twenty yards per lap they swept around the course, climbing the hill at a torturous pace. But the field was no longer a threat and had disintegrated in its attempt to catch the two leaders. So with only Brink to challenge him, Parsons attacked again. But Brink was by now no match for the master. In an unbelievable display of speed, Parsons rode away from Brink in epic style, climbing in a gear Brink could not hope to match, and won a phenomenal victory amidst the screams of thousands of appreciating spectators.

"It's the only race I really wanted to win," gasped Bob after it was over, tears of joy glistening in his eyes, adding, "In my opinion, it's the best race in the country."

The junior race was no less exciting. Setting a scorching pace from the gun, it was a flat-out contest all the way, with Portland's Nick Zeller winning by a bike length over Steve Lubin and Bob McNellis. It was Zeller's second victory at Nevada City, placing him among the finest junior riders the West Coast has produced. For Steve Lubin, it was a heartbreaker, for he placed second behind Zeller last year, and had previously missed a spot in the winner's circle by the smallest margin. It was Steve's last chance, too, for he will race as a senior in 1967.

THE SLEEPING GIANT—
INTERCOLLEGIATE CYCLING

DONALD COULTON
WESTERN REPRESENTATIVE, COLLEGIATE DIVISION,
AMATEUR BICYCLE LEAGUE OF AMERICA
September 1966

For several years a quiet development has been taking place in the world of amateur cycling in the United States. I am speaking of the emergence, or more correctly, the re-emergence of intercollegiate cycling. This aspect of amateur cycling has grown since its revival in 1959, but to those of us intimately involved the process often seems painfully slow.

Marshall Dodge, executive secretary of the National College Committee of the Amateur Bicycle League, says that for the first time he is encouraged by collegiate cycling prospects. His optimism is borne out by the increasing number of schools supporting cycling teams and the increase in races held this past year. Yet, when we look closely at intercollegiate cycling, we see that much remains to be done.

As a "graduate" of the first Western Intercollegiate Cycling Meet held at the University of California at Santa Barbara in 1963, and the faculty adviser of the cycling team at Shasta College, a junior college in northern California, I have had the opportunity to observe the numerous problems that beset a cycling enthusiast who starts out to form a cycling team and promote intercollegiate competition. My purpose in writing this article is to point out a few lessons which I have learned by experience.

Presently, the most important goal for intercollegiate cycling is to increase the number of college and university teams competing. Also, we must see that those teams already organized are continued.

One of the best ways to increase and maintain the number of teams is to find enthusiastic faculty advisers, for they can often break through red tape and gather support from the schools more easily than students. School officials frequently place so many obstacles in the way of new programs that only a person working from the inside can overcome these hurdles. Also, an active faculty adviser can be a guarantee to the school that the cycling team is more than a passing fad.

A good way to get the team rolling is to become a full-fledged campus club with constitution and officers. In many cases, if a team is recognized as a campus club, financial support is relatively easy to acquire, and economic aid can usually be squeezed more readily from student-body funds than from the heavily burdened budgets of athletic departments.

Once intercollegiate cycling begins to function as do other college sports, athletic departments will recognize its importance with financial assistance. It is too much to expect an athletic department to give full recognition to a cycling team right away. Support invariably has to come from the student government first and the athletic department second.

With an increase of teams we will see an increase of activities. More and larger races will be staged in more parts of the country. At present more areas that have intercollegiate cycling depend entirely on one or at best a very few big meets or races. The various regional championships should be the culmination of a full season of racing activities. The Eastern Intercollegiate Cycling Association is now coming close to this goal.

In the Western Region this past year, five different meets were held in conjunction with the annual championship event, and plans are being made for many additional races next year. If all schools with a cycling team would plan to sponsor at least one race each season, we would see a tremendous improvement in the sport. If a club is hesitant about hosting a large event, a dual or tri meet can suffice. In the future cycling might follow the lead of other sports by concentrating on these smaller events.

One practice which has long been common among A.B.L. clubs that sponsor road races is to take the easy way out by holding a race on some remote country road miles from civilization. It seems unlikely that much school interest can be stimulated if intercollegiate cycling adheres to this practice. Traditionally, races in the Western Region are held on campus where spectators have, in many cases, seen their first bicycle race. Using a campus course sometimes presents obstacles, but we must be ever mindful that bicycle racing needs a great deal of exposure if it is to become a truly popular sport in the United States.

To develop and maintain support on the campus, it is highly desirable to publicize any and all activities of the team or club as much as possible. Community and school newspapers are usually cooperative in printing cycling news. Sportswriters often find it a unique and novel topic. As they become more knowledgeable about the sport, we can hope that they will come to appreciate it for its many merits.

Perhaps each club would do well to find a good publicity man to see that the entire school and community know of the team and its activities by using newspapers, school bulletins, and posters to advertise its events.

There are many other ways a team can build interest in cycling on campus. Touring clubs have become popular at a number of schools and indirectly do much to support racing activities. Bicycle rallies were held at Shasta College this past year during homecoming week and a spring activities week. Both events stimulated a good deal of interest in cycling.

Shasta College also has a physical education class in cycling on its schedule this year, which is a notable step forward, but not a simple accomplishment. The proposal for a cycling class had to go to the Dean of Instruction, Curriculum Committee, Physical Education Department, the track coach, etc. Those that are interested in receiving school credit for their cycling activities might be able to get their cross-country or track coaches to allow them to meet each day with these teams.

In few cases will schools obstruct the formation of teams, although active support is something that might take time to find. Some schools, perhaps best exemplified by Princeton, are doing much for their teams by offering substantial support, both moral and financial. The student government and administration of Shasta College have demonstrated their faith in cycling by including funds for bicycling in their budgets for the coming year, and a few schools are according full athletic recognition to cycling by the awarding of athletic letters. Hopefully, all schools with cycling teams will soon follow suit in supporting their teams to the fullest.

The development of world class cyclists in the United States can be aided greatly by intercollegiate cycling but, as yet, intercollegiate cycling remains little more than an anemic younger brother of the A.B.L., benefiting chiefly from the participation of cyclists who have started their cycling activities with the A.B.L. and just happened to be college or university students as well. Some schools such as Yale have been able to break this dependence upon A.B.L. riders.

Of the eight members of the Shasta College team this past year, none had even seen a bicycle race before competing as intercollegiate cyclists. By encouraging newcomers to participate, a definite contribution is being made to amateur cycling in general.

More properly, intercollegiate cycling should be contributing to the growth of open division A.B.L. racing, rather than vice versa. When this happens we will be well on the road to producing more than just a small handfull of world class cyclists.

CYCLO-CROSSING—
A SPLASHING GOOD TIME

E. PETER HOFFMAN
April 1966

While promoters were doing their rain dances and spectators were sloshing about in the muck looking for just the right vantage point, riders all over the country were harboring second thoughts about this sport of cyclo-crossing, or so they said. A sure barometer to the success of a race might be the degree to which contestants come to doubt their own sanity. And latent in all of us, I suppose, is the desire to play again in a puddle of mud.

By no means do I wish to suggest that the cyclo-cross is a child's game for, if tackled seriously, it demands the utmost in strength, endurance, speed, and bike handling ability.

For most riders in the United States, however, the cyclo-cross has remained a relaxed form of cycling competition, a fun-type activity, a spirited event for the winter days, an enjoyable interlude between the end of a long season and the beginning of the next.

Cyclo-cross season, I suspect, is equally enjoyed by the promoters who delight in searching out the most impassable courses. If nature hasn't provided enough obstacles, you can be sure the promoter will come up with some of his own.

Watching a cyclo-cross can be as challenging as riding one. Many a time have I seen a spectator sliding down a muddy bank or fording a rain-swollen stream.

Of course, not all take the cyclo-cross quite so light-heartedly. Many fine riders have developed a high degree of skill over the years. This year's national Cyclo-Cross Championship held in Illinois was won for the second year by Herman Kron of Chicago. In Oregon, reports Erroyl Hawley, the Rose City Wheelmen sponsored a five-race series in Portland, beginning in October 1965 and ending in February 1966. The races were held on three courses: Marshall Park, Mount Tabor, and the Alpenprose Dairy. Overall standings were computed on a ten-point system with points earned in each of the five events.

Roger Brower was leading the series after the fourth race but Uncle Sam took priority and he sadly departed posthaste. Nick Zeller, the eventual winner, was only four points behind Brower going into the final event, and had he not broken his chain in the first race, might have led the competition all the way.

In Bloomer State Park, twenty miles north of Detroit, Michigan, the Wolverine Sports Club held a meet to test the mettle of the hardiest. Tom Hill reports the course was a real challenge. Among the usual hazards normally found, this one had an added attraction: a flight of stairs had to be climbed—180 of them! "The last few flights were always the hardest," Tom said. "Upon reaching the top you dropped your bike from under your shoulder, flopped on it, and continued this madness for nine more laps."

A light snow had fallen the morning of the race and the course was a blanket of white. Aside from its aesthetic value, the snow made tough going and the ground was frozen and extremely slippery.

Hill took an early lead, holding Gary Ramell, Larry Krukowski, and Bruce Watford at one hundred yards. On the fourth lap Watford caught Hill at the bottom of the stairs and they fought their way up together. Hill bounced his chain off at the top and Krukowski stormed by. Hill made up the distance, and on the next lap they scrambled up the steps as a trio. But it just wasn't Hill's day and he unshipped his chain again. Ramell and Krukowski were not to be caught this time and the race ended without further changes in position.

E. PETER HOFFMAN

This rain-swollen creek is no problem for John Gallager of Berkeley.

Steve Lubin tackles a muddy bank in Tilden Park.

E. PETER HOFFMAN

Hay bales provide an additional challenge to Bill Long in Oregon.

F. P. GIBBS

Tilden Park in Berkeley, California, was the site of another cyclo-cross series sponsored by the Berkeley Wheelmen. Two weekends of preliminary races served as warm-ups for a final championship event.

In dry weather a talented rider could remain on his bike over the entire course, but the weather was far from dry. A steady rain drenched the area several days prior to both preliminary events, and the course was oozing with mud.

Dave Brink was the strong man of the first race, and riding a fixed 73 won handily from a talented field. Brink was the only rider skillful enough to manipulate the two fords in the saddle while the others chose to go wading.

The second race required more running because of mucky conditions, and Steve Lubin of Pedali Alpini, in his last year as a junior, was able to get the better of Brink.

A cloudburst drowned the countryside minutes before the final race and the two creeks instantly became roaring torrents. Lubin was in top form and dominated the race completely, and only the fine performance of Karl Schneck of Santa Rosa posed any real threat.

And so, another winter draws to an end. Cyclo-crossing competitors, promoters, and spectators alike, surely had themselves a good time. And you can bet they'll be back out in the dripping woods this time next year.

June 1964

HARE AND HOUNDS CHASE

Robert Barriskill
June 1964

First let me tell you what a Hare and Hounds Chase is, as I didn't know myself that Sunday morning in April when the Western Wanderers decided to conduct one. You see, the Hare takes a twenty-minute head start from the rest of the group, rides like crazy in his most imaginative manner, and marks his route with arrows for the others to follow. The object, of course, is for the riders to catch the Hare by following his chalk marks; the first rider to catch, winning. The locale chosen was Golden Gate Park in San Francisco, and as it turned out, the Hare's "imaginative manner" was quite good.

They had told me a Hare and Hounds Chase is usually welcomed by the older club members, as they enjoy twiddling around the park, watching the scenery and leisurely following the arrows. Since I am an older member (having a son who can ride as well as I can), I felt safe in joining in. Below are my thoughts, as I remember them.

The fifteen or so rather placid looking riders standing at their bikes suddenly changed into tigers at the signal to start. I desperately hung on somebody's wheel, as the group sprinted for position and shot by the first arrows flat out. I soon realized I had made a mistake getting into this thing. It was a plain old cyclo-cross race, but without benefit of marshals showing you the turns. And you wear flat spots on your ten-dollar silks trying to make a quick stop and then a ninety-degree turn. Or go on your head trying to turn on pine needles . . . how do you ride on pine needles, anyway?

Leave it to the Hare. Every miserable trick in the book was in his repertoire: down stairs that I know threw at least three wheels out of line, up dirt trails a motorcycle couldn't make! (At this point an amazed motorcyclist frantically pulled his motorbike out of the way as a dozen red-faced and panting cyclists went charging up his trail.)

Up and down bleacher seats . . . shortcuts don't help . . . a quick sprint down a roadway . . . well, at least we lost half the pack of hounds . . . where's that next arrow? . . . I'll help you if you help me . . . mature adults staring with ill-concealed disdain . . . how could Hare get this far? . . . we're going flat out now . . . suppose he has us going in a big circle and he's sitting by somewhere laughing?

No, that's not it . . . over there is an arrow, and a big hole in that hedge, neatly pruned in the shape of a tall, lean cyclist. The Hare must have blasted through there at at least forty miles an hour to leave the hole that neat . . . there's another arrow on a piece of wood! Wait a minute

. . . how could that piece of lumber be in that exact spot right where it was needed? I get it . . . this thing has been carefully planned for days . . . otherwise we'd have that Hare in a pocket by now.

Funny thing, my son Ed seems to keep turning up ahead of us. I believe he had worked out a strategy of his own . . . a quick trip to high ground . . . a rapid evaluation of the general route of travel . . . a fast swoop down to intercept. But I bet this will do him no good on the long run . . . this Hare is much too unpredictable!

Where is everybody? Not a cyclist in sight . . . no arrows either . . . Dooougg . . . Laaarrry . . . not a sound comes back . . . must have taken a wrong turn. Ah . . . here's an arrow over here . . . and a little ways farther a group of cyclists searching the ground for something . . . maybe I can slip by them . . . ah . . . they didn't see me. Oh, yes they did! Here they come! But I've got a good lead now.

After an hour of this sort of thing something is bound to get very tired, and on me it's the part I used to make my living all week—my seat. As I became more and more aware of the ache in my nether regions, a solution they use in Europe flitted through my mind. At least it had previously been told me by Wally Gimber—with that very sincere look in his eyes. It seems some European riders, when faced with an especially frustrating ride, sometimes place a piece of raw steak in their shorts before mounting the saddle. Could this be an answer? Should Wally be asked to demonstrate?

Where is that Hare? He must be around here somewhere! How can that guy go this fast, and still mark arrows?

Around the next bend came my answer! I gave an elevated black-clad posterior poised in the air a well deserved swat, just as an arm reached down off the bike to make another arrow. I immediately collapsed at the side of the trail. I had caught the Hare!

TIME TRIALING FOR TOURISTS

PETER KENDAL
April 1969

To the person who happens on the scene for the first time, the proceedings make as much sense as a game of Mah-Jongg.

A bunch of bicycle riders are at the ready, but they are lined up one *behind* the other instead of side by side. They don't look like real racers, and yet in a way they do. One by one, they take off as if their life depended on it. When you come up a little closer, you see that it is a very heterogeneous group. There are boys and girls, but there are also people in their forties and fifties. While you try to figure it out, a pretty girl comes around the bend and flashes by like a bat out of heaven. What's up?

It's the monthly time trial of the San Diego youth hostelers. The idea is to ride a measured course at your top speed but as an individual. That means that you have to pace yourself. You are competing against the next fellow but without knowing you are ahead or behind. Your job is to spread your strength. It's not as easy as it sounds.

But how can you compare a twelve-year-old girl with an eighteen-year-old boy? By dividing them into classes. Girls against girls, boys against boys, veterans against veterans. The time trial is a very accurate gauge of fitness. In no other sport can physical performance be measured so well.

You learn a lot in a time trial. You learn that spinning is better than pushing. You learn that your bicycle at speed is much easier to handle than at crawl. And you learn that even a slight change in position means a big chance in efficiency.

The point is that a time-trial program will instill zest in a club that is primarily for touring and sociability like a hostel club. All you need is a course, a starter, a timer, and of course the riders.

The riders will come if you make these events interesting. One way to do this is to keep the results and to publish them in a club bulletin. In San Diego we hold our trials once a month. This way, you can measure progress. We allocate points according to the performance, and at the end of the year the top scorers get trophies. Another method we find helpful is to charge a small entry fee and award some inexpensive prizes for each event.

The course is all important. In San Diego, we picked Shelter Island. It is central, scenic, and smooth. No intersections and no traffic lights. These are prime considerations. The cyclists do not interfere with traffic because they ride by themselves and they stay on the shoulder. Our circuit is 2.08 miles. Riders make five circuits on each trial or 10.4 miles. Times run from twenty-four to thirty-five minutes. If you should be looking for a course in your city, go to a park. The site should be easily accessible, and the circuit should not be too long.

We divide the boys into two classes, A and B, according to whether they clock under or over twenty-nine minutes on their first run. Girls are in a separate class. We do not have many riders in the eighteen-to-forty-year group because these ride mostly with the local clubs. We do have a fair number of veterans. These are people over forty. Average attendance at our trials has risen to forty participants.

It has been found in England that a veteran will slow about thirty seconds over a twenty-five-mile course with each advancing year. A man who clocks one hour and six minutes over that distance at forty will clock 1:6:30 at forty-one, 1:70:00 at forty-two, and so forth. At sixty he will have slowed to 1:16:37 and at seventy to 1:22:30. These determinations came from thousands of time trials.

In summary, a time-trial program helps a hostel or touring club in three ways. It teaches proper riding, it instills vim and vigor, and it brings variety. With a successful time-trial program, clubs can mount a more challenging touring program. At least that is our experience in San Diego.

PROFESSIONAL ROADMAN—HIS EXPERIENCES AND TRAINING ADVICE

FRANS PAUWELS
March 1965

My first experience in international bike racing was the Tour of Catalonia, a seven-stage race in Spain, with the start and finish in Barcelona. It was May 9, 1940, and I had just turned twenty-one. Our team consisted of two other Dutch racers besides myself, and three Belgians.

By winning the third stage, my position in general time was second. I had never seen any real mountains in my life and now we were about to cross the Pyrenees. It was the fifth stage and everyone agreed that it was also the decisive one. Today we should cross the highest pass on the Spanish side, our destination. Except for the last twenty-five miles, most of the course was uphill. The pass ahead of us took the racers far above the timberline with snow covering the road near the summit.

The heavy Spanish food with its oils and olives had upset my stomach, but I was determined to defend my second-place position.

A dreary drizzle continuing from early morning made us look like a pretty miserable group. The Luxemburger Mathias Clemens was the leader wearing the yellow jersey, and I was trailing by one and a half minutes. Another Luxemburger, Didier, held third place and was almost two minutes behind me in the general time elapse.

At the foot of the pass, with forty-five miles to go, the race really began. A break had put eight of us ahead of the field. I was hanging on for life, with a broken spoke in my rear wheel bothering me more than it harmed me. The rain got steadily worse and the atmosphere more depressing.

It was fortunate that my friend and teammate, Ward Vissers, was there beside me. He had done extremely well in previous Tour de France races. The encouragement and advice he gave me helped me to stay with the leaders. His judgment in choosing the proper gears proved profitable for us.

There never seemed to come an end to the numerous hairpin turns. We had not even reached the timberline when I was already trying to hide my efforts. I hoped and prayed that I would be spared from flat tires. If that misfortune had occurred, I would not have known where to begin. My body was drenched, my hands were stiff, and my feet were numb. I sure welcomed the Spanish wine Ward Vissers had brought along.

Didier had been setting the pace and it seemed that the six of us, including Didier, Vissers, Clemens, myself, and two Spaniards, Bernadero and Giminez, had about the same amount of energy left. The road, which at times looked more like a creek bed than a road, did not improve much as we finally reached timberline. The rain had turned to snow, but riding seemed to become easier; perhaps the nearness of the summit made it seem that way.

Feeling better than the rest of us, Didier, the natural hill-climber, grabbed some snow off the ten-foot snowbanks along the road and threw it jokingly at his teammate, Clemens. The effect was rather astonishing. Clemens must have been the most miserable one of our group, for he fell off his bike, broke into tears, and was left behind. This put me in first place in the general time lapse but I did not have enough energy to enjoy it.

The road had been following a power line and Vissers observed its disappearance. Figuring that we were nearing the top, this put us on the alert. What a relief it was, too, to see someone waving a flag. This was the top and the next twenty-five miles would be an easy ride down to the finish.

Much to my surprise these twenty-five miles were just as bad as everything before. A mist had formed on this side of the mountains. Cold as we were, competition pushed us to risk our lives in a dazzling whirlwind of treacherous hairpin curves. Numerous times we skidded along the brink of awesome-looking canyons. The Luxemburger Didier immediately took the initiative and in no time coasted away from us. I desperately tried to stay with him, but skilled as he was he made the gap wider with every turn.

There finally came an end to this trying race. Didier won the stage by more than a minute. Vissers won the sprint of our group, Bernadero was third, and I took fourth. Fifth was Giminez and three minutes later came Matt Clemens. This put me first in the general time lapse. I had gained the coveted yellow jersey.

There was a huge crowd on the finish line in Andorra, the late afternoon sun was shining, but we hurried to our designated hotel and crawled into our beds, shivering long afterward.

I have never asked myself if the glory was worth the misery I had to endure. I do know that I have loved bicycle racing and by pursuing it a person gains a more stable character and a sense of accomplishment.

For you who are interested in the final outcome of that race, I could elaborate, but I shall conclude it briefly. The next day, Friday, was a sunny day but developed to be the most somber and tragic day in my young cycling career. Exciting visions of fame and fortune were shattered while cycling in all Europe came to a sudden halt, which was to last several years. That fatal day was May 10, 1940. Germany had begun to invade Norway, Denmark, Belgium, Luxemburg, and Holland.

Observing the American bicycle racers, it invariably comes to my mind that they lack or fail to display certain qualities essential to the success in this sport. Among these missing qualities, I think that perseverance, endurance, and determination are the most obvious.

How often have you been in a position where you allowed yourself to drop from the main field and yet after a few moments retaliate with a determination to catch them again? Did you ever get dropped at the start of a race or hill climb and in the continuing pursuit pass many riders? Have you ever decided to quit a race because it rained or the weather was too cold? Or worse yet, you did not even start a race because of these conditions?

I can recall many tough experiences I have had myself, but somehow they did not stop my racing.

This year's racing season will be here shortly and the

problem of training should be foremost in the minds of all serious racing cyclists. Here is my advice for getting into shape after being inactive for a period of time.

First of all, make up your mind that you are going to do your utmost to succeed on your bike this year—or never. This means a period of six weeks to two months of intensive training, during which time you must give up those activities and habits that will interfere with your racing.

European training usually has at least three phases, each about three weeks in length.

First three weeks: Ride alone or in a group, about twenty-five miles daily, faster than an average ride using a low fixed gear (20 teeth rear by 46 teeth front or equivalent). Ride a hilly course and if possible make the last foreleg of the ride a battle against wind and time. Use home trainers or rollers for fifteen to twenty minutes daily if you have them.

Second three weeks: Ride alone or in a group, about forty miles daily, faster than average with a fixed low gear of about 18 by 46. Hill course and back against wind, *without getting off your bike.* Make the last a rule. Fifteen minutes on rollers if possible.

Third three weeks: Alternate one twenty-five-mile day of just joyriding with a fifty-to-seventy-five-mile day of hard training, preferably alone or just one or two more riders. Hills, wind, and your time should be considered. Next day twenty-five miles of easy riding again, and so on.

Professionals add three more weeks to this schedule of training at which time they go on two training rides of 100 to 150 miles per week, alternating each with an easy ride of 25 miles. During this period one race on Sunday is usually on the program. This amounts to about three months of preparation beginning in early January.

French riders have their own method. During the last six weeks they go the same distance, choosing, however, to go with the wind at their backs only. This makes every ride a fast one.

The result is the capability to start very fast and to maintain a high speed throughout the entire race, which is important for such classics as the Paris-Roubaix, Paris-Brussels, Paris-Tours, etc.

The idea of a fixed low gear is, first, to force you to exercise your legs by continuous pedaling even though you had rather coast once in a while, and second, to develop a smooth "coup de pedal" which distinguishes experienced riders from square-pedaling novices.

It is wrong to make a bike race out of a training ride. Don't race your partners up the hills. Only the weaker riders enjoy this small victory. Save this for the real race.

Try hard to develop a *jump*. This means being able to close a gap between two riding groups in a prolonged sprint. Work on this especially during the last three-week period.

Group training should be kept to a maximum of three to five riders; more will slow you down. Two or three riders are ideal. Take turns at leading at your own pace.

And above all, learn to hang on even if you think it's going to kill you.

SO YOU WANT TO BE
A ROADMAN SPRINTER?

DON HOWARTH
July 1965

It has often occurred to me that nine tenths of all riders one sees in local road races, even many otherwise quite experienced ones, suffer a mental blockage or resign themselves to certain defeat at the group sprint finish of a road race, believing that the same known sprinters with a secret inborn talent for an explosive finish will always triumph.

This is not so. There are no "sprinter types." *Anyone can learn to sprint.* One has only to look at the European "aces" to see they come in all shapes and sizes.

All the techniques that I mention here were handed to me prior to my settling in California in 1963 by my friend and clubmate Bill Bradley. Readers will no doubt recognize Bill as probably the greatest amateur roadman England has ever produced. What may be less well known, however, is the fact that he was the finest tactitian and bike handler around. However, for years Bill was hampered and ridiculed for his lack of a finishing burst—for which he considered himself wholly unsuited. In later years Bill taught himself to sprint on the road to such effect that he could challenge anyone, even World Champion Eckstein in 1959, to within a few inches of the line.

Next let us explode another myth, that some of us are "roadmen," and some are "trackies." In this country there should be no distinction; all of us should be able to ride anything, the only possible exception being a marathon climbing event such as California's Mount Hamilton Race.

Examine the toe clips, a vital piece of equipment, before starting. These should be kept as short as possible; a medium size is adequate up to size 10 shoe. The reason for this is that a small clip enables one to "spin" at high revs, which is really all sprinting is.

Remember to clean out your cleats before the start with a coin and tighten the straps slightly with one mile to go, but not so much that they will cut off proper circulation in the foot.

Upon examining the tires of younger riders, one finds that they are almost too hard. For the road racing, the object is *not* to get as many pounds per square inch into the tires as possible—contrary to track racing practice.

The rear wheel is the "traction" wheel and should have a slightly lighter tire. If it is blown too hard it will "skip" dangerously to the side when administering a powerful out-of-the-saddle jump. A too-hard front tire will cause loss of traction on corners and "bounce" on bumpy surfaces.

The correct choice of gears is individual, but remember to keep as low as you dare, as it is only by a fast, smooth pedaling action that one can go on to become a champion. The fabulous Belgian, Rik Van Steenbergen used to win his road sprints on a modest 88 while another past great, Spaniard Miguel Poblet, won on gears 10 inches higher. However, 90 or 92 inches is a good average.

Assuming you have the ability to reach the finish with

the leaders, let us examine your actions. At one or two miles to go, sit up, relax, and take many very deep breaths, expanding your lungs to the utmost and storing oxygen. Select your sprinting gear now. As the finish rolls into sight, forget your tiredness momentarily, let your blood race with excitement, and give it your all. Hold the front wheel down. Don't jerk the arms up, as this will only succeed in lifting the wheel off the road. Keep your elbows in; "flapping" them does nothing. The power must come from your legs. Try not to slide forward on the saddle, and finally, keep that head up all the time. It is silly to emulate pictures of track sprinters, all-out, head down between arms; they do not have a spectator, stray dog, hole in the road, or rock to contend with on the finishing line.

It is impossible here to delve into how to position yourself to suit various conditions or team tactics. But one old trick to watch out for, which hardly ever fails, is when two teammates at the front on the final corner come out of the corner and the leading rider jumps. His second-place teammate does not react, and by the time his challengers have seen there is a gap they will have to sweep wide around his partner.

One more unethical but effective tactic (which I am not advocating) was that used with considerable success by one English club, the Liverpool Mercury. They would start their sprint from 250 meters in the far gutter, switching gradually to end right in the opposite gutter at the line, unnerving the pack systematically.

Another tip, employed by Bradley to win a stage in a major race, is that if the finish is marked by a banner above and across the road, ignore it. It will create an optical illusion of nearness. Sprint for the line on the road.

When it is all over and you can't all win, don't complain about the finish; you should have examined this first and if the race says that the first man through a gate into a field is the winner, just make sure you are the man.

Good luck in your final "gallop" (that's current English slang for the bunched finish).

DATE WITH DEATH

CLIFFORD L. GRAVES, M.D.
September 1965

A tense group of people was gathered on the freeway near the German town of Freiburg on July 19, 1962.

Herr Heinemann had painstakingly measured off the official kilometer. Half a dozen timekeepers of the International Timing Association were fiddling with their electrical equipment. Captain Dalichampt of the French occupation forces deployed his men at strategic points along the cleared Autobahn. Chief Schefold of the federal highway department dispatched a sweeper crew. Adolf Zimber lovingly wiped a bit of invisible dirt off the windshield of his massive Mercedes. Reporters were asking questions, scribbling notes. A photographer was angling for a shot. Jose Meiffret was about to start his date with death.

Of all the tense people, Meiffret was the least so. A diminutive Frenchman with wistful eyes and a troubled expression, he was resting beside a strange-looking bicycle. A monstrous chain wheel with 130 teeth connected with a sprocket with 15. The rake on the fork was reversed. Rims were of wood to prevent overheating. The gooseneck was supported with a flying buttress. The well-worn tires were tubulars. The frame was reinforced at all the critical points. Weighing forty-five pounds, this machine was obviously constructed to withstand incredible punishment.

On this day, at this place, on this bicycle, Jose Meiffret was aiming to reach the fantastic speed of 124 miles an hour. Everything was now in readiness. Meiffret adjusted his helmet, mounted the bike, and tightened the toe straps. Getting under way with a gear of 225 inches was something else again. A motorcycle came alongside and started pushing him. At 20 miles an hour, Meiffret was struggling to gain control. His legs were barely moving. At 40 miles, he was beginning to hit his stride. At 50 miles, the Mercedes with its curious rear end was just behind. With a wave of his hand, Meiffret dismissed his motorcycle and connected neatly with the windscreen of the Mercedes. His timing was perfect. He had overcome his first great hazard.

Swiftly, the bizarre combination of man and machine gathered speed. Meiffret's job on penalty of death was to stay glued to his windscreen. The screen had a roller, but if he should touch it at 100 miles an hour, he would be clipped. On the other hand, if he should fall behind as little as 18 inches, the turbulence would make mincemeat of him. If the car should jerk or lurch or hit a bump, he would be in immediate mortal danger. An engineer had warned him that at these speeds, the centrifugal force might cause his flimsy wheels to collapse. Undismayed by the prospect, Meiffret bent down to his task.

He was now moving at 80 miles. News of the heroic attempt had spread, and the road ahead was lined with spectators. Everybody was expecting something dreadful to happen. Herr Thiergarten in the car showed Meiffret how fast he was going by prearranged signals. Meiffret in turn could speak to the driver through a microphone. "Allez, allez," he shouted, knowing that he had only nine miles to accelerate and decelerate. The speedometer showed 90. What if he should hit a pebble, an oil slick, a gust of wind? Ahead was a bridge and a clump of woods. Crosscurrents were inevitable.

In his pocket, Meiffret carried a note: "In case of fatal accident, I beg of the spectators not to feel sorry for me. I am a poor man, an orphan since the age of eleven, and I have suffered much. Death holds no terror for me. This record attempt is my way of expressing myself. If the doctors can do no more for me, please bury me by the side of the road where I have fallen."

Who was this man Meiffret who could ride a bicycle at such passionate speeds and still look at himself dispassionately?

He was born in 1913 in the village of Boulouris on the French Riviera. Orphaned at an early age, he had to go to work to support himself and an aging grandmother. One day, as he was hurrying home from work on his ancient bicycle, he was run down by a motorist. Jose was badly shaken, and his bicycle was ground to bits. Dis

traught, the motorist offered to buy Jose a new bicycle. It
was a beauty. Before long, his bike was his life. When
he wasn't riding, he was reading. Under the skinny
frame and the deep-set eyes burned a fierce ambition.
Someday he was going to beat the world.

His first race was a fiasco. Totally unprepared, he entered a 120-miler through the mountains and was promptly
dropped. His competitors made fun of him, and a doctor
told him that he had a weak heart and should never race.
That night Jose cried himself to sleep.

The man who changed Jose's career was Henry Desgrange, the founder of the Tour de France. Desgrange had
a villa on the Riviera, and Jose wrangled an introduction.
Desgrange sensed the compelling drive in the delicate
body, and he made an accurate assessment. "Try motor-
paced racing, my boy. You might surprise yourself."

Jose did just that. With fear and trepidation he entered
a motor-paced race between Nice and Cannes. Without
any indoctrination whatsoever, he was immediately at
home. Riding smoothly and elegantly, in perfect unison
with his pacer and in complete control of himself, he was
out front all the way and finished a full seven minutes
ahead. The people went wild.

Encouraged by this success, he arranged to go over
the same course behind a more powerful motor. This ride
was an epic. Intoxicated by his speed, he barely missed
a car in Nice, grazed a dog in Cannes, scraped a sidewalk
in Antibes, had a flat five miles from the finish, and yet
hung up a new record of 1.02 for the 40 miles. He had
found his destiny.

How could a rider like Jose make a splash before he
had caused a ripple? Racing behind motors is quite different from racing in a group. Behind motors, the speed is
higher, the pedaling faster, the concentration greater. It is
like a continuous sprint. A motor-paced rider must have
suppleness rather than strength. And he must have flair.

But a motor-paced rider is not made overnight. Just as
Jose was beginning to hit his stride, the war broke out.
When he returned to Paris after five dreary years of cap-
tivity, he was as far from his goal as ever. Motor-paced
racing has a long and honorable history, but only a few
men have ever excelled in it. In America, the sport died

after "Mile-a-Minute" Murphy did his amazing ride behind a Long Island Railroad train in 1899. In Europe, the sport survived. On the road, the hour record was set in the thirties by the Frenchman Paillard with 49.362 miles. Meiffret raised this in 1949 to 54.618. Paillard immediately raised this figure to 59.954 but he was almost killed in the attempt. To beat Paillard, Meiffret selected a special circuit in Germany, the Grenzlandring. Cheered by thousands, he covered 65.115 miles in an hour and could have done more if his motor had been running right. All this required incessant training and complete concentration. Meiffret's philosophy was "to become what you are."

Although his exploit at the Grenzlandring brought him great acclaim, it did not bring him any money. In fact, none of Meiffret's rides brought him any money. All his life, he had to fight poverty. He supported himself with odd jobs and with occasional writing. His latest book, *Mes rendez-vous avec la mort,* earned him the 1965 Grand Prize for Sports Writing and the Prix Sobrier-Arnould of the prestigious Académie Française.

In an effort to improve his position in 1951, he decided to race behind cars instead of motorcycles. Cars are bigger and faster. Here, the man to beat was Alfred Letourneur, an expatriate Frenchman who had covered a measured mile behind a car on the Los Angeles freeway at 108.923 in 1941.

Meiffret's first attempt was behind a Talbot. To his consternation, he could not get past 70 miles an hour. Aerodynamic engineers told him to modify his windscreen. After months of toil and heartbreak he tried again. A 20-mile stretch of road south of Toulouse was especially cleared (even the President of the French Republic was detoured on that day). On his first run, the Talbot faltered. On his second run, he lost contact and was almost flattened by the wind. On his third run, he hit a bump and was in free flight for 50 feet, but he held on and finished the kilometer at 109.100 miles per hour. Letourneur had been beaten but not by much.

Undisputed recordman of the hour and of the kilometer on the road, Meiffret next turned to the track at Montlhéry. Here, the Belgian Vanderstuyft had ridden 78.159 miles in an hour behind a motorcycle in 1928.

But Montlhéry in 1928 was new. In 1952 it was old. The pavement was starting to crack, and the turns were atrocious. The track superintendent shook his head. He had seen many try. But Meiffret was determined. On the appointed day, he rode his first lap at 80 miles per hour. Suddenly, coming out of the turn on the seventh lap, his bicycle started bucking. Nobody knew what actually happened. Perhaps the pedals, which had less than an inch of clearance, scraped. At any rate, Meiffret flew through the air, hit the ground, tumbled three hundred feet, slid another twenty, and came to rest, a quivering mass of flesh. Horrified attendants carried him to an ambulance, and newspapers announced his imminent death. That night surgeons found five separate skull fractures. Unbelievably, Meiffret lived through this ordeal.

There followed a long period of recuperation during which he fought as much for his mental sanity as for his physical health. In search of peace, he joined the Trappists at Sept-Fons and led the life of a monk. During this time he made continuous improvements on his bicycle, wrote his first book *(Breviary of a Cyclist),* and corresponded with hundreds of people. Thus, he learned of a new freeway at Lahr in Germany where he might gain permission for another attempt on the flying kilometer. In the fall of 1961, when he was already forty-eight, he reached 115.934 miles per hour. This ride convinced him that he could reach 200 kilometers (124 miles) an hour. Thus we find Meiffret in the summer of 1962 on the freeway at Freiburg, riding like a man possessed.

The Mercedes performed faultlessly. People could not believe their eyes. What they saw was the car in full flight with an arched figure immediately behind, legs whirling, jersey fluttering, wheels quivering. "Allez, allez," gasped Meiffret into the mike. In the car, the speedometer crept past 100, then 110 and 120. Anguished, Zimber looked into his rearview mirror. How could Meiffret keep himself positioned? It was fantastic.

At the flag, the speed had increased to 127. Faster than an express train, faster than a plummeting skier, faster than a free fall in space. Meiffret's legs were spinning at 3.1 revolutions a second, and each second carried him 190 feet! He was no longer a man on a bike. He was the flying Frenchman, the superman of the bicycle, the magician of the pedals, the eagle of the road, the poet of motion. He knew that he must live in this rarefied atmosphere for eighteen seconds. When he passed the second flag, the chronometers registered 17,580 seconds, equivalent to 127.342 miles an hour.

Meiffret had survived his date with death.

Cycling for

Radiant Health

CYCLING IS NO CURE-ALL, BUT . . .

FRED A. BRANDT, M.D.
March 1969

The average American male is overfed, underexercised, tension ridden, and a cigarette smoker. Any and all of these, particularly if a hereditary predisposition and/or high blood pressure exists, can make him a candidate for coronary heart disease, and for the eventual heart attack. Male is emphasized, for the female has certain protective influences that shield her from this disease until an older age. Can anything be done to prevent or delay this disease that is now an epidemic for American men, at seemingly earlier and earlier ages?

The answer is a resounding yes, if recent medical research findings are correct. And we, as cyclists, can quite reasonably recommend our sport to help alleviate four of the six major causes: underexercise, overweight, high blood pressure, and the anxiety-tension state we all experience to varying degrees in the present-day world of unrest.

Specifically, what happens to the heart and lungs of the "nonexerciser"? The heart muscle shrinks, its beats are more irregular, its blood vessels narrow, necessary protein within the muscle cells is decreased, and utilization of oxygen is both inefficient and wasteful. Lung-filling capacity is reduced, the average nonexerciser never using more than two thirds of the lung expansion available to him.

Uncomfortable, and often intolerable, breathlessness occurs early and with relatively slight exertion. Conversely, what happens to the heart and lungs when a program of reasonable, sustained, vigorous exercise is undertaken? The heart rate is slower, both at rest and for a given level of exertion, than the sedentary person's rate. Oxygen available to the entire body is thus increased for each "beat" of the heart. Improved nutrition of the heart-muscle fibers results in better development of these fibers. This can produce the more developed, heavier, and somewhat larger heart of the trained athlete, often and unfortunately compared to the "norm" of the inactive individual. The heart muscle responds to exercise like other body muscles, and the enlarged arm muscle of a boilermaker, for example, has never been considered abnormal, although certainly "hypertrophied." High blood pressure is often decreased. Normal shortness of breath is delayed, the rate of breathing is decreased, and the lungs fill to greater capacity for any given exertion. This simply means that the physically fit can do more and recover more quickly.

Physically active men have also been shown to have lower blood levels of fats, cholesterol, and other fat fractions of the blood that are implicated in causing coronary heart disease. These substances, deposited in the walls of the heart's own blood vessels, narrow the vessels and decrease the blood supply to the heart muscle. Although over-simplified, a decrease in blood level of these substances decreases their deposition in the heart's vessels. This decrease is transitory, however, occurring within two or three hours postexercise and lasting about two days. Thus the necessity for regular exercise, at least every forty-eight hours, to achieve the desired result.

With this discussion as background then, why cycling? Medical authorities are in general agreement that swimming, running, or "jogging," and cycling are the three best overall sports to develop endurance-type body muscles capable of long-sustained performance, and at the same time, increase the "work" ability of the cardiovascular-pulmonary (heart and lungs) system. Let us examine the advantages and disadvantages of each of these types of exercises as compared to cycling.

First and foremost, cycling is interesting! No limit here

to the few repetitious routes available to the runner. The cycle's speed increases vastly the choice of differing routes and changing scenery. The cool fresh breeze created in cycling refreshes and invigorates. Yet, a stop can be made at any time to examine the scene in detail or to talk with the many, it seems, interested and friendly spectators. Twosomes or groups of almost any size can participate, with animated discussions while cycling, if this is the choice. Or one can be alone with self and nature, feeling the delightful surge of power in your own leg muscles taking you farther afield by your own effort. How clear your thoughts seem. The answer to today's and tomorrow's problems can also come so much easier here, if this is your inclination.

Second, cycling is available. The runner, limited already by paucity of differing routes, almost always needs an outdoor area to practice his sport. Inclement weather, particularly ice and snow, drives him indoors where there is simply no room to run. Not so the cyclist. The readily available indoor exercycles give the cyclist all the advantages of road touring except the changing scenery, the sounds, the smells, the feel of the fresh wind on his face, and the ability to stop and communicate with others. But there are compensations here, too. The cyclist can place a music rack by his exercycle and catch up on all that reading he neglected last summer. He can turn on and watch his favorite television program. How much better than sitting and munching goodies or drinking high-caloried drinks. The choice of activity is limited only by the cyclist's imagination. The swimmer must have a place to swim, and unless he is blessed with a tropical climate or an indoor pool, weather can also drive all but the most hearty indoors. Places where a swimming facility is either not available or at such a distance as to make regular attendance a real and discouraging inconvenience are innumerable. Again, not so the cyclist. Roads, paths, bikeways, all are always there, and the indoor exercycle solves the problems created by winter.

Third, cycling uses the largest muscle "pump" the body possesses. Dr. Paul White, the eminent cardiologist, said, "The leg muscles are an important and unappreciated accessory pumping mechanism to assist our hearts physi-

cally. Healthy fatigue of the big muscle is the best anti-
dote known to man for nervous stress, far better than the
use of the thousand and one tranquilizers and sedatives
to which American people have become addicted." This
aiding of circulation by contracture and relaxation of the
largest muscles of the thigh and lower leg, particularly
while "ankling" correctly, aids in returning the venous
blood to the heart and thus augments the efficiency of the
circulation.

Fourth, cycling is one of the most complete forms of
exercise not only for the legs but also for the arms, shoulders, back, and abdominal and diaphragmatic muscles
which are brought into use, strengthening these muscles
as well as the legs. The diaphragm, an often unappreciated
muscle, makes our chest a suction pump, enhancing blood
return to the heart and increasing circulatory efficiency
markedly. The chest during cycling can be likened to an
accordion; the bellows are more fully expanded. Because
the body weight is supported by the machine, muscle
groups can be worked individually to produce both greater strength and fluidity of motion or suppleness. Energy
expenditure or strenuousness of the exercise can be easily
adapted to the individual's abilities by speed and gearing
of the cycle. Examples of this show that calories per
minute expended in cycling on level ground are five, seven,
and eleven respectively for speeds of 5.5, 9.4, and 13
miles per hour. A wide range of levels of exertion are
thus available.

But a word of caution should be introduced. Although
medical opinion regarding exercise stress has undergone
an almost complete reversal in the last ten years, the hazards of this stress are still poorly understood. The only
real agreement is that the normal heart cannot be
"strained" by even the most vigorous exercise. Yet, irre-
versible damage can develop in certain cardiac patients
when forced to perform exercise beyond their functional
capacities. Other than in racing, cycling does not demand
the sudden extreme burst of physical effort often seen in
other sports and is therefore ideal for the potential heart
patient. Men in actual heart failure, those with recent
onset of exercise-induced chest pain, and those with other
factors indicating already present heart disease should,

of course, undertake a progressive exercise program only under the closest supervision of their personal physicians. And most important, the beginning cyclist must recognize that it may take weeks or even months to achieve the desired fitness goals.

In summary, cycling offers perhaps the best physical activity available for prevention of coronary heart disease and is fun at the same time. Such physical activity has resulted in a lower incidence of the disease in middle-aged men and, for those with disease already present, it is less severe and occurs later. One might observe in this regard that although diet, cigarette smoking, hereditary predisposition, and other factors may determine who has a heart attack, adequate exercise often determines who will survive one.

THE HUMAN MACHINE

VAUGHAN THOMAS
November 1967

The tragic death of former World Champion Tom Simpson in the 1967 Tour de France startled the athletic world. Vaughan Thomas, our English research scientist correspondent from Loughborough University, has sent us this explanation of some of the modes of operation of the "Human Engine"—which will be of interest to all cyclists, and of particular interest to top riders, and to sometimes overzealous coaches. We hope it may prevent a similar tragedy in this country.

—FRED DE LONG

Recent occurrences in the various fields of sport, particularly in cycle racing, have posed some intriguing and vital questions to those who are concerned with the development of the human's ability to produce power. This aspect of human performance is usually measured in sport by the ability to move an object such as a barbell, a discus, a javelin, or to move the body with or without a vehicle in locomotion. The most vital problems arise in the locomotor sports such as running, walking, cycling, rowing, canoeing, skiing, swimming, etc., especially when these are continued for extended distances. In their efforts to improve performance, cyclists have pushed themselves to serious collapse, and even to death. The coach, or the cyclist if he has no coach, has a tremendous responsibility to understand how the human motor works, because he is literally playing a game of life and death.

Very few coaches and performers have a more than sketchy knowledge of human physiology and body mechanics. It has been my experience that the basic concepts can best be grasped by an analogy between the human machine and the motorcar, though one can often run into difficulties if the analogy is carried too far. Especially, one must be continually aware that the higher mental processes of the human provide control mechanisms that cannot be applied to the internal-combustion engine. Still, with these provisions in mind, we can begin to examine our analogue.

No engine can do work without fuel, and the human processes the food he eats into a sugar substance called glucose, which is the basic fuel of the human engine. The liver acts as a fuel tank, from which glucose is taken by the blood to wherever combustion is to take place. The fuel pump is the heart, which has an automatic inbuilt ticking-over rate, this rate being speeded or slowed by impulses from the nervous system.

The glucose cannot burn without oxygen, which is filtered from the air in the lungs, and then joins the glucose in the blood. This fuel-oxygen mixture is then taken to the combustion chamber of the muscle fiber. However, the human engine has far more than six cylinders; in fact, there are millions, though they do not all fire synchronously. This fine control is mainly a feedback mechanism activated by demand at particular site(s).

The actual chemical combustion in the muscle is extremely complex, and even yet not fully understood. However, a broad view shows that the ignition is sparked by a nervous impulse to the muscle fiber, which then uses the energy released to contract, thus exerting a force and tending to shorten the muscle. If enough cylinders are firing, then resistance to movement will be overcome, and the muscle will produce movement. The rate of this nervous "sparking" is again under the control of the nervous system and the timing is such that one spark is followed by a short recovery phase (similar to the cylinder refilling phase) during which time the fiber cannot be reused. The smoothness and strength of the power output of a given muscle, and of the total body output, is a product of the timing (coordination) and force of all the collective muscle fibers, as is the running of the automobile engine. The development of skilled and efficient locomotion is very much a matter of ensuring that when power is desired, it will be in the correct direction, unopposed by power exerted in another direction, at just the right power output, and that the muscles concerned will be the most efficient for the job and acting within their most efficient range.

The combustion in the muscle fiber gives waste products, some of which are resynthesized within the muscle, but the remainder have to be eliminated through the body's exhaust system, in that this level is monitored at various control centers which then assess the demand for more fuel and oxygen. They then alter the rate of the heart and lung operation. Here is, then, the first fundamental difference between the human engine and the internal-combustion engine. Human control is basically by feedback of information from within the organism, whereas motorcar control is basically feed forward of information by the operator (who, being human, is still operating on his own feedback mechanisms!).

Virtually all machines have an operating temperature at which they function most efficiently, and a danger temperature at which the machine will seize up. The human is no exception to this rule. One of the products of combustion in the engine is heat, and machines usually have cooling systems which operate on the basis of feedback control. The desired operating temperature is used as a "set point," and the actual temperature compared with this. If the actual temperature is too high, then the cooling system comes into operation. In the automobile, this "set point" and comparator is a thermostat, where each locality operates its own cooling system depending upon its own temperature, and where the whole body can assist in the general dispersal of heat.

We have previously seen that the basic difference between the human and the automobile machine is the type of control. The motorist can disregard, if he wishes, the signals which reach him that all is not well with this machine, and thrash the machine until it breaks without suffering any direct inhibitory factors himself. Of course, most cars have a governor, which prevents overrevving the engine, but the human responses to all the stresses on his own various systems are virtually automatic—they are virtually all governors. Moreover, these governors are all interconnected in a complex manner, which normally prevents the human from harming his "engine" by locomotor activity.

Psychological limit: This phrase describes the subjective feelings of fatigue (pain, stiffness, heat, breathing difficulty, visual acuity, coordination defects, etc.) which will eventually cause the human to either stop or decrease activity. At that point, the psychological limit for that individual has been reached. This limit can change under a variety of stimuli (for example, training, acclimatization, motivation, drugs) and is the main point of attack for the locomotor athlete's coach, attempting to get as close as possible to the control limit.

Control limit: At this point, where body systems are being stressed to dangerous levels, some measure of "cut out" control will be established. Muscles may fail to contract, movements become totally uncoordinated, or, most commonly, so much blood will be diverted to the working muscles that the brain will receive slightly less than it needs and become unconscious. It is possible that training and acclimatization can alter these levels, and it is certain that some drugs can overcome these controls. The moral and ethical aspects of this kind of athletic preparation are beyond the scope of this article. However, it should be pointed out that some of the deaths in locomotor sport, particularly in tour cycle racing, have resulted from attempts to artificially alter this control limit.

Physiological limit: At this stage, complete control of some functions is lost, particularly respiration and circulation, resulting in system collapse and death. The normal, healthy human being cannot reach this limit. By delaying the psychological limit by some means such as stimulant drugs, the extraordinarily fit cyclist runs the risk of reaching this limit.

One probable example of this risk is the recent tragedy of the death of former World Road Champion Tom Simpson. Without intimate access to the French documentation of his death, it is impossible to speak with complete certainty, but I had given Tom some intense physiological experimentation during the previous winter and base my comments on my personal knowledge of his physical condition and habits. Here was an immensely strong and experienced rider, in good general health and with a very sound heart, who succumbed to a variety of control overriders, and died. His basic preparation was quite sound, though it is doubtful if it included enough acclimatization to fierce heat and high altitudes. He, unfortunately, did not take a great deal of salt, which indicated a possibility of salt-water imbalance. However, these slight defects would normally have resulted only in performance decrement or a blackout, quite within the capabilities of his normal mechanisms. The critical combination of intense motivation, drugs, and alcohol, which overrode his normal responses to intense heat, altitude, exhaustion, and salt-water imbalance, allowed him to reach his physiological limit. It seems fairly certain that other deaths have resulted from similar circumstances, both in the world of cycling and in other locomotor events, and not only deaths but also collapses resulting in physiological damage.

We have considered just a few facets of the complex machine that is a cyclist. Such an article can do no more than scratch the surface of the subject. It is my fervent hope that these words may lend some caution to the activities of coaches and cyclists in their search for ever-improving performances.

MUSCLE ACTION

FINLEY P. GIBBS
April–May 1966

*Believing that a basic knowledge of the function of
the body is important to both the tourist and the
racing cyclist, the editor commissioned Finley P. Gibbs
to write the following articles.*

PART I

It is a well-known fact that even though they were surrounded by mechanics and engineers, great race drivers
such as Juan Fangio and Stirling Moss had an intimate
knowledge of how their cars functioned. The ability to
tell how well the car is running out on the course is often
the difference between victory and defeat. Fangio and
Moss both had the reputation for being easy on their cars,
although actually driving them faster than their less knowledgeable competitors.

In many ways the human body resembles a machine,
although the body is of course much more complicated
than the most complex of machines. It is hoped that this
article can provide the rider with a basic working knowledge of human physiology with which he can more intelligently plan his touring, training, and racing. Of course,
it is obvious that the mere knowledge of, say, the regula-
tion of blood flow through your quadriceps femoris (thigh
muscles) is not going to enable you to beat Jack Simes in
the last two hundred meters of a match race, but at least
it might help you realize why you lost.

The discussion will begin with a brief introduction to
the actions of muscle. A young, healthy male may consist
of 50 percent muscle. Most of this is under voluntary control. Other muscle, such as the heart, stomach, and intestines, serves to move things such as blood or food

around inside the body and is controlled automatically, not by conscious effort. The only means by which muscles move the body is by contracting, or shortening. In shortening, a muscle exerts forces on its points of attachment which tend to pull them toward each other. Relaxation of the muscle, however, does not push apart the points of attachment; another muscle is needed with different points of attachment, which, when it contracts, tends to move the limb back to its original position.

When the muscle (tibialis anterior) next to the shinbone (tibia) contracts, the foot is flexed; that is, the toes are brought closer to the knee. When the calf muscles (gastrocnemius and soleus) contract and the tibialis anterior relaxes, the foot is extended. In this system the foot is the lever and the ankle joint is the fulcrum. The load is provided by, say, a pedal attached near the ball of the foot. Movement at the knee and hip joints occurs in a similar manner. In those cases, the levers are longer and consequently the muscles are bigger and stronger. The movement of the limb is then determined by the difference between forces tending to flex it and forces to extend it. It can be seen that by suddenly contracting all of the muscles in the leg at once little useful work can be performed, since the muscles would be opposing each other, and the net movement would depend on which group was the strongest. The problem is to coordinate the muscles so there is a minimum of opposing activity and a maximum amount of activity in the desired direction. This coordination is performed by the brain and spinal cord.

When you decide to push down on the pedal of your bicycle, nerve cells in the brain discharge and send impulses down their long fibers to nerve cells in the lower part of the spinal cord which lead to all of the muscles of the leg. However, only the nerves to the extensors are excited, while those to the flexors of the leg are inhibited. Impulses then travel from the spinal cord to the extensor muscles and cause them to contract. When the pedal is near the bottom of the stroke, the process is reversed and the nerves to the flexors are activated, tending to pull the leg up. During many kinds of activity, it is apparent that the muscle is contracting only phasically, not continually. We will later see the importance of this phasic activity in allowing nutrients to reach the muscle.

The pattern of muscle activation concerned with pedaling a bicycle is not as simple as it first appears, since contractions of the arm muscles are involved both for turning the handlebars to maintain balance and to keep the body steady while the legs are tending to push it from one side to the other. Analysis of this sort of coordination is beyond the scope of this article.

PART II

Physiologists classify human and most other vertebrate muscle into three types: striated skeletal muscle, cardiac muscle, and smooth muscle. Smooth muscle is the slow-moving type of muscle found in the walls of blood vessels, the walls of the gastrointestinal tract, and in various specialized places, such as in the eye where pupil diameter is changed by contraction of smooth muscles. Smooth muscles are controlled automatically by nerve impulses not under voluntary control and by hormones in the blood. In addition, they can contract without any stimulation. Skeletal muscles are large, fast moving, and powerful, serving as the source of power for moving about in the environment and are almost exclusively under voluntary control through their nerves. Cardiac muscle, found only in the heart, has features of both smooth and skeletal muscle. It is large and capable of fast, powerful contractions, yet is not under voluntary control. Its rate and force of contraction are modified by its nerves, but the heart will go right on beating with all its nerves cut, for cardiac muscle has an inherent rhythmicity of contraction. This property is in contrast to skeletal muscle which becomes flaccid and soon wastes away if its nerves are cut.

A muscle is made of cells called muscle fibers which are from ten to one hundred microns* in diameter and from one millimeter to thirty centimeters long. Each fiber is wrapped in an individual sheath of connective tissue. A dozen or so fibers are grouped into a primary bundle, or

* A micron is one millionth of a meter. The letter *i* is about two hundred microns thick.

fasciculus, which is in turn wrapped in connective tissue of a heavier sort. Several primary bundles are grouped inside still other sheaths to form tertiary bundles. The whole muscle is then surrounded by a strong fibrous coat called the fascia. Connective tissue is thus found throughout the muscle, contributing to its strength. At the ends of the muscle the connective tissue forms tendons or attaches directly to bones.

A muscle fiber or cell is composed of from five hundred to five thousand fibrils, and each fibril is in turn composed of from five hundred to two thousand muscle filaments, the basic contractile element. Thus each cell may contain as many as ten million filaments. The filaments are of two kinds: "thick" ones made of the protein myosin, and "thin" ones made of the protein actin.

During contraction, the filaments are drawn over one another causing a shortening of the fibril. The exact means by which this sliding is accomplished is still a mystery, but the tiny bridges between the thick and thin filaments are thought to somehow "crank together" the filaments. A contraction is triggered when a nerve impulse reaches the muscle cell and causes a brief period of electrical activity in the cell membrane. This electrical activity initiates a series of rapidly acting chemical reactions which somehow enable the high-energy compound ATP to transform some of its energy into the useful work of drawing the filaments together.

Nerve impulses reach a "resting" muscle at rates varying from three to ten per second (muscles are rarely completely relaxed). This establishes muscle "tone." The strength of a further contraction depends, among other things, on the total number of muscle fibers receiving impulses over their nerves, and the frequency of impulses reaching the fibers. For instance, during a moderate effort such as lifting a five-kilogram weight (eleven pounds), 60 percent of the muscle fibers in the biceps muscle of the arm would be stimulated at the rate of thirty per second, whereas in lifting a thirty-kilogram weight, 90 percent of the fibers might be receiving stimuli at the rate of fifty per second.

The ATP used up during a contraction must be replenished if the muscle is to work continuously, for the supply in the muscle is small. The bloodstream helps accomplish this by supplying the muscle with oxygen and nutrients such as glucose. The biochemical "factories" in the muscle cell then oxidize the glucose, utilizing the resulting energy for the reconstruction of ATP. It is interesting to note that energy from ATP is also required for relaxation to occur, and that a muscle "cramp" is simply a muscle that has contracted but then failed to relax when the nerve stimulation has ceased.

CIRCULATION

FINLEY P. GIBBS
June 1966

It is known that muscle cells can contract for a limited time in the absence of oxygen, building up the so-called oxygen debt which eventually must be "paid off." However, for continuous activity of a muscle for periods of, say, longer than thirty seconds, the cells must be supplied with oxygen and nutrients, and metabolic wastes such as carbon dioxide must be carried away. This is the job of the circulatory system.

In a 160-pound man, the heart weighs about a pound and is about the size of his fist. It is a hollow organ with four chambers, two atria and two ventricles. The muscular walls (myocardium) surrounding the left chambers are much thicker than the walls around the right chambers. The reason is that the left ventricle pumps blood through the entire body and operates at a pressure of about 120 millimeters of mercury (2.3 pounds per square inch), whereas the right ventricle only has to pump blood through the lungs and operates at a pressure of about 20 millimeters of mercury (.4 pound per square inch). Thus, even though the same volume is pumped by each ventricle, the left ventricle pumps at six times higher pressure.

The average amount of blood ejected from each ventricle per beat is about 80 cubic centimeters. At rest with a pulse rate of from 60 to 70 per minute, this means five to six liters of blood, so on the average the entire blood volume goes through the heart in less than a minute at rest. In a well-trained athlete during maximal exercise, this cardiac output may increase from the resting six liters per minute to as much as thirty liters per minute. Now the heart is pumping the entire blood volume every ten seconds. At this output the pulse rate would be up around 180 beats per minute, and the peak arterial blood pressure to 180 millimeters of mercury.

The blood leaves the left ventricle by way of the aorta which has a diameter of about an inch. The aorta divides into smaller and smaller arteries which deliver blood to all parts of the body. In the tissues, the blood vessels split into extremely small vessels called capillaries. The capillaries are so small that the red blood cells have to squeeze through them in single file. They are also very numerous; as many as 4,000 per square millimeter of cross section have been counted in muscle. One estimate says that there are 100,000 kilometers of capillaries in the body. The walls of the capillaries are very thin, unlike other vessels, and allow the nutrients and wastes to diffuse across easily. At rest, when the need for oxygen and nutrients in muscle is low, less than one percent of the muscle capillaries are open. In exercise, not only do the muscle capillaries open up, but also blood-flow to organs such as the liver and intestines is reduced to make still more blood available to nourish the muscles.

During a contraction, the muscle becomes very hard and the blood pressure is not enough to force blood through the vessels, for they are not rigid tubes and collapse with the pressure from the muscle. This explains why it is not possible to maintain a steady, strong contraction for more than a brief period. Only when a muscle is contracting and relaxing phasically can it perform work over a long period of time. For instance, the quadriceps muscles of the thigh contract only on the downstroke of the pedal and relax on the upstroke. Blood is flowing through these muscles only on the upstroke. You can feel this for yourself by holding your hand on the lower part of your thigh as you pedal.

Various adjustments are made by the body during the

course of training in response to the increased circulatory needs of exercise. The muscular walls of the heart thicken and the amount of blood ejected per beat also increases. The pulse rate for any given amount of work consequently goes down. Resting rates as low as forty per minute are not uncommon in well-trained athletes. The blood volume increases around 20 percent (to six liters in our 160-pound man) and the concentration of red blood cells also goes up. The number of capillaries per unit of muscle cross section may increase by as much as 50 percent. All of these adjustments are directed at increasing the delivery of oxygen and nutrients to the working muscles so that they may sustain a higher level of work over a longer period of time.

NUTRITION

FINLEY P. GIBBS
August 1966

Everyone knows that good nutrition is essential for top performance by athletes. Just what constitutes good nutrition is often a matter of controversy, however. Some extremists advocate vegetarianism, or eating everything raw, or growing all your own food so it will not be contaminated with pesticides or preservatives. The physiological value of such practices has not been demonstrated and it is well known that one can be a champion without such psychological crutches.

The human body is composed of about two-thirds water and about one-third solids. Proteins and fats each compose about 15 percent of the body weight, minerals about 5 percent, carbohydrates about ½ percent and all other substances less than 1 percent. Eating of food serves two purposes: first, it is necessary to replace structural components such as proteins continuously; and second, it is necessary as a source of energy both for just keeping alive and for performing additional work. The amount of food necessary for replacing structural components and for just maintaining normal body functions such as breathing and pumping blood around is fairly constant for most people, but the extra food required for performing work varies with the amount of work done. Riders are familiar with the increase in appetite which comes as the training rides get longer.

One of the important principles of nutrition is that the diet be varied so that even though one particular food is poor in one of the necessary nutrients, it will be compensated for by another food rich in that component. The following will serve as a guide for establishing an adequate diet. Each day the diet should include:

1. Milk. At least a pint but not more than two quarts. Two ounces of cheese or several scoops of ice cream may be substituted.

2. Meat (including fish and chicken). One large serving per day and eggs at least three times a week. Peas, beans, and lentils may substitute for meat. Liver should be eaten often.

3. Fruit. One serving of citrus fruit and one serving of another fruit.

4. Vegetables. At least two servings, preferably dark green or deep yellow and frequently raw.

5. Cereals and Bread. One serving of whole-grain cereal and two slices of enriched or whole-grain bread. Noodles, rice, or potatoes may be substituted.

6. Additional foods may be eaten to make meals taste better and to satisfy individual energy requirements.

A well-varied diet such as just suggested will provide adequate amounts of proteins, vitamins, and minerals. The individual should then adjust the total amount of calories by regulating the amounts of carbohydrates and fats.

There is really nothing special about a training diet. It involves the same principles as a normal diet except usually quite a bit more is eaten. Fortunately most people's idiosyncrasies concerning training diets are harmless. But the extremes that many people go to, such as taking huge numbers of vitamin pills or eating nothing but meat, may in many cases actually be harmful.

The principle of a varied diet still holds for training

diets, and the above recommended one is sufficient. But
although an average man may only require three thousand
calories per day, a cyclist averaging thirty to sixty hard
miles per day may require over twice that much to stay
in weight balance. This difference can most easily be made
up by eating more of the energy-rich foods, fats and carbohydrates (starches). More protein can be eaten, too, but
contrary to popular opinion, it need not be increased in
great amounts. It has been shown in several experiments
that the need for protein during prolonged periods of
exercise does not increase appreciably. In fact a six-ounce
(cooked weight) piece of hamburger per day is enough
to supply the protein requirements under any conditions
of exercise. (This does not mean not to eat more than that
if you happen to like hamburger.) So despite the fact that
the muscles are being used much more strenuously than
normally, they do not need replacement protein in greater
quantities.

Although muscles use both glucose and fatty acids
equally well for the production of energy for contraction,
experiments show that people maintained on a high-carbo-
hydrate diet have a somewhat greater work capacity than
those on high-fat diets (with proteins, minerals, and vitamins equal). The reason for this is unknown.

A meal of any great size should not be eaten closer
than two hours before a race, preferably three. It is important that the meal taste good and be easily digestible.
Fatty meals should therefore be avoided immediately before a race. A meal might consist of some protein such
as a broiled steak or hamburger and some carbohydrate
such as rice, potatoes, or toast and honey.

HEALTH SECRETS OF
A CYCLING DOCTOR

CLIFFORD L. GRAVES, M.D.
September 1968

Although I was well on my way toward middle age and respectability at the time, I still remember vividly my excitement over my first ten-speed bicycle. You will understand when I tell you the circumstances.

I was stationed in England, and bicycles had gone out of production. The streets were full of cyclists but only the utility kind. Wherever I looked, I saw only antiquated machines with dispirited people hurrying from factory to home. Finally, on a trip to Nottingham, I saw a man twiddling a fine bicycle. I immediately stopped the car and asked him where I could buy a bicycle like this now.

"Don't you know there is a war on?" he said.

"I should" was my answer. "I sure am a lot farther from home than you!"

That broke the ice. We chatted, and then he invited me to his home, which was only a few minutes away.

I met his wife, his children, and his dog. We had tea, and we talked of all sorts of things except bicycles. At length I had to go. As I took my leave, my host scribbled something on a piece of paper and thrust it into my hands. I might add that this was not the last time I saw him. We continued our friendship over the years, and I am the godfather of his daughter.

"Here is an address," he whispered. "I think this man can help you."

I did not dare look at the paper until I got back to camp for fear of breaking a sacred trust. When I did look, I saw a name and address: F. W. Evans, 32-34 Kennington Road, London. I rushed off to London.

Mr. Evans eventually built me a bicycle. It was not exactly a lightweight, but it had a derailleur gear and dropped handlebars. Right away, I had a chance to try it out. There was to be a conference at the Second General Hospital in Oxford. I could ride there.

I did ride there, ninety miles between breakfast and dinner, but I strained my knee in the process. It started innocently enough. Just a little twinge toward the end of the ride. Committed to the conference, I kept pushing until I got there. That was a mistake. When I finally drew up, I could barely walk. I made another mistake. I did not lay off for a few weeks. I could manage a few miles, but then the pain would start up. I just gritted my teeth.

Well, to make a long story short, my knee bothered me for six months. I even made a tour of Scotland with that knee, and I remember how envious I was of people who could cycle in comfort. I used to follow them with my eyes as I crept along. I did not even go to see an orthopedist because I knew what he would say. I just toughed it out.

I am telling this story because it is so typical. An inexperienced rider overtaxes himself and won't give up. He thinks that his little pain will go away if he just ignores it. Pretty soon the little pain is a big pain. In my case, it was a knee. But it can be somewhere else. These big and little pains are the occupational ills of the cyclist, and they are fairly predictable. I will list them as far as I have observed them or suffered from them.

SADDLE SORENESS

It would be hard to find a cyclist who has not, at one time or another, suffered from saddle soreness. The cause is an ill-fitting saddle, and the cure is to make it fit. Break it before it breaks you.

Every saddle on a new ten-speed that I have ever seen needs to be softened. Use neat's-foot oil underneath and a tolling pin on top. After the leather has been softened, it still has to shape itself to you. This takes time. If you are lucky, you will be sitting pretty in about a month. A saddle that is not comfortable after a month will probably never be. At this point you can cover it with a foam-rubber pad or you can start all over again with a new saddle. Another expedient is chamois in your shorts. Sprung saddles are not the answer. Neither are plastic saddles, at least not with me. Women have a special problem. They need a wider saddle.

If you should develop saddle soreness in spite of your best efforts, you can take comfort in the knowledge that you are not alone. Great cyclists have been incapacitated by this very ailment. In professional cyclists, the condition sometimes progresses to the formation of a cyst, which has to be removed surgically. That is why professional riders sometimes have their saddles broken in by a *domestique,* a second-category rider who does not mind a bit of suffering if he gets paid for it.

STRAINED KNEES

There are two kinds of leg cramps: the kind that comes cartilages, and recesses than you can shake a stick at. Every time a cyclist pushes the pedals around, he straightens his knee. All the force is transmitted from the thigh to the leg through the tendon that inserts into the top of the kneecap, the so-called quadriceps tendon. You can feel this tendon when you put your finger immediately above the kneecap and straighten your knee while you sit in a chair. This is the point where the strain develops. Occasionally, the pain is located on the side of the knee. These ligaments receive some of the force.

When you develop knee trouble, take it easy. Don't force yourself like I did because you will only prolong the difficulty. Use hot applications, gentle massage, and rest. If you don't, the period of recovery can stretch to months. The reason is that the tendon suffers structural damage. During the exercise, blood corpuscles are squeezed out of the capillaries and into the tissues. The result is multiple minute hemorrhages. The damaged tissue has to be replaced, and this is a slow process because tendons have a poor blood supply. Stop riding with the first twinge of pain. Better to be on the sidelines for a week than in the doghouse for six months.

BACKACHE

Many adults, when they begin riding a ten-speed bicycle, become aware of their back. This will be especially noticeable on rough pavement. If this happens to you, don't be discouraged. The bent-forward position is actually the strong position. Your backache will pass off.

The cause of most backache, on or off a bicycle, is the hollow of the back. This hollow is the result of our erect position. It is the price we pay for being bipeds. When man started going around on two feet, his spine had to assume an S shape. It is this S that causes mechanical stresses. These stresses are always the most severe at the lower end, in the hollow of the back. The more hollow, the more backache. The treatment is to get rid of the hollow. That is exactly what you do on a bicycle.

Without oversimplifying the situation, let me say only that the vast majority of backaches are mechanical in nature. They result from pressure on nerves and strained ligaments that are intimately connected with the spine. The treatment is mechanical also. It consists in correcting abnormal curvatures and strengthening the muscles. When you bend forward, you accomplish this. It can be shown that the spine is actually longer in the bent-forward position. Most of the exercises that are prescribed for patients with a mechanical backache consist of bending forward. Riding a bicycle cures more backaches than it causes. If your experience is the opposite, you should see a doctor.

LEG CRAMPS

There are two kinds of leg cramps: the kind that comes on while you are riding and the kind that comes on several hours afterward.

The kind that comes on while you are riding is due to overexertion or underconditioning. Usually, it means that you are riding too high a gear. The treatment is very simple. Get off and walk. Next time, don't push so hard.

The other kind is more difficult. It probably has to do with structural damage to the muscles. It has nothing to do with fitness. Some people are susceptible to it. As far as I know, there is no effective treatment. Various drugs have been tried, such as calcium, riboflavin, asparagine, all without success.

Shin Splint

Shin splint is the name for soreness along the tendons on the front of the leg between the knee and the ankle. It is due to excessive motion of the tendons in their sheaths. Some people notice it after they "ankle" too much. Heat and rest are the treatment. Recovery usually takes one to two weeks.

Painful Foot

Pain may occur in the foot where it rests on the pedal. It is due to pressure with some flattening of the transverse arch. Riders who keep their toe straps very tight are subject to it. The pain quickly disappears when you roll the transverse arch up and pinch the toes down, but you can do this only after you take your foot out of the strap. Try picking up a marble with your toes. That is the position of strength for the foot.

In summary, the cyclist is subject to various aches and pains due to pressure and muscular effort. Usually, these aches and pains are of minor importance but they can grow to major proportions. The treatment is mostly a matter of common sense. You roll with the punch.

Sometimes, this is good for a chuckle. We were sitting around on a huff-and-puff tour not so long ago, and Medwin Clutterbuck, who is English, mentioned that he had suffered a pain in his foot that day.

"A pain in your foot?" asked Jacques Faisant. "And what did you do for it?"

"Well, I got off and had a cup of tea."

"A cup of tea? How could that cure your foot?"

"I don't know, but it always works!"

Equipment and

Techniques

Bike Toter with two fully assembled bikes.

Carrier bars are spaced to accommodate the upturned bike.

YOU CAN TAKE IT WITH YOU

E. Peter Hoffman
September 1967

Today's cyclist, although he may be an avid critic of the automobile, still finds it necessary to employ the motorized beast to haul his trusty steed to distant rallies, races, on vacations, or out of urban areas to enjoy new or uncrowded roads.

Finding it impractical (or impossible) to squeeze his and his family's bikes into the back seat or trunk of the car, our enthusiastic cyclist finds himself confronted with a common problem, but an easy one to solve. "You can't take it with you" just doesn't apply to cycling.

Several bikes can easily and safely be carried on the smallest of cars, without sacrificing passenger comfort or luggage space, and at a very nominal initial cost. Two basic types of carriers are most popular: a commercially marketed rear bumper rack and the converted rooftop carrier. Both have their advantages and disadvantages and final selection will depend on one's personal needs.

The bumper rack, called the Bike Toter, is manufactured by Bike Toter, Inc., P.O. Box 888, Santa Monica, California 90406. It is designed to attach to bumpers of almost any car by four hook bolts which may be positioned according to the size of the individual bumper. The rack weighs only a few pounds and is sturdily constructed. All that is necessary for installation is a crescent wrench.

The Bike Toter will carry one or two fully assembled bikes handily, three in a pinch, and if the wheels are removed, as many as four. If your bikes are equipped with quick-release hubs, removing the wheels is no problem, but finding a place to carry them may be a different story. Several wheels can be strapped to the sides of the frames, but you will have to find space in the trunk or up front for the others. If you drive a small car or one with limited road clearance, you may wish to remove the wheels, regardless of the number of bikes carried, to avoid striking the pavement on driveways or uneven surfaces. Careful loading is necessary to avoid scratching one bike against the other.

In some instances bumper racks may make access to trunks or rear engines impossible. Inconvenience may be tolerated, but don't overlook important engine maintenance.

Bikes carried on bumpers are, of course, subject to damage from rear-end collision and will get dirty in wet weather or on dusty roads.

Regardless of these disadvantages, the rear bumper carrier enjoys a great deal of favor with small families, and is easy to install and use.

Carrying your bikes on top of the car eliminates most of the disadvantages of the bumper carrier, and is better suited to three, four, or more bikes. Any of the ready-made rooftop carriers available at auto supply stores will work. The principle is simple, and you may add many refinements to improve your carrier if you are so inclined.

Position the carrier so that, when your bike is upside down, the handlebars and saddle will rest squarely on the bars. Strap both sides of the handlebars, as well as the saddle, securely to the carrier. Securing the handlebars tightly is most important, for they will hold the bike in the vertical position. Tying the saddle will keep the bike from pivoting from side to side.

There are many ways to tie the bike down. Toe straps are very popular, and are fast and easy to use. Threaded radiator hose clamps are a sturdy substitute but take longer to operate. Sandows are useful if they are in good condition and are stretched to their elastic limit.

Pegs or eyelets may be fitted to the carrier to aid in securing both handlebars and saddle, and a sliced truck inner tube will make good fasteners. Clamps which will fit over the handlebars and are bolted to the carrier with wing nuts are the most stable method.

To accommodate more than three bikes, alternate the direction of each bike, placing the handlebar of one next to the saddle of the other.

Avoid making sharp bends in cables or pinching them between handlebars and the carrier bar. Padding the tops of the carrier bars will help alleviate this and prevent marring of handlebars and saddle.

In choosing a rooftop carrier, one with gutter clamps or some other method for positive clamping to car roof is preferred over the suction cup and hook style.

Placing of bikes on the rooftop rack and taking them off may be awkward, and if your machines are heavy, a real chore. Keeping your clothes clean while not dropping the bike is the mark of a master.

Above all, don't forget you've got your bikes on top of the car when you drive into your garage after a pleasant weekend outing.

When transporting bikes on any type of carrier, pumps, water bottles, spare tires, and any loosely attached equipment should be removed to prevent loss.

FOUR ON A VOLKSWAGEN

ROBERT BARRISKILL
October 1964

Meet Paul Brinkley! He's the athletic-looking gentleman sitting at the wheel. He's more than that . . . Paul is also one of the best boosters of cycling you'll find. This, plus the fact that he's an awfully good guy, makes him a cyclist you'd want to meet in person.

Paul Brinkley and friend, Doug Dorr, with Brinkley's ingenious Volkswagen bike carrier.

However, don't let him lure you into a bike race. Paul was one of the winners of the Veterans' Race, held recently at Lake Merced. And he recently knocked off a couple of one-hundred-mile days on a touring trip, so he's a seasoned cyclist. But this article is really about Paul's mechanical ability, as evidenced by the picture.

It started something like this: Paul, being a gregarious fellow, enjoys company when cycling. The family auto was a Volkswagen. Since the car hauls four passengers, why not four bikes? Paul pondered this problem for some weeks.

Then, one night during a lousy television show, he hopped up out of his chair, and headed for the garage. "I've got it!" drifted back to his startled wife, Frances, as the door slammed shut behind him. The idea was born into action!

After a device has been invented it often looks simple. This is true of the two carriers shown. In fact, simplicity was Paul's main requirement. Simple to build, simple to use, and as light as possible. A top rack for general hauling was also needed, and this is part of the package. However, the bicycle-carrying portion alone could be built, if a person wants only this.

Biggest features: bikes stay together; each bike takes about thirty seconds to put on and take off; racks are adjustable for just about any size bike; and both racks come off the car in about three minutes apiece. The VW probably loses a mile or so per gallon with the bikes on, but Paul doesn't hold up any traffic going down the highway.

You will notice that Paul is a proud member of the Western Wanderers. This is a dandy place to display a sign of this sort, and help boost cycling. While pictures were being taken at the All-Club Ride in August, a man and woman came up and inquired about cycling . . . attracted by the handsome rig, complete with bright yellow sign.

Here's how you can build a set of racks like those shown, and you don't have to own a Volkswagen. The racks can go on any make of car with a little adapting. Best part of the whole thing is that they are very economical to build.

You can start with a factory top luggage carrier, or you can build your own as Paul did. Side rails are attached with movable blocks to adjust for different wheel-bases. Do-it-yourself aluminum tubing and some threaded rods and turnbuckles complete the hardware for the carrier.

The rear rack is simplicity itself. Most of the working parts can be seen in the picture. Note that the bracket that holds the top bars of the two bikes is canted. This is because bikes with 22" and 25" frames are being carried, and the mechanism adjusts for this. No doubt this was part of the thinking that went on while the cowboys were chasing the Indians.

Paul has very kindly agreed to supply a materials list, and any other advice needed by fellow cyclists who want to build these racks. He can be found (when not cycling) at 44 Skyline Drive, Daly City, California. Phone: 415 PL6-6896.

I do, however, see one small disadvantage. Don't forget about the bikes being on top and drive into your garage before taking them off.

WHAT BICYCLE FOR TOURING?

FRED DE LONG
May, August 1967

PART I

A short time ago, a reader inquired, "What type of bicycle should I buy for touring?" The qualified reply was, in effect, "More information is needed." It's hard to honestly answer this question from a distance.

The touring bicycle is probably the least-known member of the field. It may be due to the paucity of experienced cycle tourists on one hand, and to the large variety of conditions that can be experienced by the tourist, on the other.

I've seen on several occasions during International Bicycle Touring Society extended trips, a lack of initial appreciation of the skills needed. We've even heard writers describe racers that don't pull all out as "tourists." All too many of the uninitiated learn the hard way that bicycle touring is a skill in itself—a skill that must be learned, as in any other phase of the sport. As one learns, one further appreciates its joys and possibilities. And shouldn't it be considered proper to *enjoy* riding a bicycle? Competitive riders sometimes never learn the joy of this lifetime sport, and "hang it up" when they are past their peak.

In *American Cycling,* October 1965, Sumner White discussed ably his feelings on the touring cycle. Yet in a conclave of tourists, there is forever animated conversation and disagreement on the required features, equipment, angles, and construction—far more so than in a group of racing enthusiasts. Why is this?

What is your definition of touring? Is it a one-day trip at moderate speed on good roads, if the weather is pleasant and the wind not too strong. Or is it Mrs. Riva Morse, on her hands and knees on a cliffside road in Yugoslavia, dragging her bicycle loaded with all the gear needed on a

Touring machine using extra wide range Huret Luxe special derailleurs, T. A. Cyclotouriste chain-wheel set, range 26 to 54 front, 13 to 30 rear. T. A. front handlebar bag balances weight distribution.

2,500-mile trip, to keep from being blown off the cliff by a savage gale?

Will you travel as a vagabond, not caring too much about appearance, or does your itinerary require that you meet with people in "civilized" attire? Will you carry all your gear, or will a sag wagon do it for you?

Are the roads you plan to use of hard surface and smooth, or will you travel on cobblestones or rutted roads with potholes? Perhaps your route will be cross-country on trails and paths, on rocky or graveled routes. Some of the most beautiful areas in out-of-the-way places are entered on roads like these, and this may be true in your local area.

What weather will be encountered? Do you really enjoy the taste of road grit splattered in your face by the fenderless rider in front, the spraying of mud and grit onto your back and legs, onto your gear, and onto the working parts of the bicycle? Or will you confine your trips to sunny terrain, or sit out cold, wet, miserable days to save the weight of rain-protective equipment. Will you ride only by day, or will it be necessary to ride at night? Or at dusk? What about the terrain? Will it be flat or hilly? Will the hill roads be moderate in grade, or steep and winding with switchbacks on the descent?

And, finally, how do *you* like to ride? What is your style?

So, in answering a request for a recommendation for a touring machine, we would take a ride. Not around the corner, but for fifty or sixty miles. We would start out slowly, then up the pace a bit. Do you take the bait, or drop behind at your own pace? If you hold in, or take the lead and step out, you've got the competitive urge. Well, fine, we'll try some hills. Do you, within your ability of course, slug to the top, or do you maintain a comfortable, steady pace? Or, perhaps, do you get off and walk—even when gearing is adequate for the grade? And finally we'll descend a winding road. Do you hold your speed conservative, applying your brakes with caution, or are you a "slope diver," making like a slalom skier madly 'round the hairpin turns?

Your riding position would be observed. Do you ride the tops—with hands near saddle height or even higher, or do you prefer the "hooks" with body inclined well forward?

And while we're riding we'd discuss philosophy, interests, and aspirations. And at the end, you will have written your prescription for a touring machine.

Sounds complicated, you say? Well, this *is* touring. A wide range of experiences, of terrain, of weather, of load, of companions. No single bicycle can satisfy all conditions. And many happy tours are made on conventional road-racing machines—some even on three-speed upright handlebar bicycles. Some temporary inconvenience can be tolerated. Touring is a stimulating experience. One lives with his mount's capabilities and rides accordingly, and enjoys the trip.

In *American Cycling,* October 1965, Sumner White

listed six requirements for a good touring machine, which bear repeating.

1. Good performance over a wide range of road conditions, including dirt roads.
2. Will handle as well with twenty-five pounds of luggage as with none, although it will handle differently.
3. No steering shimmy under any circumstance.
4. Ability to climb steep grades for long distances (five to ten miles); to be steady and fast on mountain terrain.
5. Provisions for carrying luggage with no movement of the carrier or pannier bags, nor possibility of bags fouling the spokes.
6. Weight twenty-seven to twenty-nine pounds, including front and rear carriers, fifteen speeds, fenders, and generator lighting.

It's small wonder that the touring machine, with its added refinements and niceties, is generally more expensive than a racer of equivalent quality. Note that the requirements call for performance combined with stability under a wide range of conditions. Flexibility—that is,

Featherweight tiny inside sprocket gives extra wide gear range with only ounces additional.

adaptability to easy modification to cope with varying conditions—could be added as another requirement. The ability to change wheels, sprockets, mudguards, carriers for varying tour itineraries, as well as for local use when not on tour, makes the bicycle of more value to its owner.

Insufficient stability on downgrades and under load is a common fault of many racing bicycles when used for touring purposes.

The fifteen-speed gear, when obtained with a light alloy wide-range chain-wheel set, adds almost negligible weight. It permits a better range of gears with less chain offset when the gears are selected so that only twelve maximum combinations are used. Today's front derailleurs are almost universally three-speed capability, with stops adjusted when used with double chain wheel.

Deciding which features are most important is an individual proposition, which you yourself must select. There is no absolute answer. In the meantime you can enjoy a great measure of travel on most any well-built ten-speed.

PART II

In our previous article on how to select a touring bicycle, we discussed a form of self-analysis. What will you demand of your touring mount? Will it be used for long distances with luggage—cycle camping, perhaps—or will it also be used to a major extent on short, fast trips with no extra gear? Will you traverse gravel, dirt, and cobblestones, or can you count on only smooth-surfaced, hard-topped roads?

Or do you demand flexibility—ability to cover a variety of situations? Careful consideration will pay dividends. Your horizons may change as your touring experience increases.

Recognizing at the start that the ideal specification is purely an individual matter, and that there is plenty of room for dissension, I'll go out on a limb to present some personal observations.

The Randonneur, or Cyclotouriste, bar is the tourist's favorite. Slightly wider and with a lot more forward throw than the well-known Maes bend, it is easily distinguished by its slight upsweep from center. Dimensions are about

4½″ drop, 4½″ forward, and 16″ width. This extra width allows space for handlebar bag, reduces steering effort, and the upsweep provides more hand comfort when riding on the "tops." Its proportion of drop to forward throw is more suited to the less extremely inclined riding position.

To obtain the lightest weight and the minimum of effort, some tourists use light racing rims with tubular "sew-up" tires. Others prefer the greater safety, durability, and ease of repair of the light "wired-on" tire. The wired-on is less subject to creep and roll under load, and its tread provides more security and surefootedness. A spare tube and patch kit weighs less and takes less space than spare tubulars. And if one has a bit of casing patch material in his patch kit, he has little worry about being marooned far from help of home. At less than all-out speeds, and with a uniform cadence, the slightly lower road resistance is of minor importance. Multiple punctures are an incident, not a catastrophe.

Wheels may be obtained in 16, 20, 22, 24, 26, 27, or equivalent metric sizes. Smaller wheels provide a more portable bicycle, increased luggage space, lesser spray and dousing of the legs on rainy trips. They can provide improved toe-clip and stay clearance, combined with poorer stability, greater susceptibility to road irregularities, and more difficult travel on soft or rock-strewn roads. Your requirements, as well as consideration of availability of spares will affect your decision on wheel size.

For travel on most American, British, or Irish roads, the 27 by 1½″ wheel has proven very satisfactory. Spare tires and tubes are widely available. For European Continental touring, the 700 mm. rim is comparable. Light, high-quality tires ranging from a 300-gram type that looks like a tubular, and 28 mm. (⅛″), 30 mm. (1¼″), 32 mm. and 35 mm. (1⅜″) are available. If sufficient frame clearance is provided by changing tires, the same wheels can be used for a wide variety of conditions—from fast road work to slogging over rough and soft-surfaced back roads and trails. For consistently difficult, rough routes, the 26 by 1⅜″ and 1½″ tires, or on the Continent the 650 mm. wheel size, with 35, 38, and 42 mm. sections, provide more shock-absorbing comfort, better flotation on gravel or soft roads, and are less likely to damage from stones and potholes.

The 27″ and 700 mm. size rims vary in diameter by only about 5 mm. Thus, the same brake mounting can usually be used interchangeably. It may not be possible to substitute a large section 26″ wheel and tire if brake mounting is not preplanned, or hub brakes fitted.

Toe-to-mudguard clearance is of importance in city traffic with frequent starts and stops or on roads with poor surfaces that must be traversed at low speeds. If steep ascents or descents are involved, combined with low speed because of grade, load, and road surface, clearance becomes of even greater importance.

For stability on high-speed descents or on gravel or soft surfaces, particularly when carrying heavier luggage, a shallower head tube inclination combined with a fork offset somewhat less than neutral is advisable. Indeed, the desired clearance, particularly in the case of the smaller frame, may be attained by reducing head tube inclination, while still maintaining proper stability.

Contrary to popular notions, the fine touring machine is not a long ungainly bicycle. The tourist wants performance and stability. His luggage, both front and rear, must not foul his rotating feet. Yet, the use of long and flexible chain and seat stays leads to "whip" (see *American Cycling,* September 1965, page 30) and is to be avoided. A reasonable compromise, determined by the tire clearance and the rider's foot length, must be selected. And luggage should be kept, as far as possible, between the wheel axles for best road handling characteristics.

Frame and component lightness is to be sought for. When traveling by air, total weight of bike and baggage is economically important. But all day long, while riding and when handling the bicycle afoot, light weight is a real asset. However, extreme measures—such as cutting tube diameter and gauge to the point that frame and bearing interior are reduced, and strength is diminished—are to be avoided.

We have spoken on several occasions of the advantages of wide-range gearing. Select your gear changer for capacity and rugged construction. It costs no more, and can increase the usefulness and freedom from service of your equipment. The three-speed hub gear, despite its weight and limitations in range and gear selection, is not to be entirely ruled out. This can be particularly true in rain, mud, or sandy terrain.

Because extra load and steep descents may be encountered, with rain and snow or heat, the brakes must be selected with special care. Fade and overheating of rims on long descents can be dangerous—or fatal! The extra-long brake block, or the internal expanding hub brake, or even both, have advantages.

On tour it is often necessary to ride at night to obtain supper or lodging. Headlamp mounting far forward, ahead of cape and handlebar bag, and tail lamp mounting where not obscured by luggage are advised.

PACKING FOR TOURING— KEEP IT LIGHT!

DEUX ROUES
June 1968

A few months ago we briefly reviewed the selection of a bicycle for cycle touring, and discussed its luggage-carrying accessories. However, it must be firmly understood that one's objective is not to load our bags with as much as they can carry.

Far from it! To purchase a lightweight bicycle and then load it down with gear and equipment destroys the advantage that one paid extra to obtain. Every extra pound that is added is a pound that must be carried up every hill and mountain that is crossed. And while with very low gearing it is possible to surmount the grades, a feeling of "freedom and ease" that is the birthright of the lightweight —that elusive factor termed "life" or "performance"—can be lost. One wants to enjoy the countryside and its challenges. Exercise, yes, this is something to be enjoyed. The thrill of conquering miles, mountains, and weather has to be experienced to be appreciated. But we don't want to make exercise into work or drudgery. To do so takes one's mind away from the enjoyment of one's surroundings.

Just as in hiking and camping, the experienced enthusiast is distinguished by the lightness of his equipment—by the items that through experience he has been able to cull out. We all smile at the tenderfoot boy scout who carried on his first overnight hike a pack that is almost as big and heavy as he is. And we admire the experienced hiker who carries very little, yet somehow he always seems to be comfortable, despite the weather and the difficulty of the terrain.

And so it is with cycle touring. The tourist of whom we speak will be at ease on the road, yet able to handle himself and be comfortable in heat, cold, and storm. Yet, at the end of the day, he becomes a presentable gentleman (or she an attractive lady), correct in dress and manner for wherever they may be.

Now it may be possible to send things ahead, to be picked up at the post-office general-delivery window, and to send items home on the way, but in these days of drip-dry and wash-and-wear clothing, even this can be eliminated. Of course, when you leave space in your bags, it gives you the space to pick up trinkets, a snack, or a souvenir of an extra-memorable event. These can be dispatched at the first available post office, and upon your return, you will find a "Christmas" awaiting you. You excitedly renew pleasant memories as you open the packages.

Likewise, don't be afraid to ship back the extra items you originally packed, as experience indicates they are unneeded.

On the huff 'n' puff tour through France in 1966, one of the participants was famed author and illustrator Jacques Faisant. At every town he was sought out, television cameras following him on several occasions. Yet Jacques, an experienced cycle tourist, had for luggage only a handlebar bag, and a packet of rain gear on his tiny rear carrier.

Dressed in cycling shorts and jersey during the daytime ride, after a shower at day's end he appeared in proper but informal sports attire for the enjoyable evenings. Other members of the tour carried light but crease-resistant jacket, tie, and trousers. A drip-dry polyester shirt made the "evening dress" complete.

I've been somewhat appalled at the list of suggested equipment for a bicycle trip contained in the official manual of a well-known organization which sponsors bicycle tours for American youth in the United States and in foreign countries. And having met members of these tours on the road it was obvious that full enjoyment of the trip was being hampered by the excess load being carried. It appears that there is a dearth of information available on the subject in American cycling literature.

The list of items needed on tour depends on several factors, and one must use judgment. However, the adage "If in doubt, leave it out" has much to recommend it. When planning, consider the following:

1. Are you going entirely alone or with others? If with a group, only one set of tools, sewing kit, first-aid items, utensils, spare parts, and a minimum of spare tubes and tire repair items are needed. A distribution of these between the members can be made. In a family, it is even possible to share personal items at further saving in weight.

2. Will you be off the beaten track—away from repair shops that carry needed supplies? Are stores available to buy personal items as needed, or must these be carried?

3. What variation in weather may be anticipated? If rain is unlikely and of short duration, it may be possible to dispense with rain gear. If you are planning to go from warm lowlands to cold highlands, you may wish to send warm clothing to an intermediate point, rather than to carry it all the way. And if your schedule permits, you may elect to wait out a storm or cold morning. This is for you to decide.

4. What dress will be required when not cycling? Will you be visiting churches, museums, or attending evening functions where shorts or slacks are not permitted or are inappropriate? As one tourist put it colorfully, "On the road I am a cyclist. But when I am not riding, I don't want my viewers to feel or detect by nose that I am still a cyclist." One wants to enjoy all the good things that a day's destination affords. But as previously mentioned this can be done with a very minimum of weight. On the other hand, when in vacation country, or when hosteling in

more sparsely populated areas, sports clothing may be perfectly appropriate even in the evening.

5. What accommodations will you use? If hosteling, you will require a sheet sleeping sack (in nylon, weight six ounces). You will need a small towel, soap, and may wish to carry food to cook for supper and breakfast, obtained just before you arrive. Or you may wish to camp along the way. But if you plan to use hotels or motels, the equipment needed is minimized.

Personal taste and choice are always to be considered. But it is hoped that these observations will help you learn the fun of cycle touring.

HE LEADETH BEST
WHO LEADETH NOT

DAN HENRY
April 1968

If you are new to the fraternity of group cycling, you may wonder why all this commotion concerning the leading of a cycling group cross-country. You might think or say, "Assign a leader with knowledge of the route and get on with it." It is not quite that simple you will come to learn.

Yes, you can get on with it simply, if the group is small. Even then, at best, you will fall far short of the degree of success that is potential in the occasion. If the group is large, numbering in the hundreds for instance, hopeless chaos can be your lot. Such chaotic experiences fathered the development of this method of leading cycling groups, completely unlike any other group afield.

Happy days of cross-country cycling with a group come not so much from the dedicated shepherd-type leader than from the tour leader who has done his work well beforehand.

By going over the route days or weeks prior to the event, and properly marking each turn, the participants are then completely free to enjoy the day at their own pace

The complete outfit consists of traffic paint in the feeding bottle and a one-inch brush in a spring clip between the chain stays. It is of the utmost importance to be able to remove and replace both the bottle and the brush with one hand.

A set of route markers can be put down in a fraction of a minute without even parking the bike. Road marking must be a one-hand operation.

VICTOR HIRSHFIELD

in small conversational groups. They need not maintain visual contact with the others. In fact broad separation is desirable. It adds considerably to safety, the smooth flow of other traffic, a greater feeling of adventure, and the system works equally well with a few or thousands. After marking, the route is always ready and available to be repeated again and again.

On the day of the tour, even the leader can enjoy a carefree day of cycling and mingle among all participants whether they be at the lead, somewhere in the middle, or dragging many miles behind.

The method employed in marking the route is shown in the photographs on page 253. A cyclist with a brush and feeding bottle filled with yellow traffic paint can mark a route that is easily followed.

The marks are painted upon that portion of the road surface where the cyclist normally rides. It is customary for cyclists to observe the road surface a short distance ahead. It is unlikely that one would miss directions placed in the normal line of vision.

The technique of placing the paint in a feeding bottle and using a small brush was arrived at through trial and failure of many other procedures. Also many different symbols were tried and discarded. A solid circle with arrow attached found broad favor and was adopted as standard. The use of two identical symbols together, in all cases, causes the mark to be distinctive and unmistakable. Marks and symbols painted on the road surface by utility companies cause no confusion.

The marks stand out sharply when done in yellow traffic paint, available at all paint stores. The symbol is easy to paint freehand and gives remarkable economy of paint. One feeding bottle is usually adequate for a full day's touring or approximately one hundred marks.

Usually one or more pair of marks are placed at the assembly point indicating the direction of the start and as an example of what the marks look like. Once the riders are established on their way it becomes a simple matter to follow as directed.

When traveling across a right-angled intersection, one set of markers is usually adequate. If you are on the major of two roads that cross, perhaps no mark at all would be necessary. Place marks at every point requiring a decision or to clarify intersections that are doubtful.

When traveling down an important highway and you wish the group to turn off onto a path or quiet obscure roadway, then commence with a set of marks about two hundred feet prior to the turn, a second set about one hundred feet in advance of the turn, and a third and final set right at the turn. This will give more than adequate warning of an impending turn likely to be missed. Turnoffs during high-speed descents require still greater advance warning, uphill turnoffs considerably less emphasis.

In addition to guiding one over the course, you can point out things that will be of interest to the group. Swim, stop, picnic, water, view, etc., are examples.

To alert the group of these things, a brief message between a set of standard marks is printed (no arrows in this case). For this printing I use a plastic mustard or ketchup squeeze bottle with pointed cap filled with the yellow paint. One or two such messages would be a prudent maximum on a day tour. It is best to keep our system as inconspicuous to other road users as possible. Motorists usually traverse the entire marked route and don't become aware of our marks. Such is the nature of the motorists' attention. I can conceive of but a few persons objecting to our plain marks. Printing might obviously be objectionable to many.

It is also desirable to have an instruction sheet and perhaps a marked road map for each participant. However, these sheets and maps are not essential and are merely supplementary to marking the route. The marks do much more for a greater number.

So many times have I heard, "I misread the instruction sheet" or "I didn't have time to read it" or "I forgot some of the instructions," etc. Even a detailed map is of little value in the pocket as one rolls merrily along. The marks seldom fail to get everyone to destination in a happy frame of mind.

I would recommend that route marking be done alone, or at most, with one other cyclist. Do it quickly to attract a minimum of attention. It is possible to put down a set of marks without parking the bike. I stop at the appropriate spot, dismount, and hold the bike in my left hand as shown in the photograph. With the other hand, I then remove the feeding bottle from its holder and squeeze two dabs of paint about the size of a silver dollar onto the road surface. I replace the feeding bottle and next grab the brush from its spring clip on the bridge between the chain stays. Spread the paint as required, replace the brush in the spring clip, and ride away. Set it up for a one-hand operation. With one hand be able to withdraw and insert the brush into its clip holder.

Only once in thousands of miles of road marking in fifteen years, have I had a confrontation with police. This occurred in the exclusive Hampton section of Long Island. On this occasion I was merely directed to discontinue my activity, which I did. I left the local village area and completed that portion of the tour in open country. I returned late in the day to complete the few missing links in town —without incident. The marking was then complete and the following Sunday, via the A.Y.H. Bike Train, seven hundred happy cyclists traversed the course without incident.

1. Do not use a stencil with brush or spray can. (I am sure this thought entered your mind.) After a dozen applications, the stencil becomes so messy that you are sure to become disenchanted with the whole operation. A spray can nozzle is destined to clog sooner or later and will interrupt the project. In addition, spray can paints are so weak and thin that they will not endure road traffic and inclement weather. Traffic paint will last a number of years on lightly traveled roads and a full season on a road with substantial traffic. Use regular traffic paint, not the type containing reflective crystals, which is difficult to brush and gets pesky for a number of reasons.

2. Where the road surface is dirt or gravel, place marks on adjacent poles, trees, fences, rocks, etc. You might have to move to a desired location a rock or other medium upon which to paint, in unusual circumstances.

3. Sometimes if a route is marked one weekend for use the following weekend, you might find portions of the roadway resurfaced and your marks covered over.

4. Local residents, not knowing the meaning and pur-

pose of the marks, may spray them over with black paint or otherwise obliterate them.

5. The possibility of a standing automobile or parked vehicle obscuring or hiding your marks must be considered and perhaps additional marks painted where such exposures might reasonably be expected to occur.

6. Be sure of your course before painting. The marks cannot be erased. The occasional error is corrected by painting a larger circle, thereby covering over the arrow, then doing it correctly.

Points 3, 4, and 5 each occurred but once in fifteen years. I mention them so that you may be alert to the character of experiences to expect, some serious and others quite laughable. In the main, the painted route is the mark of success.

The job is best done by bicycle. It can be done by auto, or even a motorcycle, but this proves to be awkward under some circumstances. When I have done the job by car, I ran into situations that attracted undue attention, and problems of one sort or another. By bicycle it goes as smooth as silk.

HOW DRY I AM

DEUX ROUES
April 1968

Rain protection is a broad subject involving dynamics, equipment, and accessories, as well as clothing. To the uninitiated rider, wet-weather riding may seem an impossible problem. Yet, with a little thought and preparation the cyclist can keep himself adequately dry while at the same time protecting his machine from undue exposure.

On the one hand, we have the purist. Come storm or slush, mud or mush, he slogs through, fearlessly assuring everyone as he collects a stream of grit up his back, onto his legs, chain, and head bearings, that this is the life! And indeed, once one has become completely soaked in a warm summer shower, taking a bath at fifteen to twenty miles per hour can be a unique experience.

But when the weather turns colder, and the wind is sharper, or the roads more dirty, the experience of being tarred and feathered while simultaneously being leached of what bodily warmth still remains, can be less than pleasant—if not downright unhealthful.

Protection equipment then becomes a wise investment—and includes protection for the bike, from the bike, for the rider, and from windborne rain, or from passing traffic.

Mudguards come in endless variety. The racing mudguard, only a few inches long front and rear, may reduce only slightly the impact of rain and grit on face and back of legs. The utility of these is sometimes expanded—without extra air resistance in dry weather—by insertion of a strip of steel venetian blind slat in their rolled edges. The slat is rolled up, like a steel pocket measuring tape, when not in use.

Mudguards vary in width, popular sizes being 43, 50, 55, and 60 millimeters, and in materials—celluloid, plastic, steel, stainless steel, and smooth, ribbed or hammered aluminum. Width of guard depends somewhat on the tire size to be accommodated. Weight and air resistance are lessened by narrow width and shorter lengths, but so is the protection offered.

In a light rain, almost any guard will provide protection, but as the streets become running with water near the curb or in one's path, the wider guard is worth its weight in dry clothes!

We will not at the moment attempt to compare the merits of plastic versus metal guards. My personal choice is for the light metal guard, which is rigid enough to support a carrier and a front and rear lamp, while also providing a ground path for the return current and concealing the lead wire to the lamp neatly in its rolled edge.

As streets become wetter, front-wheel spatter becomes an increasing problem. A clip-on fender flap can be carried, and slipped onto the lower section of the guard when the rain starts, and removed again in dry when not needed.

Pointed tread tires, with a heart-shaped cross section and a single central rib on the tread, are becoming more

Touring machine with Kleenfeet front and rear, front fender flap, and plastic saddle cover.

difficult to obtain. While not giving as sure a grip while cornering, they pick up and throw less water and make less spatter, and are also excellent in dry weather. Multiple ribs and other tread patterns transport the water, which with increasing speed is discharged by centrifugal force. This water splashes beyond the guard, particularly the narrow ones, and is pumped to the front, where it falls out and down, is picked up by the wind and carried as a stream or spray over the rider's legs. This can be a wind-borne stream at front or a solid stream pumped onto the back of his legs in the rear.

Side winds accentuate this condition. An excellent solution is the carrying of a couple of elastic-looped Kleenfeet attachments (see figure) which are very lightweight. These can be quickly slipped on in heavy weather and folded to a small handful when not in use.

A plastic saddle cover is helpful to keep the saddle dry, both when riding and when parked in the rain.

If the bicycle is unprotected by cape or cover, water can work its way into the seat tube at the seat pillar, into the head bearings at the handlebar stem. It can run into the bottom bracket bearings if brake or derailleur cables are run through the tubes, as is "featured" on some equipment. A silicone rubber sealant, which stays flexible, can be used to seal these spots.

Wheel bearings, pedal bearings, and bottom bracket bearings are especially vulnerable to wet weather and waterborne grit when splashed on these parts. It is simple to fashion a seal from oiled felt, cloth tape "o" rings, or other material. When so equipped, I've ridden through flooded sections of shin-deep water for short stretches without getting the bearings (except of the derailleur and freewheel) wet or dirty.

Riding clothing is a separate subject. A rain suit protects the rider, but not his bicycle or his gear. A cape protects both, but is vulnerable to flapping and loss of protection at speed or in the wind. And, while excellent with upright bars, when used with dropped bars, aerodynamic forces tend to lift the rear section. A looped string attached to the rear of the cape and fastened about the waist will counteract lifting and flapping. Southwester hats and even integral hoods of capes lift at the rear from aerodynamic forces, and block vision in front!

THE "TWICER"

FRED DE LONG
March 1968

For sheer cycling enjoyment, there is little that can beat the fun of riding tandem with a "clicking" teammate. The fun of shared effort toward a common goal, of thrilling downhill swoops as the locomotive "takes off" with demon-like fury, must be experienced to be understood. But the tandem has characteristics of its own that for both safety and pleasure must be learned. Some of these will be discussed in a future article.

One of the tandeming's advantages is its ability to "level off" riders of differing ability. One's partner cannot get lost or separated in traffic, or on a hill. The "stoker," if she has faith in her "captain," can enjoy the countryside without being concerned with balance, steering, shifting of gears, or maintaining proper spacing. Indeed, the tandem is an ideal method of teaching an inexperienced rider. The instructor can show and feel the correctness of the response, repeating each step until perfection is obtained, since the pedal action of the rear rider can be felt by the front rider through the chain.

One of the most rewarding uses of the tandem is to ride with a blind partner. He can take part in full measure, for he is not obviously afflicted—to others, no cane, no Seeing Eye dog. He can feel the breeze, hear the conversations, and actually experience his surroundings with an acuity which is a revelation to his captain.

Within the limits of space available, we can only touch lightly on the many requirements and variations in design that affect performance and cost and usefulness. Some personal prejudices will be stated, yet successful performance will be attested to by others from other equipment.

It must be remembered from the start that the "twicer" has double the responsibility and stress, yet on virtually the same frame components, and on the two wheels as compared to the single. Stress from steering, balancing, and pedaling pressure is much more severe. But stress on wheels, tires, and forks is far worse, since it is not possible to "jump" the tandem over an obstruction or pot hole, nor to cushion the blow as effectively as with a single by letting the bicycle "rock" beneath you. Thus, except for smooth roads at moderate speeds, a larger section tire is advisable. However, this does not indicate a heavy, hard-rolling tire.

Lightweight natural rubber casings with low rolling resistance are as important for performance as for safety, particularly on the rear wheel which is subject to extra-hard impact. It is easy to "bottom" a tire and break fabric and dent the rim.

For slow riding on boardwalks or level ground, and for relatively short distances, frame design and riding position may not be a critical requirement. But, for touring, and for racing, the design and construction of frame and components is of great importance. A tandem·takes off like a rocket downhill, yet must be stopped by brakes acting on the only two wheels, as with a single. Brake stresses and the forces produced by the brakes on the frame and fork mountings are proportionately greater. Brake heating effect also doubles, resulting in rapid over-heating and sometimes fading.

On the uphill stretches, the additional length of the tandem frame results in much greater distortion, further abetted by the doubling of the driving effort placed upon it. Thus, frame design to produce rigidity—without at the same time increasing impact forces on the rear rider and rear wheel—deserves considerable attention. Wide-range gearing is a must; the range of gearing required is greater, and the amount of gear shifting that will be done is likewise increased over that of a single in the same terrain.

Costs of tandems vary over a wide range, from about one hundred dollars for a domestic machine to over four times that for a hand-built touring machine or three times for a racing machine. Remember, the helmsman must not only act for but also counteract the movements of the unseen rider behind.

One point in conclusion. The top-tube and seat-post lengths of the tandem frame must permit accommodation of both riders without cramping or interference. A short frame with long rear handlebar requirement causes either cramping of the rear rider or interference with the front rider's legs. Consider this matter carefully.

TANDEMING TECHNIQUES

FRED DE LONG
June 1968

Tandem riding has loads of advantages. A stronger rider does not become separated from his partner in traffic or on hills, or due to a difference in riding pace. The more experienced rider can take full responsibility for steering, control, and shifting of gears. This makes cycling more pleasant and safer. The additional advantage of being able to carry on a pleasant conversation without concern over running into each other or with the words carried away by the wind aids sociability.

Tandeming is an ideal way for an experienced rider to instruct his partner in pedaling technique, timing of gear shifting, handling of the bike. The value of the instruction is constantly measured by improvement in response and teamwork obtained with the result that proficiency will grow. And a pouch behind the rear seat permits the "crew" to carry tidbits which she feeds to friend steersman as thanks for his efforts in making her ride carefree.

A few comments may be of assistance to those of our readers who are just starting to ride a "twicer." It may permit you to get full enjoyment sooner and with safety.

The tandem has riding characteristics that are somewhat different from those of the single. When getting on a single immediately after riding a tandem, there is a tendency to overcontrol and wobble for a while until the feel of the single is regained. Likewise, in reverse, there is greater demand on the steersman of the tandem and this must be taken into account, even if unconsciously. At both high and low speeds, on hills or on sharp turns, special cautions must be learned. The steersman must think and react—and counterreact—for two persons. Even with fixed rear bars, the rear rider can steer the tandem in a direction which the captain may not have contemplated. If a pothole is in this direction, the result can be interesting at the least, and if at the edge of the road with depressed shoulder . . . !

On the other hand, the steadiness and greater smoothness of the tandem ride with a "clicking" partner can produce a really delightful ride. I've known my long-suffering crew, with handlebars two inches wider in the rear, to rub knuckles in traffic when there seemed to be ample clearance in front. And on long steep descents, the longer wheelbase, having greater weight with less air resistance, permits the attainment of speeds with confidence that would be hair-raising on a single.

Tandeming requires teamwork, and faith of the crew in the captain. Nervousness of the rear rider at high speeds can result in a tremor being set up which can set the whole machine to wobbling, and if the captain does not maintain a constant good grip on the bars, it can cause him to lose control. On soft surfaces or gravel, it may be impossible to regain control. Any shifting of weight, lean-

ing, or turning around of the rear rider without warning
can disturb the equilibrium. I have actually twisted a handlebar stem out of shape to maintain balance when a
heavy rider shifted his weight unexpectedly. It is for this
reason that I personally favor a continuous top tube, to
reduce the loss in torsional rigidity suffered in a lady back
frame. When supporting an overhanging cantilevered load
such as the rider's body, frame twist is readily visible on
the open back type.

On the other hand, on many occasions, my favorite crew
has dismounted at a stop or traffic light to get something
from the rear carrier, unbeknownst to me. Upon starting
up, a scream from many yards behind, "Come back for
me," is the only evidence that anything is amiss! Teamwork in pedaling style makes the tandem seem a single!
A good crew provides a fair share of power and no unbalance.

Similarity of pedaling style is of utmost importance.
Nothing is of greater distress than a "plunger" who is
mated with a "twiddler." In midstroke the twiddler finds
that his pedal has suddenly disappeared from under his
foot, only to have it crash back into his foot near bottom
and top centers. If the twiddler is the steersman, the lunge
at each stroke throws the bike off-balance. It must be corrected for by a pull on the bars, and sore arms and
shoulders are added to tired legs. If the twiddler is the
stronger, he can maintain his pedal speed, forcing the
plunger's feet to twirl at a pace that he does not know
how to handle. Feet will fly off the pedals, or the plunger's
stiff legs will lift his entire body up and down, making it
feel like the entire rear of the machine is about to bounce
into midair. There are some riders who are so individualistic in their style, and so adamant on maintaining it, that
unless they can locate a similar partner, tandeming must
be discarded. Two singles may be a much wiser choice.

Short radius turns at slow speed, particularly in soft
material and with a heavy rider, must be carefully made.
The steersman must be able to remove his foot quickly
on the inside, thrusting it out for support in case the wheel
slips sideward, or the rear rider leans. It is possible in
these instances for the entire machine to flip, crashing
heavily, unless the steersman stops it by strong pressure

on the bars and aided by the outstretched foot. It is recommended that a new steersman practice slow, sharp turns with a weight attached to the carrier a few times before he carries a passenger.

Once teamwork in riding has been learned, tandeming becomes great fun. It can be likened to partners on a dance floor. It is no fun to dance with a partner who has two left feet, but two "teaming" partners can enjoy the sport to its utmost.

HANDLEBARS AND RIDING POSITION

FRED DE LONG
April 1966

Our discussion in the November 1965 issue of *American Cycling* mentioned the advantages of the dropped pattern handlebar, and described a proven method of obtaining *your* most comfortable and effective position on *your* bicycle. Some of the items affecting the rider's position on his bicycle deserve further discussion.

A bicycle is a mechanical aid to allow an individual to convert muscular energy into motion. Unless its rider is so disposed that his muscular team is most effectively utilized, premature fatigue, discomfort, or loss of performance will result.

There seem to be a lot of old wives' tales concerning riding position. A common misconception, diametrically opposed to the truth, is the statement that dropped bars lead to rounded shoulders. Actually, the more effective use of arm and back muscles strengthens the muscles that hold the shoulders erect.

The newcomer expects that a narrow, springless saddle will be uncomfortable. But the dropped-bar position reduces body weight placed on the saddle, and the reduced shock and impact permit the use of a smaller saddle, which gives less thigh friction and increased comfort.

A third misconception is that the dropped pattern bar

is fine for the male of the species, but the fair sex should be fitted with an upright riding position. Yet, the generally lesser strength, more delicate build, and wider hip bone spacing of the feminine cyclist make the advantages of reduced impact, less effort, and better muscular teamwork of even greater importance. And certainly, a slight figure in streamlined position, traveling effortlessly, is more attractive than the vertical, arm-spread stance of the bulldozer operator, which is typical of most ladies' model bicycles on the market today.

Medical doctors are more explicit. They tell us that at the small of the back, the spine curves backward and the disks and vertebrae are pinched together at the rear. Upper body weight tends to further compress this region, excess weight accentuates the condition, and road impact compounds the problem. On the front of the spine, the ligaments that hold the spine from collapsing become strained.

When leaning forward, however, the back relaxes and extends and the vertebrae separate, relieving the pinching, permitting absorption of impact without damage. If you will have someone measure with a tape, you will find that your spine will actually lengthen as much as two inches when you bend forward from the erect to the dropped-bar position.

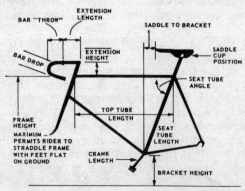

Measurements important to riding position.

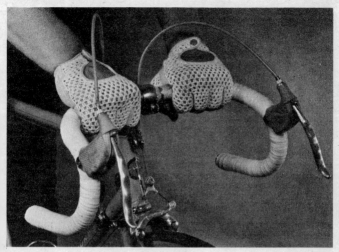

Position #1

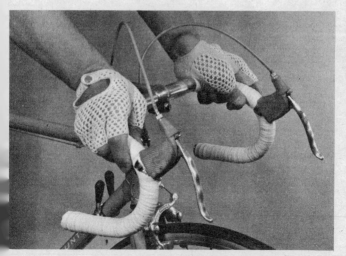

Position #2

Position #3

Position #4

Further, they tell us, this position is better for breathing. It is the instinctive position taken by an asthmatic, who, when breathing is difficult, leans over in his chair supporting his body weight on his arms, as we do on the handlebars of our bicycle. The suspended chest expands more easily, easing breathing.

Position #5

Because of these facts, the physicians of the Société d'Etudes Médicales du Cyclisme of Paris, France, corroborated by their colleagues the world over, tell us that the forward leaning position is definitely more healthful than the upright position.

When one sleeps, he turns from one position to another, throughout the night. Being forced to remain in one spot is not restful. As the modern dropped bar produces a multitude of positions for the hands, arms, wrists, and body, it reduces fatigue and monotony, and allows the best use of the muscle team for each riding condition. (See photos on pages 267, 268, and 269.)

Bicycles vary greatly in form and dimension. Handlebars vary greatly in reach and throw, frame angles and top tube lengths cover a wide range. To obtain one's position when buying a new bicycle, the dimensions shown in the sketch should be compared with those on the trusty old mount. Quite often considerable changes in saddle clip location or handlebar extension will be required.

Study your position as you ride. Note where your hands seem to "want to be" under different riding conditions. Then change your extension to suit. You will be rewarded by more pleasurable cycling.

SCIENTIFIC SETTING
OF SADDLE POSITION

VAUGHAN THOMAS
June 1967

This article, written exclusively for our readers, deserves careful attention, rereading, and filing for future reference.

I have followed the author's instructions in altering saddle heights that seemed correct to me for years on many tours. In a very short time those bikes that were not yet altered then felt amiss. The recommendations below appear applicable for both racing and touring cyclists.

Vaughan Thomas is presently doing research for his doctorate at Loughborough University, England. He was National Cyclo-Cross Champion in 1955, played Olympic basketball in 1960 and 1964, was English National Champion and International Racewalker in 1963, has coached six sports ranging from volleyball to mountaineering, and is widely known for his writings on preparation of cyclists and athletes for competition, tactical coaching, and sports physiology.

—FRED DE LONG

The Department of Ergonomics and Cybernetics of Loughborough University, England, is concerned with an overall examination into the factors affecting human performance on the bicycle. This research embraces physiological, psychological, mechanical, kinetic, and other factors. Our work is furthered by the willing cooperation of many British racing cyclists—a two-way benefit—who, by acting as experimental subjects, allow experimentation to extend to the limits of both human and machine performance. It is our hope to eventually build an analogue of cycling performance, in order that a computer may be programmed to give complete insight into all the parameters of cycling.

The most critical factor of cycling is, of course, the leg action. This may be considered as a coordination of many factors:

a. Toe-clip length.
b. Degree of ankling.
c. Crank length.
d. Pedal path.
e. Degree and position of knee flexion.
f. Amount of limb movement.
g. Saddle position (horizontal or angle).
h. Saddle composition (flexibility).
i. Pedaling rate.

These are all interrelated to varying degrees of complexity, and we decided that it would be better, at first, to standardize the mechanical variables (a, c, d, g, and h), and to combine the overall effect into one parameter—saddle height. One of the principle problems of this type of experiment is that of standardizing or eliminating variables which will affect the item being measured. There were the problems of fatigue, position, warm-up, learning, motivation, etc., in addition to those already mentioned. Consequently, the experiment design became one of a short duration, maximal power test, with all variables, except the saddle height, standardized or accounted for in the statistical analysis.

A Mueller bicycle ergometer was adapted with racing equipment, all dimensions being standardized except saddle height. A harness was designed which (1) ensured that the cyclist sat on the saddle in a position which put his axis of hip rotation as near as possible to the saddle pillar, and (2) prevented him moving from this position.

The equipment was: Christophe long toe clips, 6 ¾″ cranks, circular pedal path, Unica plastic saddle.

A heavy work load was set (500 kg/m) and the subject timed in performing this work load at four different saddle heights. One hundred subjects, ranging from beginners to world champion Tommy Simpson, thus gave four hundred readings which were subjected to statistical analysis.

The saddle heights were respectively 105, 109, 113,

and 117 percent of inside leg, the measurements being obtained (1) of saddle height from pedal spindle to top of saddle, along the line of the seat tube, and (2) of inside leg from floor to the bone in the crotch, known as pubic symphasis palpation, subject standing without shoes.

The experiment showed very conclusively (significance level of better than 0.1 percent) that for a short duration task of power output on a bicycle:

1. Alterations in saddle height of 4 percent of inside leg measurement affected power output by approximately 5 percent.

2. The most efficient saddle height is 109 percent of inside leg measurement.

These values were average figures, and there will be variation between cyclists due to individual build and idiosyncrasies. However, recent studies have shown that the better the rider (in terms of his racing ability), the nearer does he tend to have his saddle to this recommended height (rho = 0.665). Large variations tend to be compensated by alterations in the degree and even the direction of ankling.

Having obtained these results, of what use are they? The experiment was highly specific—to racing cyclists, to ergometer performance, to short-duration power output. We are wary of reading too much general application into specific facts, but in the absence of other information we can look for leads and possibilities in what facts we have. Firstly, for short-duration events such as sprints and pursuit the formula height is the one most likely to enhance power output. We believe that this likelihood will also extend to longer events, the only valid factor against this extension of application being one of comfort. However, comfort is more a case of what the rider becomes accustomed to. The skill of pedaling a bicycle is learned by very many repetitions of a very similar movement, and the most skillful cyclists usually take great care in maintaining their saddle height at the level to which they have accustomed themselves. Any alteration of this height will tend to lead to discomfort, which will become more manifest as the duration of effort is extended. The beginner cyclist will not experience this problem of alteration discomfort if he sets his saddle initially at his most efficient height. The experienced cyclist will need to make any changes in small amounts and at long intervals. For instance, the average cyclist could make up the distance between his present saddle height and the formula height by four or five adjustments of one-quarter inch at monthly intervals.

Secondly, this formula height was determined after standardizing the other parameters of leg action. Individual riders can make adjustments to the formula height by considering their own peculiarities—short feet on long legs, placing of shoe plates, position of saddle clip, "give" in saddle material, etc. We are not yet in a position to derive a formula to embrace all these details, though we are at present working on electro-myographic strabophatic assessments of leg and ankle action.

Most researchers like to discover not only "what" but also "why." Our opinions at the moment on the "why" may be summarized:

1. Changing saddle height results in alterations of the amount of angular movement made by the thigh. We have no precise figures for this as yet, but it seems that the following graph approximates to the situation.

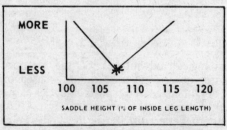

Angular displacement of thigh pedalling.

2. Muscles in particular movements have optimum strength ranges. These ranges are highly specific to the activity, and it is probable that the leg is capable of exerting more power when it approaches the fully extended position. On the other hand, fluidity of movement is also

important. The cyclist is concerned with converting angular oscillation of the thigh to almost linear reciprocation of the lower leg, and then into an elliptical path of the ankle joint and circular motion of the toes. Any complete straightening of the knee proves a disruptive factor. The formula height seems to provide the optimum conditions for both power output.

The results of this research have aroused fierce controversy in Britain. After the initial skepticism had died down, the position is now emerging as one of strong support from the ranks of international cyclists, divided opinions from the coaches, and a variety of informed support from the scientists in the field. This position is a favorable one in which to pursue our research. We hope that readers of *Bicycling!* will voice their opinions to the editors of the magazine or directly to the author. We, in our turn, hope to keep our American colleagues informed of any progress we make in this field.

PROPER FITTING OF THE MODERN DROP HANDLEBAR

FRED DE LONG
November 1965

The physiological advantages of the dropped pattern handlebar for general purpose riding as used on the majority of derailleur-geared sports bicycles are generally recognized.

This pattern better distributes the body weight, reducing road shock and providing better stability and steering characteristics and greater comfort. The bent-forward back is more relaxed; with the weight of the chest suspended, breathing is easier. The overhung body weight becomes available to propel the bicycle, and as a result, hill climbing is made easier. And even on the level the more streamlined body position reduces the wind resistance, again making riding easier, particularly against head winds.

The modern square-shaped handlebar provides four to five positions for the hands, providing a pleasant change in the points of pressure and angle of the hands, the wrists, and the back. The ability to alter position eliminates monotony, reduces fatigue, and refreshes the rider.

To obtain these advantages, however, it is necessary to fit our position carefully. If the arms are not properly placed, wrist-ache and a stretched or cramped position that is uncomfortable will result. Brake levers must be placed so that the brakes can be operated from either the top or the bottom positions.

In thirty years' experience with the dropped pattern bar, I've been acquainted with hundreds of riders, both male and female, who have changed from the upright riding position to the forward-leaning position. And when proper fitting techniques were applied, I can remember no one who was not enthusiastic. Ladies, being less strong, were particularly appreciative of the improved comfort and riding ease. Even blind riders, seated on the backs of tandems, prefer the dropped bar. Being unable to see approaching bumps, the reduced impact from road shock and the greater comfort are of particular value.

Every individual is a separate combination of leg length, body length, and arm length. For individuals of the same height, the proportions of each can vary greatly. Compare the sketch on top of page 276.

Let us place our three subjects, all of equal height, on bicycles. Clearly, since frame height is dependent on leg length, the higher-hipped person will need the taller frame.

Now let us have our riders lean their backs forward at the recommended forty-five-degree-angle position, arms extended naturally. Compare the position of the hands and you will note that it varies by several inches. It can be seen that handlebar height and forward extension length depend on the individual's proportions, the top-tube length, and the position of the grips in comparison to the point of attachment of the handlebars to its extension.

If the frame is too small, it may not be possible to raise the handlebar stem sufficiently to attain the correct height. A stem with greater vertical height adjustment than standard may have to be fitted.

Three riders of the same height, but with varying leg, arm, body, and neck measurements.

Is this important? By all means! Only a quarter-inch difference from your best position can reduce comfort and increase fatigue and prevent the most effective use of the arm pull in hill climbing.

Place the saddle in the middle of its adjustment fore and aft, set the top level, and then raise the saddle until your leg is just straight, with the heel on the pedal at its lowest point.

Place the handlebar, with its top at a height level with the saddle top. Now seat yourself on the bicycle, have a friend hold it steady for you, and settle into your normal riding position. Without changing your position, remove one hand from the bar, and allow it to hang in a natural, slightly bent manner, from your side. Rotate the free arm carefully, without stretching toward the bar. When it approaches the position of the opposite hand, note where the palm lies in comparison to the grips of the bar. This will show whether the grip should be moved forward or back, up or down.

Adjustments to obtain the correct position can be accomplished in two ways. The handlebar extension can be changed, or the saddle moved back or forth on its clip.

Placed on bicycles, with their backs at 45°, note the wide disparity in handlebar extension length required (E). Position of the saddle has been kept constant.

While adjustment for varying arm and body length can be obtained by positioning the saddle clip back or forth on the saddle wires, this is a second choice method and can lead to an ineffective body location with respect to the pedals.

Generally speaking, the more "explosively" the rider uses his energy, the farther forward is his saddle position. The short-distance sprinter on the track uses a steep seat-tube angle, with the saddle placed well forward. The sports or racing models often use a steeper tube angle to make this possible.

The average rider, however (particularly the older rider), is better suited by a more rearward position—with the saddle nose 1¾" to 2½" behind a vertical line through the crank hanger, depending on the rider's height. Therefore, when adjusting the saddle height, the fore and aft location should be simultaneously adjusted. This more rearward position permits better use of the ankles, which in turn makes riding smoother and less tiring.

Once the saddle is set to its proper height and fore and aft location, with its top level, proper "reach" is determined, using the method we described earlier, paying particular attention to proper handlebar height.

The angle at which the handlebar grips are placed is also a factor; only a degree or two of difference can adversely affect fatigue of the rider's wrists. Many cyclists set their grips at an angle of ten degrees, but this final setting must be determined after some miles on the road. A good starting point, however, is to place the lower grips at about ten degrees up from the horizontal. With the modern square bar, this places the upper section almost level—comfortable on all hand locations.

An adjustable handlebar stem with bar fitted is a good investment. This can be temporarily placed on the bicycle and adjusted to the most comfortable and effective position by trial. Then it can be measured, and an extension of proper length and height can be fitted. Satisfaction is assured!

Position of the hand-brake levers may now be set. This is important from both comfort and safety standpoints. It is necessary to be able to operate the levers from both top and bottom positions. Unfortunately, it is all too common to see levers positioned on the bottom grip, in a manner similar to the position used with an upright bar. This not only interferes with proper placement of the hand at the start of the bend on the lower grip, but also makes it impossible to reach the grip from the upper bar hand positions.

Another common error is to place the levers too far up on the bend, making it difficult or impossible to reach the lever for the female rider, or the male rider with shorter fingers.

In the event of an emergency on the road—a swerving car, a dog or pedestrian stepping into a rider's path, a hole or road obstruction—the improperly placed lever may spell the difference between a normal stop or a painful fall and serious injury.

CLEATS AND THEIR POSITIONING

DAVE STAUB
June 1964

Choice of the most durable cleat is the first consideration. There are many types of cleats available today, but the best is a durable, deep-groove, alloy cleat. There is an excellent type made in California that is a refinement of the French Anquetil cleat. The Anquetil cleat itself seems to be very durable.

Nail-on cleats are best, provided long nails are used and the ends are peened inside the shoe. Screw-on cleats are fairly risky, as you could wreck a good shoe by drilling a hole into the wrong place, whereas the nail-on type is movable once it has been put on.

It is not hard to find the correct position of the cleat on the shoe, but when one is doing it for the first time, "professional" help should be sought.

First, ride a few miles without the cleats. The pedal will make a mark on the bottom of the shoe at the approximate location of the groove of the cleat. The ball of the foot should be directly above the center of the pedal. If, when the cleat is put on, the toes point in or out, relocate the cleats quickly, as it is not good to pedal in an unfamiliar way.

After the cleats are correctly positioned, get toe clips of the proper length. Never position the cleats to the length of the toe clips; the cleats determine the toe-clip length.

A durable cleat in the correct position on the shoe is a great asset to a cyclist. It pays to use care in the selection of the cleat and in the determination of its position.

UNUSUAL MACHINES

F. R. WHITT
January 1969

In a recent visit with Frank Whitt, a practicing engineer in London, England, I was pleased to learn that this loyal subscriber to Bicycling! *was willing to present to our readers material from his long study and research into the mechanical and physiological aspects of cycling. Mr. Whitt is a member of the Southern Veterans C.C. and has restored a number of interesting cycles, tandems, and tricycles which are prize winners in veteran competitions.*

His studies have unearthed many of the fine technical advances which were devised by the best of engineering brains that were applied to the bicycle many years ago, but which have since been lost or forgotten.

The current article tells about the use of manpowered vehicles on land, cross-country, on water, and in the air.

—FRED DE LONG

The widespread development of better roads before the turn of the century made the use of the bicycle practical—and even desirable. The power needed to propel a bicycle over a smooth surface became less than that needed for walking or running at comparable rates on the same surface, and the encumbrance of a machine became justifiable.

Yet, in most of the world, good road systems were a long time in coming. As a consequence, bicycle usage, in general, was under less than optimum conditions. In addition to attempting to solve the problems associated with the use of wheeled vehicles on poor roads, inventors tried to devise bicycles for really "off the road" conditions. Machines for riding on water, on railways, and in the air have been the targets of imaginative men ever since the practical bicycle appeared in the nineteenth century and demonstrated its speed on good roads. It is most probable, however, that the bicycle's high efficiency under good conditions was taken, mistakenly, by many inventors to imply that similar performances could be expected from its use outside its proper environment.

As road building progressed, hard smooth surfaces became more common and the use of the bicycle became more efficient. It is not possible, however, to parallel this achievement with water-surfaced vehicles, since it is impossible to produce "smooth water." And, too, the resistance to movement offered by a relatively dense and viscous medium such as water is great compared with that offered by air. As a consequence, both submerged and floating objects, such as swimmers and man-powered boats, are slow compared with their land counterparts of runners and cyclists. The difference in attainable speeds at maximum human propulsive effort is about fourfold in favor of land-based movements. Water cycles can, on this account, be expected to be slow compared with bicycles running on good road. Inventors, however, have persevered over the years and many water cycles have appeared. Today, the most popular form remains the side-by-side two-seater commonly used in parks and seaside resorts, but this design is more of a recreational gadget than a serious example of water-cycle design, and was long ago abandoned as unpractical by inventors seeking the optimum vehicle. The straight-in-line design proved more efficient.

According to *A Dictionary of Applied Physics,* screw propellers, paddle wheels, and cars can all be designed to give a usage of applied-power efficiency up to about 70 percent. Also, the power absorbed by water friction on the hull of a boat can be represented approximately by this equation:

Horsepower = 0.000024 × wetted surface (in sq. ft.) × speed (knots) to the power of 2.86

Some additions of up to 20 percent have to be made for hull design and wind resistance.

The wetted surface for boats and water cycles designed to carry the same weight will be similar. Hence it can be concluded that no matter how the propulsive power is applied to the water, for a given power input by the oarsmen or pedalers the boats and water cycles should travel at about the same speed.

Some evidence of the validity of this conclusion appears in an account of the performance of water cycles in their heyday of the 1890's. A triplet water cycle ridden by ex-racing cyclist F. Cooper and two others covered 101 miles on the Thames, from Putney to Oxford, in 19 hours, 27 minutes, 50 seconds. A triple-sculls boat rowed by good university oarsmen covered the same course in 22 hours, 28 seconds. Although the water cycle was the faster vehicle, the difference in speed was not great, being only about 18 percent in favor of the pedaled machine.

Other facts about water cycles in this period are interesting. The English Channel was crossed, Dover to Calais, by a tandem water cycle in 7¼ hours, and a sextuplet water cycle ridden by girls on the Seine is credited with reaching a speed of fifteen miles an hour. Said to be ridable at speeds of ten miles an hour, Hydrocycles were manufactured by L. A. Moulton of Michigan. All these performances compare favorably with oar-propelled boats rowed by the best of oarsmen.

In addition to devising water cycles, attempts have been made to develop and popularize bicycle-type machines for running on frozen-water surfaces or on snow. Some types consist of a bicycle with a ski replacing the front wheel. Others dispense with wheels and retain the frame, with two skis attached, one on either side. Unlike the case of the water cycles, there is no published evidence concerning the speediness of these machines compared with skating or skiing. It would appear, however, that riding such machines should require less skill than either of the two traditional winter sports.

The resistance to motion offered by a steel wheel running on a steel rail is very low, much less than that associated with the best of pneumatic-tired wheels running under optimum conditions of road use. As a consequence, cycles developed for running on rails have proved practical in the sense that they were not difficult to propel. In fact, high speeds are credited to this type of machine. A drawback to this type of machine, however, as with the water cycle, is that the rider must have stretches of track available that were suitable to his needs.

The most spectacular of all the dreams and products designed by imaginative inventors is the air cycle. The design and use of this vehicle will probably continue to fire the imagination of men, until, if ever, a workable machine is built. As early as 1400 B.C., attempts have been made to fly, using only human power, by all types of men, both serious and maniacal; the challenge has proved irresistible.

It appears that the design of high-powered airplanes progressed so rapidly that the science of low-powered flight was not, as might be reasonably expected, fully explored. As a consequence, teams and individuals are, even now, engaged in unraveling the great scientific problems associated with flight at low speeds in the hope that a proper basis for the construction of a man-powered machine will be found. The whole process has been greatly accelerated by the promise of a prize of $24,000 for the first flyer to complete a figure eight over a distance of one mile.

The information published so far has appeared mainly as short articles in the daily press. As might be expected, with the generous Kramer competition still open, construction details have been held in confidence.

It appears that, in general, the latest types of machines are quite different (in the cases where opinion suggests that the design will actually fly) from those tried in the early 1900's. The modern designs include an air cycle with an inflatable wing, and two-man-power machines, both novel. The size of the machines, including a much lower lift from the wing surfaces, is greater than in earlier types.

Opinion differs regarding the use of pusher and tractor propeller systems. Some helicopters' designs are still being constructed, but as yet, none has flown. A flapping-wing machine is also existent.

An air cycle developed in Germany in the 1930's flew two hundred yards, according to reports, thus achieving much more than did those performing at the Parc des Princes at the turn of the century. G. H. Stancer, an observer of these early trials in France, wrote that only pathetic results were obtained and short "jumps" were all that were accomplished by the 199 entrants. Efforts in England in recent years have brought much more encouraging results.

A "jump" of 50 feet was made by a machine during its later stages of development at Southampton University in 1961. A week later, a "Puffin Mark 1," developed by the Hatfield Man-Powered Aircraft Club and flown by John Wimpenny, flew 150 feet at 5 feet off the ground. An improved model the next year flew the greatest distance to date—about a half a mile—in two minutes. Neither machine could attempt the turns required by the Kramer Prize conditions. These air cycles have large wingspans of close to ninety feet. The propellers of the successful machines are likewise large, approaching nine feet in length.

Among the other promising designs being developed at this time is that of a group at the University of Belfast, headed by Professor T. Nonweiler. This one, similar to a design from the South-end Airport, is a two-seater. It is believed that so much concentration on controlling is required to execute the turns and other maneuvers specified by the competition that it will be necessary to carry a "partial" passenger solely for this purpose. In addition, the weights of the machines, although light (75 to 175 pounds), are a sizable proportion to that of a man.

From informed opinion, it appears that sky-cycling is not likely to be a cheap sport. The cost of developing a machine with some expectations of its being able to fly is likely to run at $240 per pound weight of machine. This cost is more than that of standard airliners! Cost figures given for some single individual efforts, as distinct from products of teams, are, however, much lower. It is likely that any satisfactory machine will be comparatively large, so its storage and use will be limited to an airport. As a consequence there will be extra costs for usage in addition to those of the machine itself.

Although the development of air cycles is probably one of the least utilitarian types of endeavors in the history of bicycle adaptation, it is one of the most technically interesting. The latest upsurge of interest shows that it is a forward-looking part in the line of inventions associated with the bicycle and forms, as yet, an unclosed chapter in the latter's long history.

WHERE ARE WE GOING IN BICYCLE DESIGN?

DAVID GORDON WILSON
PROFESSOR, MASSACHUSETTS INSTITUTE OF TECHNOLOGY,
DEPARTMENT OF MECHANICAL ENGINEERING
April 1968

The bicycle is such a delightful gadget that it may seem sacrilegious to emphasize its shortcomings to its devotees. Yet we have been complacent for too long, and only by a healthy measure of criticism will we be stimulated to bring about some of the changes which must come if we are to propose a reasonable alternative in at least some special circumstances to completely automated transportation systems.

First and foremost the present bicycle is comparatively unsafe and unreliable, and the situation seems to be getting worse rather than better, to judge by the way manufacturers are pushing eye-level handlebars equipped with their multitudinous projections, such as brake levers, all potentially lethal in an accident. One can get unnecessarily injured by open chains and cogs, by spokes and rat-trap pedals, even by simply falling off one's machine. If one has the misfortune to have the bike driven into one's body by another vehicle the effects can be horrible. Obviously we must do something to clean up the present bicycles.

Almost equally unnecessary is the unreliability of some of the most vital components. Several times I have had handlebars break away from the machine, usually through fatigue cracks starting at stress raisers formed by ridiculous decorations. But the brakes are the worst offenders. No brakes I have ever used, even the old internal-expanding hub-brakes, have been really effective in any conditions, and rim brakes are truly appalling in the rain. In an emergency the cables of caliper brakes are very likely to fail without any warning. After hitting an unavoidable pothole the rim may carry a bump which may cause the wheel to lock even when moderately braked. No cyclist likes locked wheels in an emergency. The gears of the derailleur and the hub type are almost equally liable to slip unexpectedly because in general they don't maintain adjustment for more than a few hundred miles, and the result can be anything from a mild wobble to the rider being deposited, as I was recently, in the middle of an intersection.

The other areas in which bicycles should be improved are less important than these, but there is opportunity for a great deal of progress. It would be wonderful to be able to carry something more than a tool roll without greatly affecting the handling characteristics and running the risk of having one's belongings spoiled in the weather. Likewise it would be delightful for the rider himself to be protected from rain, hail, and snow without incurring excessive additional drag. And the aerodynamic drag is already needlessly high.

Lastly, with all these potential improvements, the first cost of bicycles should come down. If they are compared with other manufactured items produced in similar numbers, it is found that they cost two to four times as much per pound, even though they contain much less precision machining, or special finishes as, for instance, the automobile or the sewing machine. This high first cost hurts people in developing countries, where the bicycle is now a vital part of modern life, more than it does us.

Let me now discuss some of the areas that might be explored to overcome some of these drawbacks. The competition in man-powered land transport is not confined to wheeled vehicles, but it's difficult to see how leaping or walking or crawling machines can do better. If we assume that wheels should be used, how many are best? There are enormous advantages in two: the narrow width of the vehicle enables it to go places (and avoid situations) that would otherwise be impossible; a two-wheeled vehicle does not overturn at a corner; and the loads on the wheels are always in the plane of the wheel, never transverse to it. The advantages that three or four wheels bestow in obviating the need for balancing at slow speeds and in giving greater safety in the event of skids are obtained at the expense of the advantages of two wheels mentioned above —a wider vehicle, the possibility of overturning, and the necessity of withstanding side loads on the wheels and structure. In addition, unless the track width is chosen to be similar to that of other vehicles, it would make traveling in rutted roads very difficult. I remember trying to drive my first car, a 1927 three-wheel Morgan, through wet cobbled streets with deeply rutted streetcar tracks, and can recommend this sort of experience only to those wishing to set up a management test for quick decision making. For three wheels the motorcycle-and-sidecar configuration, with two instead of three tracks, has a lot to recommend it.

I think that the choice of number of wheels cannot be made a priori, but will follow from the overall design of the vehicle and from how one weighs such factors as safety and overall drag. One compromise solution which has been tried before is to run on two wheels but to have auxiliary skids which come down automatically, or on a lever being pulled, whenever balance is about to be lost.

This question of stability and balance greatly influences the range of permissible positions which may be taken by the rider. The present half-sitting, half-standing attitude is obviously desirable when one has at short notice to prop oneself up. If one did not have to do this, would it be better from the point of view of wind resistance, development of muscle power, comfort, and the ability to see and be seen, to recline backward or forward or even to lie horizontally? There are conflicting data on the best positions for power production, and I haven't seen anything that convincingly demonstrates the advantage of one position over another. I think that bicycling, or whatever traveling in a future man-powered vehicle might be called, would be more attractive to many people especially women, if they were able to sit comfortably wearing city clothes without feeling that they were performing a stunt, so that nothing too radical can be attempted.

Here again the question of attitude cannot be discussed without considering the structure of the vehicle. Present bicycles are vertebrate, whereas other lightweight structures like rowing shells are crustacean. A shell-like structure has a lot of attraction for future man-powered vehicles because of the possibility of combining the structure with a body of low aerodynamic drag which at the same time provides protection from weather and accidents and allows luggage to be carried inside. No future structure is likely to be wholly vertebrate or wholly crustacean but will probably be composite, and will depend on all the factors previously mentioned, and upon the type of power transmission used.

And I think that the days of steel chains and cogs are numbered. The synthetic cogged timing belt could right now do a better job for bikes without derailleur gears (so long as protection is given), as regards both weight and efficiency (chains are efficient when new and well lubricated, but the losses build up rapidly as dirt replaces the oil and as the tooth form changes and the chain stretches). Some interesting work has been done on the effect of various motion cycles on human power output which seems to show that a purely rotary steady motion might be considerably less efficient than one much jerkier, closer to a rowing motion. If one abandons rotary motion of the legs, and maybe the hands, too—though it seems uncertain whether human efficiency increases with the number of muscle groups being used—one is almost forced to use some mechanism which stores energy developed in one part of the cycle for use in another. If this is so, one might as well go the whole way and introduce means for energy storage over periods of minutes of full output. (There was a project at Dartmouth University a few years ago on this topic.) In turn this entails almost by necessity an infinitely variable gear. Obviously the penalties in weight, cost, complexity, and bulk of having a hydraulic or pneumatic or flywheel system, for instance, could be prohibitive. But imagine the fun of working quietly away at a traffic light and then taking off in a smell of burning rubber leaving the Mustangs desperately manipulating their stick shifts in the background.

How could all, or even some, of this be achieved without cost becoming enormous? Obviously the development and tooling costs might be very high, and could be recovered only by spreading them over a large production run. The demand for the right vehicle at the right price could also be great; however, there is enormous scope for the use of reinforced plastics and foam which, although more expensive per pound than steel, lend themselves to automatic production and the consequent reduction of labor costs. For instance, our present spoked wheels have to be assembled and trued by hand in what is a fairly skilled and comparatively lengthy operation. The use of reinforced spun glass fiber, in a technique similar to that developed for rocket casings, should enable wheels to be made lighter, more accurate, considerably more stable— and therefore safer—completely automatically.

How is one to choose among all the possibilities of construction, configuration, power transmission, suspension, and so forth? If one had all the data needed—the comparative costs and performance of every alternative—one might use the analytical methods used by the aerospace industry. One of the specifications would be a "mission profile" for the vehicle—a typical journey exactly described in terms of road surface, gradients, number of stops, speed pattern, wind conditions, luggage carried, and so forth, and when the various characteristics of the alternatives were tried, there would emerge one alternative that showed a most favorable balance of advantages over disadvantages for the rider. I doubt whether we shall ever have data good enough to do this sort of study quantitatively, but every good engineer does this sort of thing in his head when he weighs up all the conflicting factors and reaches a compromise. Of one thing I am fairly certain: The near-optimum machine will be considerably different from the present bicycle.

THE RECUMBENT BICYCLE

DAN HENRY
May 1968

The desire for more and more speed has perhaps fathered more vehicular designs than any other single consideration. And so it has been with this recumbent bicycle. I was seeking greater speed and I found it. But even more exciting, I found undreamed-of ease and comfort.

The recumbent bicycle, as such, is not a new idea. Over several generations a number of them have been shown and tried on bike tracks around the world, and outstanding performances have been recorded.

Previous versions were either ridden on one's belly in a swimming position, with the pedals at the rear, or on one's back in a reclining position quite like that assumed on a deck chair. On this second type, feet were extended horizontally forward with pedals convenient to this position. Less successful designs utilized some combination of crank and rod instead of a conventional chain drive. In all cases the prime object was to reduce aerodynamic drag by reducing the square unit of body area passing through the air. Aerodynamic drag is by far the most formidable barrier to attaining greater speeds.

All recumbent designs, insofar as I can determine, failed to prevail and never achieved mass production or distribution. Usually just a single unit was hand-built.

Much of the failure appears to have derived from the inability of the cyclist to sustain himself for extended periods on the bike because of physical distress. One or a number of physiological factors placed them in disfavor. Additionally, it is my belief that they also failed for a variety of mechanical and economic factors.

The recumbent shown in the illustration on page 290 was conceived after a careful study of photographs and drawings of a goodly number of previous designs. My goal

The recumbent in action. Note spring suspension both front and rear. The steering is done by chain drive from a false head at the handlebar position up to the true fork head in front.

was to build a speedy bicycle that would be comfortable and a pleasure to ride.

This bicycle is *fast* and has the *drive* and *float* of a tandem. A real speedster and fun machine. Fun for the person on the bike and a fascinating and amusing occasion for most spectators. Unlike any other bike that I have ridden, I find an aura, an invisible envelope of contagious excitement which seems to follow it down every road upon which I ride. Faces light up with childish delight as I pass and this adds immeasurably to the pleasure of the day's outing. The phenomena is quite unlike simple ridicule to which cyclists have become accustomed.

Except for the frame, which is silver brazed of ultralight Chrome Moly aircraft tubing, it is built from conventional bicycle parts or other equipment likely to be found around the house or in a neighborhood hardware store. Many parts have, however, been modified by heating, bending, cutting, etc. Not a single part was machined especially for this bicycle.

The most novel feature of all is the remote-steering arrangement. A false steering head supports the handlebar, and steering is accomplished by a chain drive from this false head to the true steering head at the front.

The seat is constructed of old handlebars and furniture webbing very much like the webbing of a folding chair. Sitting comfort is comparable to that of a webbed chair. The seat in its present version, shown in the illustration, is the fourth type that was tried. The three that were discarded were equal to or better than the ordinary standards of bicycle comfort but fell short of the degree of comfort that I had hoped to attain.

Both wheels are spring suspended for the elimination of road shock. This suspension is similar to the one employed on a more conventional bicycle previously described in *American Cycling,* March 1967.

The wheelbase is longer than a tandem and about twice that of a conventional bicycle. This extreme of wheelbase gives exceptional comfort. The rider being suspended well within this long wheelbase results in his receiving but a fraction of the amplitude of shock received by the wheel.

Hub brakes are employed because of the sprung wheels. The conventional rim brakes are not feasible with this arrangement.

Normal riding position is relaxed and natural, imposing no discomfort. In the photograph it is apparent that the riding position assumed greatly reduces the aerodynamic drag factor. On the recumbent, substantially the biggest reduction in drag is derived by both the arms and the legs entering the air stream endwise rather than full or partially broadside, as is the case on a conventional bicycle. The torso is about equally situated in either case.

One's thrust upon the pedal is considerably greater than can be achieved on a regular bicycle. It is quite like sitting upon the floor with your back against the wall; in this braced position a force much greater than one's weight can be imposed upon the pedals. On the conventional bike, your weight approximates the maximum thrust.

Because the recumbent rolls at a higher speed with comparable effort, exceptionally high gear ratios are employed. It has a five-speed set of conventional derailleur gears utilizing a chain wheel with sixty teeth. Several gear ratio choices well over one hundred are available. The gear-shifting lever is at the center of the handlebar. Weltmeister eight-ounce rims, eight-ounce silk tires, aluminum parts wherever possible, and egg-shell-thin tubing are many of the refinements that make the bike a very lively and responsive machine. The gross weight is within a few pounds of the conventional racing bike.

"So long for now. I'll wait for you at the coffee stop."

THE CHECKERED FLAG SPECIAL

CHARLES R. SIPLE
April 1965

In June of 1964 there came to the city of Columbus a consulting engineer from Europe. It was my good fortune that he moved into my neighborhood and that he happened to be a great fan of the sport of cycling. I learned in the course of our becoming acquainted that the '64 Tour de France was the first he missed seeing in seventeen years. Mr. Egarim's field of work is mechanical engineering and he enjoys widespread fame as an expert in the miniaturization of pneumatic control systems. His extensive library revealed his hobby to be the bicycle and its development. He mentioned that it would be entirely possible to improve upon the bicycle as we know it today, and when he did, I made the "mistake" of questioning him.

I found I had become his assistant and we embarked on a project which was to last through the summer and into the fall. In late October we put on the road a bicycle that in any competition would put all others to shame. I myself am no competitor by any stretch of the imagination, yet my first ride on the souped-up Special saw me turning twelve and a half miles in 27 minutes, 31 seconds. Mr. Egarim is twelve years my senior and on the same day over the same out and back course he posted a time of 29 minutes, 7 seconds.

In overcoming the mechanical problems in converting or modifying the bicycle, we had the cooperation of a neighborhood friend who loaned us his home workshop, and on several occasions we made use of the services of a local jeweler who fashioned parts for our shuttling check valves. The accompanying drawings I have prepared from recall. Mr. Egarim's drawings are complex and highly detailed. The drawings shown here are somewhat schematic. Nevertheless, they will permit an understanding of the principles involved.

Essentially, what this bike delivers that no other will is what might be termed a "punch line." The compressor housed in the seat tube stores a selected amount of energy

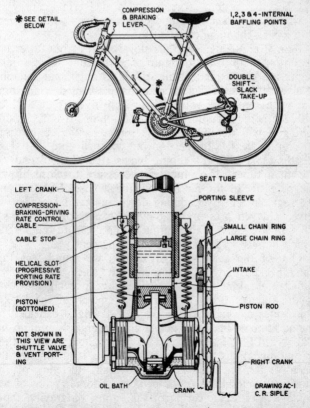

The Checkered Flag Special (top) and detail (below).

in the plugged-off tube lengths which make up the bicycle frame. This energy may be released selectively by the rider as he requires and is used to supplement his own imput. The stored energy derives from two sources: that from the crank when the bicycle is being pedaled and that from the rear wheel when coasting (downhill runs) or when braking. The five-gear wheel block has its ratcheting capability nullified, but conventional changes of gear through the usual range may still be had for reason of the double set of parallelogram changers which are mirror-image-attached, as shown. The slack throw of the chain occurs either above or below the chain stay depending upon whether the system is respectively delivering energy or storing energy. Simply put, we have a fixed-wheel system with a gear-changing capability.

Infinite adjustment permits storage rates from 0 percent of the input up to a maximum of 37 percent. Such adjustments are easily made while riding through manipulation of a seat-tube lever. The system may be vented at any time and a pressure-relief valve exhausts any overpressure which would otherwise rupture the frame tubing. It is the frame tubing, I will remind you, that serves as the compressed air-storage vessel. In the drawing you will note that short lengths of small O.D. tubing bypass the plugged ends of the main tubes. The plugs are necessary to close off the escape route of the air through the headset bearings and the seat cluster. By pedaling down substantial grades we have achieved pressure readings in excess of 1,700 p.s.i. This, incidentally, is the setting of the pressure-relief valve which allows a safety factor of 20 percent.

One of the surprising advantages we found was that hand brakes may be dispensed with, since a more than sufficient braking effect is attained by throwing the lever to the full compression position. Removal of the brakes constitutes a weight saving but this saving is canceled by the addition of the other added components. We found the Checkered Flag Special to be 9.7 ounces heavier than when the modifications were undertaken. This is not much of a penalty, for we increased the overall efficiency of the machine something like 12 percent. Another point of advantage was the lowering of the center of gravity about forty-two millimeters.

The costs involved in duplicating such a bike are high but not prohibitive. Mr. Egarim's figures permitted him to venture a guess that the average skilled mechanic might convert an existing bike for less than two hundred dollars or that the entire machine could be offered as a marketed bicycle for just over three hundred dollars.

There is the question as to the eligibility of the machine itself for competition purposes. We diligently researched the U.C.I. Rules and Regulations under Machines and their permissible Designs. Our interpretation of Article I in this section indicates we have an acceptable bicycle providing that one brake in good operating condition be fitted and that the bicycle be started in any event without pre-pressurization. With these provisions the bicycle is entirely within the rules.

Mr. Egarim was to have remained in Columbus until late in 1965, but the assignment here was finished much ahead of schedule. He has chosen to undertake a research problem for a Swiss firm which promises a lucrative return. It was necessary that he be in Zurich with a minimum passage of time. As I had helped him create the Checkered Flag Special, he told me he planned to make it available to a young Italian professional roadman of his acquaintance. He feels that the exacting demands of European road racing will be a true test for the bicycle. He has promised to forward clippings covering the successes and failures when the season gets under way. If you hear that a new rider has suddenly come to the fore on the Continent, chances are he'll be the man on the C.F. Special. I shudder to think what might happen to the record books.

> *Editor's note: Quite by accident I happened to read the name of the inventor, Mr. Egarim, backward. I wonder —do you suppose we could be the victims of an April Fool's joke?*

SADDLE AND SPRINGS—SOME ORIGINAL THINKING

DAN HENRY
March 1967

Although cycling had always been the great delight of my life, I found that advancing age brought a growing discomfort from the hard riding characteristics of the road-racing bicycle.

Each passing year amplified my need for a machine offering greater comfort without sacrificing the ease and performance of the lightweight racing machine.

I searched the marketplace for a quality spring-suspension model. The best that I could find was the heavy American truck type with front-wheel suspension only. These were all of poor quality and performance.

So I set to building one, a completely sprung road-racing-type bicycle. Up to that point I had never seen any type of spring suspension on the rear wheel of a pedal bicycle. The rear spring suspension plus the chain drive presented a formidable problem.

After only one false start, the spring bicycle assumed a pattern very similar to the product shown here. The bicycle in these photographs is the seventh generation of its type.

Each successive model brought improvements in the desired characteristics of hands-off stability and other good performance features.

As the design progressed, arrangements were added for adjusting the spring tension, so that riders of differing weights could be accommodated. These adjustable features are clearly shown in the photographs.

The bicycle pictured has traveled approximately 75,000 miles during the past twelve years. It has been thoroughly tested in the Green, Catskill, Adirondack, White, and Blue Ridge mountains of the United States and in parts of Canada, the British Isles on three occasions, Holland,

The rear spring and its adjustment. Utmost simplicity yet adequate adjustment.

The front suspension with spring and their adjustments. The end of the spring may be placed in any of the four holes provided. The nylon rope that exits from the spring and enters the top of the fork blade is a limit of travel device.

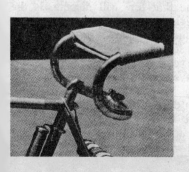

This bicycle saddle is an improvement added early in 1966. It is constructed from ordinary furniture webbing and a handlebar. I find it to be the most comfortable bicycle seat I have ever used. It concentrates one's weight upon the well-upholstered cheeks of one's sitting area rather than upon poorly upholstered bony sections of one's anatomy.

France, and Germany. Earlier models covered an additional 25,000 miles in areas near my home base of Long Island.

This grand total of approximately 100,000 miles has proved the design to be sound, simple, and successful.

From the very first model of this series, this was a machine that could be used without limitation. I used them all in the various activities of the New York Cycle Club, the American Youth Hostels, the International Bicycle Touring Society, the Cyclists Touring Club, and on vacation tours.

It very shortly became apparent that there was a performance advantage when riding this bicycle. I was usually among the first at the finish of clubs runs and similar cycling events. The longer the run, the greater was the edge over the others. Many years of experience affirmed time and time again that this advantage was most pronounced in distance events. The more hostile the road surface and the more rugged the terrain, the better it fared.

From what source does this advantage derive?

Primarily I think it comes from the circumstance of comfort and freedom from road shock. The rider is in a less hostile situation as he rolls smoothly along.

A second advantage is that the rider has a velvet-smooth pedal action. There are no sharp jolts to interrupt the even flow of effort to the pedal. One can even dispense with toe clips if he chooses. There is seldom an occasion that the foot tends to leave the pedal.

Third, I believe the resilience of the spring suspension acts something like a condenser to smooth out the flow of effort pulses.

A final source, and one that few will dispute, is the ability to equip with ultralight rims and other components. With the absence of hammer-hard blows at the rim, the ultralightweight track rims it was originally equipped with are still sound after twelve years of use. I tour with eleven-ounce silk tubulars and have about one flat per year.

The Raleigh Company of Nottingham, England, showed great interest in the design during my visit there in 1958, at which time they offered £500 ($1,400) for a ninety-day rights option. They later chose not to take up their option rghts.

During Raleigh's period of interest, the bicycle delighted many of the Raleigh staff. Among the distinguished persons of that firm that tried and tested the machine was none other than the then managing director himself, the late George Wilson, C.B.E.

The basic specifications are: The frame is of Reynolds 531 butted tubing and this frame came from a ten-speed bicycle purchased in England after the war. To this frame, minor but precise modifications were made by bending the front fork and rear triangle. Additional rocking forks with springs and fittings were added, as you can see in the photographs. All components beyond these are of standard types available in the trade. A hub brake is essential on the front wheel but some models have had rim brakes on the rear mounted at the chain stay position.

The bicycle weighs twenty-seven pounds as you see it, the coil-spring saddle included.

The webbing saddle was a new addition in 1966 and has eliminated all types of saddle discomfort. It is six ounces lighter than the saddle it replaced and I find the webbing arrangement so satisfactory that I would not consider returning to a conventional saddle.

In conclusion I would like to say that spring suspension for a pedal bicycle is not only practical but desirable. This machine, even though still in its development, is a true thoroughbred. At home on any road, in any terrain, and in any company, it gladly accepts everything the open road has to offer.

I hope that as the bicycle art develops, an increasing number of you may someday come to know the greater joy and comfort of spring suspension cycling.

STRESS, STRAIN, AND WHIP

FRED DE LONG
September 1965

With the permission of my six faithful readers, the technical section of this magazine can become a springboard for new thoughts, a crucifying ground for tradition and opinion, if these are found wanting, where rebels can debate with the experts. And we may wade in deep waters at times.

Of course, the manufacturer's viewpoint should be given fair consideration. It is of little use to build a better mousetrap unless someone can afford to buy it. A $40,000 race car may run rings around your Detroit monster, but there is no room to carry groceries. How many customers would buy one, particularly for a long drive in the rain?

When we think up ideas, let us think also about why they help, and if they are practical for the public, or just for the well-heeled connoisseur.

Our correspondents raise good questions. For example, is our frame tubing the best size for the purpose? Should we use an entirely different shape for frame members? Or as Milton Morse of Englewood, New Jersey, states, since the traditional method of threading pedals is backwards, yet it still works, why not standardize on right-hand threads for both pedals, saving cost?

And Dan Henry of the New York Cycle Club adds, "Why not radially spoke the front wheel, instead of building it like the rear driving wheel?" and goes on to explain the advantages of this type of construction.

Before we begin this discussion of some important fundamentals, try this experiment. It will enable you to visualize the end result of the matters we are considering.

Place your bicycle in a corner, parallel to one wall, with the front wheel against the front wall, the bars against the side wall. Have the cranks horizontal. Now, standing beside the bicycle, place one foot on the outside pedal, and press as hard as you dare, at the same time watching the effect of the pressure on the crank, the bottom bracket, the wheels, the chain stays. See them bend, twist, move sideways.

This is "whip" and it occurs continuously, side to side, when you "pour on the coal" for a sprint, or when climbing a hill, and to a lesser extent, all throughout your ride. This deflection wastes energy, yet *too* stiff a frame can bounce and jolt its rider, again wasting energy in a different manner.

Materials used for bicycle construction have certain basic characteristics. Also, the shape in which material is formed has a distinct bearing upon its performance. *Both* of these must be considered, and the best *overall* combination of properties, at acceptable manufacturing cost, will determine the final design. New manufacturing techniques may render past tradition obsolete, so tomorrow's bicycle may be different from the one we now know. Methods of working the materials can improve or detract from the strength of the basic materials.

Here are some of the properties with which we should be familiar if we want to look for ways to improve performance of the bicycle. Note these carefully, since the terms are sometimes loosely used, which can lead to error.

WEIGHT

Weights can be compared in terms of the weight of a solid cube of the material, one inch thick in each dimension. Steel, for example, weighs about 0.283 lb. per cubic inch; aluminum and its alloys about 0.096 lb.; magnesium, 0.064 lb.; plastics, 0.030 to 0.050 lb.; and wood, 0.020 to 0.030 lb.—a ten-to-one-range.

The use of the term "lightweight steel" is inaccurate. It usually refers to thinner sections of hollow pieces, but the basic material is just as heavy.

STRENGTH

Strength can be described in terms of the pull required to pull apart a piece of the material one inch square, or the pull to break a given-size piece, divided by its actual area in square inches. Therefore, a thinner tube under a given pull will actually be subjected to a higher material loading (called stress) than a heavier section.

For example, if the area of a tube is one tenth of a square inch, and it is being loaded to 1,000 pounds, it is stressed at 10,000 pounds per square inch, but if the area of the inner tube is only one fifteenth of a square inch, the tube will be loaded to 15,000 pounds per square inch, 50 percent greater.

However, materials cannot be used to their full strength. Long before this point they may bend or permanently stretch out of shape. The *yield strength* represents the maximum usable strength for steady loads, without permanent bend or stretch.

For loads that vary up and down, a new factor, called fatigue, comes into play. Even though the material may take high loads for a while, eventually it may crack and break without warning. To prevent this, the actual load range applied must be even less than the others mentioned. This can be called the fatigue limit. A spoke or frame tube is a good example. A spoked wheel may last for years on a stored bicycle, but breakage can occur on the road after a while, even though ridden no harder than when new. The full, or "ultimate" strength of steels may vary from 55,000 pounds for structural steel to over 200,000 pounds per square inch for aircraft steels. Yield strengths may range from 35,000 to 160,000 pounds per square inch or more.

Aluminum and its alloys exhibit yield strengths ranging from 9,000 to 80,000, while magnesium alloys may run up to 30,000 p.s.i.

Plastics vary greatly in strength, but also exhibit a property called "creep." With continued loading, a plastic part may slowly stretch or shrink, rendering it unusable. Proper design limits will limit this, while elevated temperatures will increase the problem.

BRITTLENESS

Brittleness is also known as impact strength. Window glass is an extremely strong material for its weight, yet it would not make a good frame. And while some very strong steels, alloys, and plastics have exceptionally steady load strength, they may snap under relatively small shocks, so that their great strength is not usable for our purposes.

Brittleness can be measured by the amount that a material will stretch before breaking, or by the height from which a weight can fall on a notched piece before it snaps. Think of this the next time you hit a bump while coming down a mountain.

RIGIDITY

Rigidity is described by a real jawbreaker, "modulus of elasticity," but it can be easily understood. A rubber band will stretch a long distance with a given load, but a piece of steel wire the same size will stretch only a small amount, too small to see. Try this experiment to see the effect of material rigidity. Take a quarter-inch diameter piece of different materials: wood, magnesium, steel, aluminum, and plastic. Support each at the ends, and hang a weight from the middle and measure the sag resulting. You will find the aluminum will bend three times as much as the steel and five times as much as the magnesium, while the wood and plastic will bend even more. A light alloy, where whip or twist is a factor, therefore, requires a larger section to resist this whip, even though the material may be as *strong* as the steel. Thus, much of its advantage, weightwise, can be lost since the part has to be bigger.

HARDNESS

Hardness is resistance to denting, scratching. Can you imagine a ball bearing made out of plastic? It can be done, but to support an equal load, it would have to be many times as large and the friction would be far greater. A soft cup or cone will dent easily and soon be destroyed. A soft material, like an alloy crank, unless kept tight, can be quickly damaged.

SECTION MODULUS

The shape in which the material is formed has a great effect on its resistance to loading. Try this experiment. Take a flat ruler, lay it on its flat side between supports, and place a weight on the middle. Note the amount of sag.

Now, place it tall side vertically, and using the same weight, measure the sag again. You will see that it is many times smaller.

Although the *amount* of material resisting the load is equal, its *effectiveness* in resisting bending is far greater, when the largest dimension is placed in the direction of the pull. The resistance to bending of any piece depends on the amount of material and the way it is arranged and also the rigidity of the material itself.

With a straight pull, such as on a spoke, the shape is of little consequence, but there are few members of a bicycle structure that have only a simple straight pull.

For example, a 1⅛″ diameter frame tube of 0.028-inch thickness has a cross section of about 0.097 square inches of material, the equivalent of a solid rod of material, the 0.35 inch less than ⅜″ diameter. But the resistance to bending of the tube is sixty-six times greater than the rod of equal weight, and its resistance to twist is twenty-one times as good. "Section modulus" describes the resistance to bending of different shapes, or in another form, to twisting, to provide an equal stress on the material.

Let's see why it is important. Our driving force is applied to the road at the center of the wheel, yet it enters the wheel at 1½ to 2 inches off center. We might use two sprockets and chains, one on each side, to centralize the pull on the frame, eliminating the twist from the one-sided pull, but with additional weight and complication—to say nothing about unbalance caused by unequal chain stretch.

But unless we ride facing sideways, we cannot apply our foot pressure on the frame centerline, without stamping on our own toes, since most cyclists I know are not mermaids, but have two side-by-side legs. Therefore, our foot pressure is applied considerably offset from the members that resist it.

The combined effect of off-center leg push, arm pull, and chain tension deflects the chain stays, twists the bottom bracket, twists the cranks, and bends the wheels (see how much finger pressure it takes to push the wheel rim over to the fork blade), as you have seen.

This combined effect is known as whip. And with off-center chain pulls of one-quarter to one-half tons under sprint and hill-climb conditions, this is surely a matter that is worthy of further discussion.

THE STORY OF
THE PNEUMATIC TIRE

P. D. PATTERSON
June 1967

Why the cycle? A fair question this, but not so easy to give a fair answer. In origin cycling was a sport beginning with the old hobby-horse of Georgian days in Great Britain and proceeding via the famous penny-farthing machine to the "safety cycle" of Victorian times. With the arrival of the latter, cycling really became the thing for the young man who wanted to be with it. Cycle races and touring marathons became as popular then as motor racing, trials, and stock-car events are today.

About the turn of the century another thing happened: the cycle became a common form of transport in Europe. Cars were the privilege of only the very rich (and were not very reliable at that), so that the middle classes cycled to work, to the shops, or often just to get out into the country. In Europe, even the widespread use of the motorcar hasn't completely extinguished this idea, and in many places cycles are still an accepted form of day-to-day transport.

Perhaps in America the "utility" cyclist is an extinct species, but looking at the pages of *Bicycling!* makes it clear that enthusiasts who cycle for the fun of it are rapidly growing in numbers. It could be said that this is a reaction against the idea that modern civilization is controlled by the motorcar; if it is, such reaction could be a good sign. But when cycling emerged from the novelty stage, it did something a good deal more than just create a healthy sport.

I wonder how many people realize that without the cycle there might never have been a motor industry, nor an aviation industry as it exists today. A tall story perhaps, but true enough. For the cycle led to the pneumatic tire and without pneumatics there wouldn't have been a practical motorcar; furthermore, if aircraft had arrived they would have been limited to flying boats, seaplanes, or very light affairs that could land on skids. I know it will be said, "What about helicopters?" but without the intensive development of conventional aircraft the helicopter might never have come to anything.

The way cycling led to the pneumatic tire makes an absorbing story. Look, for a moment, at the position in the early 1880's. Cycling was by then a fashionable sport for the young bloods, but their machines were equipped with tires made of solid rubber. These worked all right, but were extremely uncomfortable, rather heavy, and put high speeds right out of the rider's reach.

In Belfast, Northern Ireland, there lived a middle-aged Scotsman, who was a successful veterinary surgeon. Until he reached the age of forty-eight he had never done anything else, but to help him he had bought pieces of rubber to make his own gloves, and was fond of making little mechanical devices for his family. This man had a son Johnny, and to please him he gave him a tricycle as a present. Young Johnny rode this over the rough stone setts of the Belfast streets and was bold enough to complain to his father that it was very uncomfortable and a bit hard to push.

Now, the father was a very ingenious and practical man, who thought he'd try out a new idea. He bought some rubber sheet 1/32" thick from a local shop and built it into an air tube in his spare bedroom. He covered his tube with strips of linen taken from an old dress of his wife's, nailed these to a wooden wheel he had specially

During the early days, J. B. Dunlop (left) was often out and about with riders using the tires he made. Here he is talking to some of them during a wayside halt.

shaped, and blew up the tube with air. Then he took it downstairs to the yard which formed the reception area for sick animals. He rolled the wheel along the rough surface till it hit the door at the end. Something told him that it didn't roll like a solid-tired cycle wheel, so he took one and threw both along the yard. The solid-tired wheel went a short way and stopped, but the wheel with an air tire hit the door and bounced back.

The next step was to let Johnny try out the air-filled tires on his tricycle and he reported that the machine was a lot more comfortable and easier to push. All this was on the night of February 28, 1888; the father was John Boyd Dunlop and the pneumatic-tire industry was born in a Belfast backyard.

J. B. Dunlop was a man who looked ahead. He next bought a cycle without wheels and had some made out of metal strip, shaped by rollers to receive the air tube. The tubes were fixed in position with "gent's yacht sailcloth" and inflated, and the world's first pneumatic-tire tests were carried out over about three thousand miles. These justified his optimism and a friend named William Hume became interested. Hume was captain of the Belfast Cruiser's Cycling Club and persuaded Dunlop to supply him with a pair of pneumatic-tired wheels which he fitted to a machine he entered in the Belfast Queen College Sports. In this he was very successful, beating the crack riders on solid-tired machines in all four races. This was on May 18, 1889, and although many people laughed at the fat, clumsy-looking pneumatics, the fact remained that they were faster and more comfortable. The cycling world demanded them, and manufacture began, though at first in a very small way.

It wasn't all plain sailing, for the road from a vet's spare bedroom to a tire factory was a long and thorny one, but success came and pneumatic-tire manufacture became established. Dunlop was a skillful and practical man, but he had no liking for business or factories, so others joined up with him who were familiar with this world. Tire manufacture was moved to Coventry in England, the center of the cycle industry, and later to nearby Birmingham.

At the beginning a patent was taken out, but much to

everybody's dismay it was later found to be invalid, because an air-filled rubber tire had been patented as far back as 1845 by R. W. Thompson, another Scot, this time in Edinburgh. Thompson's tire had never come to anything, probably because rubber of good quality was difficult to get and the only potential users at that time were the horse-drawn carriages of the nobility and gentry. Patent or no patent, Dunlop's cycle tire was launched, and when the first motorcars appeared, the demand grew still bigger for a better tire.

Without the pneumatic tire motorcars could never have gone at more than walking pace, which was due to a property of the pneumatic tire that Dunlop knew nothing about. This was the fact that when a pneumatic tire is turned away from the straight-ahead course by just a few degrees, it develops what we now call "cornering force," the only force that makes a vehicle change direction under control.

The birth of the pneumatic tire is now in the history books, but in today's world maybe we can learn something from it. What led to the creation of this great industry, that in turn made motorcars, trucks, and airliners possible? Just this: the inventive foresight of a man already making a successful career who wasn't afraid to try out something new, and competition between youngsters eager to lead in a new sport. Who at that time would have foretold the great things that came from the experiments in an animal doctor's yard, who also would have claimed that cycle racing was necessary for the future of modern civilization? Nobody!

Perhaps this sort of thing could never happen again—or could it?

TIRE DISCRIMINATION FOR THE CYCLIST

D. R. HENSON
May 1966

The importance of the tires fitted to a bicycle in respect to the liveliness and performance of the machine is sometimes disregarded by the less experienced cyclist. Indeed, differences in rolling resistance between tires may vary over a range of five or more to one, depending upon the type of tire used, and the pressure of inflation. The following discussion, by D. R. Henson of the Dunlop Rubber Company, Ltd., has been prepared exclusively for American Cycling *readers as an introduction to the factors involved in bicycle tire design. If you are interested in further information, drop a line to the author.*

—FRED DE LONG

Riding comfort on a bicycle was the first consideration when John Boyd Dunlop produced his pneumatic tire. Later he demonstrated that by rolling a wheel, at first with and then without a pneumatic tire, the former traveled the longer distance, signifying a greater power efficiency. From this beginning the pneumatic tire has developed along numerous specialized channels and today one organization alone can count as many as eighteen hundred different types in production, which include over one hundred types of cycle tires.

The main classification is size, but change of size also requires tire design modifications in other directions. For example, the tread of a tire on a small wheel makes contact with the road more often than a corresponding tire on a large wheel. If one is half the diameter of the other, all else being equal, then approximately twice the tread wear can be expected. The sidewall of the tire will also flex twice as often for the same distance covered, thus putting more strain on the rubber and reinforcing cords. As result of increased flexing there will also be increased heat generated in the tire. This will not be a serious disadvantage to the life of a cycle tire, because the tire temperatures, relative to those of motorized transport, are not very high, but it will be noticeable in the power used to propel the machine.

Looking again at the above example, maintaining the same tread life on a smaller tire would require twice the tread thickness, as a logical solution; but to increase tread thickness would also increase power consumption of the tire due to heat generation. Other factors are equally if not more complex and so a simple formula is not available to redesign a cycle tire, even to accommodate a simple change in wheel diameter. Cycle tires are designed, therefore, with careful consideration of the cycle specifications and performance requirements.

Cycle tires are comparatively small in cross section, unlike passenger-car tires or more particularly tires for airplanes and earthmoving equipment. Their geometry makes possible manufacture on the simple and unique "monoband" tire-building machine. This machine is very precise, efficient, and beneficial from a production-cost angle. It does, however, limit the range of angles at which tire cords can be arranged on a tire. This range includes the accepted best cord angles of cycle tires, but there are exceptions; these include the low-angle (for lower rolling resistance) high-pressure racing tire for the enthusiast who is willing to pay a little extra.

There is a modern trend toward considerably smaller wheel diameters, which also produces a generally harsher ride. One well-known cycle manufacturer has embodied an independent suspension system to balance this feature. Where no such measures have been taken, a return to the accepted level of comfort has been achieved through the tires. These tires have an increased cross section for comfort and their cord angles are arranged to produce a lower rolling resistance; in consequence of this they, too, are not produced by the "monoband" principle.

A cyclist probably realizes more than any motorist the importance of tire cords. They are usually more apparent in the actual tire and it is reasonable to say that a cyclist more often looks closely at his tires.

Cycle-tire cords are constructed from one of four types of fiber—cotton, rayon, nylon, or silk. For general use, as in the case of the first three, the advantages between one and the other are marginal. The hypothetical strength advantages, weight advantages, and bonding to rubber advantages tend to balance each other out. Choice at times is influenced by performance in passenger-car tires and motor-racing tires, which is often entirely irrelevant to cycle tires.

Sprint or track-racing tires, however, are made from silk tire cords, which even today give the ultimate in strength to weight ratio and race performance levels.

Great importance is attached to tire cords. They should not be abused by cycling over or into objects with sharp corners, such as curbstones. By doing so the weight of the whole body and machine, increased by momentum, can be concentrated on one single cord and so damage it. This damage, although not always apparent immediately, will certainly reduce the life of the tire and possibly constitute a hazard on some future occasion.

It is also important not to cycle with flat or near-flat tires because this, too, as well as overstressing the rubber, can overstress the tire cords.

Rubber is a very versatile material, and by compounding with various chemicals and subsequently heating, it can be given a wide range of properties. One essential chemical is sulfur and the chief compounding ingredient is carbon black, which adds to the abrasion resistance of rubber and is particularly suitable for tire treads. There are, however, certain compound formulations more suitable for tire sidewalls, where most flexing occurs. For these two reasons certain high-performance cycle tires have two different rubbers used in their production, black for the treads, and translucent or biscuit-colored in the sidewalls. The main reason for the other color combinations, or for an all-white tire, is appearance. To produce these is slightly at the expense of performance.

For cycle-tire performance it is immaterial whether natural or certain types of synthetic rubber are used. One manufacturer uses synthetic rubber entirely for those types produced in the British Isles, but natural rubber for those made in Nigeria, which is advantageous for economic reasons.

In the main butyl rubber (a synthetic rubber) is used for cycle tubes because of its high degree of impermeability.

A cycle tire is essentially a performance product. For this reason the compounds of the better tires are of a high quality without dilution with reclaimed rubber or unnecessary filler materials. The high level of efficiency of a cycle tire is shown by the comparison that a sprint tire weighing 5¼ ounces carries approximately 100 pounds, that is, 300 pounds per pound of tire—whereas a car tire carries approximately 40 pounds per pound of tire.

On a smooth dry track with a reasonably hard surface a tire tread pattern is hardly necessary. The greater the surface area of tread rubber in contact with the track, the greater is the grip, no matter whether it is forward grip for propelling the bicycle, or sideways for cornering and steering.

As soon as soft surfaces are encountered circumferential ribs are necessary to key into the surface and give stability when cornering and also to support steering forces. In addition transverse ribs are necessary under these circumstances to transmit the propelling and braking forces.

On a smooth, wet, hard road, circumferential grooves, such as formed between circumferential ribs, help to channel away surface water and encourage dry-road-to-rubber contact for maximum gripping power.

A cycle tire is designed for a particular machine, or group of machines, and performance requirements. In almost every respect the design is an assembly of compromises. For instance a few:

1. For lower rolling resistance.
   a. Minimum-thickness tread and sidewalls.
   b. Cool running compounds.
   c. Low cord angles.
   d. High pressures.
   e. Small section tires.
2. For maximum tread life.
   a. Maximum-thickness treads.
   b. Abrasion-resistant rubber compounds.

3. For comfort.
   a. Low pressures.
   b. Large section tires.
   c. Soft rubber compounds.
4. For maximum road grip (or cycle control).
   a. Maximum area of rubber-to-road contact.
   b. On soft surfaces, circumferential ribs to maintain stability during cornering and in crosswinds.
   c. On soft surfaces, substantially transverse ribs to transmit propelling and braking forces.
   d. On wet surfaces, patterns to channel water away and maintain close rubber-to-road contact.

It will be seen from the above that many of these are not compatible. There is also the important factor of material and production cost. An expensive rubber compound or type cord or an elaborate process must justify itself.

A cyclist has the assurance that, for a particular use, the manufacturer supplies a tire in which these features are appropriately balanced. The above examples help the cyclist understand some of the measures taken to achieve this. For any special application it is advisable to consult the manufacturer or distributor.

Bikeways and Trails

—A New

Cycling Frontier

200,000 MILES OF BIKEWAYS

August 1968

For the experienced cyclist, capable of riding long distances, escaping the clutch of the city and finding enjoyable byroads is not a critical problem. The enthusiast is usually able to satisfy his own requirements, reaping the many benefits bicycle riding offers.

But what about the newcomer, the weekend cyclist, the family with children? Where can they ride? How can they escape the tyranny of the automobile, overcome the evolution of the megalopolis, and enjoy the natural beauty still convenient to our cities?

Bikeways!

The hope and refuge for the majority of American bike riders is a plan for utilization of secondary, lightly traveled streets, designated as "bikeways," to be shared by careful bicyclists and considerate drivers.

It took the concerted efforts of the American bicycle industry and the blood, sweat, and tears of two Floridians, Mr. and Mrs. George Fichter—long-time advocates of regular cycling for exercise and enjoyment in their town of Homestead—to focus the attention of the city fathers, Federal and state governments, and the President of the United States on the crying need for planned cycling facilities.

Back in 1961, the Fichters formed a bicycle club with their friends and neighbors in Homestead, frequently called the City of Bicycles. Discouraged by mounting traffic problems, for both motorists and cyclists, the Homestead bike club came up with a practical and highly successful answer to the problem, and they called it a bicycle safety route—secondary roads connecting residential areas with schools, playgrounds, shopping centers, ball parks, and other centers of activity. Streets designated as bike safety routes were marked with easy-to-read signs. Club members, supported by the chamber of commerce, convinced the city officials of the need for the feasibility of the project. Working with traffic engineers, they laid out the routes and raised funds for the manufacture and installation of blue-and-white metal signs. Then they enlisted the help of the police department and board of education before undertaking a citywide indoctrination and education campaign to acquaint all elements of the community with the program.

Soon, the entire town—city administration, business, schools, civic groups—supported their proposal for a system of well-marked bicycle routes where motorists would drive more slowly and cautiously. Homestead's cycling community went to bed dreaming of utopian streets where they could avoid monoxide fumes and menacing speed demons.

Their campaign climaxed in February 1962, when Homestead dedicated the nation's first "bikeway."

The idea of well-marked streets for bicycles won the support of the citizenry. Police officials responded immediately, foreseeing lowered auto speeds on bikeway streets, and more bicycles replacing autos for shopping and other short hops. Recreation-conscious citizens welcomed the plan which would encourage more people to get back on bikes for fun and fitness. City fathers found in bikeways an inexpensive new recreational facility to satisfy the leisure-time needs of their citizens.

In fact, reception of bikeways was so phenomenal that at the end of the first year, thirty-four of them were completed or under construction in thirteen states, with mileage approaching one thousand.

The success of the Homestead "experiment" had come about because of certain built-in assets—more bikes per capita than most towns, many quiet, untrafficked streets, and a small resident population—and some skeptics questioned its practicality for larger cities. Obviously bikeways are best suited to areas with little traffic.

Sprawling Chicago was the first metropolitan center to test the feasibility of bikeways. When the Chicago Park District's pioneer bikeway opened, covering some fifteen miles of lakefront paths through Lincoln, Jackson, Grand, and Burham parks, and more than a mile and a half along the North Shore Channel, it became an immediate success.

Patterned after the success of Chicago's bikeway, a second Midwest bikeway was opened in Milwaukee, followed by a third—a sixty-four-mile loop in the suburban community of Waukesha, thirty miles west of Milwaukee.

The Waukesha Bikeway passes the county's most beautiful residential areas, historic sites, hilly and timbered countryside, and lakeside. This bikeway is notable because to enjoy it, adults and their families meet at various points around the loop, riding numbered segments from one point of interest to another. Autos transport the families and their bikes to appointed meeting places.

Realizing that what originated as a safety idea had additional applications for opening up whole new areas of recreation and enjoyment for millions of people in towns like Homestead and cities like Chicago, the Bicycle Institute of America, actively involved in promoting the movement, determined to tell the bikeways story to as many as would listen.

In bikeways, the institute saw an opportunity to create a national awareness, within recent outdoor conservation efforts, of the need for designated streets for the enjoyment of cycling, and a national program of scenic bike paths and trails.

Then the bikeway idea was presented to park executives throughout the country in a survey which the B.I.A. initiated, picking the brains of experts on recreation for ideas on further bike path and trail development. The responses—from more than five hundred—were incorporated into a comprehensive guidebook, *Bike Trails and Facilities—A Guide to Their Design, Construction, and*

Operation, which for the first time made available practical information on bicycle-path construction.

The bicycle path or trail differs from the bikeway in that it generally does not use public streets. Bike trails can skirt a reservoir or lake, follow a canal towpath or river levee or an abandoned railroad right-of-way. They can penetrate the depth of a forest or slide along a seashore, enter a primitive area without disturbing the beauty of nature, yet remain within the ability of the average bike rider. In a large recreational area, the bike path can wander along golf courses, past lakes and ponds, beside meandering streams, or to and around camping areas. Bicycle paths may be planned for picnic spots—with tables, fireplaces, and shelter with comfort facilities along the way.

In our state and national parks, the bike path can take the visitor from where he must leave his car to what the National Park Service calls the Wilderness Threshold.

Stretching over three hundred miles from Kenosha to La Crosse, the Wisconsin Bikeway is the longest trail in the nation. From the Iowa state line to the shores of Lake Michigan, the bikeway travels through nine counties and some of the most scenic country in the Midwest. The Wisconsin Bikeway uses a combination of public roads and trails, the most notable section of which is a twenty-seven-mile stretch of abandoned railroad right-of-way between Sparta and Elroy.

Other states are close on the heels of Wisconsin. Ohio has just released a map of their planned bikeway from Celina, just a few miles from the Indiana state line on the west, to St. Mary's, not far from the Pennsylvania line on the east. In San Francisco, California, the board of directors of the Golden Gate Bridge recently announced that the west walkway of the span will be open on weekends for bicycle riders. Up to now cyclists have had to either walk their bikes across the bridge or risk a twelve-dollar fine. Eventually the bridge will connect a bikeway stretching from Tiburon to Lake Merced. Proposed bikeways through Indiana, Pennsylvania, and West Virginia are being considered. If all goes as planned, the entire northeastern quarter of the nation will eventually be joined by a system of connecting bikeways and trails.

The increasing public interest in and use of bikeways, public demand for more of them, and the unprecedented popularity of recreational cycling for and by adults brought strong support from President Johnson. In his message to Congress (February 8, 1965) he said: "The forgotten outdoorsmen of today are those who like to walk, hike, ride horseback or bicycles. For them we must have trails as well as highways."

In a chorus of superlatives, recreation officials, medical men, fitness and physical education experts joined the crusade for bikeways. Secretary of the Interior Udall, addressing a meeting of nearly 160 senators and congressmen, said: "I believe we need more bike paths and trails to help us offset the tyranny of the automobile," and announced government plans for the construction of 200,000 miles of them in the next decade.

Last year legislation was drafted that would lead to the establishment of a nationwide system of trails for the hiker, the cyclist, and the equestrian. The legislation provides for the expansion and development of additional trails in Federal and State Parks and Forests, as well as in our cities. The legislation would also place within the Nationwide System several lengthy trails that have natural, scenic, or historic significance, such as the Appalachian, Continental Divide, Pacific Crest, and Potomac Heritage trails.

Today, seven years after the Homestead experiment, the idea of bikeways and trails set aside for the safety and enjoyment of cyclists is recognized as a dynamic new dimension in community and recreational planning. More than seventy-five bikeways are being enjoyed at this moment, and over one hundred are on the drafting boards in communities across the nation.

There are bikeways in Kentucky's Jefferson County, in Ohio's Amish farmland, along the banks of the Sacramento River in California, at Indian Creek, Indiana, in mile-high Denver, Colorado, and in Manhattan, New York.

Dr. Paul Dudley White, internationally famous cardiologist and bicycle enthusiast, recently said: "We must establish more bike paths and trails throughout the country. I'd like to see everyone on a bike—not just once in a while, but regularly, as a routine. The bicycle should become a superb resource for the whole family to enjoy the beauties of nature, whether in our national parks, along our seacoasts, or simply in our beautiful woods and fields the country over."

CORNUCOPIA OF DELIGHTS— FLORIDA BIKEWAYS

CORAL GABLES CHAMBER OF COMMERCE
September 1968

Free from the traffic problems and limitations of visibility that hamper the motorist, the bicycling family can enjoy Coral Gables at its best. A modern bikeway, complete with its own system of signs, leads the bike rider through twenty beautiful meandering miles of the city.

The Coral Gables Bikeway represents only a small segment of the extensive bikeway system of Metropolitan Dade County. A continuous route connects Greynolds Park, north of Miami, with Homestead to the south, totaling more than one hundred miles for the vigorous cyclist.

Many bicycle rental establishments are located in the area for those who didn't bring their own wheels. So pack a picnic lunch, your swimsuit, and your camera, and let's be on our way.

Entering the city on broad, lushy landscaped Country Club Prado, the cyclist sees a gateway structure with wide-open arms, a fountain, and an arbor of bougainvillaea vine.

Moving down the Prado, one is struck by the spacious and gracious homes, set far back from the street on large lots. Next major point of interest is the sprawling University of Miami campus, studded with high-rise dormitories and other ultramodern educational structures.

On a road bordering the university is one of the world's most unusual sewage-treatment plants. Its tanks and other structures are covered with unusual murals depicting the history of Florida from the aborigines to the present day.

Now out of service and slated for demolition in a few years to make way for university expansion, the plant is often mistaken for a swank cabana club or other tourist attraction.

At the university, the cyclist has another advantage forbidden to motorists. He can tour the campus, which is closed to automobile traffic.

A highlight is a visit to the Lowe Art Gallery on campus, where permanent collections are on display in the fields of the fine arts, Oriental and classical art, ethnic art, and the decorative arts. It is open to the public at no charge.

Leaving the university, the route proceeds southward along scenic Granada Boulevard and crosses the Coral Gables waterway, a picturesque canal dredged from the soft limestone underlying the area.

Next stop is Cartagena Plaza, named in honor of the Colombian municipality which is Coral Gables' sister city under the People-to-People program. The center of interest is a replica of a famous statue in Cartagena—a pair of comfortable old shoes. A plaque explains the significance of this unusual object of the sculptor's art.

From Cartagena Plaza, the tour winds southward along Old Cutler Road, a winding, tree-shaded highway that is still much as it was in the early days when it was the main link to farming areas and the Florida Keys.

Southernmost point on the bicycle tour is Dade County's huge Matheson Hammock Park, containing picnic areas and nature trails. This is an excellent spot to park your bikes, spread out on the lawn, and have your lunch. On Biscayne Bay is a marina and a saltwater swimming beach formed much like a tropical atoll. If you're not ready for a swim yet, hold off for a few miles and try the Venetian Pool.

The route returns over the same road back to Cartagena Plaza, following picturesque Riviera Drive, passing near two of Coral Gables' unusual "villages"—small colonies of varying architectural style that contrast sharply with the city's overall Mediterranean design.

First in sight is one of the French villages, where big, somber houses are built almost flush with the sidewalk. A high wall conceals the garden on the side.

To the north is a Chinese village, including six houses with curling roofs, arched gateways, and gaily-colored galleries. Blazing colors such as scarlet, raw orange, and brilliant blue provide instant identification. In line with Oriental tradition, tiny dragons, watchdogs, and fish perch on roof ridges and eaves.

Another interesting facility is the City of Coral Gables Riviera Fire Station, a crisply contemporary building which is a far cry from the traditional firehouse. A two-story wall of glass on one side of the building gives glimpses of red motorized equipment silhouetted against a mosaic tile wall of white, blue, and orange.

The bikeway takes one past the Coral Gables War Memorial Youth Center, one of the most complete and beautiful recreation and community centers in America. Year-round classes and recreation programs are conducted here for all age groups.

The route branches off toward Venetian Pool, nick-named the World's Most Beautiful Swimming Hole. Built on the site of an abandoned rock pit, this famed showplace was designed to give the illusion of a lagoon in a Vene-tian setting. It has a grotto, a beach, a bridge, and a casino. It's open for swimming every day in the year. Spectators are welcome without charge.

Nearby is De Soto fountain, designed by nationally known architect Denman Fink, who developed the orig-inal Coral Gables city plan. The tour then sweeps south-ward to the huge Biltmore complex, where the former luxury hotel—more recently a veterans' hospital—tower over the city-owned golf course.

The tour wends its way back to the point of origin, taking in many more points of interest. Local cyclist take the tour time and time again because of its endless variety.

If you have planned wisely, and have allowed yoursel several days in Florida's bike country, you will not wan to miss the many points of interest along the bikeway i Miami. One spot of particular interest is the Coconu Grove section, where multimillionaires live next door t struggling artists, but nobody seems to mind.

Stark modern structures front on narrow, windin

streets, but so do aging villas and Tahitian-style homes—and they blend, rather than contrast.

This is The Grove, where the earliest settlement in Miami began in the 1820's, and where professionally successful people share a way of life with people content merely in their own understanding of themselves and their surroundings.

A cycling tour of the village includes the Coconut Grove Playhouse, mainstay of drama in Southeast Florida; Grove House, an artists' gallery, workshop, school, and marketplace; assorted art galleries, restaurants, shops, and an epicurean market. Just follow the neat white-and-blue signs along the well-planned bike route.

NEW FRONTIERS IN NEW YORK CITY

GURDON STUART LEETE
November 1968

A concerned nation wonders: "What's happened to New York City?"

The rumors aren't true. New York City is not a forgotten asteroid now inhabited only by hairy crazymen who live on the mounds of garbage that grow there. Many parts of New York City are in fact rather calm and beautiful. It can actually be, as Mayor Lindsay himself admits, a very nice place to live. And perhaps having some connection with all this, this summer the city has opened one of the nation's very best collection of bikeways.

This fact is doubly admirable in that traffic-flow patterns, road conditions, distribution of population, accessibility of scenic and recreational areas, and all the other factors to be considered in a large city make the job of mapping out a good bikeway system very difficult indeed.

According to the Park Association of New York City, which, together with the Department of Parks and the

Cycling in Central Park. New Yorkers enjoy weekend rid
without automobiles to watch out for.

ever-alert Department of Traffic, brainstormed the pr-
gram, the five routes are just the beginning. Projected
an elaborate network of bicycle routes linking all the bc
oughs. Trails to connect the city with the Great Lak
and Canada have even been suggested.

But now, at least, after two years of planning and pre
aration, New York City's five boroughs can boast of ov
one hundred miles of bikeways. The handsome bikew
signs will lead you through the labyrinthine confusion
Manhattan intersections to almost any part of the ci-

They'll take you past Fort Totten in Queens, along Riverside Drive above the Hudson, through the wilds of Staten Island, past parts of the Bronx and Bedford-Stuyvesant, with their three-story wooden-frame tenements and vacant lots filled with refuse, and through the vast greenery of Flushing Meadow, site of the 1964 World's Fair. And they'll steer you away from hazardous commercial thoroughfares and onto quiet adjacent streets—which might sound a little less exciting. Hardly. It'll knock you out.

In Manhattan alone you can follow official bike route signs past such spots as Columbia University, the Metropolitan Museum of Art, Cathedral of St. John the Divine, the Lincoln Center for the Performing Arts, Central Park, the American Museum of Natural History, Harlem, Grant's Tomb, a planetarium, a zoo, a swimming pool, Mayor Lindsay's front yard, and a picnic island across the East River.

And the bikeways in New York City make good sense. Parks Commissioner August Heckscher has pretty well summed it up in these words:

"Of prime importance to this administration is the provision of added programs to those areas of our city which have high concentrations of disadvantaged youth. Our feeling is that this bikeway program can provide both increased opportunities and incentives to youth to explore new areas of their city. Therefore, each of our initial routes goes through one or more of these target areas, i.e., Harlem, Bedford-Stuyvesant, Southeast Bronx, East Harlem, East Elmhurst, etc.

"The new route in Brooklyn starts at Tompkins Park in the center of Bedford-Stuyvesant, proceeds through Prospect Park, around a lake, and then on to Coney Island and the ocean. What an exciting trip for an adventurous youth—from the hot summer streets of Bedford-Stuyvesant to refreshing seashore! How rewarding it will be for that youth to make the trip under his own power.!

"This is really such a good idea. It makes use of what we already have—the streets and people's sense of adventure.

"It's like a trail through the woods."

FRESH AIR, GREEN GRASS, FOR GHETTO YOUTH

AMERICAN YOUTH HOSTELS
December 1968

The hot, dirty crowded streets of the ghetto are no place for kids to spend their summer, but for millions there is no alternative. In fact, getting out of the big-city slums and into the country is virtually impossible for ghetto youth at any time of the year.

Now, through the Pedal-Out program initiated by the American Youth Hostels in cooperation with VISTA (the "domestic peace corps"), thousands of boys and girls between the ages of ten and sixteen will have an opportunity to escape the confines of the ghetto, and bicycle into the country. The Pedal-Out program provides bicycles, equipment, and hostel facilities through A.Y.H., and volunteer trip leaders through VISTA. The program got under way in July in six cities: New York, Baltimore, Chicago, Detroit, Washington, D.C., and New Haven.

Such a program, of course, requires the availability of a good many bikes, which was one of the first challenges facing A.Y.H. Dr. Paul Dudley White, famed cardiologist and Honorary Life President of A.Y.H., approached the American bicycle manufacturers for donations to the Pedal-Out program. To date, over two hundred new bicycles have been given by the industry, and another one hundred new and used bikes have come from other sources.

As the program gained momentum, other groups lent their support, too. In New York City, the Youth Service Agency of the National Resources Administration approved a special "New York Street Corps" to aid the Pedal-Out program. One hundred and ten full-time summer workers were assigned to work in twenty-two areas of New York City. Their main job was to organize, conduct, and implement bicycle club activities with the objective of organizing Youth Hostel Clubs to operate throughout the year. Many day trips have been run, including one five-day tour of the Connecticut River Valley. Because of traffic problems, New York youngsters are bussed to the outskirts of the city.

In New Haven, the Pedal-Out program was given the name "Countryside Adventures 68." A grant of $2,000 was given by the New Haven Foundation, and Community Progress, Inc., furnished $2,700 for staff salaries for the project. Another $2,000 was donated by the New Haven A.Y.H. Council. Two enthusiastic Yale Divinity School seniors were employed to organize and run the program during the summer. Taking groups out every day, at a rate of 175 per week, more than 500 ghetto children had been served by the middle of August.

To date, the entire program has put thousands of children on bikes and given them the opportunity to enjoy the beauty and freedom of the countryside which, for most of them, had never been experienced.

Those connected with the program are enthusiastic about it, and so are many who have been approached to help.

"People are actually thanking me for telling them about the project," says a worker in one city. "Can you imagine that? It's the first time in my life that I ever heard of anyone thanking somebody for dunning them."

Many more bikes are needed to expand the Pedal-Out program and funds are badly needed. If you would like to help, send your donation to Pedal-Out, c/o The American Youth Hostels, Inc., 20 West 17th Street, New York, New York 10011.

BICYCLING BLUEGRASS STATE

LOUISVILLE COURIER JOURNAL-TIMES
November 1968

Rolling along with the trend toward greater physical fitness, cycling is enjoying the surge of the century and now tops golf, bowling, baseball, and basketball as a participant sport.

While Kentucky has no formal bikeways program at this time, Julian Walker, director of Supervised Recreation in the State Parks, reports growing support for the bikeways idea. Present interest in cycling in Kentucky is regional. In Jefferson County bike trails have been added to the parks system with one bike route each in Long Run, Chenoweth Run, and Iroquois parks.

In a way, the cyclist's biggest problem is the automobile; but in another way, the automobile is the cyclist's biggest help. To reverse the coin, simply load the bikes and drive to a good launching point for a leisurely day's ride over quiet back roads.

A short time ago, some enterprising Louisville bikers, aged ten to seventy-eight, took just this kind of a trip. They loaded bicycles and lunch into a panel truck and drove to the Knob Creek area south of Louisville in Bullitt County.

The ten-mile bike hike was a loop starting and ending in the Sunnyside school area of Knob Creek Road, trip Number 1 on the map. Two other good loops for a trip are also shown on the map. Number 2, also about ten miles long, runs along lower Knob Creek with Nichols School as start and finish. The third starts and ends in Fairdale, closer to Louisville. Ambitious riders can combine 1 and 2 for a longer and doubly delightful ride.

Really dynamic riders might join the Louisville Wheelmen, an adult group that takes several bicycle trips each month, including "century runs," trips of a hundred miles.

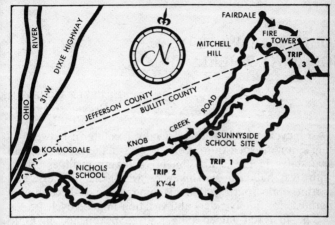

This map shows three good Kentucky bike tours.

Shorter trips, including some across the river to the Falls of the Ohio River, are also scheduled. So we see that the Bluegrass State, under the leadership of an intrepid band of cycling enthusiasts, is coming into its own as a leader in the pleasant world of cycling!

OHIO IS A WORLD ON TWO WHEELS

E. PETER HOFFMAN
December 1968

Two bicycle wheels with a friendly greeting in between—that's how to spell OHIO. Ohio is one of the most progressive states in the establishment of biking facilities. Now, with over half a dozen bikeways within her borders, and a trans-state route in the planning, Ohio is becoming a paradise for family riders and vacation-minded cyclists.

The first self-guided bike trail to be opened in Ohio was through the Amish country in Ashtabula, Geauga, and Trumbull counties. Hundreds of families and cycling groups have traveled this northeastern Ohio bikeway since its opening last year, when it was dedicated with a ceremony at the Geauga County Historical Society's museum in Burton. Roughly thirty-seven miles in length, the route begins and ends at a picnic area in Punderson State Park; points of interest along the route include a museum, an operating blacksmith shop, a Swiss-cheese factory, a harness shop, a goat farm, and a maple-sugar bush. Peaceful lanes wander through fertile farmlands, over picturesque covered bridges and along peaceful streams.

Jacob Ammon, a former Mennonite preacher in Switzerland, brought his followers to America early in the eighteenth century and settled in Pennsylvania. Members of the sect—named after Ammon, and known as Amish—arrived in Geauga County, in 1883.

Since there are no Amish churches, religious services are held in barns or homes. Their convictions forbid military service, taking an oath, and baptism of infants, and theological training is banned. Higher education is frowned upon, for the Amish believe that it takes people away from the simpler things.

Horse-drawn black buggies are used for transportation.

Up goes another sign as Ohio's bikeways expand.

The Amish shun modern conveniences, such as automobiles, electricity, and telephones. Although they like to sing, musical instruments are forbidden. Their homes are simple, being furnished without curtains, wallpaper, pictures, or other decorative materials.

Probably the most noticeable characteristics of the Amish are their costume and appearance. Nearly all clothing is homemade. Openings are fastened without buttons, which are regarded as ornamental. In place of buttons, the men use hooks and eyes, while the women rely on straight pins.

The men wear denim garments and large-brimmed, flat black hats. The women wear long cotton dresses in a standard shade of blue, and occasionally shades of purple or green. An apron and a bonnet are also standard items of attire for women. Hair styles are standardized. Men wear bangs in front and the back strands are chopped off on a level with the jawline. The women's hair is braided and coiled at the back of the head.

The Amish live secluded lives, going into town only when necessary to trade. They do not mix with "Yankees" as all Americans outside the Amish sect are called. They are basically farmers. The children are reared in an atmosphere of tradition, custom, and the religious beliefs of their forefathers, established hundreds of years ago.

Another popular trail runs through Fairfield County, which, having more covered bridges than any other county in Ohio, has been named Covered Bridge Bikeway. Other attractions along the scenic route include the famous "standing stone" of Rising Park, an old mill, the Wagnall Memorial at Lithopolis, and the abandoned locks of the Ohio-Erie Canal at Lockville. The Old Mill Bikeway, Maumee River Bikeway, Kettering Bikeway, and the Gus Husse Bikeway are other popular routes. For further information, you can obtain a free brochure on bicycle journeys from the Development Department, State of Ohio, 65 South Street, Columbus, Ohio 43215

The Romance of

Cycling's Golden Age

VELOCIO, GRAND SEIGNEUR

Clifford L. Graves, M.D.
May 1965

When a throng of cyclists from all corners of France converged on Saint-Etienne one day last July as they had done for more than forty years, they were paying homage to a man who accomplished great things in a small corner of the world. He was a man who devoted a lifetime to the perfection of the bicycle and the art of riding it, a man who inspired countless others through the strength of his character and the beauty of his writings, a man who even in his old age was capable of prodigious riding feats; in short, a man who might well be called the patron saint of cyclists. That man was Paul de Vivie, better known as Velocio.

Paul de Vivie was born in 1853 in the small village of Perne in southern France. His early years were unremarkable except that he distinguished himself by his love for the classics. If it is the mark of the educated man that he enjoys the exercise of his mind, Paul was exceedingly well educated. He graduated from the *lycée,* served an apprenticeship in the silk industry, and started his own business before he was thirty. With a beautiful wife and three handsome children, he seemed headed for a life of ease and elegance.

The change came gradually. In 1881, when he was

twenty-eight, he bought his first bicycle. It was an "ordinary" or high wheel, the safety bicycle still being in the future. The ordinary was a monster. With a precarious balance and an immoderate weight, it was a vehicle only for the strong and intrepid. That was exactly Paul's cup of tea. He began exploring the neighborhood on his newfangled contraption and he taught himself all the tricks of his wobbly perch. One day, on a bet, he rode sixty-six miles in six hours. This trip took him to the mountain resort of Chaise-Dieu. Suddenly he discovered a new world. The vigorous exercise, the fresh air, the beautiful countryside, these things took possession of him. He did not realize it but his life was beginning to take shape.

The decade of the 1880's was a momentous one, both for Paul and for the bicycle. For Paul, it was the start of an arduous and lifelong pursuit. For the bicycle, it was the end of a long and painful gestation.

This gestation had started in 1816 when the Baron von Drais in Germany discovered that he could balance two wheels in tandem as long as he kept moving. He moved by kicking the ground with his feet, and his vehicle came to be known as the draisine, or hobbyhorse.

In 1829 Kirkpatrick Macmillan in Scotland eliminated the necessity for kicking by fitting cranks and treadles to the wheels.

In 1863 or 1864 Pierre Michaux in Paris, with the help of his mechanic, Pierre Lallement, improved on the treadles by fitting pedals. This vehicle was the boneshaker, or velocipede.

Neither the hobbyhorse nor the boneshaker was a hit because of the bruising weight and the merciless bouncing.

In 1870 came the high wheel, and this did make a hit. Although the height of the wheel was a distinct and ceaseless hazard, this very height made it possible to travel farther with each revolution of the pedals. The high wheel caught the public fancy when four riders in 1872 rode the 860 miles in Great Britain from Lands End to John o'Groats in fifteen days. Clubs were formed, inns were opened, and touring started in earnest. The high wheel lasted until 1885 when it was replaced by the safety bicycle, which caused a further surge of excitement. Thus, when Paul de Vivie appeared on the scene in 1881, the bicycle was indeed on the threshold of its golden age.

Paul rode his ordinary only a year. Then he bought a Bayliss tricycle, followed by a tandem tricycle and various other early models. These were the days when the bicycle industry was well established in Coventry, while France was lagging. Fired by enthusiasm, Paul started shuttling back and forth. He was searching for a better bicycle, a search that was taking more and more of his time. Clearly, he could not push this search and also run his silk business. He made his decision in 1887 at the age of thirty-four.

In that year, he sold his silk business, moved to Saint-Etienne, opened a small shop, and started a magazine, *Le Cycliste*. Considering that he was invading a completely new field in which he had never had any training, it was a leap in the dark. In this leap, he discovered himself, and one of the things he discovered was that he could write. Words welled up within him as naturally as water tumbles down a cataract—and as gracefully. In his writing he always signed himself Velocio, and that became his name henceforth. It fitted him to perfection.

For the first two years, Velocio was content to import bicycles from Coventry. But all the time he was experimenting. For us, who have grown up with the bicycle, the design problems that assailed Velocio seem elementary. To him, they were formidable. The safety bicycle of 1885 left many questions unanswered. The shape of the frame, the kind of transmission, the length of the cranks, the position of the handlebars, the type of tires, and above all the gearing, these were matters that caused endless discussion and experimentation, not only in the shop but on the road.

Velocio's first model in 1889 was La Gauloise. It had the familiar diamond frame, a chain transmission, and a single gear of about fifty inches. It was the first bicycle produced in France, but it did not satisfy Velocio. The region around Saint-Etienne is mountainous. Velocio could see the need for variable gears. How to achieve these? In England, all the work was in the direction of epicyclic and planetary gears. Velocio struck out in a totally different direction. He conceived the idea of the derailleur.

His first attempt was two concentric chain wheels with a single chain that had to be lifted by hand from one to the other. Now he had two gears. Next, he built two concentric chain wheels on the left side of the bottom bracket. Now he had four gears. In 1901 he came on the four-speed protean gear of the English Whippet. Here, the changes were made by the expansion of a split chain wheel. Partial reverse rotation of the pedals caused cams to open the two halves of the chain wheel and secure them in any one of the four positions by pawls. Velocio took this idea and worked it into his Chemineau, the derailleur as we now know it. This was in 1906. By 1908 four French manufacturers were introducing their own models because Velocio had been too busy to take out a patent.

Incredible as it seems today, Velocio actually had to fight for the adoption of his derailleur gear. The cyclists of the period resented this marvelous invention as a stigma of weakness. They stoutly maintained that only a fixed gear could lead to smooth pedaling. Even Henri Desgrange, the originator of the Tour de France, attacked Velocio. To defend himself, Velocio wrote dozens of articles, answered hundreds of letters, cycled thousands of miles (average, 12,000 a year). At his suggestion the Touring Club de France organized a test in 1902. Competitors were to ride a mountainous course of 150 miles with a total climb of 12,000 feet. The champion of the day, Edouard Fischer, on a single-speed was pitched against Marthe Hesse on a Gauloise with a three-speed derailleur. The Gauloise won hands down. The newspapers were ecstatic because "the winner never set foot to the ground over the entire course." Still, Desgrange would not concede. Wrote he in his influential magazine, *L'Equipe:*

"I applaud this test, but I still feel that variable gears are only for people over forty-five. Isn't it better to triumph by the strength of your muscles than by the artifice of a derailleur? We are getting soft. Come on, fellows. Let's say that the test was a fine demonstration—for our grandparents! As for me, give me a fixed gear!"

Said Velocio with admirable restraint: "No comment."

The battle of the derailleur dragged on for a full thirty years. It was not until the 1920's that it was finally won. Velocio himself advocated wide-ratio gears for touring: from 35 to 85. His normal riding gear was 72.

In this battle for the derailleur gear, Velocio had a powerful weapon in his magazine, *Le Cycliste*. By 1900 this publication had grown from a fragile and unpretentious sheet of local circulation to an eloquent and influential journal that was widely read because of its incisive articles and vivid writing. Much of this writing was by Velocio himself, who never tired of describing his fantastic tours in the most colorful language. To read *Le Cycliste* is to read the history of cycle touring.

But *Le Cycliste* is more than a repository of history. With the passage of the years, Velocio became a philosopher. Having given up the quest for money and fame in the dim days of 1887, he could look at the world with complete equanimity. He read the classics in the original, and he applied their teachings to his own life. Between his articles on cycling, he counseled his readers on diet, on exercise, on hygiene, on physical fitness, on self-discipline, in fact on all the facets of what is commonly called a well-rounded life. His theme was a sound mind in a sound body. In wine-drinking France, he spoke out unequivocally for sobriety; and he warned against the hazards of smoking sixty years before a presidential commission in the United States did so. These statements he made only after he had proved the benefits on himself because he was not a man to mouth platitudes. Thus, *Le Cycliste* became much more than a magazine for cyclists. It became a manifesto of brisk living, the credo of a dedicated man, a profession of faith.

Brisk and dedicated are also the words to describe Velocio as a cyclist. By nature, temperament, and physique he was what he called a "veloceman." Something of his enthusiasm can be gleaned from his ride to Chaise-Dieu in 1881, sixty-six miles in six hours on a clumsy high wheel. His serious cycling started in 1886 on a Eureka with solid rubber tires (pneumatics came in 1889). On this bicycle he rode 90 miles from Saint-Etienne to Vichy before noon. In 1889 he made his first

150-miler, a round trip from Saint-Etienne to Charlieu on a British Star weighing fifty-five pounds.

But these were only the probings of the beginner. Partly from his tremendous drive and partly from his compelling desire to show what the bicycle was capable of, he began to extend his tours. Sometimes alone, sometimes with a small group of friends, he would ride through the night, through the second day, through the second night, and into the third day without more than an occasional rest to eat or change clothes. Consider these feats:

In 1900, when he was forty-seven, he toured the high passes in Switzerland and Italy, 400 miles with a total climb of 18,000 feet, in forty-eight hours.

For Easter in 1903, at the age of fifty, he rode from Saint-Etienne to Menton and back in four days: 600 miles on a bicycle weighing sixty-six pounds including baggage.

For Christmas 1904 he cycled from Saint-Etienne to Arles and back on a night so cold that icicles formed on his moustache.

His "spring cure" in 1910 took him from Saint-Etienne to Nice, a distance of 350 miles, in thirty-two hours. At Nice he joined a group of friends for 250 miles of leisurely touring in three days.

The following summer he tackled one of the highest Alpine passes, the Lautaret, in the company of a young friend: 300 miles in thirty-one hours.

In 1912 also, when he was fifty-nine, he undertook an experimental ride from Saint-Etienne to Aix-en-Provence. 400 miles in forty-six hours, at the end of which he had to admit that his companion, thirty-five, tolerated the second night on the road better than he. "From now on," he wrote in *Le Cycliste,* "I will limit myself to stages of forty hours and leave it to the younger generation to prove that the human motor can run for three days and two nights without excessive fatigue."

"Every cyclist between twenty and sixty in good health," wrote Velocio with the fervor of a missionary, "can ride 130 miles in a day with 600 feet of climbing, provided he eats properly and provided he has the proper bicycle." Proper food, in his opinion, meant no meat. A proper bicycle meant a comfortable bicycle with wide-ratio gears, a fairly long wheelbase, and wide-section tires. A bicycle with close-ratio gears, a short wheelbase, and narrow-section tires will roll better at first, he pointed out, but it will wear its rider down on long-distance attempts. The first consideration is comfort. His diet on tour consisted of fruit, rice, cakes, eggs, and milk.

Obviously, Velocio was a very special kind of cycle tourist. Not for him the Sunday ride with stops every half hour. "Cycling in this fashion is undoubtedly enjoyable," he wrote, "but it ruins your rhythm and squanders your energy. To get in your stride, you have to use a certain amount of discipline. My aim is to show that long rides of hundreds of miles with only an occasional stop are no strain on the healthy organism. To prove this point is not only a pleasure, it is a duty for me."

Velocio was sometimes criticized for his long-distance riding. It was said that he was hypnotized by speed and mileage and that he could not see anything of the country at that rate. He answered:

"These people do not realize that vigorous riding impels the senses. Perception is sharpened, impressions are heightened, blood circulates faster, and the brain functions better. I can still vividly remember the smallest details of tours of many years ago. Hypnotized? It is the traveler in a train or car who is hypnotized."

If anyone doubts that Velocio could see anything, let him read this short passage from a story of an Alpine crossing:

"A shaft of gold pierced the sky and came to rest on a snowy peak, which, moments before, had been caressed by soft moonlight. For an instant, showers of sparks bounced off the pinnacle and tumbled down the mountain in a heavenly cataract. The king of the universe, the magnificent dispenser of light and warmth and life, gave notice of his imminent arrival. But only for an instant. Like a spent meteor, the spectacle dissolved in the sea of darkness that engulfed me in the depths of the gorge. The scintillating reflections, the exploding fireballs—they were gone. Once again, the snow assumed its cold and ghostly face."

Could this passage have come from the pen of a cyclist obsessed by the mechanics of cycling? No—Velocio loved his bicycle because it brought him priceless freedom, because it gave him exhilarating exercise, because it opened his mind to the music of the wind, because it imparted a delicious feeling of being alive.

"After a long day on my bicycle," he said, "I feel refreshed, cleansed, purified. I feel that I have established contact with my environment and that I am at peace. On days like that, I am permeated with a profound gratitude for my bicycle." It was Velocio who coined the term "little queen" for the bicycle, a term that is still in common use in France.

And again: "Even if I did not enjoy riding, I would still do it for my peace of mind. What a wonderful tonic to be exposed to bright sunshine, drenching rain, choking dust, dripping fog, frigid air, punishing winds! I will never forget the day I climbed Puy Mary [a 5,000-foot eminence near his home]. There were two of us on a fine day in May. We started in the sunshine and stripped to the waist. Halfway, clouds enveloped us and the temperature tumbled. Gradually it got colder and wetter, but we did not notice it. In fact, it heightened our pleasure. We did not bother to put on our jackets or our capes, and we arrived at the little hotel at the top with rivulets of rain and sweat running down our sides. I tingled from top to bottom." Passages almost exactly like this can be found in the books of John Muir.

It was from experiences like these that Velocio formulated the seven commandments for the cyclist:

1. Keep your rests short and infrequent to maintain your rhythm.
2. Eat before you are hungry and drink before you are thirsty.
3. Never ride to the point of exhaustion where you can't eat or sleep.
4. Cover up before you are cold, peel off before you are hot.
5. Don't drink, smoke, or eat meat on tour.
6. Never force the pace, especially during the first hours.
7. Never ride just for the sake of riding.

Velocio was not a promoter. His efforts to create a national bicycle touring society like the Cyclists Touring Club in England floundered, and he never had an organized bicycle club even in his hometown. What he did have was a constantly growing body of friends and admirers who gathered around the master in his shop, at the rallies, and on his tours. Those who lived nearby formed a loose-knit group known as L'Ecole Stéphanoise, or the School of Saint-Etienne. A quorum was always on hand for Velocio's favorite ride to the top of the Col du Grand Bois. It was this ride that eventually grew into Velocio Day.

The Col du Grand Bois is a 3,800-foot passage across the Massif du Pilat. The road starts on the outskirts of Saint-Etienne and rises without letup over a distance of eight miles. Velocio used to make this ride as a constitutional before breakfast. In 1922 his friends surprised him by inviting all cyclists in the area to join in the ride in a gesture of reverence. Today, Velocio Day is a unique spectacle, the only one of its kind in the world.

This gradual emergence of Velocio as a dominant figure, not only among cyclists but among the people of his age, is one of the most interesting things about the man because he never made a conscious attempt to attract public notice. All he wanted was his bicycle and his friends. He never moved his shop, he never had much money, and he never rested on his laurels. Twice a year, he would have a little notice in *Le Cycliste,* inviting all and sundry to a rally. These rallies became famous. At first strictly local affairs, they eventually became national institutions and some of them are still observed, such as the Easter gathering in Provence. Velocio himself was not aware of his stature until he was invited to appear in Paris in the Criterium des Vieilles Gloires when he was seventy-six. Then it was obvious that he completely overshadowed all the others. Thousands gathered around him, just to shake his hand and wish him well.

On February 27, 1930, Velocio started his day with a reading from one of the classics, as was his custom. It was a letter from Seneca to Lucilius. "Death follows me and life escapes me. When I go to sleep, I think that I may never awake. When I wake up, I think that I may never go to sleep. When I go out, I think that I may never come back. When I come back, I think that I may never go out again. Always, the interval between life and death is short."

Velocio went out. Traffic was heavy, and he decided to walk and lead his bicycle. He crossed the street ahead of a streetcar coming from his left, saw another car coming from his right, stepped back, and was hit by the first. It was a mortal blow. He died clutching his beloved bicycle.

Today, thirty-five years later, Velocio lives on, while others, equally dedicated and equally inventive, are forgotten. Why is this?

It is because Velocio used his bicycle to demonstrate the great truths. Velocio's influence grew, not because of his exploits on the bicycle, but because he showed how these exploits will shape the character of a man. Velocio was a humanist. His philosophy came from the ancients who considered discipline the cardinal virtue. Discipline is of two kinds: physical and moral. Velocio used the physical discipline of the bicycle to lead him to moral discipline. Through the bicycle he was able to commune with the sun, the rain, the wind. For him, the bicycle was the expression of a personal philosophy. For him, the bicycle was an instrument in the service of an ideal. For him, the bicycle was the road to freedom, physical and spiritual. He gave up much, but he found more.

Velocio—the cyclists of the world salute you.

A PENNY-FARTHING FOR YOUR HEART, DARLING

CHARLES E. PRATT
February 1969

It may seem strange to some that the life story of two resolute men should hang upon a bit of ribbon. But note how trifles determine the course of events. A pebble may deflect the flying wheel and send its rider from the winning lead to a losing curb; or a ribbon may tangle its spinning spokes, or pull the pedaling bestrider by gentle impulse to the winner's goal. The tall oak and the little acorn furnish a too familiar illustration; but who stops to inquire what infant foot has pressed the acorn into the soil, or what urchin, throwing acorns at squirrels, has determined where the oak shall grow?

How few attempts to unravel the work of life and find the decisive stitches; how few, when they attempt it, stop their research at the larger events, and fail to find correctly the little things that made them occur. The silent bipedaliferous wheel has caused more happenings than have ever been written; it may even be the clue to mysteries yet unsolved.

One story out of the early days of bicycling in Massachusetts has remained untold, except in a very select circle of happy friends. It can now only be recited with such changes in names and vagueness of locality as to conceal the identity of the parties. With this limitation enough may be disclosed to entertain the resting wheelman, or to stir the heart of him or her who is not yet within that category. If the coloring, or even the weaving, of the story is not strictly in accord with the actual occurrence of events, some allowance must be made for lapse of time, and some for license of the storyteller.

In the delightful early spring of 1878 two young men, in the bloom and vigor of life, and with the good sense and pluck to keep them, began to be seen spinning over the charming roads radiating from Boston, on their bright, swift bicycles. As they grew more accustomed to the gait of their steel steeds and lither-limbed for the exercise, they sought longer communings with nature and with each other, and extended their runs farther and farther along the sinuous roads and amongst the pleasant hills and dales of the surrounding country.

In those happy days a bicycle was a bicycle, and it seemed to make little difference who made it or who imported it. They had not begun to discuss with so much avidity, not to say dilettantism, the merits or demerits of solid forks and hollow forks, of seventeen-inch and eighteen-inch rear wheels, of cones and rollers and balls, of weight and rake and tread and close-build; they did not question the rights of patentees, or look very closely at prices, or monopolies, or tariffs; there were for them no dissensions of clubs, no politics of the L.A.W., no wrangles about amateur and professional. The machines they had were not so fine as they have now, and they paid just as much for them, and they had but two or three sources through which to obtain them, but in those primitive times the bicycle was of itself a thing of beauty and a joy all the time; every wheelman was a gentleman and a brother, and the roads were the common meeting ground, the common highways, of good fellowship.

The two friends rode often abreast, often in line, sometimes rapidly and sometimes at a leisurely, sauntering rate, free as birds and jolly as yachtsmen. They drank in the fascination of motion with the fresh air and fragrance of the fields. They took the stimulus of positive exercise of limb and muscle and lung with that of the sunshine. They braced themselves to wind and grade, glided serenely through rural scenes, and partook of rustic hospitalities. With county road maps for charts, with pocket compass for direction and cyclometer for measurement, folding rule and tapeline for angles and perpendiculars, and with notebooks for incidents and memoranda, they went up and down as explorers and discoverers. Appetite was sharp, and sleep was sweet and sound; and a brave and generous life throbbed livelier through their hearts and brains. And others seeing and hearing it went and did likewise. What wonder that bicycling increased and multiplied?

Ralph and Ernest (for so their names must be called) were not exactly of the same age or temperament. Ralph was larger, strong and impetuous, of "fine old family," as the phrase goes, and full of jollity and good humor. Ernest was rather slightly formed, studious, and, in company, reticent and observing; he was finely educated and had a good position, but not so much prospect of wealth as the other. Both had many mutual acquaintances and interests, and each knew that the other had a warm personal friendship for Miss Gray, a young lady residing about three miles west-southwest from the old South Church.

They were, in reality, not madly in love, but were just in that interesting state intermediate between friendship and love, or rather where the former shades into the latter, and where one may, if he have consciousness and self-control, either halt or go forward without injustice or reproach. Moreover, whatever might have been the real feeling of Miss Gray toward either, she had shown equal circumspection and warmth of friendship to both, and indicated her preference for neither.

"I have a call to make this afternoon, and cannot go far with you today," said Ralph, as the two friends mounted for their usual Saturday spin, one pleasant day in September. "I told Annette I would come and play tennis with her and her sister, and stay to tea."

"Yes? So did I," replied Ernest, who had not known of the other's invitation. "Suppose we go together?"

Ralph hesitated. Whether it was this hesitation, or something in the previous tone of voice, Ernest was sensitive enough to perceive that there was already an impending collision or else divergence of feeling and interest. "I think, however," he generously added, pursuing his thoughts aloud, "that I will make an engagement elsewhere this time."

"No, don't," said Ralph abstractedly. "Do you think," he inquired, rather experimentally, "that Annette shows either of us any particular preference or favor?"

"I don't," answered his companion, "but I heartily wish she would, to be frank with you; and I think you do."

"Well, I do," answered the first. "I suspect we are likely to be rivals, unless we contrive to get her preference and abide by that now. We can either of us stop now, Ernest, and each of us seems to have a fair chance to win. It were better decided now."

"But how can we ascertain her preference without prejudice?" queried Ernest, brightening up. "You are bolder as well as more fertile in such expedients than I. Suggest."

"I have it!" exclaimed Ralph, after some moments. "We will go together and both ask her at the same time for the blue ribbon she wore last Saturday night at croquet. If she gives it to you, you take the lead; if she gives it to me, why—see?"

"Agreed," and they rode on together for some minutes in silence.

The friends, after circling that beautifully set gem of water, Jamaica Pond, set off toward the home of Miss Gray. Leaning their machines lightly against the fence before her father's house, they soon found themselves in her presence, and each was received as an expected friend. Her younger sister was already on the lawn, skipping about with a racquet and a ball. Annette herself, appropriately dressed for an afternoon on the lawn, and with a jaunty shade hat in her hand, wore a turquoise-blue ribbon simply folded and held with a pretty silver pin at her throat. Before she had invited her guests to the lawn, Ralph, still holding his riding-cap in hand, and advancing a few steps toward her, proffered his request for the ribbon.

"Miss Gray," he said, in a rich, manly voice, but evidently with a little embarrassment, "I have a very particular wish for a piece of ribbon—that which you wore last Saturday afternoon. Will you gratify me by letting me have it?"

"One moment, Miss Gray," said Ernest, already at her side, "I ask for that ribbon, to keep as a souvenir of the delightful game of Saturday last—and remember that I was your partner."

Annette's face was an interesting study. The look of innocent surprise at Ralph's beginning faded into a puzzled expression before he had ended; and the lips, almost posed for a half-mechanical "Certainly," parted in a smile when the other interposed; then, with a quick glance from one suitor to the other, her eyes fell and her cheeks tingled with a conscious blush. Her hesitation was momentary only, for she quickly replied, "Really, it is a trifle you ask for! and, as it is in two pieces, I will give each of you a part. But you must ride for it," she added, without waiting for a reply, as she glanced at the neat riding suits of her two friends standing before her in close-cut coats, trim knee-breeches, and stockings.

Whether she divined something of disappointment in either face which she was willing to dispel, or whether she, too, had a little ruse to satisfy a personal wish, they did not know; but they replied almost simultaneously, "I'll ride for it," and still looked at her inquiringly.

"I left it at my cousin's this week," pursued Annette, "and you may ask Miss Brown for the blue ribbon I left

"Go!" said Annette, as she watched from the window.

on her dressing case—each for a part of it—and," she added, half playfully, half earnestly, toying with the ribbon she wore, "I'll give *this* to the one who brings the other to me first."

"I'm ready," said Ralph.

"And I," said Ernest.

"Go," said Annette, as her glance fell longer on Ralph, and she went to the window to see the start.

Miss Brown lived ten miles away. It was four fifteen o'clock on the mantel as the friends left the library room for their wheels. A brisk breeze was just slackening, and the shadows grew long in the well-kept landscapes by which they passed at a quick, even pace for a mile or two, chatting of their first race and settling the route to be taken. Erect and graceful, with no apparent effort, they rode along without disparity, except in height, for one bestrode a forty-eight-inch roadster, the other a fifty-four-inch roadster, the semiracer. Perhaps it was deemed certain that the latter would win. Both knew every part of the route, and both were acquainted with Oenone Brown, a charming brunette, full of life and vivacity, and unspoiled by a course at Wellesley. Ernest had been charmed by her sweetness of voice and delicacy of execution as she sang in the twilight of a summer evening, or played accompaniment while he and Ralph sang bass and tenor duets. But with all her vivacity and apparent frankness of manner there was a dignified reserve, which Ernest had of late been half consciously debating in his own mind, without being entirely satisfied that it was not either haughtiness or dislike. He could not have explained why it was, but somehow the thought of her spurred him on more than the thought of Annette.

Gradually the conversation lessened with our competitors, and the pace quickened. To them, as their imaginations outsped their rubberhoofed courses, the bicycle became

> A wheel which turned and turned,
> With nave of burning gold and jewelled spokes,
> And strange things written on the bending tire,
> Which seemed both fire and music as it whirled.

Hedges, gardens, fields receded as they flew, and the "little hills skipped like lambs." Ralph had gained the lead and held it well, until a long hill stretched upward before them, where the surface of the roadway was less smooth and firm. Here each bent to his work, and the warm pedalers toiled harder and more slowly to the summit, to find themselves drawing a long breath abreast. A brief exchange of words and a resoluteness of movement revealed the serious aspect which the contest had assumed. The strong muscles of the older and larger rider seemed to leap to their work, and the ankles of the smaller showed their necessarily quicker action. There was nice engineering required, too; for, poised as they were, well forward on the fore wheel and moving at speed, a small stone or an unexpected rut or gulley might throw the unlucky rider and disable him or his steed. The strain became intense. Then there were passing teams and road crossings, and the irrepressible dog and small boy to be curved for.

And now, at last, within two miles of the turning goal, one of those pests of wheelmen, the driver who wants to race, entered upon the course from a side street.

Taking middle road, the man with the buggy and dark bay horse, giving a free rein and diverse encouragements, urges his beast to attempt a three-minute gait. Taking advantage of a smooth siding, Ernest gains the clear road in front and outstrips the intruder, while Ralph, waiting his safe opportunity, at last, in sheer despair, makes a spurt with the buggy for the lead, leaning dangerously near a collision, and then leaving the dust and clattering hoofs behind.

But Ernest has reached the villa where the silken trophy must be found. Springing from the left pedals, with right toe on the perch (as was the forward dismount in those days), he luckily spies Oenone just disappearing in the garden. In a moment he stands before her, glowing with the swift ride and with the moisture of physical effort on his brow. The manliness of his form and features is heightened just now by the consciousness of first achievement. He scans the dial of his watch and observes that it is forty-five minutes since he left Miss Gray's.

Explanation of the hasty errand followed quickly, and was duly appreciated by the sympathetic Oenone, who promised at once to produce the blue ribbon, but begged him to be seated while she brought it.

"There must be something more than that trifle which nerves you to this effort," said Oenone, retreating a little way and twirling a dainty willow basket in her hand. "Blue eyes are certainly more inspiring than ribbons. I have read of gentlemen fighting for a lady's glove, and all that; but this is more romantic than all," she added archly and, as Ernest thought, mischievously.

"But brown eyes are my favorites," he protested; "and I could ride farther and faster for the cherry bow on your hair."

"Blue and cherry do not go together, you know," was the quick retort.

If Ernest Hathaway had had any doubt hitherto as to which of the two young ladies he cared most for, or as to whether he was really in love, he had none now. As Miss Brown stood before him, without the restraint of the drawing room, beautiful under the overhanging maple boughs as a naiad queen, his twilight of feeling broke at once into day.

"Oenone," he said, with unaccustomed courage, "I have been playing a part today with a friend. I cannot tell you all now; but I have won the first race and am entitled to the first prize. Award me the cherry bow from your hair, and I shall be happy." And he took her hand reverently but firmly in his, and raised it to his lips.

"Mis' Brown! Mis' Brown! shure ther's a gintleman here, mum, with two o'thim bysickles, mum, 'n he's afther seein' yo roight away, mum."

"Well, go right and tell him I'll be in in a moment, Bridget," she said to the servant; and the two interrupted ones walked in silence into the house. Here Ralph repeated the request for the blue trophy, and when it was produced, he took it and handed one piece to his comrade. "Thank you," said the latter, "you may carry it all."

Ralph was puzzled, but waited for no explanation, and bowing good-bye to Miss Brown, he led the way to the waiting wheels.

On the return run Ralph was allowed to make the pace, while Ernest rode meditatively at his rear wheel for some distance. Neither spoke until the long hill was reached,

They coasted down together at almost lightning speed.

when, with legs over handles, they coasted down together at almost lightning speed.

It was a dangerous way to do. The foot rests and toe rests, which had been so much in vogue, were then becoming obsolete, really because of their temptation to coasting and its attendant danger; though, perhaps, ostensibly on account of the incoming style of "legs-over," which was urged by many as a safer method of taking hills. Hard instances of experience afterward became frequent enough to turn the judgment of wheelmen to the safer conclusion that, except on short, smooth, unobstructed declines, where play may be indulged, coasting, in any way, is unsafe; and that it is just as necessary and consistent that a bicycler should always have complete control of his steel steed as it is that a driver should retain command of his horse.

Near the bottom of this hill our riders discovered a tip-cart. Ralph, having the lead, was able to glide by without accident; but Ernest, attempting to gain his pedals, and using his brake too quickly, took that peculiar interruption to a wheelman's equanimity known as a "header." Fortunately for his limbs, there was neither wall nor curb by the wayside, but only soft gravel and turf, over which he took two or three promiscuous revolutions; then, with a half-dazed feeling, he raised first himself and then his bicycle, to find the latter with only a bent handlebar and the former with a much-soiled coat and a hand slightly scratched.

It was evident that Ralph now had the race on the homestretch. Looking back, however, at the foot of the hill, he saw his companion sitting on the ground with his machine by his side. His first impulse was to dismount and go to his friend; his second, to go on and keep the advantage he now had. He believed that Ernest was serious in the contest, and he found himself more intensely interested in the real stake than he had admitted. Surely Annette he thought, had given him a meaning glance at the start and, perhaps, counted upon his easily winning by reason of his larger wheel and finer physique. At all events he must show her some prowess now that she put him to the test, and he must not lose the advantage with her which he might now gain, however slight it might be. But he yielded to his first impulse, and returned to his friend, with genuine inquiry for his safety. As they straightened the bent handlebar against a tree, conversation ran somewhat as follows:

"I won't take advantage of your fall," he said generously. "We will wait and start fair again, when you are able. Or, perhaps, as you were first to reach the ribbon, we will complete our ride leisurely together without further contest."

"Not at all," replied Ernest; "though I thank you very much. You shall now remount first, and I will follow and pursue you. I warn you that I shall pass you if I can."

"Well, then take your part of the ribbon, and a race it is," said Ralph rather warmly.

"No, I don't care for that ribbon, but I am riding today for something as valuable as you, and shall win if I can." As he said this there was an inexplicable, faraway look in his eye which Ralph had never noticed before. The friends had found themselves for once without mutual understanding.

The remainder of the ride was a race, and a pretty one. Rim and rim for a mile; then, with a fine spurt, Ernest shot ahead and left several lengths between them. Then Ralph leaned forward and exerted himself to the utmost, and made a gallant dash ahead just far enough to alight first before the open window where Annette was watching for their return.

"Bravo! Six o'clock to a minute, and you are the winner!" she exclaimed to Ralph, as he held up the blue evidence of distance. Gratification beamed in her eyes; for she was no exception to the rule that the fair sex admire the successful man, or that other rule that they delight in gallant deeds done in either devotion or compliment to them. It was without an exhibition of reluctance that, after they had entered and were seated, she unpinned the turquoise ribbon from her own breast and fastened it upon Ralph's, with a wish that he might ever be as successful in his undertakings.

"My friend was first at Miss Brown's, and might have been first here, perhaps, but for an accident," remarked Ralph. "It was an honest race, I assure you."

"To avoid accidents is a good part of achievement,"

rejoined Ernest; "and then, accidents have their place in working out desired results sometimes," he added thoughtfully. "Ralph would also have been first at Miss Brown's, too, perhaps, had it not been for an accident. You see there were wheels and wheels, if not within wheels, today."

When the two friends had gone upstairs to freshen their toilet for tea, and had closed the door behind them, Ernest was first to make conversation:

"We have not played tennis this afternoon; but we've played a better game."

"And I have won, my dear fellow," was the reply. "And I don't believe you care. But I propose to follow up the contest for something more than this ribbon."

"We have *both* won" was the rejoinder. "I shall leave you here this evening and retrace my ride"; and without other words Ernest took from his pocket a cherry bow.

It was Oenone's; for as they had walked out to their wheels at Miss Brown's, she had taken the coveted trifle from her hair, unobserved by Ralph, and said softly, "Ernest, I will lend it to you till you can tell me all."

So far the thread of the story is clearly traceable; the main points have been verified, with ample exchange of cigarettes, on an overnight excursion, and even attested confidentially over more than one cup of tea. But there is less certainty about the immediately subsequent course of events. A peculiar reticence of two of the characters since that eventful afternoon, and also diverse ambiguous intimations by the other two, tend to preserve a veil of mystery about the ultimate award of prizes. At all events, the two young men who had found themselves that afternoon without a mutual understanding, and who apparently had in mind two other mutual understandings to be established that evening, agreed to meet again at eleven o'clock that night at Meeting-House Hill and have a confidential talk.

Just before the appointed hour Ralph approached the place of meeting with noiseless wheel. The moon had set and even the starlight was half snuffed out by cloudy extinguishers moving along the sky. Here and there a dim lamppost showed the general bend of the street and deepened the darkness between it and the next. The stillness of night was broken only by rustling leaves and occasiona footfalls of late returners to suburban homes. If any of these noticed the wheelman's passing, they could not recognize his countenance, as the headlamp, whose rays illumined for a few yards in advance the track for his soft tires, left his form more completely in the dark.

What Ralph's meditations were, as, having dismounted at the intersection of ways, he leaned with his right arm on the saddle and waited, the reader can infer as well as the writer. The fact was that after two cigarettes and several readings of the dial of his watch, he raised the wick of his lamp, remounted, and circling twice about the square, turned away and rode home. His companion of so many evening runs did not arrive until later than midnight at least, though the exact time when he passed Meeting-House Hill has never been disclosed. Ralph had no apprehensions for the personal safety of his friend, however. He knew that whatever accidents may occur from carelessness or inadvertence in the daytime, nothing serious ever befell a wheelman when riding by night.

It is to be assumed as true that two scenes in courtship were enacted that September evening; but what occurred at either remains as yet untold. In Ralph's bachelor apartments, however, a photograph of two little Hathaways, named Annette and Ralph, rests in an easel on the mantel; and there stands, too, as if it were a companion piece, on another easel, mounted with a pretty silver pin on a plain white cabinet card, a turquoise-blue ribbon.

Reprinted from The Wheelman, *December 1882.*

FIRST ACROSS AMERICA BY BICYCLE

IRVING A. LEONARD
April 1965

One morning in April 1884 the ferryboat *Alameda* from San Francisco put into the Oakland slip, and presently a short stocky figure emerged, trundling a fifty-inch high-wheel bicycle along the pier. Dressed in a blue flannel shirt of ample fit and trousers of the same color gathered at the knee in a pair of duck-hunting leggings, this solitary individual vaulted with practiced skill onto the saddle of his machine. Waving a broad-brimmed slouch hat to a small assembly of cycling enthusiasts and curious bystanders who had gathered to witness his departure, he rolled away over the rough macadam pavement toward Berkeley and San Pablo. The rider was beginning the first successful journey by bicycle across the continent from ocean to ocean and one that would later take him around the world. Within the past three years seven different cyclists in the United States had attempted the same transcontinental feat, but mountain barriers, bridgeless streams, and desert sands had, in each case, turned them back.

Our gallant and adventurous cyclist was Thomas Stevens, whose amazing trip seems utterly impossible by modern-day standards.

It is even more remarkable when one considers that Stevens accomplished this feat, not on a fast, well-equipped lightweight, but on a high-wheel ordinary, frequently called the "wheel."

The older machine was a cumbrous affair weighing from thirty-five to sixty pounds, whose mastery usually required considerable practice at no small risk of broken bones.

Compared to the modern bicycle the high wheel was less maneuverable, for the rider's position, wedged close to the handlebars, gave limited play for steering, and sharp turns were nearly impossible to negotiate. Moreover, since

Thomas Stevens (1854–1935).

the cyclist's center of gravity was only slightly off a line perpendicular with the hub of the forewheel, even a small upward gradient required vigorous pedaling. Coasting downhill, on the other hand, was likely to be precarious, since the forward pitch of the rider tended to raise the small hind wheel off the ground, which circumstance might send the unlucky cyclist headlong from his lofty perch. Indeed, skill in taking "headers" was a prerequisite of successful bicycling, and the day's run was often measured more by the number of "headers" taken than by distance traversed.

California had experienced its rainiest winter season since 1857 when Stevens mounted his wheel that April morning of 1884, the twenty-second of the month to be precise, and the dirt roads that he soon encountered, ordinarily quite passable, were muddy and unridable. Frequent dismounts and trundling limited the first day's run to an overnight stop near Suisun Bay. There a skeptical German offered to bet him five dollars that he would not get very far. The fact that the Sacramento River was in full flood made the wager look like a losing proposition when he learned that the only possibility of crossing to the other side was by the long railroad trestle.

The next day, undeterred by the prospect, he pushed his machine over this precarious means of transit for six weary miles with the sound of rushing waters beneath mingling with the monotonous bump-bump of his wheel as he stepped from tie to tie. Midway across the river the rumble of an approaching train brought alarm. Hastily looking about for a ready means of escape, he hurriedly took refuge on a projecting crossbeam on which he crouched, dangling his heavy bicycle over the flooding stream as the ponderous locomotive and its coaches thundered by.

On entering the eastern foothills of California, Stevens found it preferable to follow the railroad tracks along which, occasionally, were ridable sidepaths, for sticky red clay made the wagon roads virtually impassable. But the steadily rising gradient obliged him to walk much of the time, pushing his heavy machine before him. Rain by "bucketsful" and even melting slush added to his hardships as he trudged up the steep Sierras, where from time to time the muffled boom of far-off snowslides assailed his ears. Though it ended all possibility of riding, he was soon grateful for the shelter of the great, gloomy snowsheds of the railroad that extended, with but few breaks, for some forty miles. Otherwise he could not have crossed the wintry mountains for another month.

"Not a living thing is in sight," he reported concerning his intermittent glimpses of the landscape, writing always in the present tense, "and the only sound the occasional roar of a distant snowslide, and the mournful sighing of the breeze through the branches of the somber pines, half buried in the omnipresent snow." Groping through the smoke-blackened wooden tunnel and pushing a bicycle over the irregular surface was anything but pleasant. The reverberations of an approaching train aroused sharp dread and prompted the anxious pedestrian-cyclist to cast about for a suitable place to flatten himself against the rough wall and escape the three oncoming, asthmatically puffing engines that were tugging a long string of freight cars up the steep grade. They filled every nook and cranny of the enclosure with a raucous din and a dense smoke that darkened the whole interior to a Stygian blackness that, it seemed, could be felt. "I had to grope my way forward inch by inch afraid to set foot down for fear of a culvert at the same time never knowing whether there is room to get out of the way of the train," he wrote. Every few steps he paused, in the oppressive silence, to listen for the sound of a locomotive, and the slight rattle of the bicycle trundled over the uneven ground seemed loud enough, in his uneasy state of mind, to prevent hearing the dreaded approach of another steam engine.

Stevens finally made it to Nevada, where the character of the country changed abruptly. If California had offered the bicyclist few good stretches of riding, Nevada, Utah, Wyoming, and indeed much of the trans-Mississippi West seemed unlikely to be more generous in this respect. Indeed, nearly a quarter of a century later the roadless situation remained virtually unchanged, for in 1908, when automobilists were attempting to emulate Stevens' feat in their self-propelled vehicles, it was reported that "there were no roads west of Laramie. . . ." And even as late as 1915 it could be stated that "between Minneapolis and San Francisco there was not one mile of paved road outside the cities. . . ." Such, then were the unpromising prospects for the success of his transcontinental journey when the adventurous cyclist in 1884, passing through Reno without halting, proceeded along the Truckee River with many dismounts after short ridable patches. It was here that he reported finding himself followed "at a respectable distance of five hundred yards by coyotes."

At Wadsworth, Nevada, he prepared to cross the Forty Mile Desert, that expanse of sand, rocks, and bleaching bones so dreaded by emigrant parties in the days of the Forty-Niners. Stevens had counted upon buying a water canteen in the drab hamlet but he found none available and concluded to substitute a dozen oranges for liquid refreshment. Thus provisioned for desert travel, he boldly struck across the sands. The day was hot and it was soon evident that he was carrying the bicycle much more than it was carrying him. Now and then, however, he came upon alkali flats where he could mount and skim over the hard surface and where, as he afterward reported, "wheeling was as good as the sand-paper roads around Boston." But mostly he had to shoulder the bicycle and walk, his feet sinking ankle deep at every step and filling his shoes with sand. All about him lay "the dreary Nevada desert with no company but my uncanny shadow sharply outlined on the white alkali by the glaring rays of the sun," and it was heavy going through the "dreariest and dreadest looking country imaginable."

While coyotes, mountain cougars, wild horses, and skulking wolves were frequently seen or heard, human beings were comparatively rare in the vast expanse of land over which hung much of the time an oppressive silence. In the California Sierras Stevens had encountered an occasional Digger Indian and even in Nevada, Piutes who stared with expressionless faces at the strange apparition of a white man gliding along on a shiny high wheel. Chinese coolies and cowpunchers, the latter rarely sober, were often the sole inhabitants of the desert hamlets. In one community where a drunken spree was in progress, the cyclist found it expedient to hurry on to avoid the exuberance of trigger-happy cowboys all too likely to empty their revolvers at anything, including an object so novel as a bicycle. Reaching Carlin, Nevada, after dark, the weary traveler was compelled to give a riding exhibition to a group of insistent loafers at the local saloon who were unable to comprehend how a vehicle that could not stand by itself like a horse was yet able to carry a man over the ground. The lack of a suitable flat area for this purpose resulted in a seemingly impossible feat that Stevens was obliged to perform. "As there is no other place suitable, I manage to circle around the pool table in the hotel bar room, nearly scalping myself against the bronze chandelier."

Across Nevada, through Utah, and over the Continental Divide Stevens pushed onward.

As the Rockies grew hazy in the distance, the dominant

feature of the landscape was the flower-spangled prairie of Nebraska. At frequent intervals multitudes of prairie dogs emerged from their holes to protest in noisy and excitable fashion the cyclist's invasion of their domains. Along the South Platte River especially he observed the presence of homesteaders who, with their wagons, tents, and sod huts, were advancing westward like a picket line to dispute the hegemony of autocratic cattle barons. Between wagon ruts he rode, often wobbling precariously on his lofty perch, "and I consider it a lucky day that passes without adding one or more to my long and eventful list of headers." And more than once he was "unhorsed" by a sudden gust of wind of the prairie "that blows me and the bicycle square over."

At Omaha he crossed the Missouri and plunged into the fertile farmlands of Iowa. Then across the Mississippi and through Illinois to Chicago.

The first day's ride from the Windy City competed in difficulty and strenuous exertion with the bicyclist's arduous travels in the Far West. After fifteen miles of pleasant pedaling the road abruptly changed to deep sand through which he trudged into Indiana. The many miles along the southern shore of Lake Michigan offered no opportunity to vault into the saddle, and only on the firmer sand at the water's edge was the task of transporting the bicycle easier.

Finally, in exasperation, he shouldered the machine and struck off into the interior, scaling sand dunes until he was lost in a bewildering wilderness of swamps, sandhills, and hickory thickets, assailed everywhere by "ruthless, relentless, mosquitoes." When darkness fell he dropped his burden and sank exhausted under a wheat shock to spend the night.

In Ohio he fared much better, though the heat was excessive, and in Cleveland he was arrested for riding on the city sidewalks, from which embarrassment he was rescued by local wheelmen who had been following with keen interest his well-publicized adventure across country. Pedaling on, the road surfaces improved and became splendid in the Erie region about northeastern Pennsylvania and western New York near Lake Chautauqua, already famous for its summer religious and cultural assemblies. A brief stop at Buffalo for repairs permitted a quick excursion to Niagara Falls, after which he resumed his now triumphal course, feted along the way by local bicycle clubs. At Syracuse his route closely paralleled the Erie Canal, and by alternately riding along its towpath, on wagon roads, and between the tracks of the New York Central Railroad, he managed to stay mounted much of the time.

Encounters with temperamental towing mules along the canal's edge were not, however, conducive to peaceful cycling, Stevens soon discovered, and he humorously explained that "the greatest drawback is the towing mule and the awful, unmentionable profanity engendered thereby in the utterances of the boatmen. Sometimes the burden of the sulphurous profanity is aimed at me, sometimes at the inoffensive bicycle, or both of us collectively, but oftener it is directed at the unspeakable mule, who is really the only party to blame. The Erie Canal mule's first mission in life is to engender profanity and strife between boatmen and cyclists" was the philosophic observation of the rider of the "silent" steed.

Stevens arrived in Boston at two o'clock in the afternoon of August 4, 1884, 103 days after leaving the Oakland Pier in California. Stevens calculated he had traveled about 3,700 miles, walking, pushing, or carrying his heavy machine about one third of the distance.

Thomas Stevens, the redoubtable wheelman, who briefly enjoyed world fame during his subsequent travels, could proudly claim distinction as the first, in his own words, "to imprint the rubber hoofmarks of the popular steed of the day" all the way across the often roadless breadth of the vast continent of America.

ADOWN THE SUSQUEHANNA'S SIDE:
A HIGH-WHEEL CLUB RUN IN 1883

F. EMMET O'BRIEN
January 1969

We gazed at the nickel-plated moon in silence while Aurora shot her glided spokes athwart the zenith, and a falling star took a header down the sky. It was a glorious night to plan a poetic journey.

"Boys, I move we tour the Wyoming Valley tomorrow," said the captain; and in a moment we were discussing the routes, forecasting the weather, and carefully inspecting our machines. All were full of glorious anticipations of the morrow, except the newest member, who only hoped to keep up with the veterans a mile or two, and then sadly return. I had the honor of protecting our rear in all the runs since I had joined the club, and expected to hold that important post at all hazards, even if I had to stay miles behind to do it.

At ten next morning we started. It was Sunday; no workday in the calendar was ever fitted for such a delightful run. The cinder path between the rails had been decided on for the first two miles. Only it was too smooth. I had to exert myself to the utmost to keep up with the 54 and the ballbearing 50's and 52's, and when one of those narrow culverts between the ties compelled a dismount, I had to take a running mount while the boys mostly slipped on a narrow board or on a sleeper.

At Taylorville, the end of the cinder path, I was thoroughly blown. We stopped at the inn, where our paths were to diverge, and the boys asked me to name some of the muscles that the wheel employs. Before I had mentioned three hundred my respiration was normal, and I resolved to try for Pittston, where I could leave my wheel to be expressed back, and return by buggy myself.

So we took the path along the old Carbondale and Wilkes-Barre turnpike, while Captain Kolp told the boys how the locomotive spilled the milk. I happened to be at his headquarters when the telephone called me to a man hurt at Greenwood mines. He mounted me on one of his Columbias, and we started down between the L. & S. tracks while trains were moving on either side of us. I'll never do it again, but the captain sped between the locomotives as straight as an arrow, and I followed, with my teeth set. There were two men in our path. They saw the captain and moved enough to let him pass, but not enough to get in the way of the locomotive, which was coming down behind me. One saw me, and the other had his back toward me. I did not speak, because I wished him not to move; but just as I neared him, at full speed, the man who saw me cried, "Look out!" Of course he looked, not for me, but for the locomotive, and my handlebar took him in the back. Did you ever see a soldier doubled up by a rebel shell? He went down like a shot, and his milk can fell under the cars. Need I say that I dismounted(?), and tried to convince him that it was not the locomotive. Had I been a layman he would have convinced me that the "spine of his back" was broken into smithereens, and that the whole coal train had "knocked him speechless." The captain had just finished this incident off, with much embellishment, when we fell into Indian file, and coasted down the sidewalk through Old Forge to the wooden bridge which spans the brawling, roaring, and picturesque Lackawanna.

I began to get my second wind, and as we stopped to imbibe some ginger beer at Lackawanna, I also felt that I could complete the nine miles to Pittston without too much fatigue. The river babbled along beside us; the mountains made wider sweeps of green; and "pleasant valleys" opened up to make the transition from the somber anthracite valley to "fair Wyoming" less abrupt. I shall not attempt to describe the sweep of the Susquehanna River by Campbell's Ledge into this lovely valley. Read "Gertrude of Wyoming," or read John Eregina Barrett's less known, but scarcely less pathetic, poem of "Isabell." We crossed the beautiful river by the footpath of the lower bridge without dismounting and sped through West Pittston, and so

Adown the Susquehanna's side,
Where weeping willows, green and grave,
Salute the ever-gliding tide.

It was noon, and the speed of the party having been accommodated to the slowest member, we had only made ten miles, including stops, in two hours; but the path became gloriously smooth; the scenery grew more lovely every mile; the day was perfect, and I resolved to try for Wilkes-Barre, ten miles farther by the path. Heavens! what a magnificent run that was—past lawns and hedges, flower gardens and delightful cottages, the path sped on as smooth as ice. With congenial comrades and a perfect day, we seemed to fly along without an effort, every muscle invigorated, every nerve tingling with enjoyment, and the blood glowing like wine in heart and arteries. We made Wilkes-Barre at one o'clock, registering ten miles in the last hour, and, crossing the dilapidated old bridge, dismounted at the Wyoming House by the river side.

During the last few miles of our journey visions of roast beef, roast turkey with cranberry sauce, beefsteak and onions, etc., flitted before our minds as the landscape zipped by. The Wyoming monument suggested massacres of commissary stores, rather than of colonial patriots, and as we swept through Kingston, in Indian file, our feelings must have been nearly identical with those of Brandt's savages when they descended on the devoted band at Forty Fort: they hungered for scalps, we for rations. Our tread was as noiseless as theirs, our course more rapid.

Five years ago, upon another sentimental journey, I dined splendidly at this hotel, the slight overofficiousness of the gentlemanly waiter, which marked our failure to conceal our identity as a bridal party, being the only flaw in the feast.

The remembrance of the splendid cuisine, whetted by an occasional visit since, induced me to give free reins to my descriptive powers, and rather too free control to my Columbia; for in the midst of a gorgeous prospective feast, while following a narrow path, my off-pedal touched a fence post, and instantly I sought the rugged bosom of Mother Earth. At the same moment Fred, who was ahead, and who must have been too intently listening, touched

the same fence and spread himself on the gravel. Our
noble guide, who had modestly left the front since striking
smooth road, now struck the wreck and reposed on the
same kindly bosom. But our enthusiasm for a good dinner
was unabated, and the hardest headers we ever took
seemed light to the shock we experienced when informed
that the Sunday dinner hour had been changed to the
aesthetic hour of 6:00 P.M.

Our feelings were intense, our remarks utterly blank.
However, we could have "lunch," and a member having
suggested that we demolish it and then seek some other
hotel to devastate a square meal, the proposition was
adopted by acclamation, and we adjourned to the dining
room. My old waiter was there, and the way he spread
cold turkey, beef tea, sandwiches, pickles, coffee, and such
trifles before us must have been a revelation to his com-
patriots of the napkin; for probably never was a more
substantial lunch destroyed by an athletic party, and never
were gentlemanly waiters more gratefully tipped. Aesthetic
lunch was voted an immense success, and, on invitation,
we adjourned to the parlor of the genial secretary of the
Wilkes-Barre Club, where champagne, old bourbon, and
cigars promoted fraternal enjoyment and reminiscences
of bicycling adventures by land and water (our host has
a marine bicycle), by valley and mountain.

I will only relate one by mountain. Half a dozen of the
boys had been seeking new roads to conquer all summer,
and finally took a trip to Moosic Lake, on the top of the
Moosic mountain, ten miles from Scranton. They pretended afterward that they enjoyed it, and that though the
grades were steep they occasionally had a chance to ride
a few yards to relieve the monotony of pushing their tired
steeds upward.

The captain, indeed, asserts that as he toiled up the
last mile the boys ahead shouted that the road in front
was smooth and level, and so he found it—level water.
Then, after taking a grateful bath, the devoted band considering that the road behind was too steep to coast,
pushed on over the mountain, six miles, to Peckville, in
the Lackawanna Valley, seven miles above the starting
point, picking fine blackberries and gathering fresh laurels

as they journeyed, and finally, getting a splendid run home
on one of our *old* roads.

None of the conservative members of the club attempted
to imitate this daring exploit, but I saddled my old charg-
er, Frank, and essayed the route on horseback. I reached
Moosic Lake all right, horse and man hot and tired;
both plunged into the cool, translucent waves, which rest
serenely in the mountaintop, seven hundred feet above
Scranton, and seventeen hundred above the sea. After
this refreshing plunge we inquired the way of some of the
sojourners of the summer camp, and took the road for
Peckville. For a few hundred yards we had plain sailing;
then the road home became a grassy lane, which, in half
a mile, lost itself completely in rocks and underbrush.
Frank and I, like the bicyclists, did not wish to turn back,
but continued our way over boulders, fallen trees, and
brush.

"So toilsome was the road to trace" that I dismounted
and led my noble horse over five miles of the wildest and
most difficult mountain fastness that it was ever my lot to
encounter. Fancy pictured the handsomely uniformed gentlemen carefully guiding their nickel-plated machines over
the same lovely track.

The sun slanted westward, and far down the mountain
beneath the shadow of some rocks I thought it danced
upon some shining nickel; yes, in a moment our ex-
captain's heroic form glided out from the rock upon his
trusty 52, and one after another the members of the club
followed and ascended the precipitous hill. They rode over
trees and clove through masses of rock in defiance of the
well-known properties of matter and laws of gravitation.
Reaching the summit, they turned and coasted down over
terrific abysses and stupendous rocks, fire flashing from
their spokes, and rocks, dust, and gravel following in their
wake. It seemed as if the genii of the mountain were
awake and joining in the sport. At last, when a coast like
lightning was made by the bicycles, a perfect avalanche
of boulders hurtled down the mountain and woke me—
to find Frank pawing restlessly above me and scattering
stones and gravel over my face. We reached home in
safety, but, as before observed, none of the cautious mem-

bers ever tried that route with wheels; none of the married men, I mean, who have families dependent on them.

With chaff like this, and much more entertaining converse, we whiled away the warm hour with our host, Captain Carpenter of the Wilkes-Barre Club (the fastest rider about this region), and other visitors, and when, at 4:00 P.M., Captain K ordered "Mount," every man sprang into his saddle, more vigorous and fresh than at the starting. Adieus were waved, spoken, and I suspect even whispered by the more romantic members as we started over the Susquehanna.

Speeding back through Kingston we retraced our path of the morning, and so on through fair Wyoming. Just here a low branch over the path struck our fastest man across the eyes so smartly that he was fain to consult the surgeon on the case. Obtaining sick leave from the commander, we rode off to find a drugstore, while a hasty examination was made (en route) of the complaining optics. Nothing discovered itself, however, except a peculiar motion of the near eyelid, accomplished by some contraction of the muscles of expression. It was evidently an urgent case. Finding an apothecary, some medication was quickly instilled beneath the eyelid; but as the patient was plainly sinking from "shock" or something, and as the tremulous motion of the lid had now transferred itself to the other eye, the ancient wielder of the pestle was informed that it was imperative to produce two eye-openers at once—one to assist the surgeon's vision and one to relieve the patient. The venerable pill-compounder sadly intimated that he could not sell on Sunday, owing to local option, but he neatly filled some prescription which had such effect that patient and surgeon were able to overtake the rest of the party and speed along through West Pittston and over a footwalk of the other bridge, where a header would have cost us a plunge of forty feet into the river.

It was somewhat uphill work back through the Lackawanna Valley, but we reached home at dark, tired but happy, feeling that we had enjoyed a run such as we may wish to all your readers.

TRANS-ASIA BIKE TOUR IN 1890

IRVING A. LEONARD
November 1968

Two members of the class of 1890 at Washington University, St. Louis, Missouri, spent their senior year dreaming and planning a bicycle trip around the world, and the day after graduation in June they departed for New York to make the dream come true. The idea, they said, was conceived as "a practical finish to a theoretical education" in the liberal arts, but the recently (1887) published two-volume account of Thomas Stevens' pioneer feat on a high-wheel ordinary was probably the true inspiration. The record bicycle journey of these two spirited youths, Thomas G. Allen, Jr., and William Sachtleben by name, officially started at Liverpool, England. When, in 1894, their book *Across Asia on a Bicycle* appeared, it was a slim, illustrated volume in which they had chosen to recount only the Asiatic portion—Istanbul to Peking—of their three-year odyssey. That part, particularly western China, the Gobi Desert, and central China, they explained, was really the most remarkable and eventful. Possibly, too, the fact that Thomas Stevens had not passed through these regions of Asia, owing to adverse circumstances, contributed to the decision to confine their narrative largely to the most novel portion of an incredible journey.

The experience of crossing Turkey and Iran in 1891 on safety bicycles equipped with cushion tires resembled that of Stevens six years earlier. The roads were mostly caravan trails, and each evening, as the weary cyclists trundled their machines through the narrow streets of a town or village in quest of food and shelter, curious crowds nearly mobbed them and harassed the two youths by insistent cries to "Bin! Bin!" (Ride! Ride!), an ordeal often endured again at the morning starts. Nights in dirty khans or inns were frequently noisy and sleepless, while Turkish fare was invariably unappetizing. It usually con-

Allen and Sachtleben ready to cross the Gobi Desert.

sisted of yogurt, which the cyclists described as "curdled milk," and *ekmet,* a cooked bran flour paste, which they called "blotting-paper bread." The fact that this "Turkish peasant's staff of life" was baked in huge circular sheets inspired the young lads to punch a hole in the middle and slip them over their arms. This procedure happily provided a means of both transporting and eating, since they could nibble on the edges without removing their hands from the handlebars. And, with a favoring wind, these pastry sheets even answered the purpose of a sail! Often *zaptiehs,* or mounted guards, accompanied the riders. These horsemen liked to race with the bicyclists and generally proved more of a nuisance than a protection.

From Ankara they dropped south to Kayseri, or ancient Caesarea, with its ruins of the fourteenth-century Seljuks. There a mountain towering nearly thirteen thousand feet above them suggested their later rigorous ascent of the biblical Mount Ararat situated on the borders of Armenia, southern Russia, and Iran. At Sivas in Turkey they lingered several weeks while Allen recovered from typhoid fever, evidently contracted by drinking roadside water. At Erzurum, the Armenian capital, its civil governor accorded them gracious treatment and obliged them to proceed under guard through the pass to the east where, some three years later, another world cyclist, Frank G. Lenz, was fated to die at the hands of brigands.

After planting the American flag on Mount Ararat's lofty peak on July 4, 1891, Allen and Sachtleben wheeled into Iran, described as "one part desert with salt and the other desert without salt." At Tabriz illness again delayed them with Sachtleben succumbing this time to typhoid fever. Resuming their journey on August 15, 1891, they rode through heat, sometimes of 120°, to Tehran, the Iranian capital. There it required six weeks to obtain dubious assurances of Russian permission to pass through Turkestan. With only a promise that a travel permit would be telegraphed ahead to Meshed they pedaled six hundred miles over the "Pilgrim Road," subsisting on eggs, pomegranates, and *pillao,* or rice boiled in grease, much as Thomas Stevens had done five years before. More fortunate than he, however, the Russian pledge was kept and, accordingly, they crossed the frontier to Ashkhabad and moved on through legendary Samarkand to spend the winter at Tashkent.

Though they had won Russian consent to traverse Siberia to Vladivostok and had even forwarded spare bicycle parts along the route, they resolved, against everyone's advice, including Chinese officialdom, to take the more hazardous way to the Pacific through China. Hence, from May 7 to November 3, 1892, the two cyclists made a truly epic trek through Turkestan, western China, the Gobi Desert to the Great Wall of China, and ultimately to Peking, enduring scarcely credible hardships and privations. "Never since the days of Marco Polo," they alleged, "had a European traveler succeeded in crossing the Chinese empire from the west to Peking."

After pedaling over the vast emptiness of the desolate Kirgiz steppe region of Russia at an average speed of

seven miles an hour and lodging nights in its relatively
decent post stations, they entered western China and
reached Kuldja just over the border. In this city they made
final preparations for the long traverse of the Gobi Desert
to the Great Wall and Peking without guides, interpreters,
or servants. They stripped their equipment to a minimum
for the truly formidable journey over the route once traveled by Genghis Khan. To save weight they shortened
handlebars and seat posts and discarded leather baggage
carriers for sleeping bags of Chinese shawls and oiled
canvas; they even cut off extra parts of their clothing and
buttons and shaved their heads. These drastic reductions
were, in part, to allow for the heavy burden of Chinese
coins necessary for a journey of such length through country without exchange facilities. "Most of the silver was
chopped up into small bits and placed in the hollow tubing
of the machines to conceal it from Chinese inquisitiveness,
if nothing worse," they reported.

To the sounds of bellowing horns, boom of mortar can-
non, and dire predictions of failure the undaunted cyclists
departed from Kuldja at daybreak on July 13, 1892. With
moderate difficulties, including a broken rear wheel, shifting sand dunes, and mountain freshets, they reached
Urumchi, capital of Sinkiang province. There, curious
crowds noisily greeted them, surrounding the riders of the
"foreign horses" and "foot-moved carriages." In return
for cycling exhibitions the two youths were royally treated
and overwhelmed with gifts; their bicycles, it seemed,
were the very best passports for overcoming Chinese an-
tipathy to "foreign devils" and winning goodwill.

Resuming an eastward course, the ride to Hami on the
edge of the Gobi Desert was comparatively easy over
roads that permitted an average of fifty-three miles a day.
Then, after a brief pause for rest and repairs, they
plunged into the awesome desert "of vast undulating plains
of shifting red sands, interspersed with quartz, pebbles,
agates, and carnelians and . . . lines of hillocks succeeding
each other like waves on the surface of the shoreless
deep." Relentless, searing winds resisted their advance
and deep, unridable wagon tracks reduced progress to a
weary plodding over hot sands that burned their feet and
wore out sandals. Only passing packtrains, whose drivers

stared in silent amazement, and way stations of mud huts devoid of every convenience, varied the deadly monotony. Tea and sweetened bread, dubbed "Gobi cake" by the cyclists, were their daily sustenance, and their nights were torments of lice and fleas. Sick, emaciated, and barefoot after four hundred miles of journeying, they struggled into the hamlet at the western extreme of the Great Wall of China, where the bewildered natives regarded the mounted strangers as a species of centaur.

Though conditions now improved somewhat, misfortune dogged their progress. The most serious mishap was the breaking of one bicycle frame entirely in two. Somehow they contrived to hold the parts together with an iron bar in the hollow tubing and by telegraph wire but, "with a waddling frame and patched rear wheel describing eccentric revolutions, we must have presented a rather comical appearance over the remaining thousand miles to the coast." At last, on November 3, 1892, bare-legged, clothes in tatters, pinched and haggard, their bicycles battered, and with only the equivalent of a half dollar left, they limped into Peking. There, at the end of 3,116 miles of traversing the Flowery Kingdom, they found themselves celebrities who, in borrowed raiment, were exhaustingly feted and entertained in diplomatic and official circles of the city.

Of their subsequent careers the record is dim. Allen, apparently the chief author of their book, later published occasional articles in *Outing* magazine solely under his own name. Sachtleben (1867–1953) presently retraced their travels in Iran and Armenia in a futile effort to locate the remains of the ill-fated cyclist Frank G. Lenz. But the distinction of being the first to circle the globe on a modern safety bicycle clearly belongs to these young graduates of Washington University. Moreover, the success of their longer and more arduous journey eclipsed the hard-earned fame of the pioneer world tour on a highwheel ordinary earlier made by Thomas Stevens.

FUZZ ON WHEELS—COLORFUL COPS CUT CRIME

Law & Order MAGAZINE
August 1968

The Long Beach, California, Police Department made what it thought was a routine news announcement recently, but the story brought back poignant memories to a handful of America's retired policemen, now in their eighties.

The story involved the use of two plainclothes officers in a bicycle patrol, who speedily and quietly patrol the streets and alleys, parking lots, and even walkways between buildings in that Southern California city.

The two plainclothesmen on wheels are assigned where and when they are needed most, and the department has discovered that the bike patrol has produced more street-crime arrests, even when the incidence of crime has been reduced.

What the press called "unique" was really a rediscovery of the bicycle as a police vehicle. Prior to the turn of the century in the robust period of the Gay Nineties bicycles were the mainstay of the men in blue and were extensively used in America's largest cities.

Some of those bike patrolmen are still around to reminisce over glories that were theirs. No other city could boast sharper "lawmen on wheels" than New York City, where to be among the "crack bicycle patrol" was one of the highest honors attainable. It attracted the best physical specimens.

We must remember that in the Gay Nineties, the bicycling fad had mushroomed, and big cities were congested with men and women cycling for pleasure and sport. Up and down special paths they pedaled their single-, double-, and triple-seaters. For the first time speeding became a pedestrian's problem. Bicycles were used in little ol' New York to accomplish "scorches," or the running down of

Crack New York Bike Patrol, riding bicycles, 1904.

speedsters in horses and buggies, or the early motorists who whizzed along New York's Riverside Drive and the Harlem River Drive at 158th Street, at a racy twelve miles an hour.

Bicycles were used exclusively to control speedsters. When the fuzz on wheels overtook the motorist, he performed his arrest on the spot, and pulled the speeder off to jail. Stopping a runaway horse was a greater challenge, and a number of bicycle patrolmen were killed in the line of duty.

Probably the most celebrated police wheel group was the pride and joy of the Brooklyn Police Department of 1898 (Brooklyn was not then a part of New York City). The crackerjack Bicycle Patrol of fifty-odd men prided itself on a collection of medals and commendations for heroism and arrests of criminals in the streets. Central

Park, too, boasted an independent bicycle patrol of fast pedalers.

Some cycling cops were legendary in their own times because of their prowess and agility on the bicycle. Probably the best known of "flying cops" was Ajax Whitman, assigned to the Harlem Bicycle Patrol in 1905. It is recorded that no fewer than ten departmental citations were awarded to Whitman for his enviable ability to run down criminals in the streets.

But no "Son of Old Erin" reaped more publicity for cycling and for the Police Bike Patrol than Officer Charley Murphy, who was also a leisure-time bicycle racer. Charley beerily boasted that he could keep up with any locomotive built, provided he could get behind it with a shield to cut the wind. His precinct cronies said he was crazy. And he remarked to them: "I immediately became the laughin' stock of the world."

Murphy's three-sheets-to-the-wind boast struck a responsive chord in the heart of Hall Fullerton, publicity-wise special agent of the Long Island Railroad, who saw the possibility of a smash publicity stunt.

He went to work, and after months of preparation had a smooth and level board track laid between the railroad ties on a three-mile stretch. Fullerton kept his promise and had a hood built around one end of the caboose which cut off wind pressure from Murphy as he raced behind.

The eventful day was June 30, 1899. A mile back from the starting line, the engineer opened the throttle and they were off. When they hit the starting line, the engine was pushing sixty and Charlie was right there, too.

Just fifty-seven seconds later, Officer Murphy crossed the finish line. The smiling cop had made good his boast, and his record of covering a mile in less than a minute on bicycle stood for forty years. Thereafter, he was to be known as Officer "Mile-a-Minute" Murphy back at the precinct house.

The physical splendor of the bicycle patrolman was a matter of record in the annals of the New York City Police Department. Photographs of the trim, uniformed cyclists abound in archives and photo collections in the world's largest city.

Catapulting the bicycle back into twentieth-century

crime prevention is Long Beach Police Chief William J. Mooney, who said: "It set a fantastic record for a two-man team. For street crime, purse snatching, mugging, general malicious mischief, teen trouble areas—it's the most effective police method we've found. It's better than covering an area on foot because our men can get around so fast on bikes. It's even better than a car for these purposes because it's quieter and the officers are very maneuverable."

A Long Beach (California) bike patrolman, Gerald Heath, twenty-eight-year-old former high-school athlete, testified: "We're on our own. We're almost never dispatched. We can just wheel right into areas other police can't get near—like the time we came on a big fight and were accepted as onlookers—until we identified ourselves."

The Long Beach Bike Patrol arrest record includes eight strong-armings, five armed robberies, nine assaults with deadly weapons, eight burglaries, a narcotics charge, and thirteen cases of minors in possession of liquor.

Birmingham, Alabama, county deputies are getting back in the bike saddle in an attempt to stamp out an increase in crime in suburban shopping centers. It's the first time in the history of the department that bikes have been used. Birmingham deputies on bikes carry walkie-talkie radios to keep in communication with patrol cars and the sheriff's department. A shotgun is strapped to each bike. "Bicycle beats are a time-proved police method of patrolling," said Sheriff Mel Bailey, as he assigned six deputies on bicycle to provide closer watch over eight hundred suburban businesses, churches, and schools.

The "renaissance of police cycling" today is far less dramatic than the mass bicycle patrols of the Gay Nineties, but the bicycle is proving its worth in much the same way in helping with the apprehension of criminals.

And say, fella, the next time you're out with the boys and think you see a cop flying down the street on a bicycle, don't do a double take—it just might be.

Reprinted from *Law & Order* Magazine

A CYCLING ARTIST COUPLE

IRVING A. LEONARD
November 1967

"The road of the cyclists," warned a nineteenth-century clergyman, "leads to a place where there is no mud on the streets because of its high temperature." This solemn admonition arose from a widespread habit of cycling enthusiasts of the 1880's, an exuberant and excitable lot, to bring disrepute upon themselves by "scorching," the current word for speeding, over highways while training for attempts to break records; and these gay cyclists often incurred the wrath of horsemen and teamsters by frightening their steeds and causing runaways. Communities indignantly passed ordinances prohibiting cycle riding in parks and even on streets—restrictions which the League of American Wheelmen was partly created to combat. Moreover, cycling kept young people from going to church, it was alleged, and polite society loftily disapproved riding such contraptions. In England, too, where this innovation came earlier, the more cultivated elements of society viewed it with vast disdain. There John Ruskin (1819-1900), a high priest of aesthetic culture, scornfully declared: "I not only object, but am quite prepared to spend all my best 'bad language' in reprobation of bi-, tri-, and 4, 5, 6, or 7, cycles, and every other contrivance and invention for superseding human feet on God's ground." This disparaging attitude was reflected in the designation "penny-farthing" applied to the high-wheel ordinary whose riders were contemptuously described as "cads on castors."

In both countries cycling probably won greater respectability and wider acceptance among the higher strata of society through the activities of an American artist couple whose ramblings about Europe charmed the select readers of *Century, Scribner's, Harper's,* and upperclass English magazines. In these choice periodicals their sedately written articles appeared regularly, enlivened by admirably

382

drawn sketches. The 1880's were the vintage of magazine publishing and the golden age of illustrators before photo-engraving largely displaced these artists. Such monthly journals exuded an aura of unruffled peace and impeccable taste, betraying no hint of crudity or vulgarity in either the text or illustrative material. Hence, the advent of cycling narratives in their immaculate pages brought dignity and status to the pastime.

The male member of this pair was Joseph Pennell (1857–1926) who, more than any other artist of his time, improved the quality of illustration and raised its level as an art both in the United States and in Europe where he lived some thirty-three years. Of Quaker origin and a native of Philadelphia and nearby Germantown, he was a cycling enthusiast from the time of its introduction in the late 1870's, an energetic secretary of the Germantown Bicycle Club for years, and one of the earliest members of the League of American Wheelmen. As a somewhat nervous and moody youth he liked to draw sketches, and his exceptional talent soon brought him a career as an illustrator of the most exclusive magazines of his time. Cycling remained for him his keenest joy and the only acceptable form of exercise and distraction. Commissions for sketches soon took him to England, and there he threw himself into cycling activities serving as the representative of the League of American Wheelmen, joining groups, including the famous Pickwick Club, writing articles for British papers, and making speeches in behalf of the sport. At the same time he produced some of his finest drawings illustrating his pedaling tours; he added much artistic merit to a famous cycling manual of the time compiled by Viscount Bury. He was the artist par excellence of the new vehicle.

With his author-wife, Elizabeth Robins Pennell (1855–1936), he made extended sketching tours on tandem tricycles, and later both traveled on separate bicycles. His artistic excursions continued through the 1880's and 1890's when the vogue of illustrated travel books, largely established by him, brought steady commissions. Delighted by the relative independence of cycling, he and his wife, laden with a portfolio and small luggage, gaily pedaled to their objectives. His marriage in 1884 had resulted from a collaboration on a series of articles about Philadelphia's historical buildings for *Scribner's* magazine, for which she wrote the text and he made the drawings. With their mutual love of cycling they formed a perfect team and, as a writer puts it, "they became the most articulate couple alive, for all their reactions to art, life, and beauty were given expression in the wife's poised and cultivated prose and the husband's eloquent, graphic illustrations."

The first of their joint ventures in cycling literature was a quaint brochure, "A Canterbury Pilgrimage" (1885), a profusely illustrated account of a leisurely, idyllic trip in June 1884 on a tandem tricycle, retracing Chaucer's route over winding roads through sleepy villages and past the cherry orchards and hop gardens of Kent. This booklet, selling for a shilling a copy, was an unexpected success, for its narrative appealed to both a cycling and a scholarly public as a tribute to Chaucer and his Pilgrims, and copies were conspicuous in railway bookstalls and shop windows all over England.

In October 1884, on their Humber tandem tricycle, heavily laden with luggage and the indispensable portfolio, the young couple started from Florence on "the most beautiful, the most successful of the many beautiful, successful journeys we were to take together." Its incidents appear in a book quaintly captioned after the manner of John Bunyan's famous work: *Two Pilgrims' Progress from Fair Florence to the Eternal City of Rome Delivered under the Similitude of a Ride, wherein is Discovered The Manner of their Setting Out, Their Dangerous Journey; And Safe Arrival at the Desired City* (1885). An appropriate quotation from the seventeenth-century British preacher's classic allegory heads the recital of each episode. As the first tandem tricycle ever seen in Italy, it was a source of wonder to the peasantry and of stern puzzlement to municipal authorities who sometimes denied the cyclists the right to ride through the streets. Their journey was a succession of arduous ascents of hills so steep that Pennell sometimes pulled the tricycle by rope while his bride pushed, of glorious or bumpy descents, and of night lodgings in primitive, candle-lit inns and isolated monasteries. Most memorable of the latter was Monte Oliveto, situated on a height up which the cyclists staggered at dusk through a gloomy cypress grove, dragging their cumbrous machine. The amiable abbot rewarded them with generous hospitality, and jovially described their laborious arrival as "monsieur push-pushing the velocipede and madam puff-puffing behind him."

At Montepulciano they fell in with an Italian young blood named Sandrino who delighted showing off both his rudimentary English and a jaunty prowess of a high-wheel ordinary as he accompanied them out of town. Their greatest perils on the road were not bandits, as darkly prophesied, but herds of sheep blocking the way and causing more than one narrow escape from a disastrous spill. The Pennells' entrance into the Eternal City was climaxed by an ignominious breaking of the luggage carrier which scattered its contents over the street, and by the mortification of an arrest by the police with a fine of ten francs for "furiously riding on the Corso and refusing to descend when ordered." But nothing ever marred the joyous recollection of a happy bridal journey in unspoiled Italy.

The cultured Pennells delighted in literary associations for their travels, and their next tricycle journey, made in 1885, retraced the route of the "sentimental journey" described by the celebrated eighteenth-century writer Laurence Sterne. *Our Sentimental Journey Through France and Italy* (1888), however, does not exude the fresh joy and lyric responses infusing the pages of *Two Pilgrims' Progress,* for the tricyclists found the French customs officers irritating, the roads of France often wretchedly paved, the winds adverse, the weather perverse, and machine breakdowns both frequent and profanely frustrating. The novelty of their vehicle and cycling garb stirred wayside curiosity and derision, while a frequent Gallic coldness to American tourists and a tendency to overcharge them were practices apparently known before the twentieth century. But despite petty annoyances their "sentimental journey" provided bright moments and glimpses of beauty.

In 1889 the Pennells made the first serious trial of the newly invented tandem bicycle in Paris, creating a sensation on the crowded Champs Elysées. By 1891 safety bicycles for women had come into use, and thenceforward the artist couple cycled on separate machines. (In later life Mrs. Pennell once confided that this change was a relief, as plain-speaking "Joseph" sometimes accused her of not doing her share of pedaling.) From early youth both indulged a passion for Hungarian Gypsies, loving the music of their wild *czardas,* and so, to prepare a series of articles for the *London Illustrated News,* they cycled across Europe from Belgium to Hungary and spent the month of October in Transylvania among the Romanies seeing "picturesque towns and people and a variety of costumes beyond belief." Though Gypsy ways were vanishing, Mrs. Pennell declared in her book *To Gypsyland* (1893): "No more beautiful month of our life together can I recall."

The cycling rambles of this artist couple continued as Pennell's commissions took him about Europe. The last of their illustrated tours awheel is recorded in *Over the Alps on a Bicycle* (1898). Spiced by Mrs. Pennell's tart comments on the Swiss, it recounts a daring five-week journey over ten lofty passes, a saga of uphill plodding and hairraising descents of zigzagging roads with hairpin curves.

Though nineteenth-century guardians of the nation's morals continued to thunder from pulpits that "there is no doubt that we are dealing with a contraption of the devil himself," the effect of these denunciations was slight on their flocks, whether of high society or low. No little credit for the general indifference to such fiery admonitions may be attributed, perhaps, to the continuing series during two decades of beautifully illustrated articles and charming books presented to the public by such indisputable paladins of culture as the cycling artist couple Joseph and Elizabeth Robins Pennell.

SHAW AND WELLS, ARDENT CYCLISTS

CHARLES NEWTON
June 1968

Courtship and literature have been much enriched by the bicycle. When Harry Dacre, the English lyrist, at the end of the last century, wrote "Daisy Bell," the words were at once put to music, and took the world by storm. Even as late as my own boyhood, in the early thirties, everybody was either whistling, humming, or singing:

> Daisy, Daisy, give me your answer do!
> I'm half crazy all for the love of you!
> It won't be a stylish marriage,
> I can't afford a carriage,
> But you'll look sweet upon the seat
> Of a bicycle built for two.

Of course, it is hard to say if the bicycle has ever actually been used as a mode of conveyance for a bridal couple. But it is certain that this humble contrivance has been the vehicle of love for a considerable number of years. At one time, when a young man asked a young lady to go out cycling with him, the occasion afforded him as much pleasure as he would have derived in asking her to dance with him. Countless were the boy-girl friendships that burgeoned on "a bicycle built for two."

It is amusing to find Bernard Shaw decrying the bicycle in "An Unsocial Socialist," where he says: "I think the most ridiculous sight in the world is a man on a bicycle, working away with his feet as hard as he possibly can, and believing that his horse is carrying him instead of, as anyone can see, he carrying the horse."

Despite this ridicule, Shaw himself was an ardent cyclist even when he was well in his forties. He and his "green-eyed goddess," Charlotte Payne-Townsend, were enthusiastic cyclists, both very fond of seeking escape in the country on bicycles. And it was the bicycle that hastened the fulfillment of the playwright's most cherished desire. For when he fell from his two-wheeler, on one of his numerous excursions, he injured himself severely enough to bring the anguished Charlotte to his bedside. By the time the patient recovered, his nurse had transformed herself into Mrs. George Bernard Shaw.

Shaw's famous contemporary, H. G. Wells, too, was a keen cyclist, and began his journalistic career by contributing to a cycling journal. He describes his youthful escapades, in which the bicycle was a valued accessory, with characteristic charm in *Kipps*.

Cycling journalism found another valiant supporter in the young Alfred Harmsworth, who, a few years later, was destined to revolutionize journalism as the founder-editor of the *Daily Mail,* and to leave a lasting impression on the profession as the famous Lord Northcliffe, "the Napoleon of the Press." His biographers describe an interesting gimmick resorted to by the youthful Harmsworth to boost the advertisement revenue of *The Cyclist,* published by the House of Iliffe, with which he was associated: ". . . he invented a mysterious Chinese character whom he called Ah Fong. This personage, according to various printed reports, all of which flowed from young Alfred Harmsworth's pen, was due to arrive in Coventry by bicycle a few days before Christmas and, it was hinted, a public reception was being arranged. His mission was understood to be one of trade and goodwill, and manufacturers, it was urged, would do well to advertise their products to time with his coming. Local interest rose to a high pitch of expectation. *The Cyclist* advertisement columns were filled. Many applications were received from persons wishing to attend the reception. Ah Fong arrived in the form of the paper's Christmas number. It was a Harmsworth hoax and so successful that everybody laughed and regarded it as one of the funniest episodes in cycling journalism."

Those were the days when bicycles were the aristocrats of the road, so much so that even the famous Lord Nuffield, known throughout the world as a manufacturer of automobiles, began life as a bicycle mechanic. He set up a small workshop for the repair of punctures and other cycle ailments, but which soon became the nucleus of the Nuffield empire, and the home of the widely admired Morris car.

Supplanted by the automobile in succeeding years, the bicycle made a dramatic comeback in World War II, when petrol rationing in Britain and the Commonwealth immobilized most private cars. In wartime Delhi, it was a common sight to see red-tabbed colonels, and even generals, pedaling their push-bikes hell for leather!

My bicycle happened to be one of the first Indian-made machines, and had been placed at my disposal by an Iranian diplomat's son, who was taking lessons in conversational English from me. It was the fag end of the war, and Delhi was still very much the cycle-thief's paradise. One evening I went to see some friends who had a flat on the first floor of a building in Connaught Circus in downtown Delhi. I parked my cycle under the staircase, but did not lock it. Animated conversation and an invitation to potluck kept me at the flat till almost 9:00 P.M., when I left hastily to rush across to the office of the newspaper on which I was employed on night duty.

After working all the night through, and helping to produce the morning edition of the paper, I walked home with some colleagues in the early hours of a wintry morning, undressed, and was about to get under my blankets when I found something amiss. My bicycle was not in its customary place. It suddenly dawned on me that I had left it unlocked under the staircase of my friends' flat. Hastily, I pulled on my clothes over my night suit, and rushed down the road to Connaught Circus. It was still pitch dark, with the city fast aslumber. Inside me was the horrifying fear that my Iranian friend's cycle would not be where I had left it. When I reached the fateful staircase, I found a uniformed police constable on his rounds, but, wonder of wonders, my bicycle still reposed exactly as I had left it the night before.

I waited for the constable to turn his back, and hastily took charge of my precious possession. When I reached home, I realized that in the anxiety of "stealing" my own bicycle, I had been wheeling it along the road, instead of riding it!

Manifestly, a bicycle, too, can have a charmed life.

MOUNT WASHINGTON

IRVING A. LEONARD
May 1967

"Why anybody ever wanted to push a bicycle up Mount Washington is a mystery," wrote an historian of that highest peak of the White Mountains of New Hampshire. Why, indeed! And still more mysterious, perhaps, was why anyone ever wanted to court disaster by coasting down its steep and tortuous road to the base. Yet from the earliest years of the first era of the bicycle the records provide evidence of both feats at fairly frequent intervals. For example, the same historian reports that, on July 16, 1883, a certain E. H. Corson of Rochester, New Hampshire, trundled up the Carriage Road a high-wheel ordinary weighing eighty-five pounds, including luggage tied to the handlebars. On reaching the summit this unsung hero mounted his machine and, elevated some five feet in the air, sped down to the Glen House at the base in an hour and a half. During this wild ride he managed to keep his awkward bicycle under control with only the regular hand brake, though he afterward complained that his arm was numb for a long time from the prolonged strain of gripping the brake handle. But scarcely two weeks later H. D. Corey of Brookline, Massachusetts, lowered this record on his high-wheel bicycle to an hour and twenty minutes. A year later *Outing* magazine recorded that "the feat of riding down Mount Washington on [high-wheel] bicycles was accomplished on July 29, 1884, by C. F. A. Beckers, John S. Rogers, and Arthur Young, three St. Louis wheelmen. The descent to the Glen House was made by all three riders without broken bones, Beckers covering the distance in fifty-one minutes. A total of thirty-one 'headers' was scored on the trip, Beckers taking seven, Young ten, and Rogers fourteen."

Whatever vehicle the ingenuity of man devises to carry him over the ground faster than his own feet, or over the water, or through the air, he seems to delight in displaying his prowess with it in at least four varied uses. The first and perhaps most general is purely recreational riding and touring; the second is the competitive sport of racing, whose thrills are shared by spectators and participants alike; the third is making records of one sort or another of speed or endurance which momentarily satisfy a thirst for fame. In 1887, for example, a W. J. Morgan rode 236 miles without dismounting from his bicycle, thus beating a record of 230 miles, 469 yards, made in 1880. And lastly, special feats or "stunts," often attention-attracting activities which, by demonstrating dexterity or an impressive amount of foolhardiness, evoke surprise and wonder in witnesses, or otherwise produce responses eminently gratifying to the performer. Such exhibitions take as many forms as the inventive mind can conjure up, and surely not the least extravagant was the feat of ascending, or more particularly, descending, on a bicycle from a rugged height such as that of Mount Washington.

The treeless, rock-strewn summit of the tallest mountain of the Presidential Range, which received its exalted name in 1784 before Washington was President, towers 6,288 feet above sea level and over 4,000 feet from its base. As one of the loftiest in the United States east of the Mississippi River, it lifts its granite top to form a kind of "arctic island in the temperate zone." Geologically, it is among the world's oldest, its beginnings going back, so it is estimated, some 400 million years. Historically, it is one of the world's first great mountains to be climbed, the first white man to make the ascent in 1642 being a certain Darby Field. The subsequent three centuries have seen innumerable thousands ride or clamber up its slopes, from pioneer settlers and loggers to crowds of vacationers, with a liberal sprinkling of scientists and other distinguished visitors such as Emerson, Washington Irving, Hawthorne, Thoreau, Daniel Webster, and President Grant.

The first path to the top was opened in 1819, and the growing popularity of reaching the peak led to the construction of the Carriage Road, begun in 1855 and completed in 1861. This highway, which was essentially identical in location with the modern one, extended eight miles from the summit to Glen House on the eastern base, and it was sixteen feet wide and macadamized. While the cone at the top hardly had inclination enough to keep a wheel in motion over its hard smooth pavement, the descent soon became swift. The road had an avérage grade of 12 percent, with a maximum of 26 percent, and "there are 99 curves, more than 12 to a mile, some less than 50 yards apart."

Such, then, was the nature of the incline which quickly tempted daring cyclists to risk their limbs and lives in wild and exultant coasts down Mount Washington at breakneck speeds. This historian previously quoted reports further that, with the coming of the modern safety bicycle, the number of these perilous descents increased, though usually the machine dragged a plank behind to add to the safety afforded by foot and hand brakes. But now and then, hardy souls, with reckless audacity, challenged fate by plunging down the twisting and hair-raising road to Glen House with no braking equipment!

Proof of such foolhardiness appears in an article entitled "Cycling in the White Mountains" by Percy C. Stuart, published in the August, 1893, number of *Outing* magazine. The author, apparently with a companion whom he identifies only as "the Professor," spent a night at the Summit Hotel and arose well before dawn to witness a sunrise from Mount Washington's lofty heights. The grand spectacle embracing 150 miles of landscape enthralled them, but the exertions of climbing the previous day combined with the early rising moved them to postpone the descent until after taking a nap. From this state of unconsciousness they did not emerge until midafternoon, considerably to their surprise. They then debated whether to make the descent so near sunset time, but concluded that they could reach the base before darkness overtook them.

"We rode pneumatic safeties of the best make," the author explained, "but they were unprovided with brakes. The result was that, when the grade became, as it did at times, steep, our wheels attained an absolutely uncontrollable momentum. At such times the only thing we could do was to steer for the first heap of sand or clump of huckleberry bushes that hove in sight, and sail into it with our eyes shut tight and head down. After one such charge, which had been a particularly hard one, I found the Professor half buried under a log and snarled up among the roots of a bush so that he could not move one arm with freedom. This situation did not, however, interfere with a successful transfer of huckleberries from the branches to his stomach!

"Thus we proceeded, and I doubt not that the Old Man of the Mountains grinned sardonically as he took note of the Professor's apparel which, after every charge, became more and more 'promiscuous' until it dwindled to shreds. Within a mile of our destination, our wheels again began to get beyond our control, but we were so near the foot that we decided not to try to stop them. So down we flew at a fearful rate when, at the end of a long curve, we saw ahead in the dim light two four-horse mountain wagons passing each other and taking up the entire road. Neither of us said a word, but slid off our wheels, and were hurled through the bushes down the twenty-foot gravel embankment, and through the trees down the steep mountain slope. Meanwhile, the bicycles were running riot. The Professor's went over the embankment and flew along with increasing momentum until, with a hop, skip, and a jump, and a farewell somersault, it disappeared over the ledge and we saw it no more. The Professor himself was badly stunned, but we brought him to, going down in a wagon. Beyond a couple of tender ankles, a lame shoulder, and various cuts and bruises, he arrived at the base in, as he expressed it, 'pretty fair form.'"

Few were so foolhardy, it is likely, as to duplicate the feat of the author and the unnamed "Professor." Most cyclists made the descent slowly enough to appreciate the scenic wonders of their surroundings when not obscured by the thick, chilly mantle of clouds so often present. These fogs were frequently so dense that other riders re-reported that they were "obliged to dismount for fear of running over the edge," and that "there were few places where we could release the brakes, and we alternated in braking with pedal and hand." But the transition was swift from the bare, tundra-like, arctic summit to the treeline, which first appeared as stunted, dwarflike growth that gradually became higher and thicker, flanking either side of the road and screening deep-wooded ravines. Occasionally openings in the tall pine forest offered glimpses of wide sweeps of verdant mountains and foothills, after which the ecstatic cyclists wheeled into a quiet, welcoming glen reposing at the base like a lovely amphitheater. Then, almost without exception, they would acclaim their eight-mile descent from the "arctic island" to the temperate zone "the most delightful ride we ever enjoyed."

VALIANT VOYAGER

Irving A. Leonard
April 1969

"In spite of the opposition of every friend and relative who was on hand to register a protest (and those at a distance objected by mail) I proceeded with my preparations for riding awheel from Chicago to San Francisco. They were few and simple consisting mainly of a suitable skirt, and in having heavy soles put on my shoes. A change of underwear, a few toilet articles and a clean 'hanky' I strapped on my handlebars, and a pistol which I borrowed I put in my tool bag where it would be hard to get at in case of need. And so one morning in May I started midst a chorus of prophecies of broken limbs, starvation, death from thirst, abduction by cowboys, and scalping by Indians."

Thus wrote Margaret Valentine Le Long, a valiant representative of that new social phenomenon of the 1890's, the "bachelor girl," who, by boldly renouncing the traditionally sheltered and submissive lot of femininity, opened the way to the freedom and emancipation so largely enjoyed by her twentieth-century descendants. An important factor contributing to this liberation and the emergence of the New Woman was the new drop-frame bicycle equipped with pneumatic tires, but a journey awheel across the western two thirds of the continent in 1896—the peak year of the "bicycle craze" in the so-called Mauve Decade —was clearly a severe test of the newly proclaimed feminine independence. Her friends and relatives had ample grounds for protest against the proposed solitary Odyssey, for the roadless condition of the Great American Desert encountered by the first transcontinental cyclist in 1884 remained quite unchanged. Indeed, it was virtually the same even as late as 1908 when automobilists sought to drive their self-propelled vehicles over this route. In 1896 accommodations were still largely nonexistent and, as one moved westward, human habitations grew more primitive and widely spaced, while the character of roving cowboys, isolated ranchers, and nomadic Indians was not wholly dependable. Moreover, to a lone woman cyclist, armed only with a borrowed revolver, scattered herds of cattle and wild animals presented perils in the roadless emptiness of the western plains. But none of these acknowledged hazards daunted the determined young woman who made the arduous crossing in a little more than two months and reached her San Francisco home unscathed.

Perversely adverse winds slowed progress across the relatively smooth and level roads of Illinois, but the third day brought her to Homestead, Iowa, the largest of the seven settlements in a 57,000-acre tract of the Amana Society, a dissident German religious sect that had established a socialized community there in 1855. Its neat red-brick buildings looking all alike, wide-winged windmills, "flaxen-haired *Mädchens,* with long-skirted, short-waisted gowns, queer quilted hoods, and kerchiefs demurely crossed in front and tied behind," convinced the lady cyclist that she had inadvertently pedaled into a bit of Holland, transplanted by some vagary of fate onto an Iowa prairie. Hunger pangs moved her to hammer timidly on a huge brass knocker at the entrance of a house that faintly resembled a hotel. A response to these summons came after a lapse of time "when the fattest man I ever saw outside of a circus" appeared at the door smoking a pipe whose stem was so long that it rested on the rotundity of his ample stomach. Comprehending her unspoken query he silently led her to what seemed the quintessence of a Dutch living room with its diamond-shaped panes of glass in the windows, its large porcelain stove, and everything spotlessly clean. A bowl of what looked like "Floating Island" pudding was served and, wondering why desert

came first, the famished cyclist tasted it and gave a gasp
of surprise. It was beer soup! Startled, she was tempted to
spit it out, but the excellence of the rest of the meal, she
felt, rewarded her restraint.

On leaving behind the black muck roads and bluffs of
Iowa, the smooth gravel highways of eastern Nebraska
seemed "next door to the other place." There the abandoned sod houses of disillusioned homesteaders seemed the
epitome of desolation. "The poor, deserted 'soddies' with
the wind howling through broken doors and windows, and
flapping the remaining wings of windmills, is a midday
nightmare not soon forgotten," wrote the cyclist. In an
occasional inhabited sod hut she gratefully accepted the
humble offering of a crock of milk of "a strong flavor of
sagebrush," and heavy sour bread to appease an appetite
sharpened by the Nebraska wind.

An alleged shortcut of fifty-two miles between Cheyenne
and Laramie, Wyoming, proved a heartbreaker. In the
first thirty miles it rose two thousand feet over a sandy,
rock-strewn road, and the thousand-foot drop in the remaining twenty-two miles was plentifully endowed with an
assortment of cobblestones, boulders, potholes, and sudden turns. A coast down a long, steep hill "with a barbed-
wire gate strung across it half way down, a barrel-hoop in
the middle of the road, and a badgerhole at one side"
brought disaster. Suddenly a brown hat, a white veil, a
pea-green bicycle, scattered luggage, and a dishelved,
weeping woman formed a confused heap on the ground
eight miles from the nearest habitation.

Slowly recovering a degree of equanimity after finding
no bones broken, she picked the gravel out of her knees
with a hairpin, wondering philosophically what her sex
would do without such an adjunct. She then wiped away
her tears, straightened the twisted handlebars, and with
her hat on backward, made her way painfully to a house
at nightfall. To her dismay its inmates could not accommodate her but, harnessing a bucking bronco to a springless wagon, they transported her, crashing over sagebrush
and boulders in the black shadows of a canyon, to a
neighboring ranch where "kindly neighboring hands" lifted
her from the crude vehicle and carried her into a log

cabin. There the daughter of the family provided bandages, sympathy, supper, and two feather ticks to sleep between.

After Laramie, sand, sagebrush, cactus, mosquitoes, and road traces that expired at ponds of alkaline water or simply dissolved into the landscape were a common experience. "The dinner problem is a serious one in Wyoming where houses are twenty miles apart and the roads don't permit scorching," the cyclist wryly observed. All along she had discounted the stories of wild cattle chasing her on the plains, since most of those met had fled bellowing at the sight of a skirted human on a bicycle. On one Wyoming range, however, occurred an incident that accelerated her heartbeats considerably. After wading across a marsh she confronted a large herd of cattle blocking her way, and, contrary to the usual procedure, it began to close in upon her. The advice that she had received for such contingencies was never to run away but to advance shouting and waving her arms, but the method did not seem to work on this occasion. Without "a tree, a bush, a rock, or even a telegraph pole" at hand for shelter, panic seized her. Hastily scattering the contents of her luggage carrier in a frantic quest of her pistol, she fired its five shots in quick succession, shutting her eyes and wishing that what sounded like a popgun was a piece of artillery.

Fortunately, the pistol reports produced the desired effect and the menacing herd stampeded over the hill in wild flight, leaving her in disarray to reassemble scattered curlpapers, powder box, "hanky," and underwear. Thereafter she approached these wandering quadrupeds cautiously, first looking about for a strategic retreat, and then uttering "Comanche yells" at a discreet distance.

Ogden and Salt Lake City were welcome oases as she pedaled forward from what she called the Red Desert of Wyoming through the Great American Desert of Utah and Nevada where she kept close to the transcontinental railroad. "The wagon road has a habit of disappearing in the most unaccountable manner," she reported, "and if you are out of sight of the telegraph poles you are lost." Food and accommodations she sought in stations and section houses along the railway where the door was sometimes slammed in her face. To such rebuffs she resigned herself, alleging that "it is enough to make anyone mean

to live in that country. Of all the Godforsaken countries I
ever saw, that was the worst. Even the sagebrush refuses
to grow."

From Reno to San Francisco she found better roads
and beautiful scenery, and the roadside water tasted like
wine after the alkaline water in barrels buried by section
men along the railroad tracks upon which she had had to
rely for weeks. And to ride "one day among the snow and
rocks of the summit of the California Sierras" and on the
next spin "through orchards of the Sacramento Valley" was
veritable bliss to the homecoming San Franciscan, to whom
"the Oakland Mole seemed the entrance to Paradise, and
San Francisco, Paradise itself."

None of the dark forebodings of relatives and friends
had materialized on the long ride. Limbs remained unbroken, starvation avoided, death from thirst escaped, and
the cycling journey had posed no problems of abduction
by cowboys or scalping by Indians. On the contrary,
ranchers and section hands were usually chivalrous and
helpful, and stray Indians were unpicturesquely indifferent.
Her greatest fear, she confessed, were the tramps who
seemed to swarm about the countryside. In general, they
were what she called "the Weary Willie type" who, while
never really insulting her, sometimes manifested an unpleasant interest in her affairs. For the immunity to anything worse and for the respect generally accorded her,
this gallant, thought slightly prim, "bachelor girl" had an
explanation. This consideration she attributed wholly to
the fact that she rode a drop-frame woman's bicycle, and
that she wore "a mediumly short skirt, properly cut,"
rather than the unladylike "bloomers" that some of the
more daring members of her sex were currently sporting.

WHEELMEN OF THE PAST CENTURY

E. PETER HOFFMAN
December 1966

It is indeed difficult, even for us, whose earlier years were spent in it, to imagine ourselves back in that *dolce far niente* era of our boyhood, when Los Angeles covered a total area of thirty-six square miles, inhabited by forty thousand people and when we regarded with a sentiment akin to awe the breakneck speed of the fire engine and the milk wagon as they dashed furiously through the tree-lined streets.

We remember, too, spinning along on the old-fashioned bicycle, and some of us recall our humbled pride when inadvertently we guided the huge front wheel over a stone and took a header, to the amusement of the onlookers and not always without damage to our youthful anatomies.

Riding the "bike" in those days was confined to our own sex, but some years subsequent to the invention of the safety bicycle by Colonel Charles A. Pope in 1886, the girls deprived us of our monopoly, a deprivation to which we submitted with the most commendable grace and equanimity. During the nineties, the bicycle party became an agreeable and popular social indulgence and incidentally, the setting of many a romance, particularly after the coming of the bicycle built for two—for sometimes, proximity also makes the heart grow fonder, a statement to which I am quite certain the membership of the Wheelmen of the Past Century will render unanimous, enthusiastic and even eloquent testimony.

The world has changed mightily since we were wont to pedal our leisurely way along the unpaved streets and country roads of old Southern California; but our hearts are as warm and our spirit as buyoant as they ever were.

These are poetic lines of a romantic time, recollections of the past written by the men whose colorful history is our history, too, for these men were the rough and tumble pioneers of America's cycle sport: the Wheelmen of the Past Century.

The Wheelmen of the Past Century is a club with rich and exciting memories. Its members were the men who thrilled the Sunday crowds on velodromes now long forgotten in a day when the horseless carriage was yet a conversation piece; when a glimpse of a pretty girl's ankle caused tongues to waggle, and the world, hesitating momentarily, enjoyed a gay, carefree era which was soon to pass forever.

Their number steadily diminishing, these men gather once yearly to renew old acquaintances and talk of the good old days. Now, sixty-six years into the twentieth century, we share with them the memories of their youth, which has become our heritage.

THE 1,350-MILE SUMMER

JACK WOLFF
July 1968

Late-afternoon sunbursts bounced up into our eyes through green-yellow curtains of scrub willows. They were reflected by the mile-wide and inch-deep Platte River. Kearney, Nebraska, lay just ahead.

It was about 4:00, but we had already ridden our bikes more than one hundred miles since leaving our homes at Seward. We had started just before the sun rose about 4:30 A.M.

As we reached pavement, a policeman stepped out from the shade. "Where do you boys think you're going!"

"To the Rocky Mountain High School and College Y.M.C.A. Convention!" I answered proudly.

"It's a 'Conference'!" Herschel Gerke corrected me. He was nineteen. At sixteen, I thought "Convention" sounded

more important. Herschel was a senior at our high school.
I was a sophomore.

"Follow me!" The policeman turned on his heel. We
pushed our bikes along behind him. At city hall, we relaxed in armchairs. Soon we were restless. The chief kept
trying to get Grand Island on the telephone. Finally, he
got through. Turning to us: "You can go!"

"Why did you stop us?"

"Two boys stole two bikes this morning and headed
toward Kearney. They caught 'em."

Our Seward, Nebraska, High School Y.M.C.A. had
elected us to be their delegates. Out parents told us we
could ride our bikes west—if we really wanted to. We
never gave a thought to how far six hundred miles can be.
No one cautioned us about the lack of roads—once we got
out of the farming country. It would have done little good
to warn us.

We had New Departure brakes on our bikes. They gave
us wonderful control. We had a big bottle of malted-milk
tablets to tide us over when we had nothing else to eat.
We also had twelve dozen aluminum egg separators. They
cost only a penny. We knew we could sell them for a
nickel or dime each.

Our bicycle trunks fitted into the frame between our
legs. They held a lot. We made our dawn start as light-
heartedly as though we were heading for the swimming
hole.

West of Kearney, we slept in a pasture. An old-timer
told us to scoop out a hole for our hips so we'd wake up
limber. We woke up limber. Scooping out hip holes became second nature. Some of our hip holes were surrounded by prairie-dog holes.

The Union Pacific's double-track roadbed was ballasted
with beautiful red Sherman Hill gravel. It was our constant, reliable guide. The railroad in turn followed the
covered-wagon tracks. The Mormons heading for Utah and
the landseekers heading for Oregon's fertile valleys pi-
oneered the wagon-train routes, starting in 1843. Then in
1848–49, the goldseekers followed the Oregon Trail to
blaze the way for hundreds of thousands of additional
goldseekers. When our rear ends began to get sore from

the bumps over the railroad ties, we packed our bikes back to the wagon ruts.

The sun had burned my forearms badly during the first several days. Now huge water blisters—wrist to elbow—almost doubled the circumference of my forearms. They didn't hurt. But they weren't pretty, either! Shortly, I forgot them.

The Union Pacific passenger and freight trains fascinated us. Whenever a train approached from east or west, we relaxed. The passenger trains set us dreaming of soft seats and no exertion. But the freight trains provided excitement that was as breathtaking as anything in a circus. Every long freight had one or two brakemen riding on top of the rolling and lurching freight cars.

Sometimes they sat on the roof. Usually they stood up —an unforgettable sight. They faced forward, leaning into the wind at an angle of almost forty-five degrees, balanced by the pull of gravity against the fifty-mile-per-hour wind pressure. Wonderful fearless skill!

We looked forward to Buffalo Bill's hometown. Young Bill Cody had been a Pony Express rider at fourteen and fifteen. He was a fearless, expert rider and shot—a boy younger than we. The Pony Express contributed mightily in building the West.

Buffalo Bill had also been a Kansas cavalryman in the Civil War. He had risked his life countless times on the western plains.

Buffalo Bill was no hero in North Platte. While he gallivanted all over Europe, his wife sat alone at home. He lived high off the hog with European royalty and high society. His wife was alone. His neighbors felt that Buffalo Bill should have been home with his wife. Perhaps they were thinking of themselves, too.

West of Buffalo Bill's Scout's Rest Ranch, we were in the real West. The prairies were wide open as far as we could see.

I loved geometry. No geometric drawing equaled the beauty and perfection—excitement, too—of dozens of absolutely equidistant wagon-train ruts that curved ahead of us in marvelous uniformity. Sweeping grandly away from a long since dried up mudhole. Sweeping magnificently around the rise of a low hill.

The lines ran perfectly parallel until they fused into a single line. They stretched into infinity.

Day after day, we watched the wagon-wheel ruts merge with the rut in which we rode; to stretch far ahead.

When we were particularly tired, the endlessness could be discouraging. Even worse!

These ruts also frustrated us. When we got fed up of being thrown when a pedal snagged the side of the rut, we pushed our bikes to the Union Pacific tracks and ties and ballast.

We stopped one day to drink water and visit with a construction party. We asked about the beautiful, uniform red Sherman gravel. The party chief told us the story. Years before, the Union Pacific built its line around Sherman Hill, west of Cheyenne, to avoid the time and cost of tunneling through. Decades later, they decided to straighten tracks and lessen grades by tunneling through Sherman Hill. To save money, they specified that the contractor owned the rock which he blasted out of the mountain for that tunnel. That would force him to pay for removing trainloads of rock from the railroad's property. This would bring revenue to the railroad for hauling away its own rock.

Kilpatrick Brothers of Beatrice, Nebraska, got the contract. This was their first really big chance. It could bring them a big future. They gambled on finding ways to get rid of the rock.

They moved their great shovels to the bottom of the mountain. Day after day, they hauled away loads of Sherman gravel. They never reached solid rock; never had to blast through the mountain; never had to haul away anything from Sherman Hill.

The Kilpatrick Brothers made a huge fortune of shoveling instead of blasting their way through Sherman Hill. They made a second fortune by selling back to the Union Pacific Railroad the rock that had originally been the Union Pacific's rock. The little company had become a giant-killer.

The Union Pacific construction crew enjoyed the story. So did we. We bumped along over the Sherman gravel of the eastbound track with new strength and renewed spirit.

My forearms had long since turned to watery blisters,

raw spots, and then a beautiful brown tan. We were veteran vagabonds on bikes as we approached Julesburg, Colorado. I had pinned back the front brim of my battered felt hat. Both of us had acquired terrific self-confidence. I had proven to be somewhat more at home on a bike than Herschel was—probably a better coordination of muscles and mind. I usually led the way.

We crossed the North Fork of the Platte River to follow the South Fork toward Denver. Here those pioneers heading for Utah, Oregon, and California had run into big trouble. Rocky Mountain snow waters had caused the South Platte to run dangerously deep and wide.

Famous pioneer artist W. H. Jackson crossed the South Fork of the Platte near Julesburg in 1866. One of his many Early West paintings shows the mile-wide South Platte with more than twenty wagon trains and additional Indian parties scattered widely over the visible area. They were endangered by quicksand in the shallows; by rushing torrents in the shallows of the unexpectedly deep channels. Many were washed far down stream. We were following history-making trials.

Here we became aware of a phenomenon. We saw the white crests of the Rocky Mountains far to the west. At the end of each day, they were still as bright and clear—and far away—as when we first saw them in the early morning light. We passed many railroad water tanks, stations, grain elevators—town after town. We knew we were going farther west. But the white mountain peaks told us we were standing still. By the time we reached Fort Morgan, the Rockies had moved closer.

We headed for the Union Pacific station to use the facilities and to stretch out on the benches. A young fellow in Slav costume walked around with his blouse hanging down over his pants. The town constable took him to the men's room. When he came out, his blouse was tucked inside his pants. As soon as the constable walked out—out came the blouse. This happened again and again. Finally, the constable gave up. Americanization, he discovered, takes a little longer and means a bit more than tucking shirts inside of pants.

Somehow, the Rockies had moved closer during the

time we were in the station. As we mounted our bikes, we felt that Denver was just around the corner.

After two nights in Denver, we started on our last lap to Cascade Canyon. Denver had broken the spell of the prairies.

The gravel road led south, skirting rocky hills that had broken off from the eastern edges of the big Rockies. With ninety miles ahead, we kept moving. Shortly, on an upgrade, a swank brougham passed us. Impassively, the driver in uniform sat in the unprotected front seat. Inside, an elderly gentleman leaned forward on his cane. His bushy white moustache pointed horizontally to each side. I speeded a bit to observe him better. He stared dead ahead.

At the next long downgrade, we passed the brougham. Neither driver nor millionaire changed expression. Farther along, this particular grade began to wind down the side of a small mountain toward a narrow valley. Far below, a crystal stream skirted the mountain. Pressing back down on my New Departure brake, I kept the speed just under recklessness. A few sharp turns later, I saw white water below. Within seconds, I swooped around a turn and saw clear water rushing across the road, its bottom sprinkled with small boulders. I barely got my feet up as we swooped through without hitting a stone and coasted up the other side. Dismounting, I turned just in time to see Herschel's front wheel strike a boulder. He shot over the handlebars and aquaplaned to a prone stop in about two feet of water. He was unhappy. Also unhurt.

As we stood beside the road for Herschel to drip-dry, the brougham put-putted up the grade. The driver and the owner could have been wax figures.

We turned west at Colorado Springs for the climb up into the Rockies to Cascade Canyon. We were thirsty. At Manitou, we saw a small Greek temple of pillars with a fountain in the center. We swerved aside and headed for the iron-stained dippers chained to the fountain. I took one full swallow. Choked! It was the foulest water I had ever tasted. I banged the dipper against the stone and rushed back to the bicycle.

We pushed our bikes most of the eight long, crooked miles from Manitou up the narrow, deep, and twisting canyon. To our left, the rock reached far above us in vertical lines. To our right, the rock fell straight down to the water rushing white over and between great rocks. As a youngster, I had spent three summers in Hot Springs, South Dakota. I had thought of the Black Hills as mountains. Climbing up Ute Pass, I got another impression of mountains.

My memory of the Y.M.C.A. Conference vaguely reproduces a vision of a wide-covered veranda encircling a generous structure, waiting on tables for our board and room, evenings discussing subjects in front of a huge stone fireplace. But clear are the memories of our cycling adventures.

There was the climb up to the top of the mountain—a shoulder of Pike's Peak. It was a hot climb. Far below— a jewel of a blue, blue lake with a tiny island in the center. On a shelf of the mountainside. "Last one in is . . ."

Several of us hit the water at about the same moment. It was liquid ice. Our swimming dive carried us a good way toward the island. We touched a rock and hurried back. Who won the race? Who cared?

Some memories stand out clearly after many decades. Others fade fast. Beth, my wife, started her diaries in her teens. They have been full ledger size for decades. In reading back over our eventful lives we occasionally find an event about which Beth wrote: "We shall remember this as long as we live!" We read what happened, where, when, and with whom. But neither of us has the slightest memory of the event and the people.

However, I clearly remember many events of our 1910 venture. A Mr. White, a Y.M.C.A. official from Kansas, photographed Herschel and me just before we started our return trip. It fortifies memories about the bicycle and clothes—particularly my corduroy trousers, high-laced boot-shoes, the brim-up felt hat I used as a pillow.

Our Y.M.C.A. Conference was ended. We started the long downgrade trip to Manitou on the stagecoach mountain road. It wound back and forth between vertical canyon walls shooting almost straight up—and the vertical drop to our left. The raging mountain rapids and falls below—among great chunks of rock that had broken away from the wall above us.

At one place, the downgrade road appeared to climb upward again. I took my foot off the brake and gathered speed to help coast that upgrade. I quickly realized that my eyes had tricked me. Coming down a steep mountain road, a decrease in downgrade can appear to be upgrade.

My life depended upon getting my bike back under control.

Heavy, iron-tired stagecoach wheels through decades had ground the road surface into fine gravel. The road sloped toward the canyon at my left—particularly at right turns. I was very conscious of the jagged rocks and white water below. And I was afraid. Slightest excessive pressure on the brake bounced my rear wheel toward the precipice. I had to use the brake to get around turns. My life depended upon a cool assessment of exact brake pressure—to slow gradually without skidding. I had to maintain rolling contact between rear wheel and road surface.

It was truly wonderful when I recovered control of my bike.

My Uncle Louis Hartman was assistant chief engineer at Denver's Brown Palace Hotel. The ornate lobby amazed me. The underground plant doubly amazed me. Stories deep. Endless galleries, tunnels, furnaces, rooms, the yellow glow of electric-light globes.

I had never even dreamed of such an underground complex dug out by people. My uncle was the number-two man in running this complex of caverns and its complicated machinery. I was proud of him!

New country lay ahead as we headed north from Denver. Cheyenne was 110 miles beyond the rolling hills ahead—along the east battlements of the great Rocky Mountains. Before end of the first day, my front tire had collapsed. Herschel pedaled slowly ahead. Then waited. Before long, he waited with his flat tire. Together again, we pushed our bikes north.

It's a hardship to push a bike along rutted roads that wander over and around a hilly landscape. We were pushing our bikes well toward the top of a long gentle slope when we heard an automobile puffing up behind us. The driver yelled, "Put your bikes in the back end and climb in!"

It was already an old car—a one-cylinder Cadillac. Red. The next minute, the engine began to falter. "Get out and push. Hurry!" yelled the driver. We pushed.

As we crested and started down the long wavering ruts on the other side, he yelled: "Jump in! Quick!"

Once more we clambered up the back steps into the little tonneau which was already crowded by our bikes. This get-out-push-get-in-quick formula lasted several miles. As we crested another rise, we saw a long gradual descent into a town. A lumberyard on the left. The railroad depot on the right—farther along. A few straggling buildings beyond the elevator. The road leveled off in front of the lumberyard. The Cadillac engine coughed. Died.

The driver jumped down and hurried toward the railroad depot.

"Where you going?" we called after him.

"To buy a ticket out of here!"

"What about the car?"

"The heck with it!"

Hours later, we slept the night with our hip holes.

The dawn chill awakened us. We headed north. The Rocky Mountain peaks to our left kept pace with us. Hours later, the same peaks were still with us. Finally, we ignored them.

It became a long afternoon after a long, long morning. Since mid-morning we had found no place to trade egg separators for food. The sun dropped fast toward the peaks when we saw distant ranch buildings—towards the mountains. It looked inviting. But it would be a long, long hike out of our way. We were tired from pushing our bikes. They might turn us down. Our appetites decided the issue.

"Sure you can eat with us," said the rancher. "But my brother and I are going to look over a new fence line before supper."

He pointed to a new white Buick runabout with two bucket seats in back. "Want to come along?" How could we say no?

It was miles to the fence line, miles along the fence line. The sun dipped behind the Rockies. The familiar chill began to penetrate. As we started back, early darkness fell fast.

The brother got out and lighted the headlamps. Playfully, the driver began to dodge in and out between the posts. Each dodge to the left brought a fence post rushing toward the car where I sat. One post didn't get out of the way. Before I could shudder, it hit the car. We skidded to an almost instant stop.

The post had jammed the right running board into the rear tire. They couldn't pry the running board away from the tire. No luck!

Once more we hoofed it across a prairie—this time in the dark. We were stumbling along by the time we reached the ranch buildings—tumbled into bed within minutes after our late-late kitchen-table supper.

At Cheyenne, we stopped with Herschel's cousins. Everyone drank homemade root beer. The water was too stinky to drink. We had sent our bikes home express-collect. Our bike-riding summer was over. We were going to hike the rest of the way home.

Feminine Freewheeling

BICYCLE WIFE

Evelyn P. Murray
December 1965

Ladies (wives, sweethearts, mothers, and concerned sisters), I would like to tell you the secret of how to live with an impossible man. If any men are reading, and consider themselves in this category, please read on!

Everyone has his own brand of impossible man, but Tom is the kind that when we were married, his mother cheerfully handed him over to me, saying that now it was my turn to worry.

The starry glint in his eye which I had fallen in love with I discovered to be the burning light of racingitis (an unusually active desire to race). But marriage made his cure impossible, for now he could never afford to race a sports car or even a motorcycle. At the point of poring over immigration information to decide which country he and his mechanical books would disappear to, Tom accidentally discovered bicycles, first of all for the exercise, then for the escape from our apartment. Then, it was inevitable, Tom found that people really do race the things and that's all he needed to know.

From this point on Tom was a new man. Of course I blame him completely for the former electrical static that upset the atmosphere of our marriage, because I am still the same person with the same faults, but Tom . . . let me tell you about the change.

Instead of endlessly complaining about the terrible state of business, about his unfortunate state of having to work for a living, work is merely a necessary interlude between bicycling, and who worries about anything anyway when there's a race only two weeks away?

No longer does he relentlessly expose my ineptitude as a housewife and run his fingers over the moldings or hold nightly inspections to check up on work done or undone. Now he overlooks the dust because this is the bicycling season and he's never home long enough in daylight to notice it. His fingers are busy pinching his muscles to see if they pass the pinch test.

Instead of handing your man a drink to calm him when he enters the door (remember he's in training), hand him his bicycle instead, and I guarantee that any ensuing arguments will be your fault completely, for he'll be in an excellent mood that will last until he leaves for work. The same act repeated will bring the same results, and you'll never need to worry about him again. Even rainy evenings pose no problems; just give him his accumulated stockpile of bicycle magazines and you won't hear anything but happy sighs of impatience to be on his bicycle again.

Disregard his desire to quit work to bicycle all day, and although he's last in the pack, be sure to encourage him to take you with him to Mexico for the next Olympics.

Whenever he wants any new equipment, like a third bicycle for instance, be sure to let him have it. He'll feel so guilty about your being such an understanding wife (of course he won't take back the bike, that's part of the guilt) that whatever big thing you've fought for years to have, or the official permission to pursue, it is as good as yours.

That's my secret for peace in one's midst (small apartment or no). Your time together as a family will be one of relaxed happiness and pleasant memories. When the children are old enough to imitate their father, a whole family on wheels will even calm down the tensions of the young and give everyone a shared experience that mends a family together.

I'd trade in my engagement ring for a carload of wheels and tubes just to have the thrill of living with a happy man.

HOW TO LOSE WEIGHT ON THE WAY TO THE SUPERMARKET

J. RAY CHENOWITH
December 1968

"That's the way I looked a year ago," says Karen Davids, slim, trim, brown-eyed, auburn-tressed suburban mother, as she stopped to chat.

She displayed a photograph of a girl very much over-weight. "I was dieting and losing weight. But it was so slow. I decided to exercise."

This routine decision, once made, she explained, necessitated a purchase. Now, while other mothers buzz into the supermarket parking lot with the family station wagon, Karen, six-year-old son, Gregg, and eight-year-old daughter, Chris, pedal up on the ten-month-old bicycles.

"I might sound like a commercial but I mean it. Bicycling helped me drop from 225 pounds to 150 pounds in about ten months," Karen says.

Karen began to enjoy her newfound motivity, she says, once the trick of riding and the enforced exercising were mastered and incorporated.

Her first bicycle ride, however, was near disaster to the program. Even though it was short—less than a half mile —she arrived at her destination so exhausted she was unable to pedal home. An understanding and indulgent friend packed both Karen and bicycle into the family station wagon and delivered them to the mobile-home park where Karen lives in South San Jose, California.

"After I got over that, it started to be fun," says Karen. "Then I began to lose weight. Within ten months I had lost the 75 pounds."

She wouldn't think of driving to the shopping center for small items now, she adamantly states.

"It's so much trouble to get the car out and we'd much rather ride our bikes. Besides," her brown eyes sparkled, "it's darned good exercise."

It takes only two or three minutes for the threesome to be bike-mounted—ready to depart their home in the small mobile-trailer park which fronts on Monterey Road, before it becomes Highway 101, as it winds through South San Jose.

"The traffic is really no problem, either," Karen says. "After a brief safety-training program for the children, all it takes now is patience. We just line up on the shoulder of the highway, wait, and watch. When there's a traffic lull, I say 'Go!' and we all *go!*"

She and the children then quickly push their bikes across the highway to the center dividing strip where they mount and take off.

"It makes you feel so good," Karen said fervently, as she and the children began to line up on the edge of the highway.

"It's fun," said Gregg, hurrying to join his mother and sister in line for one of their daily caravans to the shopping center near their home.

"Your sense of well-being improves. It just makes you feel good all over. Really makes you feel fit!" Karen glanced up and down Monterey Road. *"Go!"* she commanded.

"I like it, too," Christine's comment drifted over her shoulder as she approached the cycle-mounting side of the highway.

Karen's effervescent smile flashed, "Oh, I forgot—it's so much easier to change a bicycle tire, too."

I nodded glumly—and set the bumper jack in position. Putting the spare on a station wagon is also a healthful exercise, I thought; that is, if you look at it in the proper perspective.

FROM HOOPSKIRTS TO NUDITY—THE BICYCLE'S EFFECT ON WOMEN'S DRESS

BICYCLE INSTITUTE OF AMERICA
December 1968

If Grandma didn't have the spunk to go bike riding in her bloomers way back there in the nineties, there is considerable doubt that the young ladies of today would be wearing strapless bathing suits, baring their midriffs, or sporting the tricky shorts-and-bra costumes that are so familiar to us now.

The freedom of dress enjoyed by today's women is directly traceable to bicycling, and it would be quite appropriate if the ladies made some salute to the American bicycle industry for their emancipation from bustles, petticoats, and wasp waists.

About the time the first American bicycle was being manufactured in Hartford, Connecticut, in 1877, America was in the grip of staid Victorianism which was based on the contention that the morality of a nation could only be improved by keeping the sexes rigorously apart. It was even scandalous for a woman to appear in a hotel dining room or other public place. It was a man's world, and woman's place was in the home. Consequently, there wasn't much bike riding on the part of women. The clinging-vine type—crinolined and swooning—was the world's ideal woman. In those days, Dame Fashion decreed that women should wear plenty of clothing. Six starched petticoats and assorted underclothing underneath an ordinary dress were considered proper. Add a bustle to that combination and every woman walking down the street looked like a small circus tent in motion. If milady desired to go bathing, and few did, her bathing suit required at least twelve yards of material. A few hardy women defied the conventions and wore the so-called bloomers designed by Mrs. Amelia Bloomer of New York City in 1849, and were subject to bitter ridicule in the

BICYCLE INSTITUTE OF AMERICA

Oh, you beautiful dolls! Women cyclists at the turn of the century.

press and in the bar-rooms. Incidentally, the bloomer costume, consisting of a short skirt and a pair of Turkish trousers gathered at the ankle, or hanging straight, was first given the aesthetic name of "camilia" by Mrs. Bloomer, but because of the widespread notoriety, it came to be known by her name.

It was not until the nineties that women began to throw off the shackles that bound them to the Victorian way of life and started to show some sign of the independence that characterizes them today. Prior to this time, a woman seen bicycling was labeled "fast" and unfit to mix with proper ladies. Besides, with those voluminous skirts sweeping the ground, women didn't care so much for the cycling sport. Some of the more daring demoiselles let their ankles show just about the shoetops and there were many hoots of "twenty-three skiddo" and "Oh, you chicken," as they rode their two-wheelers in town.

America, as all countries in that period, depended on Paris for its fashion guidance. It was not until the gay Parisiennes took up cycling seriously that the emancipation of the fair sex as far as dress was concerned got under way. Mrs. Carrie A. Hall, noted fashion authority, writes about this tradition-breaking happening in her book, *From Hoopskirts to Nudity,* thus:

> The great change in this period [the nineties] from the staid gentility of mid-Victorian times was brought about in no small degree by the advent of the bicycle for women. The Parisienne, always keen on new pastimes and ready for new sensations, was the first to take up this sport which had hitherto been regarded as a purely masculine form of exercise.
>
> The early part of the nineties therefore saw the bicycle the rage of feminine Paris (and America) and from the moment that it was conceded that a lady did not lose caste because she rode one, the emancipation of the fair sex began. This called for a special pair of knickerbockers, not unlike the bloomers in shape; stockings, with high boots, or shoes; a simple shirt, with collar and tie, and a soft felt hat with no trimming. Later, the knickerbockers were superseded by a divided skirt.
>
> Because of the bicycling fad, the playing of golf by women was much influenced, and it was possible now for women to ride their bikes to the links which had before been accessible only by a train journey. Dress reformers had attempted sixteen years previously to do what the bicycle now achieved without self-advertisement.

In the nineties cycling was more than a sport, or something new in the transportation line. It was a craze, and very much the thing to do. Every city and town had its cycling clubs. Every major city boasted hundreds of such organizations, most of them luxuriously furnished. In the clubs and out, bicycles, cycling, cycle racing, and the petted heroes of the racetrack were the ever popular topics of conversation. Everyone who could possibly afford a bicycle owned one. Bicycles were not cheap, either. The average price was $100 to $150, and in those days a century note was a respectable sum of money.

On Sundays and holidays, women cyclists joined the men and crowded the streets, parks, and adjacent country lanes in towns all over the country. The languid lady of the old-fashioned school became transformed into a new being, a new creature evolved with modern ideas. With her change of ideas also came a complete reaction as to her notions of fashion.

Natural outgrowth of the bloomer biking costume was the mannish-tailored suit and the shirtwaist. The latter was popularized all over the world when a young artist by the name of Charles Dana Gibson showed his "Gibson Girl" of magazine-illustration fame wearing one of the new doodads, which featured deep pleats over both shoulders. Skirts gradually became shorter, as high as four inches from the floor, and women's ankles were becoming visible for the first time. Menfolk thought the new fashion changes were scandalous, and there were many discussions on this subject in the popular saloons and sporting places of the day. In fact, male indignation was so great that several lawmakers introduced laws in Congress forbidding the wearing of such apparel by women. As they are today, women must have been powerful persuaders even then because such laws never got beyond the introduction stage, and male criticism of women's dress decreased as the years rolled by.

From 1900 to the beginning of World War I, women reveled in the new fashions influenced by their bicycle-riding predecessors. The hourglass figure became a thing of the past, and women began to think in terms of the straight-fronted silhouette with clothes more closely following the lines of the normal female body. If variety was, or is the spice of life, the fashions of the early part of the twentieth century were highly seasoned. Fashion trends of that period spent themselves lavishly in every direction. American women began to ignore Parisian modes and adopted purely American clothes which were made for ease and comfort as well as style. From bike riding, they went on to other sports—horseback riding, golf, tennis, swimming, etc. All these sports demanded a new, different, and radical costume, and the sports clothes era of American fashions was under way.

Next big change in women's fashions came with the entrance of women into the Armed Forces during World War I to replace men who were being shipped overseas. They wore uniforms that were mannish, comfortable, and economical. When the war was over, the women in service were reluctant to give up their uniforms. Consequently, they adopted a new mode of clothing as closely akin to the boyish form as possible. This was the beginning of the flapper age when, as one observer noted, "Not since Eve wandered out of the Garden of Eden attired in a fig leaf has woman gone so lightly clad." Short skirts, rolled stockings, flat chests, no hips—that was the fashion order during the Roaring Twenties.

The bicycle, too, had its troubles. The motorcar became the backbone of American transportation and the bicycle served principally as transportation for children to and from grammar and high school, for errands, recreational jaunts to nearby playgrounds, and visits to friends and playmates. In the early years of the Depression, the bicycle industry seemed destined for ruin. But the leading manufacturers refused to give up the ship. Improvements were made and an aggressive public-relations and merchandising program instituted. As a result, the bicycle business improved rapidly in spite of the backwash of the Depression and was one of the leaders in the recovery period, 1933–36.

The heavy interest in cycling prompted a new fashion change. The ladies took to wearing slacks, but these garments were a nuisance to the bike rider. So, the shorter version of slacks, which were immediately dubbed "pedal pushers," was devised. Originally designed for female cyclists, pedal pushers, however, were used for other sports and became a "must" item in every girl's wardrobe for many years.

More abbreviated attire, especially in sportswear, was the fashion edict following the years of World War II. Midriffs were bared, and halter and shorts, covering only the bare essentials, was the approved costume. Bikini bathing suits became the rage on the Riviera, and finally achieved some popularity in the United States. Plunging necklines also became the vogue. Many fashion historians like to believe that woman's passion for near-nudity in recent years is her answer to the charges that she lost her feminity during World War II when she competed with men in defense-plant jobs and even in the military services. Suffice to say, the abbreviated sports costume is here to stay and the bicycle can also take another bow for this. Feminine cyclers were the most enthusiastic purchasers of such costumes.

Because of the ban on gasoline, many women rode bicycles to and from their defense-plant jobs during World War II. It was not an uncommon sight in the summer months to see Rosie the Riveter blithely pedaling her way to work in comfortable shorts and halter. When times returned to normal, Rosie still liked to bike and that is one of the principal reasons that the bicycle industry grew in post-war years.

Today, the emphasis on health and recreation has created a bicycle boom of fantastic proportions. From a low in 1932 of 200,000, the sales of bicycles in America has climbed to over 4.5 million in 1967, and 1968 is expected to be a 5-million year. An estimated 60 million people rode bikes during the past year, and again, styles reflected the functional demands of the trend, with such innovation as the pants dress becoming widely popular.

Yes, the bicycle has played a commanding role in women's long fight for freedom of dress. Sports costumes are just about as brief as they can get. Being fickle creatures, what will women do next?

It will be interesting to find out.

THE NEIGHBORLY THING

Ticki Lloyd
April 1968

I once heard someone say that bicycling can put the "bloom of youth" on a woman's face. All I can say is that I must be riding the wrong bicycles. Nothing like that has happened to me.

However, I must admit bicycling can be lots of fun and very rewarding, too. What better way can a woman eliminate the "battle of the bulge" than by riding a bike? And what better way can she really see the city and the surrounding areas than by taking a slow cruise on a cycle?

Bicycling can be a neighborly thing, too. When you're riding in a car, it is not likely you'll apply brakes and jump out to greet someone. But a bike offers a different mode of transportation. It's a friendly sort of thing. If you're riding along observing the traffic laws, you're naturally riding close to the curb, and if you're riding close to the curb, you're close to your neighbor's yard. What woman is going to bypass a chance to stop and have a friendly chat with another woman?

Riding a bike can be very beneficial and lead to many wonderful adventures. As a matter of fact, bicycling led to my collection of geraniums. Whenever I stop to chat, I look around my neighbor's yard to see what kind of flowers are growing, and then I "move in" on the unsuspecting citizen something like this . . . I might say, "Your geraniums are perfectly beautiful. How in the world do you get them to grow like that?" This approach is always flattering to the gardener, and before you know it, I'm pedaling down the street with cuttings of geraniums, some exotic bulbs, and an assortment of various species of plants.

Later on, when my cuttings start producing, and I see someone pedaling by my house, I am impelled to start passing out cuttings. This plan is excellent for beautifying the city, too. If we get enough women cycling around the city, passing out cuttings of geraniums, roses, daisies, etc., we'll be actively participating in the beautification program.

Bicycling is fine for collecting recipes, too. I got a marvelous recipe for poppy-seed bread over on P Street one day while cycling in the sun. A charming old lady was busily engaged pruning bushes, and I pulled over to pass the time of day with her. A delightful fragrance circled round my head and filled the air with spicy fragrance. At first I thought the odor was coming from one of the lovely shrubs in her garden. Then, with a smile, my guide led me into her charming kitchen and proudly popped a beautifully puffed load of baked poppy-seed bread out of the oven. Needless to say, not only did I get a sample of the bread, but before I left, I had the recipe tucked in my tote bag. It is always a good idea to have some sort of bag with you to carry cuttings and recipes, etc.

I do not think there are enough women around these parts riding bikes. At least I don't see them on my runs. Perhaps this is because I ride early in the morning, when the dew is fresh on the plants and the ozone still has that earthy odor I love so much.

It is amazing to discover how much beauty is around us—it's ours, and it's free. Sometimes when I'm riding in the outlying districts of town, I begin to feel so close to Creation and become aware of all that has been created for us. I particularly love to ride in those sections that have a wealth of pine trees, and listen to the needles whistling in the breeze and inhale their fragrant aroma. It is so exhilarating, it makes you feel "freshly scrubbed" all over.

I have listened to beautiful concerts early in the morning by artists who are willing to devote time and talent, and ask nothing in return but appreciation. I refer, of course, to the singing of the birds. These tiny creatures are real opera stars, and they have much to teach us of joy.

Bicycling is for all seasons: I like to ride in the winter, with the wind whipping my face; in the spring when the azaleas, wisteria, and magnolia trees are dressed in all their finery to present a veritable wonderland; in the summer when the light rain is falling like jewels from the sky and kisses the face with its light touch; in the autumn when the trees are dressed in brilliant shades of red, yellow, and orange. It's a joy to ride on the beach and watch the sea gulls float over the briny deep and come to rest on a rippling wave.

Fun Is Where

You Find It

A MISSISSIPPI BIKE HIKE

DUANE THOMPSON
AGE TWELVE, BOY SCOUT TROOP 227,
CHALMETTE, LOUISIANA
September 1967

On June 2 we left New Orleans just after we got our report cards. We had been planning this trip since February. The ones in our Boy Scout Troop who went were Orlando Peterson, the patrol leader; myself, assistant patrol leader; Mark Jones; Dennis Dobson; Danny Thompson (Explorer); and the counselor, Mr. Thompson. We decided on the name "Big Wheels" for our patrol. To go you had to do some phase of civic duty.

We started our hike at Wiggins, Mississippi, north of Biloxi. Among the six of us were two 10-speeds, one 5-speed Stingray, and three 3-speeds. All of us made it in fairly good shape, except for the Stingray which reared up on steep hills because the pack was on the back.

We took a wrong road out of Wiggins and after three or four miles of pedaling, we got back on 29 and proceeded to De Soto National Forest. The people along the way were very friendly and our packs didn't give us much trouble so we made good time.

When Mark, Danny, and I got to the intersection of another highway, we stopped for a rest until the others came. We could see rain in the distance so we got our ponchos on. Mark and I went out first. In a couple of

The author with camping gear and patrol flag, studying a road map.

minutes it was pouring down, but our ponchos and campaign hats kept us fairly dry.

We made very good time in the rain. It was refreshing. We stopped at Black Creek where Dennis and Danny caught up with us. There we refilled our canteens in those old-fashioned pumps. We turned down a gravel road. There our progress slowed down because of the wet gravel and the mud. On some of the steeper hills, Mark, Dennis, and I had to get off. Almost everywhere we looked we could see corn fields, cows grazing, pine forests, and blue ridges in the distance.

We finally arrived, after twenty-three miles, at Cypress Creek. While my father and brother went to get food at a store, six miles distant, Orlando, Mark, Dennis, and I put up the tents and started the fire. It started to rain heavily and the fire died out. At about 9:00 P.M. my father and brother came back with food. We (except for Dennis, who was sleeping) went under some trees which provided some shelter from the rain and cooked with our mess kits. We used a light alcohol stove. Then we hit the sack. The next morning Mark and I went fishing in Black Creek, but didn't have any luck. We cooked our breakfast over an open fire, cleaned up the area, and fixed our tents and packs on our bikes. It was a little drier than yesterday so we made better time on the gravel roads. We stopped for lunch at a country store. We told the owner the route we were taking and she said that a bridge was washed out and we would have to take a detour. She described a route for us, which proved to be an excellent road and good scenery. People like that are very helpful.

Every once in a while cows would appear on the highway. All we did was ring our bells and yell at them. My father and I stopped at Paret Fire Tower. It was a grand view looking from the top. You could see breaks in the pine forests where country roads sliced through and you could see dim, distant blue ridges stretch out into infinity. The wind was real brisk up there.

Finally we started on and stopped at Moody's Landing situated on Black Creek. The river ran in a wide curve where pine trees came down to the edge of the creek. We finally arrived at Brooklyn, Mississippi, which is about four million people less than Brooklyn, New York.

We passed over a one-lane wooden bridge that spanned Black Creek. From there my father and I traveled about two miles to Ashe Lake. This lake is 33⅓ acres and averages about five feet deep, but is very scenic. There is an island in the lake which had great big blackberries. It also had an excellent diving place ten or eleven feet deep. Nearby is a bamboo forest where, with the sunlight filtering through, it looks like you are in a yellow room with poles. Mark, Dennis, Orlando, and I slept on some benches in the shelter of Ashe Lake while my father and brother slept in a tent.

The next day we had breakfast, cleaned up the area, and then had a little church service. After that we went swimming again. At about 1:00 P.M. we left Ashe Lake and proceeded toward Wiggins. I was with my father

again and we stopped a couple of times to pick blackberries. Once we stopped at a crystal-clear stream called
Beaver Dam Creek. It was ice cold. We followed a little
stream that was a tributary of Beaver Dam Creek. Beaver
Dam Creek had a perfect swimming place, just off the
highway, but we had to go on.

Finally, after many miles we arrived on the main highway about a mile from Wiggins. It was smooth pedaling
from there to home. The back roads that we had been
on were a heavy mixture of gravel with asphalt.

When we arrived at Wiggins, we bought a gigantic,
ice-cold watermelon, feasted on it, and went home. We got
some medals for it that say Bike Tour.

WHY NOT BICYCLE TO WORK?

ROBERT PETERSEN
December 1968

> *Dr. Petersen is a research psychologist on the staff of
> the National Institute of Mental Health. Thirty-seven
> years old, married, and the father of three children,
> he has been cycling for "almost as long as I can re-
> member." In addition to being an active cyclist and
> hiker, Bob is a photographer, ham-radio operator, and
> bird watcher. Between times he writes scientific articles
> on the problems of drug abuse.*

Cycle to work? "An appealing idea, but impractical" may
be your first reaction. But is it? I and many of my co-
workers at the National Institute of Health (N.I.H.) in
Washington, D.C., do just that. What's more, many of
us do it four out of five days of the week. Recently the
Washington *Post* newspaper even proclaimed the bicycle
the new status symbol at N.I.H.! The benefits? Better
health, real savings in commuting costs, and the added
bonus of cycling regularly year round.

Let's examine how we do it and just how practical an

idea it is. To begin with there's the question of distance. Just how far from work can you live and still use a bicycle as a means of commuting? I live five miles away and can make the trip comfortably in fifteen or twenty minutes. That includes several hefty hills and a few stoplights on the way. Up to ten miles away would still be well within the limits of reasonable commuting. And when you get there, there's no need to waste time trying to find a place to put the car or paying expensive parking fees. You can usually park in or near the building in which you work at no cost whatever.

What about the weather? In the Washington area summers are notoriously hot and humid. Winters, while they do not rival those of Maine or Minnesota, are still well below freezing part of the year. The solution? During the warmest part of the year, you are riding to work early in the day—before it's had a chance to warm up. I usually leave by about eight. By making maximum use of the wide range of gears of the modern lightweight bicycle it's possible to choose ratios that are minimally likely to overheat your personal radiator. I usually leave off my tie and suit jacket in warm weather, unbutton an extra button on my shirt, and can count on being sufficiently "air-conditioned" to arrive at work without needing a shower. Since I can shower after returning home, I often make the return trip a more active one. I place my tie in my suit-jacket pocket and carefully fold the jacket inside out— as you might for packing it in a suitcase. I then place the jacket on the luggage carrier secured by an elastic band or so-called shock cord (this can easily be obtained from your local cycle dealer). As a result my jacket and tie arrive as unruffled as I do.

During the winter I generally wear a coat over my business suit. A car coat is of convenient length for cycling and yet formal enough for attending a business lunch. My particular coat comes equipped with a hood attached to the collar which provides extra warmth and yet folds out of sight when not needed. On the very coldest days I add a wool sweater or suit vest for additional warmth. Part of the secret of being comfortable when cycling in winter is in wearing a hat and gloves. As the army discovered in World War II, the use of a hat and gloves greatly reduces heat losses and adds greatly to your comfort in cold weather. The other part of the secret lies in using your bicycle's gear ratios wisely. While in summer I choose among my gears for mimimal effort so as to avoid becoming overheated, in winter I make my choice so as to insure enough effort to keep me warm. Hard as it may be to believe until you've actually tried it, the effort of cycling even in cold weather will keep you comfortably warm. And unlike the closed-in, overheated feeling you get in an automobile in winter, you're breathing really fresh air.

The only time I skip cycling to work is when it's actually raining or snowing when I start out in the morning. I suppose by a careful choice of rain gear I might even be able to ride in the rain. I generally avoid snow and icy-road conditions because of the reduced stability of two-wheeled vehicles under these conditions. Despite eliminating riding when it's raining, snowing, or icy, I've been able to use my bicycle to commute more than 80 percent of the time. Even in more severe climates it's possible to cycle for much of the year.

People frequently ask me about traffic problems in commuting by bicycle. But remember, by cycling to work you're combining business with pleasure. What is the most efficient route by car is not necessarily the most efficient or most pleasant by bicycle. You're frequently better off choosing those secondary streets or roads disdained by the motorist as too narrow or slow for him. But by contrast, you're likely to find them fine for riding and delightfully freer of carbon-monoxide fumes. You may even discover you're able to observe the world around you in a way you never could traveling by car. Even when it's necessary to use a major thoroughfare for part of the distance, I've found that there is frequently a shoulder out of the mainstream of traffic which is perfect for cycling. Motorists generally seem to give cyclists a wide berth. Perhaps it's because they associate bikes with children, but even on streets without shoulders, I've found that the typical motorist is usually considerate. He generally passes me with far more than enough room.

What type of bicycle is best for commuting? I myself now use a fifteen-speed touring model equipped with dropped handlebars and a generator set. Before that I used a ten-speed bike with higher gear ratios, but I found it too highly geared for cycling with minimal effort in summer. My present bicycle is the same one I use for recreational riding. I chose the dropped handlebars because they offer a wider choice of riding positions than do other handlebar shapes. Most prospective cyclists have visions of themselves contorted into a pretzel-like shape if they use dropped bars. But as more experienced riders know, the advantage of that type of handlebar is that it provides a wider choice of riding positions for greater comfort and efficiency. You can ride with your hands on the upper or middle portion of the bars—in a more or less upright position—or with hands on the lower part of the bar for extra power.

While fifteen-gear ratios are convenient for touring under heavy load, ten-gear ratios with a sufficiently wide range of choices are more than adequate for commuting.

I personally use toe clips on the pedals, since this makes for more efficient pedaling. By keeping the straps loose enough, there is plenty of room for even heavy dress shoes to enable you to remove your feet quickly from the pedals as needed.

The generator set is especially convenient in winter when it is usually dark by late afternoon. I used to have a battery operated headlamp, but the generator eliminates worries over dead batteries. I also have a rear light and a large red reflector on the back of the bicycle. To be absolutely certain of being seen, you can even add an orange visibility vest over your outer clothing. If that seems a bit too conspicuous, the reflector, reflecting tape on the bicycle, and the headlamp make it pretty difficult for any motorist to miss seeing you.

Because I often carry a briefcase to work, my bicycle has both front and rear luggage carriers, although one or the other would really be enough. Instead of a luggage carrier, a basket might be substituted with equal ease.

Another point sometimes brought up is any problems that might arise from riding in good clothing. Actually by wiping off excess oil from the chain drive and using fenders, this has never been a problem for me. Extra oil serves no useful purpose anyway, and lightweight fenders add very little to the weight of the bicycle.

Now that you're more than half convinced that cycling to work just might be practical after all, what are the health benefits? Dr. Kenneth Cooper, author of a best-selling book on physical fitness, *Aerobics,* highly recommends cycling as one of the best means of maintaining general fitness. By cycling as little as three miles to work and back at a pace just over fifteen miles per hour, it's possible to earn the thirty points a week Dr. Cooper suggests for optimal fitness. That level of fitness is, by the way, a higher level of physical well-being than Dr. Cooper found in nearly two thirds of air-force recruits—all men in their late teens or early twenties.

As for commuting costs, even if you figure as little as six cents per mile for operating the cheapest car, my ten miles of daily cycling save me at least 60¢ a day, $3 a week, or $150 a year. That's without taking into account extra auto-insurance costs, parking fees I don't pay, and other commuting expenses. In addition, using my bicycle for commuting has eliminated the need for a second car despite suburban living—a very substantial savings.

Last, but probably the biggest bonus of all, is the sheer pleasure of cycling regularly and feeling better for doing so. Perhaps I could discipline myself enough to exercise regularly, but bicycle commuting makes it a certainty. Cycling brings me closer to the world around me in a way that driving never would. I watch the changing seasons and the small events en route to my office in a way I never could while driving. Whether it's the arrival of the first birds from the south in spring or the changing colors as summer turns into fall, I am a more relaxed observer, better able to enjoy the panoply of seasons. And after the accumulated tensions of the workday, what better way to unwind than by pedaling home dissipating your tensions as you go?

HOW TO ORGANIZE A BIKE CLUB

E. Peter Hoffman
March 1969

Bike clubs come in many forms, but all have one common objective—to increase your cycling pleasure.

Basically, there are two types of clubs: racing and touring.

Racing clubs are generally made up of young men and women of high competitive spirit. The club provides the opportunity for regular organized training sessions, racing instruction, club races, group buying power, and in most cases, the chance to sponsor one or more "open" races during the season.

An open race is one in which anyone can enter (regardless of his club affiliation) and as such must be sanctioned by the Amateur Bicycle League of America. If this is one of the goals of your proposed club, affiliation with the A.B.L. will be necessary. Club membership in the A.B.L. is fifteen dollars per year, and in addition to race sanctions, entitles the club to vote in league matters, which include decisions regarding state and national championships and participation in international competition.

Touring clubs range from informal to highly organized, and club life encompasses a wide spectrum of activities. There are clubs with no formal meetings, no dues, and no scheduled activities. Such groups attract members who are interested in impromptu rides—and nothing else. On the other hand, there are clubs that meet bimonthly, publish a newsletter, schedule three or four rides per week (ranging from local breakfast jaunts to tough "overnights"), organize and promote large bike rallies, plan extended vacation tours and trips to Europe, run races and time trials, promote bike trails, work for favorable bike legislation, hold auctions, and intersperse the year with a number of social events to boot.

In many areas of the country where climatic conditions

make cycling impractical in winter months, club activities may swing to ice skating or skiing. In some cases, hiking, canoeing, sailing, and other outdoor activities go hand in hand with cycling throughout the year.

Although touring clubs may be independently organized, most are affiliated with the League of American Wheelmen, the American Youth Hostels, or both.

The League of American Wheelmen (L.A.W.) will provide clubs with assistance in promoting rallies, initiating new bikeways and trails, and in fighting for cycling legislation. On the other hand, in belonging to L.A.W., a club aids in strengthening this organization, which in turn is working toward betterment of the sport.

American Youth Hostels (A.Y.H.) provides clubs with the opportunity to use Hostel facilities throughout the country, as well as advice and leadership from a full-time staff of trained individuals.

Of course, many of the benefits of A.B.L., L.A.W., and A.Y.H. may be obtained by individual membership, and whether your new club will wish to affiliate with one of these organizations will depend on the interests of your group. But whether you affiliate or remain independent, you're on your own when it comes to making your club a success.

First, decide what you want your club to do. History shows that a precise purpose is the best way to get things started. Later on, as your club grows and interest broadens, you can include other activities.

Once you know what you want, you can begin to look for others who want the same thing. Start with a small "steering committee." It only takes a chosen few to set preliminary plans. A steering committee should formulate the purpose and objectives of the proposed club, as well as lay plans for an open meeting, at which time the pro tem club becomes an official organization.

Business at this first organization meeting should include such pro tem policies as name, objectives, type of membership (mixed, "singles," family), and size of membership. Suggest the amount for dues. This can run anywhere from one dollar up, depending on whether you must rent a room for meetings, publish a newsletter, hold an annual banquet or party, etc. You should decide on a temporary chairman and secretary along with committees to set up (1) the open meeting, (2) officers, and (3) a constitution.

Preparation includes setting a date, time, and place for the first meeting. If you want to be selective about who is going to be in your club, word of mouth is the best means of gathering prospective members. For a larger group, plan written invitations or telephone calls (a local bike shop may often give you a good list of names or allow you to post a notice). Radio, television, newspapers, posters, and handbills are also at your disposal.

For the open meeting have a well-prepared agenda. The meeting should consist of two major parts: explanation and action. The explanation, or program, part of the session can be presented by using short talks, bicycling movies, demonstrations, and other devices that will hold your audience's interest while building enthusiasm for the club.

Since no club business can be carried on without a constitution, the first order of business is to elect officers and adopt a constitution.

Embellishments that will help the first official meeting are refreshments, name tags, a "welcome committee" to make each guest glad he came, paper and pencils in case on-the-fence guests want to make notes to take home and think it over.

It is wise to collect dues as soon as possible. One way of enticing members to be "in good standing" quickly is to set a date that will close charter memberships. Everyone who pays his dues before this established date will be enrolled as a "founding father," a point of pride once the club proves its permanence.

Once your constitution is set and officers elected, you're in a position to form working committees to carry out activities.

If regularly scheduled rides are your main purpose, a committee should be formed to plan these rides well in advance, and see that the schedule is published and sent to all club members. The ride schedule should also be posted in local bike shops, at college campuses, and sent to other clubs within your area. Also, each ride should be led by a ride captain, who can be appointed pro tem for specific rides. If you plan to promote a race, a rally, or even an interclub ride, committees should be established for these purposes. You may wish a committee to be responsible for social events, such as a club Christmas party or annual awards banquet. And if awards are to be given to members for their participation or accomplishments in club activities, you will need a committee for this.

By all means, don't overlook a membership committee for further recruitment. This is the lifeblood of any good organization.

PROFILE OF A CYCLE TOURIST

PIERRE ROQUES
November 1965

Writing in *Miroir Cyclisme* of June 1965, Pierre Roques gives a neat and hilarious description of the cycle tourist. According to Monsieur Roques, a cycle tourist has these characteristics:

He is eccentric. He is extremely fond of physical exercise, but he does not give a hoot for competition. He despises fashionable hotels and would rather stay in a quaint old hostel. He is bored with small talk but fascinated with a whispering tree. He can give you the name of every little village in a hundred-mile radius but he does not know the latest football score.

He is bullheaded. He undertakes tours that are completely beyond reason. The more tired he gets, the less he admits it. Then, when he is back, he wants to show you his pictures, exhibit his souvenirs, lick his wounds. Even when his tour has been a complete washout, he will tell you that this was the best one he has been on. For him, the bicycle can do no wrong.

He is fussy. You should see him when he discovers a scratch on the frame. You should see him spit on his finger to wipe off a smudge. You should see him filling his bags with all sorts of ridiculous articles. You should see him trying to take a picture: his body contorted, his neck twisted, his face convulsed, his duff in the brambles, all to get his eye to the viewfinder.

He is nosy. Invariably, he leaves the highway to explore the byway. Then, when he still has miles to go, he stops to poke around ancient buildings, size up rustic bridges, fathom gurgling streams. Completely unconcerned, he drags his bicycle through dingy alleys of decrepit villages. Night or day, he is always on the prowl.

He is incomprehensible. At the very moment his train gets to the mountains, he gets off to continue on his bike. Then, after crossing the highest passes, he pitches an impossibly small tent in a far-out corner while everybody else settles down in a normal tent in a normal spot with normal people. Apparently, he is not happy unless he does battle with weather, barriers, and terrain.

He is illogical. He does not want anything to do with racing, but he pushes himself to the limit on a century run. He belongs to all sorts of touring societies but he rides mostly alone. He will start on a long ride against the wind, knowing full well that the wind will turn when it is time to go back. When you stop your car to offer him a lift, he says no thanks, even though sweat is streaming down his face.

He is prejudiced. In full knowledge of his shortcomings, he does nothing to correct them. He does not even try to deny them. Instead of listening to normal, sensible, rational people, he gives them the cold shoulder and goes merrily on his way. It is as if he lived in a different world. All he cares about is his bicycle. On his bike, he is brisk, bright, and easy. Off his bike, he is dreamy, drippy, and droopy.

Riddled with these taints, vices, and infirmities, he is really nothing but a freak. In polite company, he should be banished and not befriended, rejected and not adopted, dismissed and not pitied. He will thank you!

THE LEAGUE OF
AMERICAN WHEELMEN

E. PETER HOFFMAN
August 1965

Once upon a time, there lived an organization called the League of American Wheelmen. It was an institution that played a vitally important part in fostering and promoting the cycling movement in America.

When cycling was very young it needed care, encouragement, and protection. The L.A.W., as the league was commonly called, fought for the right of wheelmen to use the public streets and highways. It started the good-roads movement in the late 1880's. It opened the parks and drives to cyclists. The objects of the league were "to promote the general interests of bicycling, to ascertain, defend, and protect the rights of wheelmen, and to encourage and facilitate touring."

In the early 1880's a bicycle-touring wave hit the United States. Wheelmen began to venture on long tours into strange parts of the country. The league established a touring bureau to furnish information as to routes, maps, etc. Members were asked to send in detailed information regarding their routes. Each state division gathered information relating to its own roads, and many of the divisions published road books. Hotels that granted reduced rates to league members were listed, together with railroads that carried bicycles as baggage. It was the league, by the way, that finally forced the railroads to make this concession.

Starting its second decade with a membership of over 18,000, the league enjoyed a truly remarkable growth. In 1893 there were close to 40,000 members. Then the well-remembered bicycle boom started. Fashion set its stamp of approval on cycling and everybody wanted a bike. The cycle industry expanded tremendously. In 1895–96 there were about three hundred bicycle factories. Production reached a top of nearly two million bikes in 1897. League expansion kept pace with the cycle trade until the membership soared to an all-time high of 102,636 in 1898. Many famous people whose names have become part of our nation's history were members of the league, including Orville and Wilbur Wright, Commodore Vanderbilt, and Diamond Jim Brady.

Then the bubble burst! The public, excepting the real cycling enthusiasts, turned from the bikes to the new "horseless carriage," and bicycle production dwindled along with the cycle industry. The league lost membership drastically, and by 1902 only 8,629 remained. Each year more members deserted the sinking ship. The league did not cease to function, however, and was carried on through the efforts of its secretary, Abbot Bassett, until 1942.

Once upon a time may seem like eternities ago. Yet today, right now, cycling in America is struggling through a period closely paralleling the time when L.A.W. was organized. The industry has reached an all-time high. Millions of bicycles are being bought yearly by a health and recreation-oriented public. Higher incomes and increased leisure time along with the need to escape the hectic pace of modern society has led to a rediscovery of the delights of cycling.

The problems facing today's cyclists are very similar to those that faced the league in 1880: Denial of right of way, expanding freeway systems, and the menace of the "horseless carriage"—multiplied millions of times over.

One of the greatest assets of the league was its influential power as a large collective body. All the members working together achieved more than if the same individuals had worked separately or without a common goal.

The first case affecting the rights of the wheelman with which L.A.W. dealt was the Haddenfield (New Jersey) Turnpike Case. The Pike Company refused to allow bicycles on the pike. The league proposed making a test case and supported the Philadelphia Club in starting suit. The company backed down and revoked its anticycling policy.

In 1879 the New York Board of Commissioners excluded bicycles from Central Park. L.A.W. decided to take the case to court. For eight years the struggle went on, and finally, in 1887, the "Liberty Bill" was signed by

Governor Hill revoking all laws discriminating against bicycles and established the rights of wheelmen to ride on any parkways, streets, or highways in the state of New York. Many states soon followed with the passing of similar bills.

L.A.W. fought and won many cases in which drivers had crowded cyclists off the road or had deliberately run them down.

Now, after many years of inactivity, the league is being reorganized. During the early months of 1964, Joe Hart, onetime officer of the national League of American Wheelmen and active cyclist with the Columbus Park Wheelmen, set out to promote a reunion of former Chicago Council League members. With the help of Ben Altman of the Wandering Wheelmen and Art Clausen of the Ramblers, the reunion was a complete success.

But most important, the revival of the national organization was initiated. A national convention was held on July 2 and 3 of this year, officers were elected, and the League of American Wheelmen again became a reality.

Inquiries from individuals and touring clubs are enthusiastically invited. For information, write to Mrs. Dorothy Hart, 5118 Foster Avenue, Chicago, Illinois 60631.

FUN IS WHERE YOU FIND IT

JOHN FULTON
November 1968

A mound of dirt, a bicycle . . . and the nerve to take a tumble . . . That adds up to *fun?*

Well, it can. If you're a youngster and you have enough imagination to see yourself daringly zooming a motorcycle when you're really straddling a mini-bike!

The dirt's for real. So are the hills and gullies and the huge mounds of dirt in the vacant lot down the street.

Bump humps. Dump humps. Mini-mountains. Zooo-o-o-m!

Ride around the dusty craters at a forty-five-degree angle.

Nerve and heart the heroes of the Tour de France would envy.

And at the end, home. Washing machines. Band-Aids. Hearty dinners. And Mom.

TOPEKA CAPITAL-JOURNAL/JOHN FULTON

He's down!

TOPEKA CAPITAL-JOURNAL/JOHN FULTON

Slam the brakes! A cloud of dust. A safe and sudden halt.

"When both wheels are off the ground, you fly over a hill," says Gene Carpenter.

"I want to go up. And up." Steve Watkins tops a mound.

Index

For the Sunday cyclist... for the cross-country tourist... whether you ride for better health, for sport, or for the sheer fun of it,

GET

THE COMPLETE BOOK OF BICYCLING

The First Comprehensive Guide To All Aspects of Bicycles and Bicycling

JUST A FEW OF THE HUNDREDS OF EXCITING TIPS YOU'LL FIND:

- A simple way to increase your cycling efficiency by 30 to 40%—breeze over hilltops while others are struggling behind.
- 13 special safety tips for youngsters.
- How to read a bicycle's specifications to know if you're getting a superior one or a dud.
- How to know whether to buy a 3-speed to start with, or a 10-speed.
- How to select the right kind of equipment for touring or camping.
- How to minimize danger when cycling in the city.

▼ AT YOUR BOOKSTORE OR MAIL THIS COUPON NOW FOR FREE 30-DAY TRIAL ▼

C4/1